AF412173

LONDON'S BURNING

London's Burning

Pulp Fiction, the Politics of Terrorism and the Destruction of the Capital in British Popular Culture, 1840–2005

Antony Taylor

continuum

Continuum International Publishing Group
The Tower Building, 11 York Road, London SE1 7NX
80 Maiden Lane, Suite 704, New York, NY 10038

www.continuumbooks.com

First published 2012

British Library Cataloguing-in-Publication Data
A catalogue record for this book is available from the British Library.

ISBN: HB: 978-1-4411-1887-5

Library of Congress Cataloging-in-Publication Data
A catalog record for this book is available from the Library of Congress.

Typeset by Newgen Imaging Systems Pvt Ltd, Chennai, India
Printed and bound in Great Britain

To Marsha Healy

Contents

List of Figures

Abbreviations

ARP	Air-Raid Precaution
ASU	Anti-Socialist Union
BUF	British Union of Fascists
CND	Campaign for Nuclear Disarmament
CPGB	Communist Party of Great Britain
ILP	Independent Labour Party
IRA	Irish Republican Army
IWMA	International Workingmen's Association
NATO	North Atlantic Treaty Organization
PLO	Palestine Liberation Army
SDF	Social Democratic Federation
SNP	Scottish National Party
TUC	Trades Union Congress
US/UK	United States/United Kingdom
WEA	Workers' Educational Association
WITCH	We Intend to Create Havoc

Acknowledgements

This book has been a number of years in the making. What began as a relatively modest study of a number of little-known texts on anarchism grew remorselessly into an analysis of popular fiction, its relationship to national political decline and further importance in the formation of attitudes towards the capital. Inevitably I have accumulated a large number of debts (academic and personal) along the way. Thanks go in particular to Chris Hopkins at Sheffield Hallam University, for suggesting avenues of research and little-known texts, and then patiently listening to my misreadings of them. Thanks too to Mary Grover and to the Middlebrow Network at Sheffield Hallam, for the stimulating forum for debate they have made available to scholars interested in the intersections between literature and history over the years. My especial thanks go to John Baxendale, who, in his work on J.B. Priestley, has blazed a trail to demonstrate the ways in which historians can intrude on the study of literature. His influence is apparent in this book during the course of numerous conversations over a malfunctioning photocopier. Thanks as well to literary specialists at Sheffield Hallam who have shared their expertize with me, notably Sue McPherson, and Steve Earnshaw. My particular thanks go to Gill Campbell, who has reminded me throughout the research for this book that many of the volumes cited are of dubious literary merit, and there are better books out there to read. Perhaps I'll do that now! Thanks too to Martin Carter for his insights as a genuine Londoner and to participants in the 'Lost London: Explorations of a Dark Metropolis' conference at Sheffield Hallam in June 2010 for ideas emerging during the course of the conference. I'd also like to thank my fellow historian of nineteenth-century radicalism, Matt Roberts, for his input and suggestions for further reading, and Karen Morton, my co-teacher on the 'London: Literary and Historical Perspectives' module at Sheffield Hallam for her enthusiasm for the project and her interest in all things metropolitan. Thanks as well to Livi Michael for her encouragement. Thanks in particular to Fergus Wilde, and to Chetham's Library, Manchester, for their help with the illustrations. This book only looks the way it does as a result of Fergus's hard work on the presentation of the pictures. Above all, my thanks go to my partner, Marsha Healy, for her insights, wisdom and companionship over the years. I dedicate this book to her.

Introduction

The traffic murmured sleepily in the distance. How nearly it had come, thought Bond, to being stilled. How nearly there might be nothing now but the distant clang of the ambulance bells beneath a lurid black and orange sky, the stench of burning, the screams of people still trapped in the buildings. The softly beating heart of London silenced for a generation. And a whole generation of her people dead in the streets amongst the ruins of a civilisation that might not rise again for centuries.[1]

The destruction of London has been more often imagined than seriously contemplated. From the early years of the nineteenth century, cultural pessimists imagined the political forces that might bring about a destruction of the metropolis. Much of this dystopic material traded in images of political and social upheaval. Periods of popular protest or radical activity generated fiction that considered the methods and tactics insurgents might use to bring the city to its knees. In highpoints of such concern in the 1840s and 1850s, in the 1890s, in the 1930s and in the 1970s and 2000s, writers have allowed their imagination free rein in describing the aftermaths of terrorist attacks, anarchist bomb plots, Bolshevik revolutionary upheavals or the consequences of a right-wing putsch. Confined usually to the pages of popular fiction, there has been a tendency to dismiss such writings as the lurid imaginings of the pulp novel market. Dismissed as a 'literature for the masses' until recently, these books received almost no serious critical attention. They certainly don't merit literary acclaim. Yet recent work on spy thrillers and detective fiction has demonstrated the extent to which popular fears and moral panics about the security of the metropolis find a place in these usually overlooked musings. Drawing on popular literature from authors like Pierce Egan Jr., Edgar Wallace, through 'Sapper' to John Burmeister, in work that is usually omitted from the canon, this book seeks to re-evaluate the contribution of popular fiction to the construction of the terrorist threat. It analyses the highpoints for the production of such works and locates them in their cultural and political context. From the 1840s, when a fear of Chartist insurgency was paramount in the minds of authors, this book moves through the anarchist thrillers of the 1890s to 1900s, considers the fears about Bolshevik revolution in the East End that obsessed writers of the 1920s and 1930s, explores British fears of Fascism in the inter-war years and assesses the concerns with underground counter-cultural forms that feature in the thriller literature of the 1970s. It concludes with a re-evaluation of the metropolitan background to the figure of the Islamist terrorist. A 'deep' reading of the fears that surround the figure of the militant Islamist demonstrate that the image of the terrorist is mediated through numerous prior visions of terrorism in London with roots in cultural constructions of anarchism and direct action radicalism dating from the 1890s and before.

I

The vision of a destroyed and decimated London imagined by James Bond in *Moonraker* is in a long tradition. Perhaps the most traditional of Ian Fleming's Bond books, both in its setting and in the nature of the threat faced by Londoners, *Moonraker* drew unashamedly on memories of the Blitz and on the thriller fiction of the 1890s. The images used by Fleming emerged from a common pool of popular fiction that provided the threads linking Bond with older pulp heroes like Bulldog Drummond and villainous enemies familiar to himself and to many of his readers from his Edwardian boyhood.[2] The threat of a destruction of the capital and the impact it might have both on the empire and on British interests abroad provided a long-standing motif. The object of pulp villains from Fu Manchu through to the repellent ex-Nazi Hugo Drax in *Moonraker*, the imagined destruction of the capital represented the collapse of British power, authority, cultural values and moral leadership. The avowed aim of the majority of pulp villains was to plunge Britain into a new age of barbarism.[3] Following 7/7, such fears have resurfaced in response to the emergence of a militant Islamist terrorist threat. This volume grows out of recent academic interest in terrorism and the impact of terror on popular sentiment and media opinion. In the wake of 9/11, numerous books have appeared on terrorism (by John Gray, Paul Berman and Michael Ignatieff, in particular), but none have adopted a thoroughgoing historical approach.[4] The existing histories of terrorism are often partial, polemical and impressionistic. In its examination of the much-overlooked genre of popular fiction and discussion of its relationship to the history of the capital, this book explores new avenues in the understanding of popular literature. Unusually for a history-based study, this book crosses disciplinary boundaries. It seeks to connect the history of terrorist threats in Britain with recent debates about the ways in which historians approach the task of using literary sources. In addition, it locates the image of the terrorist in the work of those currently reappraising popular fiction as a cultural product. In so doing, this book draws on a range of other disciplines including sociology, urban studies and political theory. The pertinence of the book's key themes – Britishness, urban identity, fear of terrorism – place it at the centre of debates about identity, popular culture and recent political threat.

This, then, is not a conventional account of terrorism and political militancy in London. Its object is to chart the course and direction of popular fears. In so doing it examines material that is traditionally ignored or overlooked. By these means, it arrives at a highly unorthodox view of popular politics. This book draws primarily on popular fiction. It seeks to re-evaluate its importance for historians working on local, regional, national and imperial identities in the twenty-first century. The novels of prolific popular writers such as Edgar Wallace, Arthur Sarsfield Ward, Ian Fleming, John Buchan and Dennis Wheatley have long inspired their own enthusiasts.[5] Indeed, the heroes that have emerged from such material have often established themselves as popular and culturally significant icons in their own right. Such books, however, are only intermittently read for indications of how they negotiate and present shifting conceptions of national and imperial strength and for the national, racial and political ideas that underpinned these notions.[6] Recent years have seen a renewed interest in popular literature on the part of historians. Once derided as the poorer end of the literary marketplace, unworthy of academic study, popular fiction is now read as a manifestation of popular identity and as a cultural phenomenon in its own right. Works of popular fiction are no longer dismissed simply for their variable literary merit, but for the first time are beginning to be examined for the light they shed on political sentiments and social trends.[7] Study of this material opens up possibilities for a new analysis that stresses the manifestations of popular opinion, imperial ideas and the cultural identities carried by popular novels and serializations. The sheer volume of popular fiction and the genres it spans provides opportunities to consider the inter-related nature of culture and the ways in which different visions of British identities serve to undermine or to consolidate one another. In a different sphere, whilst there has been a renewed interest in regional and metropolitan identities in recent years, this has not been matched by an adequate reappraisal of the popular works that represent such identities. Much yet remains to be done in linking the work of pulp fiction authors to audiences, whilst questions persist about the degree to which the messages underpinning such fiction found wider support or otherwise.

These concerns fix the chronology of the book. Beginning in the 1840s, it draws on arguments about the emergence of a recognizably modern publishing market. In its analysis of the content of popular fiction, this book sits broadly in agreement with Philip Waller, by placing the origins of mass publishing in the middle years of the nineteenth century.[8] Throughout, it follows Ian Haywood, in seeing the place of origin for many of the forms and styles of popular literature in the expansion of popular print media in Victorian Britain after the repeal of the 'taxes on knowledge' and the failure of the 'moral middles' either to police or to stem the flood of cheap publications.[9] Taking the 1840s as an optimum period for the growth and development of techniques for the production of popular, garish and widely consumed mass market publications, it analyses the fears and popular concerns that marked out the sensationalist terrain and content of this material. Thereafter it follows such material through to the explosion of the cheap paperback market in the 1970s and recent lurid imaginings of terrorism in popular fiction.

In itself, this book is not simply another study of terrorism. It offers few insights into the reasons for individual acts of terrorism, or for the dynamic behind terrorist networks, organization and initiatives more broadly. It does, however, provide a generalized definition of terrorism for the purposes of this study. In line with Walter Laqueur's seminal study, *The New Terrorism*, it chooses to interpret terrorism very broadly indeed.[10] Spanning movements of the right, and the left, and taking cognisance of religious and secular variations to terrorism, this book represents terrorism as a fanatical form of politics, reliant on extreme displays of political violence and utilising sophisticated technological methods of destruction to bring about its aims. The anarchist groups discussed in Chapter 2 fit conventionally into this framework, but movements like Bolshevism, Irish republican terrorism and extreme sub-cultures amongst some student militants are also included on the grounds that their subversive and conspiratorial forms of organization locate them within a recognizably distinct world of 'underground' political forms. Following Lacqeur, this book includes a chapter on Fascism (Chapter 4), on the basis that under certain circumstances, Fascism's emphasis on demonstrative violence leads it to imitate the subversive political format of movements of the militant and conspiratorial left.[11] Al-Qaeda and Islamist extremism fit firmly into a spectrum of terrorism in which the primary motivations are religious rather than secular. To interpret what radicals themselves thought about political violence in their own writings, this book includes an opening chapter on the historical memory of peasant revolt amongst reformers in Britain. As Laqueur allows, along the way terrorism can take many forms, from the state-directed, through the inventive, to the exotic, often making it explicable only in comparative terms.[12] It is to be hoped that this volume appraises some of these different dimensions to a complex phenomenon.

II

In Britain, London, rather than the regional centres, provided the backdrop to the apocalyptic visions contained in such material. A further function of the arguments presented here is to provide a contribution to recent cultural debates on the role and position of London during periods of perceived political threat. For this reason, this book gauges the importance of the metropolitan background to terrorist thriller literature more generally and considers the neuroses surrounding historical debates about the vulnerability of the capital to attack. It concludes by considering the importance of previous generations of thriller writers to the cultural construction of the threat posed by al-Qaeda, and the reactions of media and fiction writers to the London bombings of July 2005. This volume is not a literary treatment of the books under consideration, but, rather, provides a reading of the popular fiction market historicized in its cultural context, while assessing audiences, key themes and cultural responses to it. The book is strongly rooted both in the political and in the historical contexts it describes. It reflects a burgeoning interest in all things metropolitan, mirrored in the proliferation of material on London geared towards a more popular audience and a revival of interest in the local history of the capital. There are other books on terrorism, but this one revisits the subject and returns it to its urban context. This book might also be seen as a contribution to recent re-evaluations of London that highlight the hidden cultural and political dangers of the metropolis.[13]

This book is not primarily a study of genre. Nevertheless, the material examined throughout this study falls loosely into the category labelled popular crime fiction, or the thriller form. Such material has a long provenance and bequeathed a significant legacy for inter-war and post-war writers. Widely read, but frequently held in contempt, these books demonstrate a lineage of form and ideas that take their origins back into the world of mid-Victorian sensationalist fiction. Most standard accounts of thrillers and spy fiction place their point of origin in the 1890s and the years before and after the Great War. Anthony Hope, H. Rider Haggard, William Le Queux and John Buchan are often seen as grandfathers of the genre. As Allan Hepburn comments, this period was formative both for the style and content of popular fiction, dealing, as it often did, with spies and shadowy conspirators who transcended national boundaries, crossed frontiers at will, spoke numerous languages and adopted multiple identities and disguises. Such books posit the external threat of invasion from without, matched by duplicity and treachery by unreliable elements from within.[14] As Michael Denning notes, in many ways, these books were a counterpoint to the traditional imperial adventure story, acting as a compensatory and consolatory literature for a Britain past her imperial zenith and reflecting the country's global contraction.[15] As Kevin Foster has commented, the figure of the spy became both 'a symbol and the source for national decline'.[16] Most of these novels and the majority of the works cited throughout this volume might be seen as occupying the same space as the output of

Edgar Wallace that Dorothy L. Sayers categorized as 'the purely sensational'.[17] Such authors were seen as venal and in thrall to debased popular tastes. A. R. Orage captured this sentiment in his view of Wallace as 'the counterpart of the profiteer'.[18] Nevertheless, these books held a peculiar fascination for many contemporary writers. George Orwell spoke of 'good bad books', and Graham Greene in particular sought to inject a greater depth of characterization, plot and a more rigorous standard of writing into the traditional detective and thriller form. He again quoted Le Queux, Anthony Hope and John Buchan as instrumental and formative in the development of his writing.[19]

Despite literary curiosity about the genre, Britain has never either embraced or exalted its popular fiction writers. Embarrassing, unrespectable and with few pretensions to acceptability, they are the epitome of the 'low brow'. Recent interest in the 'middle brow' grows out of a tacit sense of the exclusion of this literary form and constitutes an attempt to reclaim some authors (but not others) for the canon. Contemporary notions of the 'middle brow' have problematized popular fiction. The lack of consensus about the 'middle brow' itself reveals continuing confusion about literary form and style, and demonstrates little more than a widespread rejection of Bloomsbury and modernism. Popular fiction, whilst sharing some of these traits, lacked the middle brow's sense of seriousness, embrace of self-consciously archaic styles and overweening self-importance. Equally, popular fiction fits uneasily into the reading material seen as shaping the development of respectable, aspirational and self-improving working-class culture.[20] For Orwell, an exciting fusion of low and middle brow was possible in the muddle of genres and literary product he encountered in Francis and Myfanwy Westrope's 'Booklovers' Corner' bookshop in the 'social borderland' of Hampstead and Chelsea in the 1930s. For him it provided a heady brew of the popular and the didactic, frequently reflected in his own writing.[21] For most authors, however, these books and writers inhabit a space that Richard Hoggart believed belonged alongside the liminal, the marginal and the transient in popular culture. In *The Uses of Literacy* he describes a profusion of literature including serial shockers, cheap novels, 'sex-books', pulp fiction and hobby magazines circulating as part of a polyglot form that flourished in station bookstalls and was freely available to the commuting and travelling public:

> The 'blood-and-guts' sex novelettes can be bought not only from the 'magazine shops' but from some railway-bookstalls. They are usually in a corner, all together, lying beneath the cards of aspirin and the styptic pencils. There are the dailies and weeklies, the welter of little 'hobbies' and 'handicrafts' magazines, the Penguins and the Pelicans; and then the sex-novelettes – they all make a picture of some of the stresses within our culture.[22]

This literary product overlapped with a burgeoning industry of authorship. As Christopher Hilliard has demonstrated, the inter-war and immediate post-war years were a period in which amateur authors prospered. Large numbers of aspiring writers sought to learn the writers' craft at reading circles, in correspondence courses and in regional writers' groups. Some of these figures achieved some limited success, but most remained in obscurity.[23] As Hilliard comments, these figures often eschewed traditional approaches to literature; a number of them were willing to experiment with style and form, contributing to the modernist departures in literature after World War II.[24] Many simply added to the weight of traditional thrillers and poor crime fiction in circulation that became a staple of the British reading public's diet, pre- and post-Word War II. Few of the authors cited in this book may be seen as displaying literary merit, whereas many fall into the bracket of journeyman authorship or aspiring hack writers, but only a very few received plaudits for their work. Some like Dennis Wheatley and Cyril McNeile are notorious and have become by-words for the worst excesses of the popular thriller form. 'Pulp', when the term is used in Britain at all, refers to authors of this nature and calibre.

A strong point of contrast emerges here with regard to the United States. There the term 'pulp' as a description of popular fiction is far more frequently employed. The British disdain for low-brow fiction is to some extent inspired by a dislike of American paperback novels and their penetration into the British fiction market in the years before and after World War II on the back of a stream of cheap US imports.[25] Characterized by poor production values, cheap paper and garish illustrations, for contemporaries in Britain, this material embodied the worst aspects of American popular culture. The term 'trash fiction' is sometimes used to describe it. In the United States, responses to 'pulp' are very different. Attitudes to 'pulp' fiction oscillated, between affection and fear, finding their natural level after the 'Red Scares' surrounding the effect of horror comics on adolescents ended in the 1950s.[26] These days, pulp fiction evokes nostalgia and is often celebrated, rather than derided. Pulp writers like Ayn Rand and L. Ron Hubbard have attained major followings and taken their place on a podium within a 'pulp' hall of fame. Their influence in the world of ideas in the United States is out of all proportion to the quality of their literary product and their abilities as writers or social visionaries. On the back of a much greater acceptance of thrillers, science fiction and the lower end of the literary marketplace in the United States, writers there have shown themselves more prepared than their British counterparts to adapt and to experiment with the forms and styles of popular fiction. Philip Roth, in particular, has demonstrated that there is great potential in plundering established plots from science fiction and invasion panic novels to explore and decode particular historical episodes.[27] Much imitated for their brash, salacious and 'hard-boiled' elements, the proliferation of popular fiction 'pulps' derived from the American model, traditionally stoked fears about a coarsening of style amongst British thriller writers.[28] Pulp proper in Britain might be seen as encompassing the works of semi-pornographic and titillating writers like Hank Janson and the 'yellow-backs' of the 1930s. In the inter-war years 'pulp' elements migrated upwards into the crime fiction genre. Writers like Eric Ambler, who aspired to something more original in the fiction they produced, acknowledged their debt to this material. In his 1936 novel, *The Dark Frontier*, the novel's hero, Henry Barstow, is involved in a car accident. Following a head injury, he spends the remainder of the novel convinced that he is the hero of a detective novel he reads in the hotel before his accident. The moment of discovery of the book is an important one in the novel: 'It lay open, face downward, displaying the full expanse of a bright yellow jacket. One half of this was devoted to a list of the publisher's other offerings while, on the front cover, above a three-colour reproduction of a lantern-jawed man with a blue jowl and an automatic pistol, was the title, in blood red letters: CONWAY CARRUTHERS, DEPT. T.'[29] In Britain, 'pulp' remains defiantly unrespectable. It is usually labelled as 'crime fiction' or thriller writing, but also has a manifestation in popular romance stories. As Clive Bloom has demonstrated, an energy, vibrancy and vigour is common to both British and American popular crime writing. For him, this strong overlap in style and content is indicative of a transatlantic definition of 'pulp' in which definable characteristics recur.[30] For Bloom, the category of 'pulp' is a portable one, useful in both British and American contexts. Bloom defines it as a 'lower grade literature' that symbolizes 'a type of infiltration by hackdom into the realm of the sacred (that is the serious novel)'.[31] This book follows the notion of a pulp marketplace in fiction that circulated (and still circulates) widely in the United Kingdom, whilst drawing on numerous constituencies of readership. Despite the ubiquity of such material, its exclusion from the canon and traditional concerns about the demeaning and degrading experience of those readers exposed to it means that it remains a largely un-researched area of study. Such novels, nevertheless, traditionally act as a vector for many of the popular concerns of the periods. As Bloom shows, there is something gleeful and irreverent about these books in both a British and American context.[32] The themes and ideas they consider provide a unique insight into the popular mindset. In 1941, at the time of a potential German invasion of Britain, it was to popular authors like Jules Verne that contemporaries turned to make sense of the situation.[33] Easily transferable, dealing in only a limited number of plots and ideas, their contribution has allowed for a context in which alternative versions of British politics, British identities and even possible futures and apocalypses might be explored. It is this genre that provides the bulk of the reference material for the study that follows.

The setting and landscape of London looms large in much of this material. London provided the appropriate background to crime fiction, political thrillers, studies in governmental corruption and police stories. Here well-known public landmarks and disparities of wealth and power gave a recognizable context to plot devices and characterizations rooted in the experience of living in or knowing the capital. Thriller writers reflected the varying moods of London, from the quietness and respectability of the suburbs through to the noise and vulgarity of the East End and the superficiality and glitz of the West End and the City. Fogs, crowds, squalor, plenty and want feature markedly in the work of authors like Margery Allingham. The fusion of a recognizable landscape and the established image of metropolitan rootlessness are typified by the demobilized, armed and unemployed ex-servicemen who run amok in her classic study of post-war criminality, *The Tiger in the Smoke*:

> Meanwhile, Crumb Street, never a place of beauty, that afternoon was at its worst. The fog slipped over its low houses like a bucketful of cold soup over a row of dirty stoves. The shops had been mean when they had been built and were designed for small and occasional trade, but since the days of victory, when a million men had passed through the terminus, each one armed with a parcel of government-presented garments of varying usefulness, half the establishments had been taken over by opportunists specialising in the purchase and sale of secondhand clothes. Every other window was darkened with festoons of semi-respectable rags based by bundles of grey household linen, soiled suitcases, and an occasional collection of surplus war stores, green khaki, and air-force blue.[34]

For the crime writer Peter Cheyney, London was quite simply the capital of the underworld with all the moral failings that this statement implied. In *The Urgent Hangman*, his detective hero, Callaghan, muses: 'For a few moments he saw London objectively. Saw it in a glance mainly consisting of two parts – a very thin upper crust and a damn thick lower one. The upper crust was the veneer of respectability, 'niceness', cleanliness, which London showed the world; the lower crust – the thick one – all the rottenness, cheap crookery, and general lousiness that existed in that jungle in the heart of the metropolis whose boundaries are known to every intelligent police officer'.[35]

III

The destruction and moral squalor of London is a major theme in much of this material. There is a long lineage to these visions. The great fire of 1666, often attributed to a Catholic conspiracy, was frequently cited as evidence of the fragility of the city when faced with a natural disaster or political violence. Thereafter, the unprecedented growth and expansion of the city in the eighteenth and nineteenth centuries inspired numerous fantasies about its downfall. Since the writings of Macaulay and the etchings of Gustave Doré, images of London's destruction were always contained within its success as a city. In the eighteenth century, it was a commonplace to depict London as a 'Babylon' or a 'new Rome' built on slavery and suffering, rooted in unsustainable bursts of commerce, and inevitably destined to decline into barbarism.[36] Pride and vanity, it was believed, characterized the sophisticated urban dweller, blinding him to the possible fate of his endeavours. In many cultural readings, London was portrayed as a place of low morals, poised to collapse into impotent decadence and disintegration or brought low from attacks by new vandals and barbarians. From the eighteenth century onwards, there were fears that the success of London was unsustainable, making the capital vulnerable to riotous behaviour by the excluded, or to attack from great power rivals. The rapidity of social change, the upheaval of nineteenth century re-building programmes and the unprecedented expansion of London outwards meant that the capital was about erasure, creating a cityscape dominated by the ruins of its past. As Lynda Nead remarks, London at the height of its growth and power in the nineteenth century 'was also possessed by dystopic visions of its future'.[37] Lord Macaulay best typified this outlook. In 1840, his review of Von Ranke's *History of the Popes* speculated whether a New Zealander, returning from the colonies in the distant future, would still find the Church of Rome standing. The image was a potent one, taken up and adapted by writers and authors to imagine a lone colonial visitor inspecting and recording the ruins of London following an unspecified apocalypse in a dim and distant future.[38] This vision of national and social collapse became a convention, drawing on the ideas of writers like Volney, and presenting an admonitory rebuke to proud and avaricious Londoners in periods of national peril like the American War of Independence.[39] As Patrick Wright has observed of the twentieth century, many of the images of London rebuilt, remodelled or reconceptualized by conservationists, town planners, architects and literary pedestrians are contingent upon the city's destruction in the first instance.[40]

Many of the fictional destructions of London mimic the destructions imagined for other major cities. Prophetic destructions of iconic urban centres occur throughout the Anglophone world. From the inter-war period onwards, authors like Oswald Spengler predicted the demise of urban civilization. In his *Decline of the West*, written in 1918, he announced that human society had reached an unsustainable plateau of civilized urban culture in the great cities of Europe and North America, but was destined to fall back into barbarism and self-immolation.[41] As Max Page comments with regard to contemporary visions of the destruction of New York, certain themes recur in relation to images of urban catastrophe. In periods of crisis, London, like New York, bore the weight of catastrophic expectation. Britain, as in the United States, shares a ruralist image of the nation, dislikes cosmopolitan complexity and harbours a fear of unregulated urban expansion, and the immigration that accompanies it. For many writers who deal with the destruction of London, the city displays an ambiguous relationship with 'Englishness'. It provided an anti-England of cosmopolitanism, immigration, race-mixing and unpatriotic values.[42] Moreover, as with New York, London is a 'provisional' city, in which demolition and re-building creates constantly shifting vistas of change.[43] This process fostered a sense of the transience and impermanence of urban space. Significantly, both New York and London are financial centres that are often subject to environmental and political violence in fiction and cinema, high-lighting the fragility of financial markets and the disruption of the institutions and services that depend upon them. As in depictions of the destruction of New York, the collapse of London releases uncontrolled crowd violence and mob behaviour, destroys financial stability (and the seat of government) and presages disarray in communications and the stability of other urban centres. As Page points out, such themes demonstrate the most grudging type of acceptance of big-city finance, acknowledging the necessity for such centres, but speculating about a society no longer dependant on them.[44]

Strongly embedded in popular culture, many of these predictions for the political and social collapse of the capital had implications for the fate of empire. Imperial themes were consonant with the tradition of a decayed and decrepit London. The city's pre-eminence was an expression of the country's imperial reach and power. Her financial and trading culture was coloured by an impe-rial swagger. The 'heart of the empire' and characterized by monuments to imperial endeavour and overseas adventurism, the collapse of London would herald the obliteration of British overseas interests.[45] The twin themes of the collapse of London and the disintegration of empire frequently took a parallel route. Rome was frequently invoked as a proxy for the decline of the British empire.[46] The image of a London in decline inspired J.A. Froude's advice to the white settler colonies that their societies would flourish best through a rejection of urban life. For Froude, the best hope for the British race lay in a regenera-tion of urban man away from the constraints of city life in the challenging and invigorating environment of the Australian bush or the 'back-blocks' of New Zealand. Froude believed this would revive the fortunes of the race, imper-illed 'in the enormously extended suburbs of London and our great manu-facturing cities: miles upon miles of squalid lanes, each house the duplicate of its neighbour'.[47] These themes were portable to parts of the empire where 'new Londons' arose. When writers in the Australian colonies imagined their new-world cityscapes, and the possible destruction of their own cities, due to greed, over-expansion or conquest, they often saw future catastrophes in terms of the precedent provided by London.[48] Much popular fiction betrayed a strong interest in the themes provided by imperial London. Many popular novels traded in the threat posed by returned adventurers, retired colonels with an arsenal acquired from days spent on the North-West frontier or dangerous colonial types, plotting colonial independence, revolt or international drug deals. Such stereotypes abound in post-war crime fiction, typified by the writings of Agatha Christie, against a background of Britain's diminishing role in the wider world.[49] Here rapid political change in the empire matched accelerated social change at home, providing fertile territory for the authors of popular fiction.[50] For Neville Shute, writing in the coronation year of 1953, about a projected British future in the 1980s, post-war emigration policy has emptied the country and Britain and London are in terminal decline. The best have emigrated to Australia and New Zealand, leaving a dwindling and listless population without enterprise, still facing food shortages, and in thrall to a statist socialist and quasi-republican government.

> He came to the National Gallery on the north side of Trafalgar Square and crossed the road and stood for a time looking out over the square at the corner by Canada House. There was a bus stop near him, and a long queue of white-faced, patient Londoners waiting to go home. He thought of the vigour and beauty of the people in similar bus queues in Brisbane and Adelaide, comparing the tanned skins with the sallow, the upright carriage with the tired slouch. It wasn't the fault of these people that they looked white and tired; hardships had made them so, and overwork, and the errors of dietary scientists who planned the rationing back in the Forties and the Fifties, when most of them were children. Badly treated people, out of luck, yet with a quality of greatness in them still, in spite of everything.[51]

When the queen leaves London to reside permanently in the Australian commonwealth, the act provides final confirmation of Britain's impotent status and the rejection of her history and traditions. These sentiments extend Froude's vision of a declining London into the twentieth century and followed Macaulay's vision of metropolitan energies flowing outwards to the peripheries.

IV

Much of the popular fiction that deals with the destruction or collapse of London provides a counter-narrative to the utopian literature of social visionaries like

William Morris. In *News from Nowhere*, the upheaval and social collapse accompanying a revolution that begins in London gives way to a verdant rustic utopia in which an artisanal culture of individual creativity and communal values flourishes. The novel gained wide currency on the political left, inspiring a new generation of socialists and creating a usable political narrative in which riot and disorder initiated by a massacre of reformers in Trafalgar Square paved the way for a better world.[52] The London rebuilt by the revolutionaries in *News from Nowhere* is a verdant garden city, in which peach trees bloom in Trafalgar Square and the destruction of the slums of the East End is marked annually by a festival of country-dancing and rural recreations.[53] Many of the popular accounts of a capital spiralling into chaos and disorder were written in opposition to Morris' vision of a violent, but ultimately successful, transition into a peaceful and prosperous future. Most popular fiction authors posited instead a country plunged into a future of anarchy, social disorder and political chaos by irreconcilable radical and socialist elements. The fate of Paris during the Commune of 1871 provided a possible model for the potential destruction of London in these events, much commented on by the press and contemporary popular fiction writers. As Matthew Beaumont demonstrates, the Paris Commune, which provides a counterpoint to events in *News from Nowhere*, casts a long shadow across the fiction writing of the period.[54] James Harvey writing in *The Republican* newspaper in 1871 quoted the apocalyptic visions of Carlyle on the contagion of French revolutionary sentiment and its threat to the British government and the loyalty of the army:

> These, these men may for a time may be true; once, twice – nay, a third time, they may mow down their brothers, friends and companions with musketry, but not always. Thomas Carlyle points to the helmeted giant posted at the Horse Guards, and prophecies that, regularly as he is to be seen in his sentry box, so long things may hold together, but his co-mate at the Tuileries has disappeared. And how long will he be seen in London?[55]

The events of the Commune, and the forces contemporaries believed it released, which Goldwin Smith described as 'political Satanism', were seen as an overt threat that thrived in London's slum districts.[56] As Beaumont remarks, in the nineteenth-century, any intimation of social breakdown or governmental collapse carried automatic connotations of the Commune. In the Victorian environmental thriller by William Delisle Hay, *The Doom of the Great City* (1880), in which a poisonous fog asphyxiates Londoners, a vacuum in authority gives rise to the killing of policemen, rampaging mobs, looting, and genocide.[57] Such images of a disintegrating London dominated by radicals, and *in extremis* throwing up forces of social disintegration and decay that hastened its decline, lingered into the twentieth century. In John Christopher's 1956 environmental thriller, *The Death of Grass*, in which famine leads to a collapse of urban society, a small group of survivors listen to events in London on a car radio. With food stocks exhausted and the government in disarray, London has been taken over by a Citizens' Emergency Committee: 'The voice began suddenly and, with both radios now on, seemed very loud. The accent was quite unlike what might be expected on the BBC – a lightly veneered Cockney. The voice was angry and scared at the same time'. Roger, the cynic of the group sneers: 'At my guess the Emergency committee's a Triumverate, and composed of a professional anarchist, a parson, and a left-wing female schoolteacher. It would take that kind of combination to show such an ignorance of elementary human behaviour'.[58]

The fact that so much of this fiction trades in plots that show the consequences of a vacuum in authority, and, thereafter, either a restoration of order, or a dystopic alternative future, raises questions about the political orientation of the form. Much of this literature resists categorization. In conventional terms, however, the usage 'conservative' is sometimes employed to describe it. George Orwell detected a counter-revolutionary tone in much of it. Writing about the anti-socialist polemical fictions of Ernest Bramah, he remarked: 'Ernest Bramah . . . was a sensitive, idealistic man whose private fears of the mob turned him into a passionate anti-democrat'.[59] Eric Ambler echoed this view, writing his left-wing thrillers in conscious rebellion against a form that promoted an established kind of fiction, lacking in both characterization and plot, in which the hero 'could be a tweedy fellow with steel-grey eyes and gun pads on both shoulders or a moneyed dandy with a taste for adventure. He could also be a xenophobic ex-officer with a nasty anti-semitic streak. None of that really mattered. All he really needed to function as hero was abysmal stupidity combined with superhuman resourcefulness and unbreakable knuckle bones'.[60] As Ambler suggests, the protagonists in fiction by Haggard, Buchan and Kipling were frequently 'batchelor gentlemen', opposed to the 'new woman', scornful of the working classes and patrician in their protection of Britain's rural landscape against influences from the encroaching towns.[61] Alison Light has demonstrated that the inter-war period is a formative one for such literature, in which notions of particular styles in popular reading became strongly established. As she points out, this fiction was only seldom about country houses, 'old maids' and retired majors. In her study of the novels of inter-war women writers, she suggests it was often a static form in which there is an emphasis on rural respectability, and in which the rootless, downwardly mobile aristocracy and the 'feckless' and 'adenoidal' working class or domestic servants are distrusted alike. For her, popular fiction turns inwards towards the insular English and the domestic environment in these years.[62] More often than not, in the crime fiction of many inter-war authors, popular fiction is traditionally characterized by the inability of its authors to clothe their work in the outward garb of respectability. In its nineteenth-century origins, much popular fiction was ephemeral and marginal. This notion harmonizes with Clive Bloom's definition of 'pulp' as 'always illicit, rarely controllable, maybe actually illegal, but only sometimes subversive'.[63] The popular thriller form in fact constitutes a fusion of genres and styles, in which particular styles of politics (socialism, trades unionism, pacifism, etc.) are seldom tolerated, and in which the keynote might be described as 'populist' in tone. Indeed, the essential components of this fiction follow the definitions of populism outlined by Ernesto Laclau in his *On Populist Reason*. Mainstream, yet excluded from the respectable, held in contempt, raucous in its approach, this fiction is informed by a conspiratorial mindset, in which a fragile Britain is constantly under threat and repeatedly imperilled by unreliably led unpatriotic elites and politically compromised governments. True virtue resides in 'the people', 'the little man' and the stoical middles in alliance with patrician figures who stand outside the structures of power and authority and who foil the plots of foreigners, the unpatriotic and the cosmopolitan. Only through the role of these elements can the nation itself be redeemed.[64]

At the heart of such fiction resides the vision of the capital. London's preeminence in such writing demonstrates the centrality of the metropolis in the national imagination. London is home to many of the symbols of nationhood and Britishness, from Buckingham Palace, through the National Portrait Gallery to the Bank of England. London as a backdrop to national calamity provides a short-hand for state, nation and government in crisis. References to London in much of the literature discussed here mirrored the city's place in national history and were reflective of its fortitude in World War II. Such images were consonant with London's resilience and survival during the German Blitz of London in 1940. Then totemic buildings like St. Paul's Cathedral that expressed English creativity and notions of national and historical continuity floated unscathed above the destruction to achieve a lasting place in the national imagination.[65] Community values, a steadfast determination to carry on and a smiling indifference to danger were the characteristics of a besieged, war-time London that worked their way through into the popular image of the city under attack.[66] They are routinely revived whenever Londoners experience difficulties or crisis. A London imperilled or actually fallen carried with it connotations of national defeat and humiliation. For many fiction writers, the state of the nation could be mirrored by events in London. From Eric Ambler's vision of London as a nest of conspiratorial city financiers in the 1930s (reflected in recent reporting of the 'credit crunch') through Wyndham Lewis's description of the carcass of the capital as a free city, rotting under the weight of bureaucratized socialist rule 'reeking in their nostrils of freedom' in the late 1940s, London is a cipher, acting as a barometer of the position of the country.[67] In most depictions of dystopic events, it is this space that London occupies within popular fiction, and one reason why any discussion of pulp literature must involve a discussion of the capital. Unapologetically, therefore, London, as a place of disorder, governmental collapse, destruction or renewal, is at the heart of what follows.

It should be emphasized that this book offers only a limited contribution to the currently popular form of 'alternative' or 'counterfactual' history. Often concerned with military history, the actions of 'great men', international diplomacy and great power rivalry, 'alternative' history displays some of the 'populist' tendencies of imagined popular fiction.[68] Niall Ferguson, in the introduction to his 1997 *Virtual History* collection, acknowledges the presence of counterfactual history as a component of popular literature, but dismisses works like Robert Harris' *Fatherland* and the German victory in World War II he describes, as a mere 'extrapolation' of past trends, explored in insufficient depth, in which 'a Nazi victory in the Second World War becomes merely a titillating backdrop for a good departure-lounge yarn'.[69] In these comments, he shows the desire of historians working even in the field of 'speculative' history to distance themselves from the excesses of the popular fiction market. Whilst most of the novels under discussion here offer alternative or 'virtual' versions of British political development, rather than analysing the likelihood of the competing historical scenarios invoked, this book seeks to understand the context and background to the 'departures' in historical events outlined.

V

This book is organized into the following chapters.

Chapter 1 provides the 'deep context' for fears about popular revolt in the capital and their implications for national stability. Drawing heavily on Pierce Egan Jr.'s *Wat Tyler* (London: Simpkin, Marshall and Co., 1841) and James Cooke's *Jack Cade, the Insurrectionist* (London: T. White, 1841), this chapter considers the historical precedents for attacks on London. The first real concerns about radical attempts to subvert London solidified around the Jacobin and Chartist movements of the early to mid-nineteenth century. Radicals themselves paid homage to Wat Tyler and evoked his march on London in 1381 as a possible blueprint for action against the government in the metropolis. Pierce Egan's popular novel about Wat Tyler's life captured the imagination of many radicals and was part of a radical cult surrounding Tyler's political memory that persisted through the early socialist movement into the traditions and popular memories of the Labour Party. This chapter considers the fears of a revived peasant revolt generated by such revolutionary visions and describes the importance of Pierce Egan's conception of a tumultuous and ungovernable London, both to radicals and to the opponents of reformism. Furthermore, it analyses subsequent depictions of the events of 1381 by those writers who, from a conservative perspective, saw Tyler worship as a phenomenon that bred dangerous radical notions, in particular, the children's author, G. A. Henty, in his *A March on London* (New York: Charles Scribner's Sons, 1897). Chapter 2 continues the theme of radical disruption of London and the concerns about national safety and collapse raised by radical insurgency. These manifested themselves particularly in the apparent threat posed by anarchist conspiracies in the later nineteenth century. The anarchist panics of the 1880s and 1890s coincided with the emergence of a more recognizably modern pulp fiction style and of new technologies for the construction of explosive devices. The origins of recent thriller-writing about bomb plots in London are here. Authors like E. Douglas Fawcett in *Hartmann the Anarchist* (New York, Arno Press: 1975), Richard Whiteing in *No. 5 John Street* (London: Thomas Nelson and Sons, 1902) and Edgar Wallace in *The Council of Justice* (London: Pan Books Ltd., 1973) were prepared to imagine the consequences of a successful terrorist bomb plot in London. Their concern to identify possible terrorist communities or suspects painted a lurid vision of a dark and dangerous London that harboured deviant communities and individuals prepared to target central government in its home. Such fiction overlapped with similar work on the continent and drew inspiration from the new detective and spy fiction genres. In turn, it contributed to the creation of a new 'literature of terror' that has implications for later 'Red Scares' in the inter-war period.

Post-1919, the strongest fears manifested by thriller and detective fiction writers clustered around the Bolshevik menace. Indeed the merciless and fanatical Bolshevik agent rapidly assumed a central role in all subsequent thriller writing up until the 1950s. Between 1920 and the mid-1930s, this figure dominated concerns about possible insurgency in London. Communist writers like John Sommerfield in *May Day* (London: Lawrence and Wishart, 1984) imagined the circumstances in which a popular uprising might become possible in the capital; in return conservative thriller writers shuddered at the possible implications of revolution in the metropolis and urged preparations against its apparent inevitability. John Buchan's Richard Hannay and Sapper's Bulldog Drummond clashed directly with circles of Communist agents, often against the backdrop of conspiratorial activity in London. Less well-known novels like Dennis Wheatley's *Black August* (London: Arrow Books Ltd., 1961), or Hugh Addison's *The Battle of London* (London: Herbert Jenkins Ltd., 1926) described the steady descent of the post-revolutionary metropolis into chaos and disorder, and warned against the secret forces, both inside and outside government, that were prepared to collude in a Bolshevik takeover of London. Such works carry a strong sense of the centrality of the usually overlooked British 'Red Scare' in the inter-war years.

Throughout the twentieth century, the rise of the extreme right troubled many British writers. From the 1930s, a speculative literature emerged that imagined a British Fascist state, imposed either by indigenous Fascists or emerging as a consequence of defeat in World War II. In novels like George Shipway's *The Chilian Club* (London: Mayflower Books, 1972) and Arthur Wise's *Who Killed Enoch Powell?* (London: Weidenfeld and Nicolson, 1970) informed by contemporary fears about the rise of the National Front, authors sometimes flirted with visions of a right wing, sometimes Fascist, attempt to subdue London, converting it into the headquarters of a revived, now ultra-conservative, nation, purged of radicals, intellectuals, liberals and trade union-ists. Much of this literature emerged out of the political volatility evident in Britain from the late 1960s. Typical 'Fascist Britain' novels like Peter Van Greenaway's *The Man who Held Parliament to Ransom and Sent the Queen Packing* (London: Penguin, 1968) and Robin Cook's *A State of Denmark* (London: New English Library, 1970) actively imagined a weakened British democracy under threat and the ensuring possibility of a right-wing coup. The beginning of the 1970s witnessed the starkest messages about the inevitability of political disintegration in London. Against the background of the metro-politan counter-culture inspired by the events of 1968, the squatting protests in South London, and the flaunting of trade union power, authors were only too willing to imagine the possibility of an incendiary, revolutionary, anar-chistic or post-putsch London. Transatlantic terrorist threats inspired by the American 'Weatherman Underground' and compatible with a similar ten-dency apparent in American popular fiction are particularly marked in such books as John Burmeister's *The Weatherman Guy* (London: Michael Joseph Ltd., 1976). In addition pulp fiction writers like Pamela Kettle in *The Day of the Women* (London: New English Library, 1970) speculated about feminist or extreme left takeovers by urban guerrillas. Such fears are also grounded in concerns about the emergence of Celtic nationalism, with a number of such volumes examining the implications of Welsh, Scottish or Irish extremist cam-paigns in the capital. Here popular fiction mirrored contemporary fears about the 'break-up of Britain'.

The final chapter charts the significance of previous decades of thriller-writing on the construction of the al-Qaeda threat, and the model it provides for an attack on the capital. 'Radical Islamism' has come to occupy the space formerly reserved for anarchists and Bolsheviks in recent metropolitan fic-tion. Drawing on the experience of the London bomb plot of July 2005, media responses to it and recent popular literature about al-Qaeda [notably Chris

Cleave's *Incendiary* (London: Vintage, 2005) or Stella Rimington's *At Risk* (London: Hutchinson, 2004), this chapter seeks to analyse the image of the terrorist in twenty-first century Britain and unravel its meaning against the background of the popular literature that has contributed so markedly to its construction. Finally, it assesses the contribution to cultural readings of the metropolis of the image of the bomber and his victims in more recent popular literature.

London, and the fiction that describes its collapse, are inextricably intertwined with British national identity and debates about the state of the nation. In common with other societies and cultures, Britain has spawned a literature of anxiety that acts as a barometer of the state of England. Sometimes badly written, often wrong in its assessment of British malaise, this literature found (and continues to find) a wide audience and a ready readership. It, and the moral panics fostered by it, are the subjects of the remainder of this book.

Chapter 1

Wat Tyler, Jack Cade and the Threat of Peasant Revolt in Nineteenth-Century London

For Wat Tyler of old, a hearty-chorus bold,
    Let Labour's children sing!
For the smith with the soul that disdain'd base control,
    Nor trembled before a king;
For the heart that was brave, though pierced by a knave
    Ere victory for Right was won –
They'll tell his fair fame, and cheer his blythe name,
    When a thousand years are gone!
    (Thomas Cooper).[1]

And Kett the Tanner whipt out his knife,
    And Wat the Smith his hammer brought down,
For ruth of the maid he loved better than life,
    And by breaking a head made a hole in the crown.
From the Saxon heart rose a mighty roar,
    'Our life shall not be by the king's permit,
We will fight for the right – we want no more'.
    Then the Norman found out the Saxon grit.
    (Robert Collyer, 'Saxon Grit').[2]

In recent years, much has been written about the role of the past in shaping the nineteenth-century political platform. In Britain, Chartists, reform radicals and socialists had a deep sense of the past. The oppositional politics they espoused was frequently enmeshed with notions of popular memory and ancestral rights. As on the continent, memory and tradition suffused the platform of nineteenth-century British radicalism. Many recent studies of popular politics have noted the appeals to history and memory mounted by reformers intent on a purification of the state through a return to pre-lapsarian notions of English liberty. The doctrine of 'Old Corruption' itself presupposed traditions of arcadian simplicity and Anglo-Saxon peasant purity prior to the Norman Conquest and postulated a historical fall from the virtues of long-standing English freedoms. The return to an imagined past emphasized the continuities between nineteenth-century reformism and previous moments of historical reform as well as lending precedent and depth to the nineteenth-century platform experience. Such convergences of history and tradition sustained the radical agitation into the early years of the nineteenth century and throughout the period of transition from Chartism, through popular liberalism, and into labourism after 1900.

The British tradition of historical memory is, however, a selective and promiscuous one. Some of the figures that have traditionally proved central to the radical tradition have been ignored by historians. In most secondary literature, peasant revolts, and those who led them, have been expunged from the catalogue of historical injustices that radicals drew on in support of their position. Wat Tyler, Robert Ket, Jack Cade and An Gof, insofar as they are remembered at all, are seen as part of a somewhat affected retro-kitsch leftism. They are portrayed as rural rather than urban figures, having little relevance to the mass movements rooted in the travails of nineteenth-century towns.[3] Moreover, their role is overshadowed by seminal and better-known events like the English Civil War, the Glorious Revolution of 1688 and the betrayal of the 1832 Reform Act. For radicals prepared to embrace 'direct action' tactics, however, the peasant revolts set up important precedents. The march of An Gof, Wat Tyler and Jack Cade on Blackheath, and thereafter the capital itself, supplied important examples of stalwart defenders of liberty, prepared to take their grievances to London and to seek restitution from their betters. These were men of the people, confident in their power and ability, gaining moral strength from the vigour of their supporters and unabashed in face-to-face contact with their social superiors. In this sense, the peasant leaders set up an important counter-point to aristocratic chivalric and heroic traditions in which those at the lower end of the social scale were prepared to hold government and crown to account. Moreover, the example of peasant revolt provided a framework of action for radicals bold enough to take a stand, as well as furnishing a narrative of popular revolt, much emulated in the popular literature of the 1840s and 1850s. Moments of decisive radical change, like the Liberal landslide of 1906 in Norfolk, were distilled down to 'something left over from Litester's Rebellion or Kett's Rebellion, something that while it left them (the peasantry) docile and good-humoured for years at a stretch, less likely than any body of men in Europe to break into rebellion, bubbled up in them on these occasions'.[4] In sum, the historical example of peasant revolt provided a canvas on which those who speculated about the future direction of reform might revisit the causes and consequences of revolt. In the absence of other alternative readings for the course a British revolution might follow, the peasant revolts of 1381, 1450 and 1497 became hugely important. Prophetic, and emblematic of a potential radical departure from the constitutionalist mainstream, they showed the degree to which government and crown might potentially unravel against the background of the relevant social and economic injustices. Moreover, the near success of the 1381 peasant rising in particular held out possibilities for the destruction of London and showed the capital's vulnerability in the face of potential riot and disorder. Unsurprisingly, then, mention of peasant revolt provided a politics of threat, in which the capital became the backdrop for a riotous and unrestrained incendiarism. In the popular literature that referred to the events of 1381, the keynote is danger, destruction and despair in which the metropolitan revolutionary impulse is awakened, and the arguments for and against drastic political change are rehearsed.[5]

I

In 1934 Labour regained control of the London County Council following a closely fought local election. In the weeks after the campaign, it resurrected a plan proposed by previous Labour administrations for naming one of the newly constructed streets on Lewisham Hill, close to the camp-site of the 1381 rebels on Blackheath, 'Wat Tyler Road'.[6] This issue had a long provenance. Proposals for the change of name had come before the council on previous occasions and had been opposed by the derided 'Lewisham respectability'. Herbert Morrison, the leader of the council, was keen for the change of name to go through, and received the backing of the Labour group on this issue. The choice of name, however, badly divided the council. The Local Government Committee baulked at the idea and countered the proposed with the suggestion that the road should be named after Anne Boleyn instead. Discussions remained inconclusive, but at a council meeting on February 13, it was alleged that 'Wat Tyler was more worthy of memory by respectability than Anne Boleyn'.[7]

The controversy surrounding the proposal for a 'Wat Tyler Road' indicates the centrality of the myth of Wat Tyler for radicals and reformers. Alternatively, for those who opposed the use of the name, Tyler evoked a spirit of rowdyism and disorder inappropriate for the nomenclature of the metropolitan suburbs. At the heart of the appeal of Tyler and other peasant rebels was the notion that this was a suppressed tradition that underwent a constant process of redis-covery and reclamation from the 'thousand defamatory pens (that) have lied away the characters of Ball and Tyler'.[8] From the eighteenth century onwards, the name became synonymous with dissenting causes able to summon up the spectre of Tyler, Cade or Ket. Twentieth-century evocations range across party and political divides from socialists, anarchists, Tory radicals, through environmental campaigners to motorway protestors and poujadiste groups or petrol protestors on the political right. Almost any act of radical opposition to the status quo could earn political reformers the sobriquet of 'Wat Tyler'. From Jack Jones as the 'pensioners' Wat Tyler' to José Bové as the 'Wat Tyler of Europe', Tyler has come to stand for an adamantine opposition to the accepted order of things.[9] His spirit was strongest amongst metropolitans groups, and those who saw themselves as operating outside the constraints of conventional norms. In the 1970s, squatters in South London took the notion of peasant rebellion to their hearts. The counter-cultural squatting agency set up by the self-styled hippy leader Heathcote Williams bore the legend embossed across its doorframe 'established by Wat Tyler, 1381'.[10] Tyler also re-emerged during the Poll Tax riots of 1990, when the slogan 'Avenge Wat Tyler' was appended to pamphlets and leaflets that sought to capitalize on the disturbances.[11] The spirit of peasant revolt was continued in the many commemorations and pageants that sought to keep the themes of the movement alive. During periods when the Labour Party has been torn about its future direction, Tylerism provided the opportunity for a re-examination of political goals, and for the exercise of fantasies of democracy.[12] The 600th anniversary of the revolt in 1981, which provided a rallying call to the Bennite Left within the Labour Party, and was commemorated with particular vigour by the Communist Party, had many precedents and drew on a strong vein of people's history.[13] For trades unionists, the 1381 rising was quite simply 'John Ball's strike'.[14] Republicans, freethinkers and anarchists also embraced some of the connotations of peasant revolt. Republicans saw the action of Richard II to suppress the peasant movement as demonstrating the bankruptcy of kingship and the beginning of a rebel tradition linking: 'Tyler and Ball, and Cade and Kett, Vane and Blake, and Harrison, Priestley and Cartwright, Spence and Owen, Vincent, Ernest Jones and Bronterre O'Brien'. Anarchists revelled in the massacre of lawyers and the resulting threat to the legal and social underpinnings of government: 'Ball's teachings were distinctly of an anarchist character. Preaching the establishment of a new order of things founded on social equality, he denounced and rejected all laws, and declared every person who upheld them to be a public enemy. In his opinion it was not sufficient for the rebels to kill the lords of the kingdom, they must also kill all the lawyers – advice which the insurgents were quite willing to follow'.[15] Tylerism, then, put later movements in touch with the shade of an irreconcileable folk violence and tradition of the 'people militant'. It survives in unexpected places, not least in the real ale movement where beers like 'Kett's Ale', 'Wat Tyler Ale', and 'Cornish Rebellion' demonstrate the historical pull of a movement that seemed to shrug off Victorian notions of sobriety and respectability and embrace instead the darker and more spontaneous mood of the people in revolt.[16]

Through such treatments, Wat Tyler and Jack Cade became the generic peasant revolt leaders. In them were distilled the violence, anger, rage and, indeed, temerity that were believed to characterize peasant protest. The ideas summoned up by his name were feared quite as much as they were endorsed. The abhorrence of Tylerism expressed by opponents of 'Wat Tyler Street' was in a long tradition with roots deep in the seventeenth and eighteenth centuries. By the middle years of the nineteenth century, Tyler had become a hobgoblin for respectable opinion. As early as the 1650s, popular histories used the Tyler legend to brand the Levellers as potential subversive Tylers.[17] The years 1789 to 1815 also witnessed an outpouring of pamphlet literature that stigmatized reformers as wolfish amoral Jacobins, keen to emulate the excesses of the peasant revolts of 1381 and of the later sixteenth century. Some of this literature set up Socratic dialogues between loyalists, demagogues and militant reformers in which the cause of reform is revealed as a sham opening the way for revolution. Most adopted a format in which Tyler is exposed as a foolish mountebank and wavering loyalists are won back to faith in cottage, throne and alter whilst Tyler leaves the stage lamenting his failure.[18] In 1815 the town of Norwich staged a loyalist public drama about Robert Ket's 1549 rising to celebrate the end of the Napoleonic Wars and to repudiate the threats posed by the resurgent Jacobinism of the post-war years. With one eye on contemporary events, its preamble read:

> The memorable rebellion headed by Kett the tanner was one of the most formidable of the numerous insurrections which, in elder times, have agitated this country; while, at the same time, she was bestowing peace and quietude on surrounding nations. It wore an aspect so appalling as to threaten consequences subversive of the constitutional authorities of the realm; and, in its devastating progress, called forth, from the public functionaries of the time, all the energies of loyalty, firmness and intrepidity to stem the furious torrent of desolation which rushed through the broken flood-gates of sedition.[19]

These fears of a revived Tylerism on the part of the respectable classes who saw in him a symbol of revolt was much satirized, not least by Charles Dickens in *Bleak House*. Here Sir Leicester Deadlock's recurrent fear is that any meddling with the proceedings of the Court of Chancery 'would be to encourage some person in the lower classes to rise up, somewhat like Wat Tyler'.[20] The names Tyler and Cade themselves became by-words for sensationalist and attention-seeking platform appearances by demagogues: Joseph Arch, Joseph Chamberlain, the Tolpuddle Martyrs, David Lloyd George, John Burns and even the Fenian movement were all compared to Cade.[21] Others sought to avoid the title, and were reluctant to act in ways that might evoke comparisons with the past history of peasant protest. Contemporaries feared that the Wilkeite reform movement of the 1760s could fall into the hands of extreme and violent Tyler-figures, fears that were apparently confirmed at the time of the 1780 Gordon Riots.[22] To be tarred with the image of a Tyler, then, was to drift from the constitutionalist mainstream into the wilder fringes of political radicalism. Seismic moments of social and political change also carried under-tones of social rage from below, channelled through the persona of the peasant rebel. Land reform in particular was believed to be the harbinger of broader social unrest, eliciting contact with the shade of peasant protest in the past. Some radicals depicted Tyler as an overt land-reformer whose campaign for rent reductions particularly incensed the Southwark slum-landlord, William Walworth, and brought about his death in 'a vindictive blow for landlordism'.[23] The custodian of radical memory, Joseph Clayton, made the link with peasant *jacquerie* and land reform explicit, writing in 1910: 'The leaders of the Labour Party, in their speeches at public meetings, use much of the old revolutionary talk of John Ball and Robert Ket, and the arguments of Winstanley for the popular ownership of the land'.[24]

II

There is a sense that a great deal of Tyler-worship is of comparatively recent vintage. It is traditional to attribute interest in the events of 1381 to William Morris' *The Dream of John Ball* first serialized in *The Commonweal* in 1886–7.[25] For Morris, the peasant revolt was an unambiguous harbinger of socialism. A time-travelling narrator is propelled back in history during a dream, to the eve of the final climactic battle of the rebellion. Revealing his fate to Ball, he outlines the future rise of industrialization and the inevitable emergence of the socialist utopia from the structural injustices of the relationships between capital and labour. Ball's defeat, he suggests, is a necessary sacrifice on the road to a more just society and part of an incremental struggle for liberty. Men who come after, argues the narrator, learning from the mistakes of the rebellion will understand: 'How men fight and lose the battle, and the thing that they fought for comes about in spite of their defeat, and when it comes turns out not to be what they meant, and other men have to fight for what they meant under another name'.[26] The book went through a number of cheap imprints, and was reissued as an inexpensive paperback in the inter-war years.[27] Thereafter images of 1381 abounded. The early radical and Labour movement was steeped in the popular memory of Wat Tyler's revolt. Immortalized in Edward Burne-Jones' frontispiece for the 1892 edition of the book in illustration of Ball's famous couplet 'When Adam Delved and Eve Span, Who Was Then the

Gentleman', the work became a socialist classic, performed by Morris at meetings, discussed by him with his audiences, and allegedly found as a cherished item in the homes of impoverished workers who had pawned all their other possessions.[28] The book gained such a wide readership that it circulated frenetically amongst radicals in the White Settler Colonies.[29] In Australia, the émigré radical and socialist William Lane wrote under the pen-name, 'John Miller', the password used by the fellowship of peasant rebels in Morris's fantasy of the rising.[30] In the 1880s, Henry Hyndman used the peasant revolt of 1381 as the starting point for his theoretical discussion of socialism in England, creating an influential and lasting chronology of labour that enabled Hugh Broadbridge to assert that the revolt marked the first occasion when 'the cry "socialism in our time" was raised'.[31]

Wat Tylerism thrived particularly amongst Christian Socialists. Stressing the primitive spirituality of the Medieval Church, Christian Socialists looked back to a pre-Reformation ideal characterized by unmediated contact with the poor, philanthropy and a close relationship between clerisy, lay members and congregation. There was a strong perception that this tradition arose from the same impulses that produced Wycliffe's vernacular Bible and the open air ministry typified by the teachings of Ball.[32] Those who argued this line suggested that the Reformation ruptured the close ties between cleric and flock, leading to a falling off of the pastoral traditions of the Church, with the suggestion that poor relief was no longer carried on with the same vigour once it fell into non-religious hands.[33] Commemorations of 1381 connected strongly with such ideas. The Christian Socialist writer Joseph Clayton, who had arrived at Labour politics through the Ruskinite Guild of Saint Matthew, was a vigorous celebrant of this position. A friend of Keir Hardie and Edward Carpenter and agent for Will Thorne in 1900 when he stood for West Ham, Clayton reappraized the peasant revolt tradition, and, against the backdrop of the House of Lords crisis of 1909–11, made it integral to the mythology of the Independent Labour Party. In a stream of publications, he rescued the reputations respectively of Robert Ket, Jack Cade and Wat Tyler.[34] This is a tradition also exemplified by the exuberantly anachronistic work of Bede Jarrett, who in *Medieval Socialism* reclaimed John Ball as 'a preacher of communism'.[35] Most famously of all, Conrad Noel, the 'Red' bishop of Thaxted in Norfolk, liked to think of himself as the spiritual successor to John Ball, and consecrated 'the Chapel of Blessed John Ball, priest, martyr – inspirer of the Peasants' Revolt, 1381' as part of a homage to him.[36]

Raphael Samuel has demonstrated the promiscuity of this tradition.[37] Even embraced by Home Rulers and proponents of Celtic nostalgia like Keir Hardie, Tyler worship grew out of Liberal narratives of political progress.[38] Drawing on the work of J. E. Thorold Rogers, liberal 'peoples' histories' focussed on the political obstacles to reform posed by the great territorial dynasties.[39] In these writings, the people struggled against the corrupt and oligarchic landed dynasties that exercised an influence disproportionate to their political talents, and whose presence disfigured the political history of Great Britain by manipulating parliament, throne and altar to their own ends. In much of this work there was a move away from traditional icons of Whig historiography, amongst them Hampden, Coke and Pym, notable for their gradualist approach to political reform, to figures who embraced a more aggressive vision of the English Commonweal. For some, the continental radical tradition embodied by the slave revolt against the Roman Empire led by Spartacus imparted a more respectable classical pedigree to reform history.[40] Many radicals, however, liked to see the English in particular as latent revolutionaries. For some, the presence of apparently revolutionary moments in British history like 1381 or 1549 enabled them to move away from appropriations of rebels in antiquity, French Revolutionary thinkers, or later, the images of the Bolshevik Revolution. This allowed for an indigenous tradition of revolt, wrested from the middle classes, that demonstrated the restiveness of the British population without recourse to alien and imported revolutionary traditions.[41] *Justice* relished the struggle for the soul of the national past from the grip of the bourgeoisie: 'There are Englishmen who know nothing of Ket, and little of Lilburne or the Chartists. History is written by the middle classes, for the middle class'.[42] The Independent Labour Party (ILP) in particular felt an affinity with the experience of 1381; its propaganda was steeped in this milieu in areas of its strength. When ILP branches in Kent were reorganized into a United Socialist Council in 1908, the event was inevitably described in the *Labour Leader* as 'The Peasants' Revolt in Tory Kent'.[43] The tradition, however, thinned in other parts of the United Kingdom, and Scottish radicals, for example, were more readily drawn to Scottish romantic heroes, particularly William Wallace.[44] For many English radicals Tyler worship became something of a historical catch-all, pointing up the despotic tendencies of restricted dynastic rule and allowing the first generation of Marxist historians to appropriate the long history of political injustice that traditionally featured in the radical canon. Christened 'Marxist Medievalism' by Raphael Samuel, this radical history provided a beacon for unity on the left and served the purposes of the Popular Front in the mid-1930s when Tyler and Ball featured alongside Oliver Cromwell and Richard Cobden in 'March of History Pageants' that showed the inevitability of a socialist triumph.[45] The cast of characters for a 1936 Communist Party appeal to history included 'on the road trodden by the great names of England's people – Simon de Montfort, Wat Tyler, Hampden and Cromwell, John Wilkes, Charles James Fox, the Tolpuddle Martyrs, Willliam Cobbett, the Chartists, William Morris, Keir Hardie, Tom Mann'.[46]

III

Whilst some memories of Tyler were revived by William Morris, Wat Tylerism
was already strongly embedded within the 'deep' memory of popular radicalism. Scrutiny of the political literature of the nineteenth century unearths
a robust tradition of radical militancy rooted in Tyler's politics dating back
at least to the 1760s. By the 1820s, a tangled history of the revolt was familiar to many working-class readers. Instrumental in this process of transmis-
sion was the juvenilia of the Romantic poet, Robert Southey. The story of
Southey's poem *Wat Tyler* is well known. In later years, after his elevation to
the Poet Laureatship, Southey sought to renounce the radicalism of his youth
and became a social and political conservative. In the 1790s, however, he was
a fiery romantic reformer, inspired by the events of the French Revolution.
Outraged by the trial and imprisonment of the London Corresponding
Society Jacobins, Southey was moved to write a long poem, *Wat Tyler* in protest at their treatment, and in celebration of the British revolutionary tradition. This he hoped to present to the imprisoned radicals. Never formally
published, the manuscript of the poem languished until 1817. During the
radical movement of the poet-Napoleonic War period, the poem fell into the
hands of radical publishers William Sherwin and Richard Carlile.[47] By this
time, in a conventional progress, Southey had moved away from the radical ardour of his younger self. Byron, Henry Brougham, Hazlitt and William
Smith were amongst those who denounced him for his change of heart. Keen
to prevent publication of the poem, Southey tried to suppress publication
of the work by suing Sherwin for breach of copyright. Lord Eldon, the Lord
Chancellor, shocked by its inflammatory tone, refused to grant him an injunc-
tion on the grounds that its wide circulation might foment revolutionary feeling.[48] Without any formal licence, the poem was open to repeat printing and
publication. The controversy drew attention to the work, and resulted in its
widespread dissemination in cheap pirated editions. Indeed, in unlicensed
editions, *Wat Tyler* sold three times as many copies as all the rest of Southey's
output put together. Southey's son later estimated that this amounted to
between 30,000 and 40,000 copies in individual sales.[49] James Epstein sees
the work as one of the great radical publishing phenomena of the nineteenth
century. The proceeds from it helped sustain the printing businesses of both
Shewin and Carlile for a number of years in the 1820s and 1830s.[50] At the
time, the fact that it was published to apparently coincide with the March of
the Blanketeers in Manchester brought it a considerable notoriety in radical
circles.[51] It was through this pirated edition that most of the literary encounters with *Wat Tyler* occurred. It was a favourite of the young Chartist militant, George Julian Harney, and circulated amongst the apprentices in the

print shop where W. J. Linton trained.[52] In later years *Wat Tyler* was quoted with approval by the Chartist press. Extracts from it appeared in a number of publications, and it featured in collections of Chartist verse and ballad sheets for distribution at public assemblies and radical camp meetings.[53] John Ball's testimony before Sir John Tresilian was a particularly popular excerpt from the play, still widely reproduced in the post-Chartist years. In it Ball doesn't deny that his rhetoric inflamed the already angry mob:

> That I told them
>   That all mankind are equal, is most true,
> And the blood-cemented pyramid of greatness,
>   Shall fall before the flash.[54]

Radical exposure to Southey's *Wat Tyler* was not, by itself, responsible for the large radical audience the story of the peasant revolts attained. By the early twentieth century, it appears to have languished somewhat; Jesse Collings was seemingly unaware of its existence when he appealed for the composition of a national epic dedicated to the subject of 1381 on the model of Schiller's *William Tell*:

> Vivid accounts have been given of the exploits of the peasantry in other countries. Splendid dramas and poems have been written in another country on the deeds of Tell; but the field is still open and the materials abundant for some able writer of prose, verse or drama, to bring home to the people of this country the feats of the peasant leaders throughout the centuries – these obscure heroes to whom the liberties of Englishmen are so largely due.[55]

There was, however, a significant residue of tradition relating to peasant revolt that persisted and provided a lived exposure to the story. Much of this was captured in the material culture of nineteenth-century public politics and the civic pageants of municipal histories. The metropolitan memory of peasant revolt was an especially potent one. Tyler lingered on as a character in the Bartholomew Tailors' Fair at Smithfield Market until its closure in 1855. Here nonsense and comedic plays were performed about him.[56] He was also a presence in the Lord Mayor's Parade, an appropriate reference given that it was William Walworth, Lord Mayor of London, who was responsible for his demise. Walworth had been a member of the Fishmongers' Livery Company. On those occasions when a member of the Fishmongers occupied the mayoral chair, they provided a float for the Lord Mayor's procession in which an effigy of Tyler's decapitated head was paraded in front of a knife-wielding Walworth.[57] It was witnessing this burlesque and the rather unpleasant imagery surrounding Tyler that persuaded William Morris to rescue the story of the 1381 revolt: 'All the more as it has become a sort of nursery tale in which the figure of the wise and pious kingly youth, the sturdy loyal citizen, and the ruffiany agitator have been made to stand out against a dark background of foolish and ignorant armed peasants, knowing not what they asked for.'[58] Tyler and Cade, in particular, remained lived presences in London literature. The chap-book tradition continued to refer to them although there was much ambiguity (and some downright hostility) in their depiction. As Dobson rightly points out, though, in these essentially loyalist productions the devil 'was inadvertently given the best tunes.'[59]

For some reformers there were clear continuities with the world depicted in the peasant struggles and post-1867 radicalism. In many instances, the received memory of Ket in particular seemed a positive one. Described as an 'English Gracchus', poetic laments circulating in London cherished his memory:

> Years rolled away before the plough again,
>   Went over Norfolk in Eliza's reign;
> And then each ploughman told his son of Ket,
>   His life and suffering till his eyes were wet;
> And girls wove garlands in his name,
>   Who had no grave – and hung them up to fame.[60]

Furthermore, Wat Tylerism was deeply entrenched in the iconography of the reform movement. Radical naming traditions often included references to Tyler. The name 'Wat Tyler' itself was a recurrent 'nom de plume' for angry correspondents to the reform press from the days of the Chartists, via the Reform League, to the early socialist and Labour agitation.[61] Alongside Ball, or Straw, his name became a popular alter ego for the most fiery platform demagogues. In the 1880s the ultimate accolade remained a comparison with Tyler, Ball or Straw, with Tyler retrospectively christened 'the John Burns of 1381'.[62] Admirers barely stopped short of seeing Joseph Arch as a reincarnated Wat Tyler.[63] Betrayal of established leaders and factionalism might lead to imputations of 'back-stabbing' and comparisons with Walworth's fatal blow to Tyler during the parlay at Smithfield. G. J. Harney compared the position of Chartist leader Feargus O'Connor, subject to considerable venom as a consequence of a power struggle within the movement, to the fate of Tyler: 'stabbed in the back by Walworth's dagger'.[64]

IV

By the 1920s, these diffuse traditions about peasant revolt had merged in numerous pageants and amateur dramatics with Tyler, Ball or Jack Straw and

Ket as their hero.[65] There was an *agitprop* quality to much of this work, and a socialist realist style that strongly influenced the post-World War I depictions of Tyler as a proletarian radical. In Halcott Glover's *Wat Tyler: A Play in Three Acts*, Tyler is an unequivocal socialist and bone fide hero of labour. As part of this symbolism, Tyler's blacksmith's hammer is prominently displayed throughout, and following his death, his body is carried from the stage with the hammer placed across his chest 'like a sword' in a subversion of the chivalric knightly tradition.[66] This celebration of the manual tools employed by peasant rebels from Tyler's hammer to the German peasant 'shuh' through to the sabot of the French *jacquerie* and saboteurs normalized the rebels as industrial 'working-men' or artisans, militarising the tools of their trade.[67]

So authentically proletarian did Tyler appear by the 1920s that there was criticism of those books and plays produced about the subject of the 1381 Peasant Revolt that were beyond the pockets of a working-class audience. *Freedom* was particularly scathing about William Chandler's 1927 play about the subject *Thirteen Eighty-One: An English Tragedy*, the text of which, whilst handsomely printed on a hand-press in a limited edition of 250 copies, sold at a price that 'put it completely out of the reach of a working-class reader'.[68] Tylerism was such an ingrained tradition within the politics of labourism at the end of the nineteenth century that it was almost obligatory for prominent radicals to pen some epistle or play to celebrate Tyler and the other rebels. This tendency is accurately captured in Howard Spring's novel of betrayal in the North Country Labour movement, *Fame is the Spur* in which the hero, Hamer Shawcross, an aspiring platform demagogue, writes a popular history of revolt to add to his democratic credentials:

> *Tyler, Ball and Company* had an extraordinary success. It was a history of popular revolt, threaded along the names of the people's leaders: Wat Tyler, John Ball and all the rest of them down to the tale of Orator Hunt and Peterloo . . . Historical pundits could have picked him to pieces, but he wasn't writing for pundits: he was writing for the millions, and at least he reached the hundreds of thousands. Like Blatchford's *Merrie England* his book came at a moment most opportune, voicing a growing unrest, feeding it, and giving it an objective. In its blue paper covers it made its way into the homes of northern artisans, of miners in South Wales and Durham, of chain-makers in Cradley Heath, and of seamen in a hundred ports.[69]

Drawing on themes of martyrdom and spiritual sacrifice, the cult of Tyler encouraged secular pilgrimages to places associated with the past history of peasant protest. Tom Paine famously lamented the absence of such a monument to his memory at Smithfield, the place where Tyler was killed. This theme was taken up by a later generation of radicals who derided the erection

Figure 1.1 Wat Tyler murdering the tax-collector with a hammer, the tool of his trade as a blacksmith. From Pierce Egan Jr., *Wat Tyler* (London: Simpkin, Marshall, and Co., 1841), p. 447. (Author's Collection.)

of a statue to Walworth, whereas Tyler's acts lacked any memorial.[70] For many reformers, however, visiting the topography and physical survivals of the various revolts became part of a counter-cultural experience, in which claims to a radical geography of the nation were asserted. This was radical politics as tourist-trail. There were attempts to treat some places as hallowed ground, effectively converting them into shrines. The WEA and Labour Colleges tutor Mark Starr wrote in *Lansbury's Labour Weekly*: 'It would be worthwhile, for example, on visiting the East End of London to trace Wat Tyler's march on the city, the subsequent attacks on the lawyers of the Temple, and the final incidents in Smithfield. We have no Wall of the Communards as in *Pere Lachaise*, but here is a fourteenth century memory of a deceived peasantry'.[71] The same notion underpinned attempts to lay claim to the square below Norwich Castle, on the grounds that it had been sanctified by the blood sacrifice of Robert Ket, whose body was hung from the castle walls following his abortive rising in 1549. Starr believed that this made the square into sacred ground, and validated its use by socialist and radical orators.[72] Some radicals even walked the sites of the battles connected with the various revolts. In a dedication at the beginning of his study of Ket's rising, Joseph Clayton recorded his thanks to John Burns, for accompanying him on walks at the alleged location of Ket's camp. He wrote 'To the Right Hon. John Burns M.P. Once a popular rebel, now an unpopular Minister of State, but always a large-hearted lover of the common people. This book is inscribed by his friend the author in memory of a certain joint pilgrimage to the scenes of the Norfolk Rising'.[73] Even the most dubious of survivals could double as places of radical assembly. Jack Straw's Castle on Hampstead Heath, a public house that had no convincing provenance or connection with the 1381 rising, was ostentatiously and impishly patronized by Tory radicals and supporters of Randolph Churchill's Fourth Party.[74] Marking or setting up monuments at such places was also commonplace. In Norwich there were a number of campaigns to erect a statue for Robert Ket.[75] He was finally commemorated by the unveiling of a plaque at Norwich Castle in 1949, at which, despite attempts to create distance from 'the Left-wing', there were indirect references to the rapid social change of the post-war years ushered in by the 1945 Labour Government. Dr Joan Evans, stressing that the present generation could identify with the societal changes Ket experienced, commented that he 'lived at a time when everything in England was in the melting-pot, religion, the language, the system of education, the style of building, and the feudal system, which was shifting to another class structure with a money basis, and even the English idea of state and monarchy'.[76]

Ultimately, the tradition of Wat Tyler was an unequivocal rallying call to revolt. At moments of legislative reform or of particular radical militancy (notably in 1831, 1842, 1848, 1866–7, and 1884) emotive appeals were made to his memory. The most extreme reformers unashamedly embraced Tylerism. In Sheffield, his name was closely associated with the unsuccessful rebellion by Samuel Holberry in 1840. At his funeral, George Julian Harney declared that 'with the Tells and Tylers of the earth, the name of Holberry will be associated'. The Sheffield Chartist Club in Fig Tree Lane featured a shrine to Holberry in which there was a bust of the martyred leader, and banners inscribed with the name of Tyler. Bingley, near Bradford, could boast its own 'Wat Tyler', a brawny blacksmith called Isaac Jefferson, who propounded an extreme physical force doctrine, and whose determination to resist arrest sparked off the Bradford riots of 1848.[77] Highpoints of political radicalism witnessed dramatic resurgences in Tyler's reputation. In 1858 his example was much cited in relation to the Bernard conspiracy to assassinate Napoleon III. *Reynolds's Newspaper* portrayed the 1381 rising as entirely justified in the face of illegitimate and despotic state action; from its perspective, and against the background of the politically sensitive assassination attempt on a widely disliked European head of state in which some British radicals colluded, it apparently provided a clear argument for tyrannicide. The paper described Tyler as 'goaded to rebellion by the most accursed and diabolical tyranny' by 'the execrable monarch Richard II'.[78] Most Tyler associations were, however, unambiguously metropolitan. The name was prized particularly by metropolitan radical groups. In the capital in 1817, and again in 1848, there were 'Wat Tyler' clubs and a Wat Tyler Chartist Brigade. The Wat Tyler Chartist organization especially was riddled with informers, its militant body language having attracted large numbers of police spies and agent provocateurs.[79] In London, Tyler stood for an irreconcilable tradition of political militancy. In 1867 the Chartist poet John Bedford Leno oversaw the design of a banner for the Bloomsbury Branch of the Reform League '3 ft 6 in. by 2 ft. representing Wat Tyler and the Tax Gatherer, and on the other side a full rigged ship in full sail to be called the Manhood Suffrage and the Ballot'.[80] The presence of Wat Tyler on a banner added a provocative and inflammatory tone to public gatherings and protests. A banner adorned with the image of Tyler (possibly the one Leno had a hand in designing) flew at the second Hyde Park meeting of 1867 asserting the popular right of entry to the royal park.[81] Other metropolitan reformers found themselves retrospectively ascribed with the characteristics of the fourteenth- and fifteenth-century rebels. Many of the open spaces of London, where clashes with the police and authorities occurred, carried memories of Tyler. Public space agitations organized to preserve access to Plumstead Common across the Kentish border in the 1870s inevitably drew on the memory of 'The Men of Kent'. A long-standing campaign to prevent enclosures and military exercises by the army from restricting popular recreations on the common was orchestrated by John De Morgan, an anti-vaccinator, Fenian, member of the International Working Men's Association (IWMA) and rights-of-way campaigner, who modelled himself on Tyler. De Morgan felt that popular agitations needed the touch of 'Kentish Fire'.[82] At a meeting on the common, he defied the police and detectives sent to report on proceedings: 'He knew that Wat Tyler was a man of Kent and that the basis of all his agitation was the right of the people to the commons. Wat Tyler assembled 40,000 or 50,000 of the men of Kent and it was only by treachery on the neighbouring Blackheath that the king was enabled to conquer the men of Kent. No number of detectives in plain clothes could injure their cause. The mark of the beast was upon them.'[83] Other open ground with a Tyler connection also attracted the attention of radicals and reformers. Clerkenwell Green, a place of long-standing radical assembly, and from 1890 the starting point for the May Day marches in London, gained a reputation for militancy after the burning of the Priory of the Order of St. John by Tyler's men. In addition, the display of his severed head there made it something of an unofficial shrine to Tyler in the aftermath of the rising. Thereafter it became a democratic space associated with proletarianized religious and political freedoms. In this, it bore some similarity to Blackheath, the site of the hustings for the Greenwich elections, which, despite its association with Gladstone who frequently spoke there in his role as MP for Greenwich, defied attempts to convert it into a tamed, domesticated liberal environment.[84]

Radical poets and authors were much attracted by 1381 and other peasant risings as symbols of revolt, and for the failure of the lost and hopeless political dreams they conveyed. The anniversary of Tyler's death was frequently commemorated by the publication of amateur songs and verses in his memory.[85] In 1850 the established Chartist poet Thomas Cooper was moved to write a full-length novel about the impact of the 1536 Lincolnshire Rising; the glamour of these risings also inspired more obscure amateur poets to chance their arm on this subject matter.[86] Writing in the *Northern Star*, a minor Chartist poet imagined the return of the wraith of the murdered Tyler, who, disappointed by the collapse of the rebellion after his death, laments the events that have stalled the reform project, and the lack of fervour apparent amongst radicals:

> A shadow called reform I see,
> > Exulting over the nation,
> Though Cade was slain ingloriously,
> > For seeking reformation.
> Muir and his fellow martyrs brave,
> > Their memories unrespected,
> You scarce can trace Fitzgerald's grave,
> > And Emmet lies neglected.

Hoping the example of 1381 will stiffen the cause of reform, Tyler flees, pursued by the vengeful shade of Walworth, and imploring the Chartist movement to remember him in his suffering:

> Many kindred spirits still survive,
> 　　To raise for coming glory,
> Till not a Briton but will strive,
> 　　To profit by his story.[87]

The ambiguities of the Tyler legacy are expressed through the popular literature that dealt with the rising. Many of these poems and short epistles accentuated the ambivalence within the radical community about the nature of the revolt, and the divisions between reformers that existed over the character of peasant protest. In both 1831 and 1871 at the time of the reform bill crisis and the republican agitation against Queen Victoria, Tyler and Cade were held up as vulgar demagogues who perverted the course of reform and undermined the impulse towards graduated democratic change and individual self-improvement.[88] Cade in particular was a figure who was quintessentially anti-Victorian, stigmatized for his ignorance and illiteracy and, despite the attempts by some worker historians to rescue his reputation, frequently portrayed as a 'tool of aristocratic tyrants' and a mere dupe of aristocratic faction.[89] The term 'Jack Cade legislation' was sometimes used by critics of progressive and levelling acts of parliament to demonstrate the subversive nature of such reforms.[90] The Tyler and Cade who emerged from such treatments were little better than blood-thirsty brutes. Both figures became pantomime villains for the anti-reform course. In John Walker's poem a malevolent Cade broods:

> Strike down these ermined ruffians, lords and all:
> Clergy, and squires and Commons – they must fall.
> Down with the middle classes, merchants too,
> Strike them to earth, the scoundrels yet shall rue;
> Their castles, churches, palaces, shall blaze,
> And all the world on this bold action gaze:
> Then, gallant brethren, when the battle's o'er,
> And all the rich are butcher'd in their gore,
> We'll seize their treasures, and need work no more.[91]

For some reformers, these same attributes made the rough justice meted out by the peasant leaders an acceptable code of conduct for prototype British revolutionaries. John Watkins, an enthusiastic North Riding ultra-radical, who proposed the guillotining of the leaders of the Lovettite Chartist faction, fantasized about the extreme violence associated with the revolt and lauded its excesses in his own amateurish poetical compositions.[92] For many radicals, however, the violence associated with Tyler and Ball made them too unpalatable for incorporation into the pantheon of the radical elect. For them, Ball was a more acceptable alternative, a priest and an ascetic, distanced from the worst excesses of the revolt, whose actions were sanctified by Morris' work, and whose career placed him firmly within the forms of fellowship associated both with the early Christian churches and the ILP. J. Bruce Glasier, locating him alongside other radical saints, was moved to ask: 'What is it that has from the beginning of society stirred men to forsake their own comfort and plunge into the hard, thorny ways of reform and the scorching furnaces of revolution – the John Balls, the William Wallaces, the Toussaints the Winkelrieds, the John Browns, the Sophia and Petrovskayas . . .?'.[93] Here Ball featured in a strong vein of quasi-mystical and spiritual populism within radical movements, in which he propounded an early gospel of 'social equality'.[94]

V

For both admirers and opponents of Tyler, the set-piece descriptions of these writings centred around the burning of London, the opening of the Marshalsea prison and the destruction of the Palace of Savoy. References to Ket or to Tyler abounded in later periods of political ferment characterized by public disorder, especially during the Gordon Riots of 1780, when Lord George Gordon sought to distance himself from memories of Tyler, and Horace Walpole appropriately 'ransacked', among other precedents, memories of the Ket rising of 1549.[95] Some writers treated these events with sympathy, seeing Tyler as a noble guerrilla leader, too trusting of his followers and betrayed by the rioting urban mob mingled with the semi-criminalized elements released from the gutted Marshalsea. For them, the rebels were pushed into the unwise cause of revolt by short-sighted and inflammatory state action.[96] Pierce Egan Jr's *Wat Tyler*, written in 1841, best encapsulates this tradition. Written at the height of the Chartist agitation, and reaching a wide readership, Egan Jr's *Tyler* continued in the vein of his previous work, in which considerable sympathy is evinced for key historical figures with a radical appeal, amongst them the Netherlands ultra-Protestant Quentin Matsys, the American rebel privateer John Paul Jones and the long-standing emblem of outlawry, Robin Hood.[97] Egan has some of the characteristics of Harrison Ainsworth. He specialized in historical romance fiction and excelled at descriptions of a dark and fearsome Middle Ages, dominated by ravening aristocratic gangs, abducted blue-blooded ladies, brooding castles and cruel dungeons, filled with instruments of torture. Lavishly illustrated by Egan, these works had a folk art quality. In contrast to his loyalist and apolitical father, Egan Jr. dabbled in the radical politics of the 1840s, becoming a well-known jobbing illustrator and writer in the popular journalistic circles of the capital. Subsequently he contributed to newspapers of a mildly liberal persuasion like the *Weekly Times* and *Home Circle*.[98] Through his writings, the vision of a landlord-ridden Middle Ages became a staple of advanced liberal fiction, in which social and political progress was retarded by monarchs, courts and their aristocratic and priestly retainers.[99] Written in 1841, Egan Jr's *Wat Tyler* captured the reforming mood of the early 1840s and attracted a wide Chartist readership. His Tyler was a man driven beyond endurance by the exactions of a corrupt and lascivious tax collector, and the inequitable treatment meted out by the most fanatical of the king's followers. This echoed the traditional account in which Tyler's daughter is sexually molested by the king's tax gatherer under the guise of investigating her age and thus her fitness to pay the poll tax. The tax gatherer is killed by Tyler, 'the neighbours applauded the deed, prepared to support Tyler and so gathered a large force'.[100] To reinforce this positive view of Tyler, Egan Jr. invented a spurious pedigree for him in which his slim biography is fleshed out by a career as a soldier, fighting patriotically by the side of the Black Prince at *Crécy* and the siege of Cambrai in the Hundred Years War. This portrayal depicted Tyler as a 'Freeborn Englishman' incarnate, loyal, trustworthy and righting wrongs introduced by delinquent advisers, and scheming aristocratic families.[101] Many of the virtues of the true-born Saxon persisted in these images. Tyler was frequently seen as a man of Saxon blood, who opposed the tyrannies of Normanism. 'The rebels got to London and committed all kinds of depredations against the Normans', wrote the land and poor law reformer Thomas Costley, adding 'this was not class against class, but was a fight of the old blood against the new blood'.[102] This was a model transposed onto Cade in a similar fictional treatment of the peasant leader's career by James Cooke written in 1840. Again in this treatment, Cade is a reluctant rebel, who suffers abuse at the hands of unscrupulous Norman courtiers, including the sexual molestation of his wife on their wedding night. In a final speech of defiance before he is cut down by the king's men, Cade declaims:

> Thous asketh me or rather these men for whom I answer what we have to complain of. I will tell thee officer of oppression that hath turned trust, deity and love into suspicion, revolt and hatred. Thou art the servants of those who have ridden over the prostrate forms of hundreds, yea many thousands – who have put a tax upon the sweats that drippeth from the toil-worn peasant's brow; have classed their fellows like oxen; and from the serf's bridal bed pulled the blushing partner of his toils and simple wants to become liveried menials, the victims of the rich man's gross desires . . .

His aim, he cries, is 'of taking from the worn their burthens; of ripping the rich, purple ermine and gold from the shoulders of mankind's oppressors'.[103] Far from being looters of the capital in 1381 and 1450, the peasant rebels that emerge from these popular fictions were stalwart defenders of the weak and fearful. In Pierce Egan's account of the rising, Tyler attempts to rein in the mob and prevent the destruction of London. The backbone of his peasant army are 'small tradesmen. . . who were not guilty of the excesses which the lowest order of their companions were'. Even the most riotous members of the peasant invaders are excused. In Egan's eyes, the depredations and looting are a reaction to the ill-treatment of the poor and the brutal conditions they experienced at the hands of their social betters. Their actions were 'easily accounted for in the fact that these poor creatures, having been held no better than brutes, treated in all degrees as such, fed, housed, beaten, made to slave and toil as such, were, in reality scarcely removed from brutes. Shame upon those who had made them so!'[104] Other radicals highlighted the degree to which looters were punished by the peasants themselves, stressing the incident in which plunder taken from the Duke of Lancaster's House was flung back into the burning building.[105] This honourable view of Tyler and other peasant leaders and followers (amongst them the Duke of Monmouth and Cade) stressed the position of the rebels as victims, the prey of judicial tyrants and an inflexible state that meted out excessive punishments to the innocent or misled.[106] In 1848, the trial of the Orange Tree Tavern Chartist conspirators in London and the suspension of habeas corpus in Ireland drew exaggerated comparisons with the 'Harvest of Heads' at the end of Cade's rebellion and Judge Jeffreys' 'Bloody Assizes' in the West Country.[107]

The model of Irish insurgency lay behind many of the fears about a new peasant rising. The rising in Ireland in 1798 and attempts to initiate a revolution in 1848 by Young Ireland militants, placed Irish concerns at the forefront of contemporary anxieties about political instability and imperial disintegration. During the reform bill crisis of 1831–2, the moderate reformer William Napier stressed that he would never take the path of a Wat Tyler or a Jack Cade: time spent in Ireland as a military officer during this turbulence had taught him the folly of revolt.[108] For many contemporaries, the Irish situation in 1798 demonstrated the potential for success of an Irish peasant rising and provided a blueprint for the violence that might be visited on the capital. The 1798 rebels were largely a peasant army, whose massacres and depredations became intertwined with representative images of a successful and destructive *jacquerie*.[109] In fictional accounts of 1798, many of the excesses attributed to Wat Tyler and his men in 1381 are reproduced as representative features of debased and degraded peasant armies. Like British peasant rebels, Irish rebels in loyalist discourses were driven by predatory animal urges, plotted in secret and bound themselves together in demonic legions by secret and blood-curdling oaths.

There was a strong gothic element in fictional accounts of peasant rebels desecrating the dead or licking the blood from their own pikes. There were also counterparts of Ball in the role of Irish Catholic priests in fomenting the rebellion. In many accounts they were seen as fanatical priest-warriors, inciting their superstitious and ignorant congregations to violence, and using religion to blind them to their true interests.[110] There were strong fears here manifested by the urban, against the rural. Within British radicalism, the romantic cult around Robert Emmet, the doomed leader of the 1803 rising in Dublin, also evoked some of the romantic and romanticized features of leadership that surrounded Tyler and Straw.[111]

Collisions between rural and urban life are a feature of the attack on London narrative. For loyalist critics, 1381 symbolized unrestrained mob violence at its worst. The spectre here was of a unity between militants in the towns and a turbulent peasantry. Bringing these two combustible elements together was seen as destructive of the existing political order.[112] There was also little here of the popular petitioning tradition 1381 is conventionally said to express. Rather, the destruction of a number of prominent public buildings in London in 1381 cemented the image of peasant revolt at the heart of popular lore relating to riot and disturbance in the capital. The pulse of popular rebellion beat strongly in the pulp literature of the period and mirrored prevalent concerns about the mob. In Silas K. Hocking's novel *The Broken Fence*, which begins with an anti-enclosure riot in Cornwall, the crowd marches rhythmically and ominously in step to tear down the land fenced off by the local squire. As they march, they sing the traditional verses of support for Archbishop Trelawney, clerical opponent of James II in 1687:

And Shall Trelawney die,
　　　Then Thirty thousand Cornish men,
Shall know the reason why.

Similarly, Charles Gleig's thriller, *When All Men Starve* set in a futuristic England of food shortages and bread riots follows the fortunes of a rebellious peasant army of rioters and radicals who march on London in a 'straggling column, devoid of discipline, devoid of artillery, devoid of all martial necessities save dare-devil courage born of desperate resolve'.[113] In this work the bread rioters are an amalgam of previous images of peasant rebellion. Like swaggering freebooters they wear black feathers in their hats reminiscent of the 'wisp of wheaten straw', the generic Jack Straw ostentatiously wears in his cap in Morris' *Dream of John Ball*.[114] For most critics, the strongest images left by the rebellion of 1381 were of a London in flames, where mob law ruled against a backdrop of the destruction of major landmarks like the Palace of

Savoy and the Priory of St. John at Clerkenwell. One much-reprinted critique of the events of 1381 described Tyler's men as a 'parcel of low ruffians' and talked of he 'whose arm was for robbing the City of London and the extirpation of all who were any ways noted for learning with twenty thousand of the dregs and scum of his rake-hells'.[115] The most graphic depictions of a London in flames occur in the fiction of the patriotic children's writer G.A Henty.[116] In 1897, his *March on London* put a strongly loyalist inflection on the events of 1381. Against the backdrop of Queen Victoria's Golden Jubilee of 1897, Henty sought to reclaim the jingoistic dimension to the rising. The heroes he places at the heart of the action were not the peasant leaders, rather they were the knights and courtly retainers who served Richard II, and helped overcome the revolt. For Henty, Richard II, 'the boy king' was the undisputed hero of events. At a time of much introspection about the reign of Queen Victoria, his story of a child monarch, brought unexpectedly to the throne, overcoming rival claimants and an unsupportive family, against the turbulence of a rapidly changing, riotous England and warfare abroad, bore more than a hint of the loyalist narrative of Victoria's reign that underpinned the Jubilee.[117] Indeed, Tyler makes only two brief appearances in the book, stepping out from the crowd as a sullen and resentful demagogue, and later in a standard vignette, felled for his 'threatening and insolent' manner by Walworth at Smithfield.[118] Henty saw 1381 as emblematic of the forces released by socialism and the early Labour Party. In such treatments, Tyler became a symbol of the crowd, an embodiment of an unstable, shifting crowd *mentalité* in with he was prominent in either restraining, or encouraging, its excesses. Henty dwelt excessively on a London alive with social ferment, and close to destruction. Even attempts by the peasant leaders to restrain the mob he portrays as bestial. His scene of the looting at the Duke of Lancaster's Palace is alive with fear and anxiety about mass popular action:

> With shouts of triumph they broke into it and scattered through the rooms, smashing the furniture and destroying everything they could lay hands upon. Some made for the cellars, where they speedily intoxicated themselves. Loud shouts were raised that nothing was to be taken. The silver vessels and jewels were smashed, and then carried down to the Thames and thrown into it. In a short time flames burst out in several parts of the palace. One man was noticed by another as he thrust a silver cup into his dress. He was at once denounced and seized, and was without further ado hurled into the flames.[119]

Henty is clear that by their actions in looting London, and their attacks against the Flemish community, which feature prominently in the book, the peasant

army have absolved themselves from all pity. In his final descriptions of the
rout of the peasantry, they are cut down, without mercy, by his child-heroes:

> The two lads kept together so as to be able to give each other assistance
> should any stand be made. None, however, was attempted; the greater por-
> tion of the rioters had thrown away their arms, and when overtaken they
> raised cries for mercy.
>
> 'You gave none to the Flemings', the lads shouted in return, infuriated by
> the scenes they had witnessed in London; and for an hour they followed the
> fugitives, sparing none who came within reach of their swords.[120]

VI

For plebeian reformers, interest in peasant revolt was more than simple
'ancestor-worship'.[121] Radicals valued the tradition for the lineage it gave to
the reform cause, and for the light it shed on the motivations behind physical
force militancy. A popular concern to revisit the career of the famous rebel
pushes the origins of English radical memory back beyond the seventeenth
century, which Margot Finn sees as the starting point for a particular brand
of folk radicalism.[122] Tyler was an 'uber-militant', driven to embrace direct
action by extreme personal privation and despotic unjust rule. For some radicals, the Tyler tradition impelled a historical momentum towards liberty that
the aristocracy of England were simply unable to snuff out. Pierce Egan Jr.
wrote that the aristocracy of fourteenth-century England was 'so very high
in Toryism, they could believe no improvement in the people's condition less
than a crime'.[123] Writing in 1899, the socialist James Leatham saw reform as
incremental, and the failure of the peasant revolt as a consequence of under-
developed social and political institutions in Great Britain. He wrote that only
the graduated reform of Britain's civic polity would allow the energy of the
revolt to be harnessed to the reform platform and then 'the cause of the people
could go marching on'.[124] This view was echoed by some foreign observers who
discerned the same concerns and a similar trajectory towards reform in both
the peasant revolts and the movements that followed them.[125] Often radicals
completely misunderstood the risings they embraced so enthusiastically. Even
the most unlikely risings were pressed into service to reveal the full extent of
'Old Corruption' within the state. The 1549 'Prayer Book' rising in the West
Country for example, which advocated a restoration of the traditional Latin
liturgy, an end to Archbishop Cranmer's Book of Common Prayer as well as
to the iconoclastic attacks on Catholic shrines, in Chartist eyes was shorn of
its deeply conservative underpinnings to emerge as a moment of liberty and

Figure 1.2 Wat Tyler as a popular demagogue rallying his peasant army. From Pierce Egan jr., *Wat Tyler* (London: Simpkin, Marshall and Co., 1841), p. 468. (Author's Collection.)

renewal. Writing in 1854, Ernest Jones embraced it unreservedly. For him, it demonstrated the persistence of historical traditions of liberty that might be absorbed by the Chartists to re-establish their base in the West. He stressed the continuities between a revolt that had been suppressed by an army of mercenaries under the command of Lord John Russell and Lord Grey, and the continuing depredations of the great Whig dynasties still in government during the middle years of the nineteenth century: 'The seed of evil sown then is growing now, and will continue to grow till the strong hand of freedom tears up the deadly upas of monopoly and wrong' he asserted.[126] The peasant revolt was an entrenched part of the visual grammar of political militancy. There can be nothing more emblematic of Chartist radicalism in particular that the vision of the man with the pike.[127] Such visual references provided a frame of reference for movements of political protest into the twentieth century. For other reformers, the peasant rebels were an example of the people militant. The notion of a people prepared to defend themselves by training with the bow and staff featured strongly in the ideas of radicals opposed to standing armies, their aristocratic and courtly officers and the tax exactions they required to support them.[128] For most radical reformers, the peasant revolt signified the longevity of the people's cause. Moreover, it demonstrated that the traditional idea of liberty remained the same down the ages. In this sense, the tradition acted as an antidote to liberal constitutionalist histories, and provided a plebeian variant on Whiggish readings of the national past. Radicals were happy to view the past anachronistically (and even eccentrically) in their search for similarities with their cause. In their eyes, the popular petitioning tradition that was a frequent feature of fifteenth-century revolt bore many of the same aspects of the Chartist petitions of the 1830s and 1840s.[129] The Revolt of the Commons was also seen as an outdoors revolt with strong similarities to the campaigns waged around the metropolitan open spaces in the 1860s. For most radicals, the same traditions of liberty that dwelt under the Oak of Reformation in Ket's camp outside Norwich continued to reside in the brown field sites and open spaces where radicals and reformers met and congregated to discuss republicanism and parliamentary reform in the 1870s and 1880s.[130]

This chapter has stressed the centrality of historical memory to nineteenth-century radical reformers and excavated the less well-known aspects of this constitutionalist tradition. Concentrating on radical images of peasant revolt, it suggests ways in which radicals who looked to an indigenous British tradition of revolt sought to resurrect the memory of peasant leaders like Wat Tyler and Robert Ket. Chartist radicalism in the 1840s drew strongly on nativist notions within popular reformism. In line with their long-standing concerns to purge 'Old Corruption' from government, British radicals extracted their own version of history from the national narrative. Within Chartist rhetoric, there was

a celebration of figures associated with turmoil and disorder in British historical memory. Drawing on Southey's celebration of Wat Tyler in 1794, peasant
heroes were particularly lauded, amongst them Tyler himself, Jack Cade and
Robert Ket. Moreover, events in Europe in 1848 and 1870–1 led same reformers to reconsider the English Civil War, the Monmouth Rising in 1685 and
the Glorious Revolution in 1688. For many radicals, the same social forces
that historically repressed liberty in a British setting were again in the ascendant in the middle years of the nineteenth century. Amidst the period of reaction following the Orange Tree Tavern Conspiracy in August 1848, memories
were stirred of the tyranny of Charles I in the English Civil War and of Judge
Jeffreys at the 'Bloody Assizes'. For many radicals Tyler, Ball, Ket and Cade
provided an answer to the aristocratic traditions of chivalry that marked off
landed and aspiring aristocratic society in the middle years of the nineteenth
century. *Reynolds's Newspaper* saw Tyler as a plebeian hero and worthy lower
class response to Simon de Montford: 'What Simon de Montford did for the
trading or middle classes at the cost of his life, was hardly surpassed by what
Wat Tyler effected for the serfs by the sacrifice of his'.[131] This, then, is a chapter
about the manipulation of British historical memory in 'the Age of Reform'. It
demonstrates the emphasis reformers placed on well-established notions of
popular liberties, radical constitutionalism and the continuing power of the
tradition of 'Norman Yokery' throughout the nineteenth century.

Chapter 2

Anarchism and the Literature of Terror in the Metropolitan Imagination

And in sight of the battlements of wealth and power, striding over the blood-stained paths of the past, the anarchist reaches out his hand to destroy the whole rotten fabric of today! It shall not be reconstruction, but destruction! It cannot be! It must be destruction! The twentieth century shall be ushered in by the crash of falling thrones. One decade remains. Our motto, 'No Quarter,' our weapon, dynamite. 'Terror' in the Old World is our means of attack! And in the New! To grasp at money, to control votes, to ally ourselves with party, to get a hold on officials, can we thus prepare for the bloody fields of nineteen hundred![1]

Michael Koffman hurled a bomb – and fled.

Undetected in the panic, unseen through the reek of dust and smoke, he quickly reached the river and dived like a rat over the quay edge. Immediately below him lay a small sailing ship. Silently he dropped aboard, and vanished into the hold. There was only one man on deck at the time. He came aft slowly, and quietly closed the hatch. Then he lay down and affected to sleep on it.[2]

Anarchism provided the cultural context for the terrorist panic of the last quarter of the nineteenth century, and the first decade of the twentieth. The years between 1880 and 1910 were bracketed by anarchist atrocities. According to the *Saturday Review*, between 1865 and 1900, 'two reigning sovereigns, one royal consort, and at least one leading statesman were killed by anarchists and "vulgar regicides".'[3] For better or for worse, these assassinations stamped their imprint on anarchism. Subsequently it was unable to escape from its close associations with the politics of terror. For contemporaries, anarchism distilled many of the social fears of the *fin de siecle* period and reflected prevalent anxieties about the collapse of the cultural and political certainties of the nineteenth century. During this period, it became a metaphor for the broader dissolution of European society. Assassination attempts and bomb-plots were compounded by the presence of individuals from the upper echelons of European society within the ranks of the anarchists themselves. Mikhail Bakunin, Count

Tolstoy and Peter Kropotkin were all from notable families and could boast connections at court, and relatives amongst the gentry, causing *Reynolds's Newspaper* to characterize the movement in Russia 'as an aristocratic as well as a democratic organization'.[4] This phenomenon of renegade aristocrats and 'titled' assassins convinced contemporaries that the social order was in the process of dissolution. For some observers, the status quo was weakened by the spectacle of the aristocracy and upper tier of European society rending itself into chaos and disarray. Above all, anarchism carried connotations of social fragmentation, disorder and imminent governmental collapse. The executions of prominent French anarchists like Emile Henry and Ravachol, which were the first political executions since the Paris Commune, served to highlight an apparent drift into chaos and disorder.[5] These anxieties are expressed in the remarks of W. E. Adams, 'that madness was in the air in the eighties and far into the nineties. There were German madmen, English madmen, French madmen – all thirsting for blood, like so many ghouls or vampires'.[6]

I

Anarchism is a movement that is much misunderstood. Those hostile to anarchism saw it simply as an agitation rooted in the doctrines of conspiracy and dedicated to the propagation of terror. Terms like 'nihilism' that carried strong cultural resonances, but which contributed little to an understanding of the complexities of the movement, were frequently substituted for 'anarchism' by its detractors. Despite the moral panics surrounding anarchism in the 1880s, the movement itself has left minimal traces in British, political, social and cultural history. Described by Peter Marshall as a river 'fed by many currents', anarchism has few stable core components.[7] David Weir points out that anarchism's ideas were largely subsumed in other political movements, recurring in socialism, liberalism and to some degree, conservative individualism.[8] Inconsistencies abounded within anarchism. The Bolshevik Victor Serge recounted that the anarchism he encountered in Paris in 1906 as a young man was 'shot through with contradictions [and] fragmented into varieties and sub-varieties'.[9] Some variants of anarchism espoused a primitive communitarianism, others a robust and strident individualism.[10] Displaying some affinities with Marxism and social democracy, anarchism preached individual hostility towards and militant non-compliance with the status quo. Whether peaceful or militant, anarchism was about non-conformity and individual self-expression. Drawing on George Bernard Shaw, Willard Wolfe defines it as nothing less than 'the complete and consistent defence of human freedom, combating monopoly and coercion in every form'.[11] Differing from Marxism

Figure 2.1 A bomb explosion attributed to anarchist conspirators during a public meeting in Haymarket Square, Chicago in 1886. From M. J. Schaack, *Anarchy and Anarchists: A History of the Red Terror and the Social Revolution in America and Europe* (Chicago: F. J. Schulte and Company, 1889), p. 142. (Author's Collection.)

in its appeal to the peasantry and to the 'lumpenproletariat', anarchism advocated individual revolt and an end to centralized state institutions.[12] For most contemporaries, anarchism was a movement that was fixated on the individual, the decentralized and the regional at the expense of the national and the collective. The term 'anarchist', however, has found expression in literature, art and politics and recurs frequently as part of an anti-statist or sometimes bohemian outlook. Highly theatrical, flamboyant, attention-seeking and, at times, near-hysterical in its denunciations of oppressive systems, anarchism may be regarded as the anti-programmatic Left. It stands against power and authority, against the power of the state, against bureaucracy ('Red Bureaucracy') in the case of socialism, against militarism and war, against the domination of women by men, against clericalism, and against censorship that hindered the free circulation of ideas.[13] The Labour leader William Anderson captured the spirit of anarchism when he recalled the anarchist Harry Duncan, who 'spoke with a good deal of force, and with one vast oratorical sweep used to level in the dust statesmen, politicians, parliaments, lawyers, priests, monopolists, capitalists, landlords, powers and principalities'.[14] In Britain, however, anarchism has tended to take a more 'ethicist' road.[15] Positively, it stands for egalitarianism, co-operation, individualism (Ibsen's 'the minority is always right), regionalism and small units of production. It distrusts government, seeing it as the product of forces that manipulate the state for its own ends.[16] The maxim of the Russian peasantry 'only fools exult when governments change' was much quoted by anarchists throughout the nineteenth century. Anarchists abstained from voting, refused to pay taxes and preferred 'delegation' or 'voluntary co-operation' to centralized leadership.[17] In 1891 its visionary components led George Bernard Shaw to talk about 'the impossibilities of anarchism'.[18]

Moreover, anarchism had strong peasant roots. It was significant in those parts of Europe where there were unreformed systems of land tenure and little or no democratic representation. 'Land and Freedom' became its slogan in Russia and Spain. Anarchism's violent associations are a consequence of its origins in non-participatory state systems. It drew its most dedicated adherents from the nations of eastern and southern Europe, which were left untouched by the changes of the French Revolutionary era, and where there was little popular democracy. In these areas, its supporters tended towards the volatile. Anarchists turned frequently and readily to violence. Anarchism's emphasis on 'propaganda by deed' led its many opponents to characterize the movement as one of senseless, unthinking destruction. There was something of the millenarian in its determination to undermine and cast down all existing religious and political institutions and replace them by a renewed and vital brotherhood of man. For Wagner, the fiery utterances of Michael Bakunin, anarchist high-priest and leading advocate of physical force, prompted him to describe the anarchist leader as 'a destroyer of gods'.[19]

Anarchism's disregard for social, sexual and political convention made it vulnerable to the taint of criminality. Like other terrorist organizations, it showed a tendency to diversify into crime. The apparent overlap between anarchism and the criminal underworld was noted by many contemporaries. For its critics, the spirit of freedom that permeated anarchism readily turned to licence. As Bertrand Russell commented, 'anarchism attracts to itself much that lies in the borderland of insanity and common crime'.[20] In France, anarchists christened themselves 'illegalists', and talked about 'revolutionary expropriation' and 'individual expropriation' as coded language for pure theft. The celebrated French anarchist, Ravachol, was a criminal opportunist, only retrospectively granted anarchist status. In addition, the French anarchist group, the Bonnot gang, were pioneers of motorized bank raids and the use of acetylene torches used in safe-cracking to boost the revolutionary war chest.[21] J. Bruce Glasier recalled that in London the Autonomie Club became 'bolder and bolder' in its resort to illegality, preparing 'to issue a few years later (1894) leaflets entitled "Vive le Vol" ("Long live Theft") and even to justify theft not only on the part of the poor from the rich, but by comrades from comrades'.[22] Other anarchists flirted with unconventional illegal or semi-legal sexual experimentation that defied social convention and sometimes carried legal penalties. Emma Goldman in the United States and John Henry Mackay in Germany preached contraception, free love, non-monogamous sexual relationships and homosexuality.[23] The most frequently read and well-known anarchist today remains Alex Comfort, author of the classic sex manual from the 1970s, *The Joy of Sex*.[24] For its critics, anarchism attracted the criminal, the immoral and 'the deviant', including abortionists, members of the 'long firm', confidence tricksters and arsonists. W.C. Hart, an apostate anarchist, wrote of the organization and sub-groups he encountered within metropolitan anarchism:

> At the back of a small shop in a certain street in St. Luke's, Clerkenwell, as choice a set of desperadoes collected as ever met under one roof. They styled themselves the 'Free Initiative Anarchist Group'. Amongst its members were (well-known to the police) anarchist pick-pockets, burglars, long-firm schemers, clever jewel thieves and so on. Here was hatched many a successful burglary and jewel robbery, 'smash and grab raids' on jewellers, arson on insured premises, etc.[25]

Surrounded by fellow travellers, constantly prone to schism, and a magnet for state informers and the criminally inclined, non-anarchist radicals saw even 'the most generous and noble among their number' as likely to 'fall victim to official plotters'.[26] In Edith and Hubert Bland's novel of anarchist emigres, *The Prophet's Mantle*, the nihilists are stalked by predatory spies and blackmailers 'with deeply-set, hollow eyes'.[27] For some progressives, the language and actions of anarchism were so criminalized and extreme that they depicted the movement as a fiction, merely providing a cover for *agents provocateurs* who, financed and supported by industrialists, used anarchist groups to discredit conventional reformist political programmes.[28]

Anarchism, then, presented a fearsome face to the British nineteenth-century reading public. Framed by fear and hysteria, it expressed many of the social concerns of the late nineteenth and early twentieth centuries. Anarchism's residue in the British context is mainly a literary one. Anarchist bomb-making rings feature prominently in the fiction of the last quarter of the nineteenth century, and embody many of the popular fears of the period.[29] From the middle 1880s, a sensationalist literature developed, which became obsessed with the 'dynamite congresses' and 'Black Internationals' of desperate and 'asocial' adversaries of society. This chapter draws primarily on literary sources that were preoccupied with anarchism. Anarchism's literary footprints testify to its fascination for a whole generation of novelists who used its concerns as plot-device and backdrop. In this literature of 'social panic', anarchism itself came to symbolize a broader series of social problems relating to the advanced urban areas of England. Most famously discussed in Joseph Conrad's *The Secret Agent* in 1907, anarchism spawned an entire genre of 'dynamite romances' in which plots and characterization revolved around criminal conspiracies and bomb attacks on London. Whilst overshadowed by Conrad (a relatively late addition to the genre),[30] this literature found its most significant outlet in the pulp fiction of the late nineteenth century, reaching its peak at the beginning of the 1900s, when it connected up with fears of national decline, military defeat and debates about the reform of existing asylum practices for political exiles seeking safe haven from illiberal governments in Europe. Fears of anarchism mediated through fiction played a prominent part in the introduction of the 1905 Anti-Aliens Act, whilst the Siege of Sidney Street in 1911 accentuated concerns about political exiles in London, and led to parliamentary debates about stricter controls on firearms.[31]

The anarchist tale proper stood midway between older invasion panic narratives and a popular literature that revolved around conspiracies and secret cabals. The spectre of anarchism and the 'Black Panics' it engendered drew on concerns about a secret and opaque network of global terrorists, rooted in a disavowal of established government that imported the tyrannies of the despotic East into the capital of the empire, and cloaked its activities in mysterious codes, revelations and the paraphernalia of secret societies. The secret oath-taking that traditionally haunted the Victorian imagination and coloured attitudes towards trades unionists and Irish Republicans also fired the imagination of those who explored anarchist themes.[32] Anarchist tales could bring together fear of foreigners, invasion panics and concerns about secret forces suborning high society. Whereas once these themes had been the exclusive preserve of popular stories targeting Germans in Britain, or drawing attention to German or French expansionism, increasingly they became part of the popular realm of the anarchist tale.[33]

Drawing inspiration from the aristocratic pedigree of a number of the early anarchist leaders, early anarchist tales depicted anarchists as social deviants, often from the upper echelons of society who infiltrated and destroyed high-ranking families.[34] In Guy Boothby's *The League of Twelve*, the sinister anarchist Carlitz, inveigles his way into a fading aristocratic family. Holding the daughter of the family, Inez de Montalva, hostage in a rented castle in the English countryside, he hopes to exert pressure on her brother to assassinate the Spanish minister of war.[35] Anarchists in popular literature often sought to enrich themselves and their cause by manipulating vulnerable members of the European financial and landed elite. The plot of Richard Henry Savage's *The Anarchist: A Story of To-Day* revolves around the attempts by an anarchist circle to gain access to the fortune of a wealthy American society heiress for the purpose of bankrolling revolution in North America. Set against a background of society intrigue, this tale provided opportunities for opulent and exciting backdrops in the United States, Austria and Italy. Anarchists as powerful and wealthy figures directing secret and all-encompassing conspiracies also feature in John Buchan's *The Power-House*, published before World War I, but only released in 1916 as a thriller for soldiers at the front. Here the anarchist leader, Lumley, is an aesthete, bibliophile and collector of fine porcelain who maintains the public façade of a philanthropist, but secretly intrigues to further the sinister 'power-house' and its plans for 'super-anarchy'.[36] Confronting his deadly adversary, Buchan's barrister adventurer, Leithen, captures the essence of the anarchist super-villain: 'You have been highly successful in the past, but why? Because you have been above suspicion, an honourable and distinguished gentleman, belonging to the best clubs, counting as your acquaintances the flower of our society. Now you will be a suspect, a man with a past, a centre of strange stories'.[37] In such images lie the origins of the refined, cultured, but thoroughly amoral villains who provided the adversaries for Ian Fleming's James Bond. Moving beyond recent treatments of the crime thriller and the rather well-known depictions of anarchists in the *The Secret Agent*, this chapter probes the sub-stratum of popular and pulp tales that drew on anarchism for inspiration, and considers the motifs that recur throughout the genre.

II

The anarchist was a ubiquitous presence in late nineteenth-century popular literature. The gentler side of anarchism is displayed in Edith Nesbit's *The Railway Children*, where the children help a displaced and herbivorous Russian nihilist exile, essentially a hybrid of Stepniak, Count Tolstoy and Kropotkin. Their mother patiently explains that the anarchist is an author whose book about the sufferings of the Russian peasantry resulted in his wrongful imprisonment by the Tsarist regime for many years: 'He was three years in a horrible dungeon with hardly any light, and all damp and dreadful. In prison all alone for three years'. As a Fabian socialist, Edith Nesbit was well-acquainted with cerebral anarchist circles in London, had agitated on behalf of anti-Tsarist organizations and brought her insights to bear on the creation of this character.[38] In 1885 she and her husband, Hubert, had penned their own anarchist fiction about a nihilist exile in London loosely based on the career of Kropotkin.[39] In adult literature and popular fiction, however, anarchism survives largely in terms of the ideas attributed to it by its detractors. The vision of anarchism presented here was less nuanced than that of *The Railway Children*. Some of those authors who wrote about anarchism had direct experience of its violent side. The crime fiction writer Edgar Wallace witnessed the assassination attempt on Alfonso XIII in Madrid at his wedding to Princess Eva of Battenberg in 1906. In his memoirs, he remembered seeing the bomb-thrower, Morel, hurl an incendiary device concealed in a bunch of flowers at the royal couple. He recalled: 'The force of the explosion almost lifted me off my feet, and in a second I was in the middle of a confused, screaming throng of people, mad with fear. I had a glimpse of dying horses, of blood lying in the roadway, of a half-fainting queen being assisted from her carriage, her white dress splashed with blood'.[40] Wallace was also present at the famous Sidney Street siege in 1911. Using his journalistic credentials, he gained access to the house across the road, and glimpsed the shadowy figures of the anarchist gunmen at the windows.[41] Both Wallace's first novels, *The Four Just Men* and *The Council of Justice* had anarchist themes.[42] His vision of anarchism was framed by the attitudes of its critics. For its opponents, anarchism was an aberrant bacillus. Defined as cancer, canker and disease, anarchy was depicted as an expression of the impure. *The Spectator* compared it to the 'seeds of cholera' that it was the duty of all men to stop.[43] In these descriptions, anarchists were a kind of revolutionary detritus. In the work of George H. R. Dabbs, a doctor-turned-crime writer, the anarchist characters are demented and near 'hydrophobic'. In his *The Ladder of Pain*, descriptions of the anarchist conclave in Zurich express the physical revulsion many contemporaries felt for the anarchist':

> They were of various nationalities and yet of one type. They had each one the dreamy, fanatical face associated with the evangel of destruction. As you glanced at them sitting there – these spiders of the world's web – you did not think them so much cruel, as inevitable. In that one room were gathered together the very ganglia of the disordered creeds of Europe and America.[44]

H. Barton Baker's anarchists in his *Robert Miner, Anarchist* are 'a sea of awful faces, of men and women, blood-craving as tigers, merciless as hyenas, vicious as monkeys. It was as though the gates of hell had been opened to reveal a glimpse of lost souls'.[45] Even in Joseph Hocking's relatively benign treatment of anarchism, in which his hero, David Baring, retreats to an anarchist commune in Cornwall, the vision of the anarchists remained ambivalent at best. He reports of his new colleagues: 'Some of the faces he saw were thoughtful and refined; others again showed signs of coarseness. There were a few who appeared to be foreigners; these wore a ferocious aspect – at least, most of them did. One man almost made him afraid; his eyes shone so brilliantly, while his long hair hung in tangled masses down his shoulders'.[46]

Such treatments tended towards the sensationalist. Wallace in his *The Council of Justice* rightly saw links in the popular perceptions of anarchism, and a populist press (typified by his fictional *Daily Megaphone* based on the *Daily Mail*) that battened on the strident revelations it provided to uncover potential threats at the heart of empire.[47] For admirers of Kropotkin and other exile anarchists, the excitable exposures surrounding anarchism were unfounded, but demonstrated the moral panic this particular political tendency invoked. In an interview late in life, George Bernard Shaw recalled of the media's treatment of Kropotkin, who he christened 'the saint of the century':

> He was built up by the press as a desperate character, a terrorist with revolvers hidden in his pockets and all the time conspiring with similar criminals the downfall of all the things the world held sacred: property, royalty, government, morals and freedom. I found him, as you say, a man so filled by social conscience that he could not bear the thought of anyone being poor and suffering. A tramp greeted us and he took out all he had and gave it to him at once without question.[48]

In at least some of the stories produced by radicals themselves there was a tendency to scoff at the conspiracies anarchism allegedly fomented and to ridicule the over-reaction of the authorities. In the short story, 'The Dynamiter', by Harry Quelch, a socialist finds his house raided after an informer alerts police to the presence of apparent bomb-making equipment at the dwelling. In fact, he is repairing his gas pipes. The narrator, a police detective, who organizes the raid, becomes an object of ridicule and retires from the police service soon after.[49]

III

The imaginary social geography of anarchism tied the movement closely to the capital. For most observers, anarchism's associations were overwhelmingly metropolitan. This mirrored the attitudes of anarchist themselves, who saw London as a place of unique spiritual desolation and unrelenting poverty that vindicated their non-compliance with social and political convention. In the anarchist paper *Freedom*, London was 'the vampire city' or 'snakeland'. In the works of the anarchist writer, John Henry Mackay, 'the metropolis on the Thames' is 'the greatest wart of the earth'.[50] There were also unconfirmed anarchist conspiracies against targets in London. According to a story by the émigré anarchist Rudolf Rocker, he played a major part in talking conspirators out of planting a bomb at the Lord Mayor's Procession in November 1909.[51] For popular fiction writers, their stories about anarchism began and ended in the East End.[52] Fiction writers overlooked the fact that the only anarchist bomb-making ring to be successfully broken up in Britain was a cell of militant 'Dynamitards' in Walsall in the West Midlands in 1892.[53] Moreover, confusion occurred over responsibility for the various terrorist attacks in the capital. In the existing literature, anarchism became a repository of blame for other 'dynamitard' atrocities and various unsuccessful attacks on public buildings and monuments. In most cases, the anarchist threat clouded and occluded the threat from Irish Republicanism. Henry James's *The Princess Casamassima* was inspired largely by the bomb attacks of Irish Fenian associations, rather than by anarchist outrages.[54] The bombs planted in railway stations and public places in the infamous 'Year of the Dynamitards' in 1884–5 were the work of extreme Irish republican splinter groups, not anarchists, as the metropolitan press frequently alleged.[55]

For many contemporaries, the violence initiated by Irish Fenian-inspired irreconcileables in the mid-1880s was interchangeable with the anarchist threat. Fenians pioneered the first street bombings in London, detonating gunpowder outside Clerkenwell gaol to free one of their leaders in 1866. The presence of Fenian bombers and dynamitards in London added to the landscape of danger that marked out the capital. Anarchism and Irish republicanism were commonly seen as sharing joint aims and profiting from a drift towards chaos and the destruction of government. The 1885 targets of the Fenian bombing campaign in London included traditional anarchist targets, amongst them the Tower of London, Scotland Yard and Westminster Hall.[56] Pre-anarchism, Irish Fenians were seen as great innovators and pioneers in techniques of irregular warfare and political assassination. A number of them had enlisted on both sides in the American Civil War. Here they trained in the arts of 'scientific warfare' that provided the blueprints for aerial warfare, irregular naval piracy at sea, submarines and basic manuals for explosives.[57] Thereafter many of the traditional characteristics of the terrorist menace accrued around Fenianism. Like the anarchists, they were believed to sit at the heart of a vast pan-global conspiracy, and to control enormous resources throughout the empire. In the manner of anarchism, the Fenians were ultimately believed to favour the destruction of civilization itself.[58] Their activities also entered the same fictional realm as anarchism. By the 1880s, a number of sensationalist accounts of Fenian depredations were in print, notably Donald MacKay's *The Dynamite Ship*, in which Fenian dynamitards plot to ram an explosives-laden vessel into the Houses of Parliament.[59]

In myriad plot-devices, the capital provided an image of dissolution and dislocation that created the perfect environment for anarchist characters in literature. The capital best embodied the spirit of a turbulent and unruly 'mobocracy' wherein anarchism found its natural home. In addition, the *dramatis personae* of anarchist fiction tended to drift further towards the bottom of the social hierarchy as the genre progressed. The anarchist flitted through the shadows and fogs of London. Apparently rooted amongst the shifting and itinerant poor and most visible as a belief system amongst Eastern European migrants in the East End, anarchism was represented as a creeping murrain that threatened to overwhelm the cityscape of London in the later part of the nineteenth century.[60] The homeless migrant or political exile was commonly seen as a vector for anarchism. In 1911 the anarchists who battled the police in the siege of Sidney Street were characterized as 'alien desperados'.[61] Even the radical press was inclined to blame migrants from Eastern Europe for the import of anarchist ideas.[62] Such migrant characters are a staple of the pulp fiction genre. H. Barton Baker's anarchists are 'hulking, scowling Germans, French, Italians, indeed the scum of all nationalities'. Gathered together, 'the whole air was faint with the sickening odour of their unclean mass and garlic-tainted breath'.[63] Thriving on rejection and social isolation, anarchism was perceived as an embodiment of social decay and national dissolution. For some observers, society had withered and declined, providing an opportunity seized by anarchists who battened on the social injustices that relegated the poor to the churning rookeries and warrens of the East End of London, where anger and dispossession readily turned to violence. Others depicted anarchists as elaborate confidence-tricksters, preying on the weak and the vulnerable. In some treatments, anarchists are wastrels or opportunists, who sense the power and position to be gained from exploiting the gullible and the poverty-stricken in the ghettoes of the East End of London. Here anarchists were just updated mountebanks, with unreliable 'quack' remedies for society's metaphorical and figurative ills. In Arthur Morrison's short story 'The Red Cow Group', the tables are turned when the dupes of an anarchist's plan for a terror attack convince him, in turn, that a quite harmless substance is a deadly explosive. Left bound and tied as an apparent human bomb, he is humiliated, unmanned and exposed as an empty windbag, rather than a revolutionary hero.[64]

The plots of many of the novels about anarchism, however, pivot on the journey to the dark and subterranean East End.[65] In Henry James's *The Princess Casamassima*, the dilettantish radical Princess remarks to Hyacinth Robinson: 'I want to know London . . . the huge, swarming, smoky human city. I mean real London, the people and all their sufferings and passions. . . Perhaps you can help me'.[66] In epiphanies of conversion, the exposure of conditions in the East End confirmed, directed, deterred or encouraged heroes and anti-heroes along the road towards physical force, or its renunciation. After touring the East End and observing conditions there, the hero of *David Baring* turns his back on a large fortune inherited from a distant relative who is an East End 'sweater' and eschews modern life to reside in an anarchist commune in the West Country, loosely modelled on the anarchist colony of Whiteway outside Stroud.[67] The East End he experiences is a place of poverty, fear and brutishness:

> The people dressed differently, walked differently, and, what was more, they had a different expression on their faces. He could not define the differences, but he felt it. The look in their eyes, the cast of features, was to him strange. This did not apply simply to the very poor who swarmed in the alleys and back streets, but was evident amongst those who kept shops, and lived in comfort . . . as far as he could judge, the great masses seemed to live for the animal pleasure of the present moment.[68]

Also strongly apparent in such literature is the notion of transgression and changed social roles. The notion of a man like David Baring from a high social station converting to anarchism connects with the prevalent fears about a collapsing social order in the larger cities. Anarchists themselves drew on their own experiences of the capital to explain their resort to terrorism. *The Anarchists*, by John Henry Mackay, is perhaps the sole literary treatment of anarchism by an anarchist author. An extended Socratic dialogue between individualistic and collectivist anarchist theoreticians, it begins with the by now conventional perambulation through the squalor of London. Appalled particularly by an example of child prostitution he encounters, the hero, Auban, uses the episode as the opportunity for a meditation on social and political injustice. For most anarchists, child prostitution was the example incarnate of exploitation of the weak by the strong, and of the itinerant and helpless, by the wealthy, the powerful and the propertied:

> He saw a face rise before him which he had never since forgotten: the features of a woman, frightfully disfigured by leprosy and bloody sores, who, with an infant at her breast, was dragging, rather than leading, a fourteen-year-old girl by the hand, while a third child, a boy, was clinging to her dress.
>
> 'Two shillings only, gentleman, two shillings only . . . she is still so young, but she will do anything you want'.
>
> And with that she drew the girl near who turned away, trembling and crying.
>
> A shudder ran through him. But the beseeching and piteous voice of the woman kept on . . .[69]

The repellent images of the East End in Mackay's work aroused the curiosity of other anarchists, establishing a tourist trail around deprived areas of the capital. Rudolf Rocker was one such reformer who found his principles reinforced after a visit to the poorer parts of London in imitation of Mackay's journeys through the city.[70]

Anarchism, then, resonated in the architecture and public space of London.[71] Most studies highlight the interweaving of the social geography of London with the cultural context of literary anarchism. In contrast to more open and overt forms of radical politics, which for reformers, socialists and liberals involved the colonization of the open ground and public spaces of the metropolis, anarchists plotted in dark corners and behind closed doors.[72] Anarchists were frequenters of the dangerous 'lurks' and bolt-holes of London, that from the days of Henry Fielding and Patrick Colquhuon, were seen as a component part of the dangerous and transgressive landscape of the capital.[73] In such terrain, Fu Manchu's assassins and willing slaves navigated a system of tunnels and secret caves below London where the henchmen of the evil genius reigned supreme.[74] Much the same territory provided the landscape of anarchism. It was here that intrepid reporters and hack writers sought them out to provide horrifying descriptions of their blood-curdling meetings for mainstream newspapers.[75] These descriptions provided the basis for investigative and revelatory treatments of the anarchist menace. In Helen and Olivia Rossetti's autobiographical *A Girl Amongst the Anarchists*, the anarchist lair is a 'fetid . . . den', the atmosphere of which

> [w]as laden with the smoke of divers specimens of the worst shag and cheapest tobacco in the metropolis . . . Past the type racks and cases, which occupied the first half of this apartment, were grouped benches, stools, packing-cases, and a few maimed and deformed chairs for the accommodation of the assembly. Then came a hand printing-press, on which were spread the remains of some comrade's repast: the vertebral column of a bloater and an empty condensed milk, among other relics. The floor, from one extremity to the other of the 'office', was littered with heaps of unsold revolutionary literature, the approximate age of which could be gauged by the thickness of the dust in which it was smothered.[76]

In H. Barton Baker's *Robert Miner; Anarchist*, a similar vision prevails. The anarchists gather in a smoke-grimed, mould-covered room, where the flickering lights throw distorted shadows on the walls of 'the seething mass that writhed and gesticulated on their seats, or sprang to their feet in their mad excitement'.[77]

In such accounts, anarchism mapped and delineated the social landscape of London. H. Barton Baker's narrative covers the full range of dubious anarchist headquarters from 'frowsy clubs in the neighbourhood of Fitzroy Square . . . cheap restaurants in Leicester Square . . . secret dens in Soho to which

Figure 2.2 An illegal anarchist fraternity subdued by the intervention of Edgar Wallace's anti-anarchist vigilantes, the Four Just Men. Cover of Edgar Wallace, *The Council of Justice* (London: Ward, Lock and Co., 1930) (Author's Collection).

admission can only be gained by a pass-word' to degraded former habitations of the gentry near Oxford Street where there were 'foreign clubs' and crumbling premises of which 'the upper parts . . . are let out in tenements to the regenerators of the human race'.[78] The geography of London is reflected in the names of anarchist groups like 'the Charlotte Street Anarchists', and in literary meeting places like Greek Street, Soho, a traditional haunt of radicals where Edgar Wallace's fictional 'Red Hundred' gather.[79] Henry James famously experienced the characters for his *The Princess Casamassima* emerging from the streets of London.[80] Unsurprisingly, James Connell on his well-known train ride across London during which he scribbled down the verses of the 'Red Flag' incorporated references to the assassination of Alexander II by Russian nihilists and to the anarchist Chicago Haymarket Martyrs, whose cause was widely supported in London and provided the occasion for the capital's first workers' May Day demonstration in 1890:

> In Moscow's vaults its hymns
>> Are sung,
> Chicago swells its surging
>> Throng.[81]

Within this environment, and drawing on the heightened fears generated by the popular disorders and dynamite outrages of the last quarter of the nineteenth century, anarchists apparently subverted and usurped other organizations. Their actions provided a reproach to the misguided philanthropy of the higher orders. In *The Princess Casamassima* the working-men's Sun and Moon debating society is simply a screen for more extreme gatherings by an inner circle of fanatics; in *The Council of Justice* the convention of the Red Hundred gathers at a disused philanthropic Mission for Russian Seamen. This mirrors contemporary fears that the power of anarchism lay in its ability to 'warren' kindred organizations and groups. Claims that they were doing so were repeated even in the radical and socialist press.[82]

Unsurprisingly, anarchism became the canvas on which contemporary fears of the dissolution of the metropolis were projected. Both Edgar Wallace's *The Council of Justice* and E. Douglas Fawcett's *Hartmann the Anarchist* rely on a vision of the impending destruction of London. The potential fate of London is carefully charted during the course of the novels, capturing the attention of an audience, which perceived anarchism largely in terms of social threat. Late nineteenth-century fears about immigrant radicals in the East End, the concerns of polite London in the aftermath of the Paris Commune, and notions of a riotous and disorderly London cohered around contemporary obsessions with the figure of the 'Dynamitard'. Popular memory also drew on celebrated assassination attempts in Europe, with many, like the Orsini assassination conspiracy against Napoleon III, involving plots hatched amongst gatherings of exiles on British soil.[83] These popular fears were stoked by the public utterances of the anarchists themselves. Both Kropotkin and William Morris hoped for an end to the great 'abnormal' cities of the industrial age, and a return to a more devolved Medieval conception of urban living.[84] Morris found solace from the injustices of the modern city in Richard Jefferies' *After London: Wild England* in which, following an environmental disaster, London collapses into a bog and society reverts to peasant subsistence farming and Dark Ages-style anarchy. In this ecological and social indictment of the metropolitan, the ruins of the capital emit toxins that poison England, and the fearsome bog where the capital once stood drags those to their doom unwise enough to search for the buried treasures, wealth and technology of 'the Ancients'.[85] For some critics, anarchist interest in urban improvement and town planning implied the demolition of existing cityscapes. Furthermore, the genre of anarchist *expose*, which featured significantly in the popular literature of these years, dwelt on the violent utterances of secret and bloodthirsty anarchist congregations intent on the destruction of government in its seat of power. According to one such memoir, at a secret conference of anarchists in the Tottenham Court Road, proceedings ended with the song:

> Arms! Arms! To make our Rulers fly!
> Bombs, powder, pikes and lead
> Shall bring our brothers bread
> Cold on the earth shall tyrants lie![86]

These sentiments are echoed in the song of the Dynamitards in *Hartmann the Anarchist*, where, in a vulgar parody of Tennyson, the anarchist Schwartz sings:

> The dynamite falls on castle walls
> And splendid buildings old in story.
> The column shakes, the tyrant quakes,
> And the wild wreckage leaps in glory
> Throw, comrades, throw; set the wild echoes flying;
> Throw, comrades; answer, wretches, dying, dying, dying.[87]

In a contrast to such apocalyptic visions of physical force, *The Master Crime* by Joseph Lyons and Cecil Raleigh imagined a more subtle anarchist attempt to destabilize the institutions of the City of London, and by extension European finance capitalism itself. By substituting an anarchist impersonator for the powerful financier, Lord Ashcroft, the evil Prince Peteroff Kalytzin 'Chief of the Terrorists' is able to cause a run on the banks, and undermine confidence in the Bank of England. By these means he hopes money will be siphoned off to pay for the revolution at a time when economic turmoil will paralyse the old order and render it incapable of defending itself. Peteroff exults:

> The world has not got gold for one thousandth part of its demands. Stop what little there is from flowing – and the end is chaos! . . . The Bank of England is the Fountain Head . . . at the hour when the Bank of England breaks, and closes without warning – at that hour the Credit of the World will disappear! At that hour there will be Nothing – a wild struggle even for bread – and at that hour the Army of Freedom will march rich in Men and Gold – Money in rivers, to pay the good men or buy the bad – Money, hard Gold clinking with their sabres, while the rulers of the nations stifle screaming in a welter of bankruptcy.[88]

IV

More than anything else, the Paris Commune hangs over the anarchist 'moral panic' literature of this period. The Commune provided a lived example of a context in which society disintegrated into its constituent parts. Exalted and revered by anarchists themselves, it became a key motif in contemporary depictions of the movement. Anarchists represented their agitation as emerging from amongst Communard survivors, and serving as an act of reprisal against the bourgeoisie, through the 'bomb of the slain'.[89] There was some substance, then, in the tendency for popular authors to elide images of the Commune with anarchism, and to depict 'the younger brood' as 'the revengeful spawn of unforgiving fiends of the Commune of '70'.[90] Critics of anarchism also noted the movement's propensity to celebrate the anniversary of the event in orgiastic excesses attended by 'a small crowd of boozy, beery, pot-valiant, squalid, frowzy, sodden Whitechapel outcasts'.[91] In many treatments of anarchism in literature, the Commune provided a dreadful portent and example. The anarchist Azrael in Richard Whiteing's *No. 5 John Street* is a former Communard, whose professionalism and revolutionary dedication is contrasted with the eccentricities and impotent sloganising of an elderly British veteran of 1848.[92] Images of death and destruction hover about Azrael. ' "Azrael" . . . this . . . is the name of the Angel of Death' remarks one character prophetically; 'Sort o' gives yer a nasty taste in the mouth' suggests another after listening to Azrael's inflammatory anarchist rhetoric.[93] In his biography, Richard Whiteing claimed that the character of Azrael was based on the French anarchist, and former Communard, Élie Reclus. Elder brother of the anarchist, earth scientist, and close confidante of both Jules Verne and Kropotkin, Élisée Reclus, Élie was the most militant of the brothers, reminding Whiteing of 'those animals whose jaws lock on what they bite'.[94] Images of revolutionary 'blood martyrdom' also feature prominently in *The Princess Casamassima*. Eustace Poupin is a former revolutionary street-fighter of 1871 and the quintessence of 'the political exile'; Hyacinth Robinson believes his own grandfather to have died 'in the blood-stained streets of Paris, on a barricade, with his gun in hand'.[95] Commune imagery abounds in *Hartmann the Anarchist*; during the 'tempest of dynamite' Hartmann's aerial flying machine unleashes liquid petroleum on London in an echo of the Parisian *petroleuses* prepared on ignite Paris in the final days of the Commune.[96] Again in images drawn from the events of 1871, the West End and Bayswater are looted by anarchist mobs wearing caps of liberty, and working in tandem with Hartmann's aerial offensive.

Such images tied in with a long-standing tradition of the threat posed by an insurgent London. In Bracebridge Hemyng's *The Commune in London, or Thirty Years Hence* of 1871, and John Drew Gay's *How John Bull Lost London, or the Capture of the Channel Tunnel* written in 1882, London is imperilled by collusion between unpatriotic radicals in the East End and the forces of

Figure 2.3 'Drunk with Slaughter'. Hartmann the Anarchist's attack on London using aerial zeppelin technology in E. Douglas Fawcett, 'Hartmann the Anarchist, or the Doom of a Great City', first published in *The English Illustrated Magazine*, Vol. 10 (1893), p. 778. Illustration by Fred T. Jane (Author's Collection).

Figure 2.4 'The destruction of the Houses of Parliament by Hartmann the Anarchist' in E. Douglas Fawcett, 'Hartmann the Anarchist, or the Doom of a Great City', first published in *The English Illustrated Magazine*, vol. 10 (1893), p. 741. Illustration by Fred T. Jane (Author's Collection).

invasion, in the latter overwhelming the capital by an invasion of French soldiers dressed as tourists through the Channel Tunnel.[97] The burning of London was a set-piece of much of the sensationalist literature that imported Communard-style anarchists into the capital. In Charles Gleig's *When All Men Starve*, imperial commitments lead to an international war between Britain and all her colonial rivals that she inevitably loses. With food supplies interrupted, London is attacked by a peasant revolt of bread rioters. After slaughtering the metropolitan police on Wimbledon Common, these 'forces of anarchy' sack London, their depredations culminating in an orgiastic destruction of the West End and Buckingham Palace:

> From all quarters come men and women and slatternly, drunken girls, until thousands are gathered round the glowing building, shouting, cursing, dancing a mad can-can in the flicker of the leaping flames. Higher, higher, rises the fire till the whole great building becomes a glowing patch of brilliant light, and the red sparks, caught by the rising wind, shower in golden cascade upon the neighbouring houses. The mob dances its mad dance of anarchy, revelling in the downfall of the Respectabilities, forgetting in this brief hour of its triumph, the curse of Labour, the squalid wretchedness of vanished years.[98]

For Hartmann the anarchist, his technological apocalypse in London evokes memories of the disintegration and sacking of Rome, which had obsessed metropolitan prophets since Macauley's famous vision of the sterile landscape of a vacant and ruined metropolis. 'Within three days' time', Hartmann declares, 'London will be in ruins, and Lord Macauley's New Zealander will be able to commence his survey'.[99]

Literary images of anarchism were divided in their reading of the potential for destruction and devastation posed by the anarchist threat. Prevailing visions of contemporary anarchism were confused and inconsistent. Some observers were misled by the different approaches to social change espoused by different anarchist groups. The movement was characterized by a tension between pacifism and anti-militarism, and a more revolutionary platform that advocated a violent upheaval within society. Beatrice Webb noted this tension, commenting, 'it is a strange irony that this faith in violence has been in nearly all countries, intertwined with Tolstoyan cosmopolitan pacifism – this unnatural alliance being due to the possession of a common enemy the Law-and-Order Imperialistic Capitalism'.[100] Even the more peaceful anarchists recognized the necessity for a transitional phase of revolutionary expropriation. Some anarchists, however, preached a withdrawal from the world and a restoration of the human spirit by an exposure to the simple verities of peasant life and the eternal certainties of pastoral farming. Inspired by the ideas of Tolstoy and Kropotkin, this outlook coloured the many back-to-the-land schemes of the late nineteenth and early twentieth century.[101] Something of this Tolstoyan outlook is evident in the Christian Commune attended by David Baring as an escape from the horrors and sophistries of urban life and the strains of estate-owning in the shires:

> Each morning, after breakfast, (a) blackboard was uplifted, on which was written the thoughts of great men, which were to be a guide and an inspiration through the day. The writers whose words were most frequently quoted were Epicetus, St. Francis of Assissi (sic), Emerson, Thoreau, Ruskin, Carlyle and Tolstoi . . . Nearly all the maxims poured scorn on wealth and on the comforts which men usually believe that wealth commands. In fact, David was not long in discerning that civilisation, as it is usually understood, was regarded as a curse, and they held that the nearer they could get to primitive standards, so much would it be better for them.[102]

Other anarchists, however, derided this notion of a restitution of the human spirit through rural smallholdings, and preached instead the liberation from drudgery and wage-owning that technological innovation might bring. Kropotkin himself experimented with new and more sophisticated forms of greenhouse and different rotation systems for an increased agricultural yield.[103] Many of these images of a sophisticated and highly technological anarchism derive from the advances in explosives that made portable pocket bombs and small explosive devices possible for the first time. After 1864, Alfred Nobel had found ways of stabilising the notoriously temperamental nitro-glycerine in a solid compound. For anarchists, this created 'a poor man's artillery' or 'Nobel's awful portable volcano' to counteract standing armies and conventional military equipment.[104] Delivery systems were simple, but effective: seemingly innocent pedestrians, or horse-drawn carts.[105] Many of the prevailing images of anarchism acknowledged the movement's mastery and command of these new forms of technological innovation. Bomb-factories, elaborate fuses and 'infernal engines' for assassinations were an integral part of the arsenal of literary anarchism: 'In hidden mechanical workshops and chemical laboratories, the coward's weapons, were studied, practised on, and every dark refinement of devilry applied to the discovery of methods for *removal*'.[106] Instead of turning their backs on the world of science, in Victorian and Edwardian pulp fiction, anarchists positively embraced it. Hartmann the anarchist invents a new form of aerial flying engine that includes flame-throwers and other weapons of mass destruction. In Edgar Wallace's *The Council of Justice*, anarchists use zeppelins in an attempt to destroy London from the air in a highly derivative plot-line clearly influenced by E. Douglas Fawcett.[107]

Prefiguring the plots of many later spy thrillers, the anarchist conspirators in George H. R. Dabbs' *Ladder of Pain* drop carbolic acid into a closed room to kill the hero of the novel alongside his adopted daughter. The anarchist leader exults: 'When we leave we shall liberate carbolic acid into the room. It is painless and fairly swift. To-night you will repose together in the lake in one winding-sheet'.[108] In much anarchist pulp fiction, wily and devious means are used to bring mayhem to the capital. In Arthur Morrison's short story, 'The Case of the Lost Foreigner', bombs are concealed in French bread-sticks and a plan orchestrated for simultaneous explosions around London – 'they were to be distributed, probably in broad daylight, in the most natural manner possible, in a baker's cart'.[109] Anarchists themselves came to believe that they controlled huge reserves of highly sophisticated death-dealing devices. Quoting from the New York *Home Journal*, *The Anarchist* recorded the potential of the new weapons provided by dynamite:

A barren rock in the secret mountains of Switzerland with its dynamite laboratory and convoys of air and land may set at naught all the standing armies of the proud German empire, and drop annihilation upon its walled cities at any hour by day or night. At this moment, a single wayfarer, with

Figure 2.5 Aerial Anarchists hovering over London in E. Douglas Fawcett, 'Hartmann the Anarchist, or the Doom of a Great City', first published in *The English Illustrated Magazine,* Vol. 10 (1893), p. 653. Illustration by Fred T. Jane (Author's Collection).

dynamite in his pocket throws the cities of England in greater terror than would an army of a hundred thousand men landing at Dover, with only the ordinary weapons of guns and sabres . . . Jupiter with his lightenings was scarcely more of a master of the ancient world than is the mob with its bomb of dynamite, the avenging fate of modern monarchies.[110]

V

Frequently, contemporary fears of anarchism as destroyer of the metropolis fused with conceptions of the 'aberrant individual'. Impelled by the 1880s debate about the social fragmentation and polarization of London, the image of anarchism thrived on the revelations of Alfred Mearns, Charles Booth and Charles Masterman. Anarchism heralded the disintegration of group loyalties, community life and of the family. In the anarchist press, leading anarchists declared themselves opposed to the institution of the family unit, which they portrayed as a coercive institution, calling for the 'letting of fresh air in upon the whole idea and practice of the family'.[111] Following Lombroso, some contemporaries believed that anarchist tendencies thrived within dysfunctional households and were accentuated by an absence of parental restraint – truants, professional malcontents and delinquent barrack-room lawyers were amongst those likely to succumb to the lure of anarchism.[112] Leading anarchists like Mikhail Bakunin and Emma Goldman came from troubled or authoritarian family backgrounds. Orphans who lacked all parental guidance were believed to display the greatest propensity towards the movement. Johann Most, Ravachol, Emile Henry and the assassin of Elizabeth, Empress of Austria, Luigi Lucheni, were abandoned or orphaned at a young age and were frequently cited as representative of this trend.[113] Anarchism, then, traded in the wreckage of nineteenth-century society. Beatrice Webb noted the existence of an anarchist or syndicalist type, who epitomized this tendency, the discontented rootless 'angry youth, with bad complexion, frowning brow and weedy figure'.[114] In a foretaste of late twentieth-century moral panics about youth, such delinquents might be recognized by their liking for tattoos and other inappropriate bodily adornments.[115] The popular literature about anarchism frequently portrayed the impressionable and the vulnerable from delinquent or troubled family backgrounds as the fodder of anarchism. In *David Baring*, the orphaned hero seeks stability within the false family of anarchism; Helen Rossetti's thinly disguised autobiographical heroine in *A Girl Amongst the Anarchists* drifts into anarchism after her father dies.[116] Similarly, the plot of George H. R. Dabbs' *The Ladder of Pain* revolves around a family feud, in which an unloved brother establishes a worldwide anarchist conspiracy to exact revenge on his more favoured sibling. In his letter to his brother in which he reveals all before his suicide, he declares:

> It is within an hour of midnight, and within that hour I die. We were brothers by name, but never brothers in heart. I always hated you. You were my mother's favourite, and she was the only woman I ever loved on earth. Even when you quarrelled with home (but not with her, curse you) you still heard from her, she still kept your picture by her bed. And when she was dying and you were far away in Australia it was your name that was the last on her dying lips and in her fading thoughts. She divined my hatred and kept us apart in boyhood.[117]

Broken families allegedly formed the recruiting ground for anarchism. Critics saw anarchism as an attractive credo for the members of the rootless refugee congregations in the East End. In anarchist figures like Alexander Berkman and the Russian terrorist, Nechaev, the tendency towards suicide and self-immolation was sometimes seen as a consequence of ruptured family backgrounds. Brooding and malevolent, both Nechaev and Berkman believed that worldly connections diluted revolutionary zeal and should be subordinated to the terrorist impulse. In their writings, they preached a distance from everyday ties and total immersion in the cause of the revolution. For them, violence was a redemptive act, bringing an awakening of the masses.[118] Lombroso famously argued that such anarchist bomb-throwers and assassins were simply selfish suicides that lacked the courage to take their own lives openly.[119] In *Hartmann the Anarchist*, the use of violence is gleeful and depraved, an apparent consequence of painful family separations. The French refugee and murderer Emmanuel Barthelemy provided a figurative model for these aberrant figures (a wax-work of him was an early literal model in Madame Tussauds). His death-mask was a frequent illustration in phrenology textbooks, which under the category 'revolutionists, infidels, murderers' provided the prototype for Cesare Lombroso's anarchist heads in his *Criminal Man* (1911).[120] Helen Rossetti recalled that her anarchist colleagues enjoyed phrenological readings and revelled in the possession of the correct anarchist characteristics: 'Nothing afforded the comrades more satisfaction than to be informed that their bumps showed undoubtedly criminal propensities'.[121] Such figures were depraved harbingers of metropolitan disintegration more broadly. Anarchists were 'hyenas', asocial lone individuals who comprised the social wreckage of the East End. In popular literature, anarchy was compared to 'a werewolf' and the anarchist crisis of the 1890s was ascribed to 'anarchistic wolves who would storm the fold and destroy sheep and shepherd in one mad rush'.[122] The names that anarchist groups like the French 'Panthers of Batignolles' or 'The Pariahs of Picardy' and

'The Wild Boars of the Marne' allocated themselves, seemed to confirm their marginal and aggressively militant outsider status.[123] In both Britain and the United States, transience and absence of familial and community roots hinted at anarchist affiliations; respectable opinion saw tramps, hobos and itinerant workers in makeshift camps and shanty-towns as the natural breeding-ground for anarchism. The plot of H. Barton Baker's *Robert Miner, Anarchist* begins with the death of the patriarch of a family of anarchist tramps, who, in a shattering revelation at the end of the novel, is revealed to have abducted Robert Miner from his aristocratic parents.[124]

Women and gender issues were integral to the plots of many of the 'dynamite romances'. Here they fuelled concerns about the 'New Woman' and the 'Woman Franchise Question' that increasingly preoccupied Edwardian reformers and their conservative opponents.[125] Women inflamed by anarchism and ultra-radical ideas were a disturbing presence in otherwise conventional novels of devotion, duty and piety.[126] They also cemented the setting of such literature in the capital, which was believed to be the heartland of the free and emancipated female of the early twentieth century. One of the major contemporary concerns about anarchism was that its advocacy of free love, and gender equality made it uniquely attractive to female reformers. Male anarchists noted a preponderance of women in the organization.[127] A shadowy female guerrilla was allegedly present at the robbery in Houndsditch that sparked off the Siege of Sidney Street.[128] For its opponents, anarchism posed a major threat to hearth and home, upsetting the balance between the sexes and luring impressionable women away from their duties to parents, children and spouses. On these grounds, female anarchists were particularly feared and loathed. A number of them were notorious and became emblematic of the threat anarchism apparently posed to society. Louise Michel, 'The Angel of the Commune', was the quintessential female anarchist. An unrepentant Communard imprisoned and exiled in French New Caledonia, she became a full-fledged anarchist in the 1880s. Appearing regularly on platforms throughout Europe she proved an inspiration to the celebrated female anarchist, Emma Goldman, in particular.[129] Goldman was also much impressed by the example of the Russian anarchists and nihilists. Russian nihilism had a strong female dimension, radicalized by Chernyshevsky's novel *What Is to Be Done?* in which the heroine escapes from a loveless marriage to establish a sewing cooperative and to train as a doctor, thereafter dedicating her life to the people.[130] The strong female component within nihilism exerted a powerful influence on female recruits. Vera Zasulich, who shot Governor General Trepov of St. Petersburg, and Sophia Petrovskaya who was executed for her complicity in the assassination of Tsar Alexander II, created a model for the activist, militant woman in the front-line of revolutionary activity.[131]

Figure 2.6 'The Red Sisterhood'. An unflattering portrayal of female anarchists in the United States, 1889. From M. J. Schaack, *Anarchy and Anarchists: A History of the Red Terror and the Social Revolution in America and Europe* (Chicago: F. J. Schulte and Company, 1889), p. 207. (Author's Collection.)

These were the 'squaws' and 'red sisterhood' much loathed by opponents of the movement.[132]

Unsurprisingly female anarchists often played the part of *femme fatales*, luring innocent and naive men into conspiracies and assassination attempts. In H. Barton Baker's book, *Robert Miner, Anarchist*, the descent of Robert Miner into anarchist militancy begins through an encounter with the mysterious and alluring Wenda Zaluski at a society party, who subsequently becomes his revolutionary muse.[133] In G.A. Henty's boys' own adventure, *Condemned as a Nihilist*, the young Godfrey Bullen is flattered by a nihilist agent, Katia, into involvement with a plan to secure the escape of a revolutionary leader. Unsuspectingly implicated in the conspiracy, he is exiled to Siberia but escapes to regale his friends at home with his adventures. His uncle, warning of the subversive role played by women in nihilism, concludes:

One of the most extraordinary things connected with the movement is that women play a large part in it. Being in the thick of every conspiracy they are the life and soul of the movement, and they are of all classes. There are a score of women for whose arrest the authorities would pay any money, and yet they elude every effort. It is horrible. This is what comes of women going to Switzerland and learning to look on religion as a myth and all authority as hateful, and to have wild dreams of an impossible state. Of affairs such as has never existed in this world. It is horrible, but it is pitiable.[134]

The dynamite romances traded heavily in compliant images of women, and sought to return female anarchists to the home. Having fought off the machinations of the German anarchist Carl Stein and his confederates to secure the fortune of the American heiress Evelyn Hartley, her new husband, Philip Maitland concludes that 'no woman is at heart a communist!'.[135] In Whiteing's *No. 5 John Street*, the 'Amazonian' flower-seller, Tilda, stands as an emblem of the traditional woman. Adopting a nurturing and support-ive role to a young girl dying of consumption, she assumes all the mater-nal characteristics and family responsibilities anarchist women traditionally lacked. Ultimately, it is she who foils Azrael's plan to explode an anarchist bomb in a society party, dying in the blast herself to prevent the fulfilment of the outrage.[136] The strongest attempt, however, to reverse the deleterious impact of anarchist teachings on women occurs in Wallace's *The Council of Justice*. Here the lead is taken by a female terrorist, the mysterious 'Woman of Gratz' who appears as a compendium of the various prominent female anarchists of the late nineteenth century, coloured with a hint of mystery and of sado-masochism.

> There were other women in the movement, heroic fools seeking a frowsy martyrdom. As ruthless, as merciless, as wicked as the worst men of the Red Hundred. . . . (but) . . . the Woman of Gratz leapt to greater fame. She had been arrested half a dozen times and whipped twice; but they could prove nothing against her and elicit nothing from her – and she was very beautiful.[137]

Resorting to many of the conventions of the popular romance novel, Wallace's *The Council of Justice* pits the vigilante group, 'The Four Just Men', against the anarchists of the 'Red Hundred', led by the 'Woman of Gratz'. Finally, however, a love interest is introduced, and the dedication of The 'Woman of Gratz' to the anarchist order is undermined by her love for her putative enemy, Manfred. Betrayed by her emotions, 'The Woman of Gratz' renounces violence and becomes an ally of the vigilante group against her former comrades. Thus is the female anarchist disarmed, by love.

VI

The anarchist 'dynamite romance' flourished in the years between 1880 and 1914. During this period, it put in place the characteristics of a distinctive genre in thriller fiction. By the outbreak of World War I, it was gradually supplanted by a new style of literature that anticipated other menaces, either future, high tech wars or more traditional mass popular risings. Nevertheless, at their height, the 'dynamite romances' of the early part of the twentieth century had already established the ground rules of fiction dealing with anarchism in London well in advance of the publication of Joseph Conrad's *The Secret Agent* in 1907. Against the background of a crumbling urban polity, anarchism heralded the disintegration of families, the collapse of established gender hierarchies, projected a threat from the 'New Woman' and demonstrated the terrible power of terrorists who revelled in death, whilst ignoring the value of life. In many ways, Azrael in *No. 5 John Street* is Conrad's 'Professor' in embryo, aligning himself with a cause that, as in *The Secret Agent*, brings tragic and unintended consequences. Moreover, popular fiction relating to anarchism created an archetypal anarchist, that was the Victorian era's legacy to a later generation of thriller writers. Oscillating between visions of anarchist organization as a vast faceless international conspiracy, and as a matter of small group dynamics, pulp fiction writers nevertheless portrayed anarchism as a primal and elemental force that brooked no negotiation, and whose depredations, and the methods taken by governments to contain them, threatened long-standing English liberties.

At the height of the 'Dynamite Panic' of the 1880s, the socialist newspaper *Justice* commented that 'dynamitists and state socialists appear as lurid figures on the horizon of society'.[138] The anarchist figure in pulp fiction provided more than just literary colour. As Donald Rooum comments, "The "anarchist bomb-thrower" is a folk-myth, mostly derived from literature. It was originated in the "penny bloods" of the nineteenth century and revived with gusto by the writers of "boys' stories" in the early 1920s, when war was out of fashion but fictitious heroes still needed enemies".[139] From the 1880s, low art and literature collided around the issues provided by anarchism, whilst anarchists themselves became part of the furniture of the metropolitan novel. Analysis of the many novels about anarchism in their metropolitan and historical contexts connects up with contemporary fears about an impure and rootless feral proletariat. Anarchism stood for the divided physical space and social geography of the metropolis. Repeatedly, anarchism provided ready fodder for thriller and pulp fiction writers. These novels deserve consideration as documents that framed the preoccupations of early social investigators in London. For many contemporary writers, anarchism was a disease-like phenomenon that attracted the criminal and the deviant, and acted as a harbinger of metropolitan disintegration more generally. Many of the popular stories that detail anarchism emphasize these criminal dimensions to the agitation. It represented everything that was most debased and uncontrolled about the urges of metropolitan low-life. In this reading, anarchists were a form of moral pollution, hastening the breakdown of the collectivities of East End communities. Most often, the bomb was quite literally about the atomization of the capital. It symbolized the collapse of families (as in Conrad's *The Secret Agent*) and belongs to the 1880s debate about the fragmentation and social polarization of London highlighted by Charles Booth's social survey, and expressed through William Booth's Salvation Army crusade, mobilized to remedy the spiritual malaise of the capital that in the popular imagination, anarchism sought to exploit.

Chapter 3

Red Scares and Inter-War London

But my friend, that million and a half of a few years ago, is nearly four million today. Every day thousands of young people are graduating from the universities under high pressure, and every one of them is a Communist. That is one great factor in their favour; they control the intelligent youth of Russia, the other is their fanaticism. With them the Communist ideal is a religion: ambition, comfort, leisure, personal relations, everything must give way to that. That is why I believe in the long run they are bound to triumph.[1]

'One reads about spies in books and things' she said absently, 'and it all seems – unreal. Not the sort of thing that could possibly happen in one's life. And then – well, it does.'[2]

The inter-war years have been described as a 'golden age' of detective fiction and the thriller genre. By the end of the 1930s, detective fiction comprised one quarter of all new novels published in English. Much has been written about crime fiction both as genre and as metaphor. The social conservatism and jingoistic tone of these novels are often noted.[3] Conventionally these years have been seen as a period in which popular fiction became defined by traditions of patriotism, and a conservative regard for the maintenance of the status quo. In this, they mirrored the political ascendancy of conservatism itself during this period. Murders at country house parties, aristocratic sleuths and villains, amateur detectives and an acute eye for social manners and conventions have apparently marked out a genre that proved distant from the social realities of the 1920s and 1930s. As Julian Symonds has remarked, 'In the British stories the General Strike never took place, trade unions did not exist, and when sympathy was expressed for the poor, it was not for the unemployed, but for those struggling along on affixed inherited incomes.'[4] This chapter re-examines the inter-war thriller and crime novel. Challenging views of a de-politicized genre, it focuses attention on those novels that proposed an explicit set of political convictions. A considerable sub-element within the crime fiction of these years tackled directly the threat posed by radicals, socialists, Bolsheviks and Irish Republicans. Often overt, rather than covert, sometimes overlooked altogether, or simply described as inherent in the form itself, these political statements merit further consideration. This chapter argues that the conservatism of inter-war fiction is recognized, but seldom explored in any detail. Moreover it asserts the failure of historians to link up the literary forms of these years with recent historical work on Red Scares and 'anti-Redism'. In these novels resides the spirit of the British 'Red Scare' of the post-1919 to 1939 period. Finally the chapter explores the 'Londoncentric' view of much of the popular 'Red Menace' stories of these years, tracing the links between the anti-anarchist fiction of the 1890s and the fears about socialism expressed in inter-war crime novels via the journey through the landscape of the capital.

I

The late nineteenth and early twentieth centuries saw the emergence of the popular thriller and spy fiction genre. There is now an extensive literature on crime fiction and related thrillers. Much of this work concentrates on definition.[5] Categories of definition revolve around crime novels, detective novels, police fiction and the thriller proper. Traditionally, academic authors have been preoccupied with exploring the provenance of such fiction. Other perspectives concentrate on the American influences and audiences that shaped responses to the genre. Particular authors attract their own strongly partisan admirers.[6] Moreover, some popular crime authors have sought to create a respectable pedigree for their craft, locating themselves in a tradition dating back to Wilkie Collins and William Godwin. Recent research on juvenile popular fiction has demonstrated the continuities apparent from the pulp pro-imperial 'boys' own' adventures of the Edwardian period, with their explicitly nativist and patriotic agendas, through to the crime serial magazines and potboilers of the 1920s featuring Sexton Blake and other celebrity detective figures.[7] Such resonances were noted by a number of contemporaries. They often evoked both nostalgia and enthusiasm in equal measure. George Orwell recalled, somewhat wistfully, in 1944:

> The great fascination of these old magazines is the completeness with which they 'date'. Absorbed in the affairs of the moment, they tell us about political fashions and tendencies, which are hardly mentioned in the more general history books. It is interesting, for instance, to study in contemporary magazines the war scare of the early sixties, when it was assumed on all sides that Britain was about to be invaded, the Volunteers were formed, amateur strategists published maps showing the routes by which the French armies would converge in London, and peaceful citizens cowered in ditches whilst

the bullets of the Rifle Club (the then equivalent of the Home Guard) ricocheted in all directions.[8]

Orwell discerned the link in popular fiction through to issues of defence, invasion and patriotism inherent in such material. In this he followed the judgement of A.J. Balfour in the 1900s, who, when asked what he could possibly see in the invasion panic novels of William Le Queux, replied 'several thousand votes for the Conservative Party'.[9] Balfour's admiration for Le Queux was echoed by Stanley Baldwin's enthusiasm for the novels of John Buchan in the 1930s, and his role as an advocate for his contribution to literature.[10] Orwell provided the most famous judgement on the popular fiction of this period, suggesting that left politics always failed through its inability to establish and exploit more established popular literary forms, whether juvenile or adult.[11] In line with this assessment the political opinions of many thriller writers have been subjected to a scrutiny that reveals conservative, or even ultra-rightist political opinions. Whilst the canon was never solely rightist in nature, and descriptions of thrillers as a conservative genre must always be subject to qualification and exceptions, from Peter Cheyney, through Dennis Wheatley, Dornford Yates and John Buchan, there is a marked propensity towards Conservatism (sometimes active) and revanchism amongst the leaders in the field.[12]

In this chapter, questions of definition are placed at one remove in order to analyse the framework, conventions, personalities and themes of a popular fiction characterized by anti-socialism and anti-Bolshevism. Without discriminating between different fictional forms, it ranges across thrillers, detective and police novels, and even some science fiction. The intention is to illuminate the cultural context in which Red Scare ideas proliferated during the inter-war years. 'Red Menace' ideas found a natural home in such literature. The theme of the 'Red Menace' attained such potency during these decades, that most of the established crime and thriller writers of the period produced at least one novel drawing on such notions. It even worked its way into drama. Arnold Ridley's play *The Ghost Train* about an allegedly haunted station and Bolshevik conspiracies in the West Country found fame as a favourite piece of amateur repertory for many years.[13] From Agatha Christie to John Buchan, many writers found that they had at least one anti-Bolshevik romance inside them. For some, like Hugh Addison, anti-Bolshevism was their only defining idea. This chapter therefore draws on the work of more established authors and of lesser figures that produced works of anti-socialist fiction. Placing such ideas in context, it seeks to illuminate both the nature of the inter-war 'Red Scare' and to suggest alternative routes whereby the notion of a British 'Red Scare' might be explored. Following the literary form described by Martin Priestman, the majority of novels outlined here might best be described as a variant of the 'anti-conspiracy thriller'.[14]

II

Hostility to socialism and radicalism accompanied the emergence of movements of popular protest. The 'forward march of labour' created an opposing current of hostility to ideas for the representation of labour in parliament, protection for the rights of trades unionists and suggestions for the redistribution of wealth. Anti-socialism was rooted in Victorian and Edwardian preoccupations with a perceived monomaniacal and confiscatory radicalism. Colonel Willoughby de Broke recalled with nostalgia the days when 'the freak, the faddist, the schemer and the doctrinaire were either not returned to the House of Commons at all, or else, if returned, were made to feel out of place in an assembly composed of those whom an orator of blue blood once called "people like ourselves"'.[15] Despite the pragmatic and non-doctrinaire programme of British labourism, the Labour Party became associated with visions of political and social extremism, and of social and economic turmoil from an early stage in its existence.[16] The rhetoric of early socialism was shot through with apocalyptic and revolutionary images, feeding the mood of hostility towards it. Marx's acolyte in Britain, Henry Hyndman, predicted that an English Revolution would take place in 1889, and saw the Social Democratic Federation fulfilling the role of a Committee of Public Safety.[17] The radical agitator and later Manchester Labour MP, J.R. Clynes, recalled the antipathy towards the 'red tie fanatics' who moved in the socialist circles of the 1890s. Elsewhere in the empire fears were raised about 'disordered imaginations' and 'red-tie maniacs'.[18] Socialism evoked a peculiarly toxic form of counter-politics. Stewart Grahame, who examined examples of socialist ideals amongst utopian communities in Latin America, commented: 'Those who have studied at close quarters the manners and customs of primitive races will see a close correspondence between their habits and the ideals of socialism. It is difficult to resist the conclusion that State Socialism amounts to nothing less than a hideous form of state-enforced barbarism'.[19]

Opposition to 'socialism' ranged from the philosophical, through the religious, to the moral and the economic. For some of its critics, the word 'socialism' continued to evoke images of unbelief and free love associated with the older Owenite and secularist movements. In Bermondsey, in the early twentieth century, the Conservative election candidate, John Dumphries, railed against socialism as 'atheistic' and 'something even graver, something usually concealed – Free Love'.[20] The careers of Edward Carpenter and H.G. Wells suggested a continuing tradition of such influences within the movement. Some critics foresaw a joyless and regimented society in which the family became redundant and children were raised in state-regulated barracks. Wells commented: 'People are told that socialism will destroy the home, will substitute a sort of human stud farm for that warm and intimate nest of human life, will bring up our children in incubators and crèches and institutions generally'.[21] Others stressed the apparent impracticality of socialist models of political and economic organization, leading to increased bureaucracy, the paralysis of financial markets and chaos in the system of distribution and supply.[22] For its critics, a socialist society would be an acquisitive and potentially amoral one, in which there was license for theft and personal gain.[23] There was often speculation about the social cost of socialism; it was frequently represented as encouraging selfish materialism, but perversely depriving the population of the opportunities required for satisfying their desires. Austin Hopkinson, the independent, but Tory-inclined, MP for Mossley in Lancashire, believed that though the doctrine had started out as a 'dream of kindly and foolish men', it had rapidly mutated into 'a monstrous tyrant, spreading abroad envy, greed and hatred'.[24] Much of this sentiment was couched in apocalyptic terms. A.J. Balfour remarked in 1907: 'The basis upon which our civilisation rests – the central fact which has guided its evolution from the condition of a mere savage horde to that of the greatest empire of the world – is being sapped and unless that is stayed we shall be led to the enervation which characterised the latter days of the Roman Empire and which has heralded the decay of most of the great civilisations of the past'.[25]

By the 1920s, there was a common acceptance that the rise of labour meant a commensurate collapse in the wages and conditions of the respectable classes, imperilling the livelihoods of the aspirational and upwardly mobile. Conspiracy theories abounded, and the feeling mounted that labour governments would spell economic chaos and national collapse. Some of this extreme antagonism was stoked by pressure groups. The main vehicle for the anti-socialist platform became the Anti-Socialist Union. Established in 1908 and inspired by the Army and Navy Leagues and the National Service League of the period, the Union sought to channel anti-socialist ideas and provide practical help for the opponents of organized labour.[26] As Kenneth D. Brown has pointed out, the Anti-Socialist Union (ASU) planted the association in the popular mind between the Labour Party and the imported doctrines of continental socialism.[27] It highlighted deficiencies in socialist planning, issues of socialism and national defence, campaigned against socialist academics in universities and provided a focal point for attacks on left ideologies more generally. The *Labour Leader* spoke of the organization's appeals for money 'as carefully calculated to make the flesh of dukes, rack-renters and nervous old

Figure 3.1 Humorous depiction of the triumph of socialism. The comic tramp, 'Weary Willy' enjoys the benefits of a transformed post-socialist society. Postcard 'When We're Socialists', 1910 (Thomas Arthur Browne) (Author's Collection).

ladies creep'.[28] As Brown comments, if before 1914 the ASU had seen as its task the job of authenticating a link between the Labour Party and socialism, in the inter-war period the organization tried to 'create a similar association between communism and a more socialist-orientated Communist Party'.[29] After its demise it became superseded by a plethora of other organizations with the avowed aim of resisting the encroachment of socialist ideologies. A full-blown anti-Communism emerges in the rhetoric of its successors groups, particularly the Economic League, in the 1930s. The League pioneered political blacklisting, and was instrumental in much of the orchestrated victimization of trades unionists and Communists during these years.[30] Anti-Communist literature conveniently ignored the expulsion of known Communists from Labour ranks in 1924, and the extreme anti-Communism of leading Labour moderates. Herbert Morrison was the most prominent amongst them, describing the formation of a popular front with the Communist Party of Great Britain (CPGB) in 1936 as 'the road to ruin'.[31] It also overlooked the historical weakness of British Communism, which suffered severe financial problems, and, except in 1926, enticed very few international Comintern officials into Britain to foment revolution.[32] Instead, contemporary pamphlets revealed a subversive Communism 'that works in secret . . . The real truth of the matter is, of course, that, preaching a doctrine of revolution and destruction, the Communist Party of Great Britain would like to enforce in Great Britain what its Parent Party has enforced with the penal settlement and the firing squad in Russia, namely complete suppression of free speech and free criticism.'[33] These ideas reached their peak during the early 1920s, and were much in evidence during the 1924 general election, which saw a concerted attempt to topple the first Labour government. Conservative Party campaign leaflets insisted that under Labour, the monarchy would be swept away, and the empire placed in circumstances of extreme peril.[34] The fabricated Zinoviev Letter, which alleged the infiltration of Communist agents into the upper echelons of the party, asserted that the Labour Party promoted propaganda to erode the loyalty of the armed forces and hasten the advent of revolution. The forgery was widely accepted and is often seen as costing Labour the election.[35] Thereafter a series of 'Red Panics' kept the issue of Bolshevism at the forefront of the British public's mind. The exposure of Arcos, the Soviet trading bureau in London, as the front for an international spy ring in 1927, provided ready fodder for popular writers.[36] As the Labour MP J.R. Clynes recalled, 'Communist talk and tactics have for years been the most precious possession of the Parliamentary forces ranged against British Labour. Whenever the Communists applaud some absurd foreign idea, that idea is promptly fastened upon us by the Tories, as though it were our official label'.[37] The prevalence of anti-Bolshevik rhetoric was frequently satirized. It features in Allen Clarke's Lancashire dialect literature to disturb the peace of his fictional Tum Fowt Debatin' Club when some mildly liberal sentiments are expressed: '"Disgraceful!" roared Tommy Dod. "He owt to be expelled. I shouldn't wonder if he isn't bein' subsidized by th' Red Men of Moscow. He's in their pay. They're on wi' their dirty sacret work everywhere, doin' aw they con to ruin eaur glorious Empire"'.[38]

Behind much of the popular fiction about Bolshevik insurgency and secret influences lay the spectre of the Irish question. Many writers of popular fiction saw Irish republicanism and Bolshevik plots as virtually interchangeable menaces. Events in Ireland in 1916 and during the civil war cemented the view that the empire was in crisis, poised on the brink of imminent disintegration. A number of authors feared that the culture of political martyrdom, marital law and political breakdown might spread to the mainland of the United Kingdom after 1919. Guerrilla warfare in Ireland, armed conspiracies and the exodus of the Anglo-Irish aristocracy created a vision of a society in dissolution. In much fiction, the disintegration of British rule in Ireland and the outbreak of civil war there presented a vision of future circumstances on the British mainland.[39] For many writers, the menace to hearth and home posed by Irish separatism made Britain a beleaguered state, threatened both by Irish militancy from within, and imperial rivals from without. In her novel of subterfuge and conspiracy, *The Secret Adversary*, Agatha Christie's Bolsheviks and Sinn Feiners work closely together to sow disharmony, using money from the

American Irish community to support their aims: The Sinn Fein terrorist at her gathering of Bolshevik agents declaims: 'In a month from now – sooner or later as you wish – I will guarantee you such a reign of terror in Ireland as shall shake the British Empire to its foundations'.[40] So strong were these images of all-embracing threat that the informer, Gypo, in Liam O'Flaherty's *The Informer*, a tale of betrayal and revolutionary justice amongst republican militants, depicted the 'conspiracy' of his confederates as an autonomous entity in its own right, with its own internal dynamic of revolt:

> But they were not merely two men, two human beings. They were something more than that. They represented the Revolutionary Organisation. They were merely cogs in the wheels of that organisation. That was what he feared, what rendered him powerless. He feared that mysterious, intangible thing, that was all brain and no body. An intelligence without a body. A thing that was full of plans, implacable, reaching out everywhere invisibly, with invisible tentacles like a supernatural monster. A thing that was like a religion, mysterious, occult, devilish.[41]

III

A proliferation of socialist and progressivist fiction during the early years of the twentieth century reinforced the notion that socialist and radical ideas were in the ascendant. A publication sponsored by the American Jesuit Order, which drew largely on British examples, commented: 'It has become quite the "rage" with the third rate literati to float their intellectual wares on the radical market by the use of the catch penny term socialism on the title page'.[42] Utopian novels rapidly became the staple of the radical publishing market from the 1890s onwards. Such utopian fiction abounded in the early days of the British Labour Party.[43] Whilst ever willing to expound about the form a utopian society might take, these novels were often uncertain about the exact process whereby a transition to a post-capitalist state might be effected. Even radicals themselves, sympathetic to the aims and outcomes of a utopian social transformation, questioned the assumptions behind this kind of literature. Cecil Chesterton wrote: 'How do you get to Morris' ideal society in *News from Nowhere* – he shows us heaven. When we ask how this state of things was brought about, we are told that it was by a series of riots in Trafalgar Square, followed by a general strike, an economic crisis and the capture of power by insurgent workers'. As he pointed out, there was a limit to what might be accomplished by such methods.[44] Philip Frankford's 'The Coming Day for the Worker', which provided a story of the English Revolution and drew derivatively on Morris, posed many of the same problems. The action takes place in a futuristic Croydon, modified by post-revolutionary social planning. Experiencing the delights of a new civilization at first hand, the protagonists who arrive by airship from another planet find the road to socialism gradually revealed by their hosts.[45] The centrepiece of the novel, told in flashback, revolves around descriptions of the symbolic burning of the East End. Frankford writes:

> But at last the day came when humanity would be denied no more. The hour of reckoning, and of revenge, had arrived. The people arose like giants refreshed with wine. The oppressors of the human race were now led – as were the swine in scripture – down the abyss into the deep sea below . . . Then came the grand clearance of the London slums. Those foul rookeries, kept up so long in order to provide gold for the greedy capitalists, were raised to the ground. Our great historian, Harvey, tells us how the multitude welcomed with shouts of joy the burning of these sickening dens. Every time the flames leaped and danced, every time the fires added to the great burning mass yet another of its victims, the shouts arose anew. For the multitude hailed these flames as a harbinger of their deliverance from bondage. The nightmare of capitalism was over, a fresh birth was given to man. A new London arose built upon the ashes of the old.[46]

Literature from abroad also found a place in the canon of predictive writing. Jack London's vision of the emergence and overthrow of a plutocratic oligarchy in the United States, in his book the *Iron Heel*, found a wide readership in Britain, and was enthusiastically reviewed in the labourist press. George Benson wrote: 'We are led through a maze of plot and counter-plot, through street fighting and the annihilation of whole cities of revolting workers. This tale grips with a double force, for not only are our sympathies naturally with Everhard as the hero, but he is a socialist fighting our battle, and we await the outcome of each move with a personal interest which it is impossible to feel in an ordinary tale.'[47] The format of these novels was duplicated in the White settler colonies, where radicals hoped that the example of reforms adopted in the dominions might impact on the domestic environment at home. In New Zealand radicals speculated about the impact of energies released by colonial land-reforming zeal, and imagined a Britain turned into a republic by the refusal of the large landowners to nationalize the land.[48] Other domestic socialists sought consolation from the past, painting fanciful images of Chartist-style popular agitations that might overturn the state in a single blow. Told from the perspective of the imagined brotherly commonwealth of 1950, the serialized novella *The Second English Revolution* by Fabian and guild socialist Holbrook Jackson, portrayed the English revolution of 1920 in much the same terms as

Frankford. His story, however, drew nostalgically on memories of the Chartist petitions. He imagined a mass petitioning campaign against poverty under the leadership of Enderby, a Chartist-style demagogue and the 'Cromwell of the English Revolution':

> The procession was one of the longest ever seen in London. It still had barely left Hyde Park corner before its head appeared in Whitehall. At it head marched Enderby carrying the flag which became the flag of the revolution and which now waves over the commonwealth of Britain: the Union Jack in the centre of which on a white ground was emblazoned the Cap of Liberty. We knew ourselves to be patriots, but we demanded freedom to live for our country as well as die for it. Behind Enderby came the hundred delegates who were to deliver the petition to the House. The huge roll containing the four million signatures followed on a great market cart painted scarlet and drawn by four handsome dapple-grey shire horses. It looked like an enormous Eastern scripture in the roll from which preceded the invention of the book. Indeed it was a scripture, an inspired document, but instead of announcing the will of God, it announced the will of the people.[49]

Connotations and memories of the mass movements of the nineteenth century were very evident here. There follows a rapid escalation of conflict during the presentation of the petition at the bar of the House of Commons. With the death of hundreds of protestors, a declaration of martial law, and the assassination of Enderby, the tide turns in favour of the rebels, allowing revolutionaries and moderates to unify around the memory of the martyred leader.[50] In a similar tongue-in-cheek tale by Cecil Chesterton, the future revolution ends badly, provoking a 'White Terror' and the public hanging of the movement's leader, Charles Murray, Victor Grayson, Conrad Noel, and Chesterton himself in Trafalgar Square.[51]

IV

The 'Londoncentric' nature of this material is very marked. These were the fantasies and 'imaginary barricades of London's Jacobin journalists'.[52] The plausibility of a possible British insurrection in London was made more likely by the famous panic surrounding Father Knox's satirical play *Broadcasting from the Barricades* in 1926. A gentle spoof, which satirized the conventions of British radio broadcast media, and English cultural *sang-froid*, it sets the stage against which the increasingly preposterous events of a popular rising in London unfold. From a demonstration by the 'Abolish-the-Queue Society' in

Trafalgar Square to the sacking of the National Gallery and the Savoy Hotel, events rapidly escalate through the shelling of the Houses of Parliament with trench mortars and the lynching of the Minister of Transport, whose body is hung from a tramway-post on Vauxhall Bridge Road. A famous example of a media hoax, and instilling panic at the time, the events of 1926 demonstrated the febrility of British public opinion and its susceptibility to ideas of imminent political and social violence.[53]

Much of the popular fiction of these years that speculated about the possibilities for a British revolution framed these imaginary insurgencies in purely metropolitan terms. Political and social change was to proceed from the centre. Despite the economic and social unsuitability of the capital for a literature that considered the declining days of pre-revolutionary society, and depicted the death throes of late capitalism, London was seen by many Communists as the cradle of the British revolution. In John Sommerfield's *May Day*, an industrial landscape more suitable to the Industrial North is transposed onto London. Here an overstretched and underpaid factory proletariat work in machine-shops where 'the floor is slippery with oil and graphite, as with some horrible blood'.[54] Generally these authors avoided the expedient of situating their conflicts in smaller communities, and then working through the tensions between rebels and counter-revolutionaries that might emerge in such circumstances. Only J.D. Beresford attempted this treatment in his book *Revolution* published in 1921. In this study, located in a commuter suburb of London, the intention is to examine the impact of national events on the psychology of a small town. Charting the collapse of the British government in the face of a general strike led by the charismatic demagogue, Isaac Perry, Beresford's novel examines the social tension within his chosen community, and the winners and losers as power changes hands from the squire and the vicar, to the politicized mob and the agricultural labourers. Even here, however, the book's early chapters revolve around the increasing anxiety on the streets of the capital in the face of the paralysis brought about by the strikers.

> There was a remarkable effect of general apprehension in the thoroughfares of the city, and they were more crowded than was usual at that hour of the afternoon. Men and women were not hurrying to their secret destination, intent upon their own affairs. They were loitering, and what was more noticeable still in that place, observing each other, finding excuses for casual conversation, with perfect strangers. And in Throgmorton Avenue, except for some occasional and obviously facetious quotation of Government Stocks, no business was being attempted. Men stood in groups talking together nosily, a trifle boisterously. Their attitude seemed to express an excited determination to see the thing through, albeit with just a shade of uneasiness showing behind their assumption of nonchalance.[55]

J.D. Beresford presented a rare example of a non-aligned author; his hero, Paul Leaming, seeks to remain above and apart from the two sides in the new English Civil War. His quasi-mystical aim is to create a common doctrine of religious humanism that will bring both adversaries together.[56] In the 1920s and 1930s, a new generation of authors (the most passionate were Communists) added to the tally of such fiction. Communism created a second generation of authors fixated on the imminence of revolution.[57] Many of these works gleefully depicted the details of fighting in the streets of the capital itself.[58] Works by Philip Toynbee and John Sommerfield were especially partisan. Sommerfield depicts the rush of events towards an outbreak of revolution on May Day, 1937. Concentrating on the logistics and organization of revolt, Sommerfield sacrifices his hero, James, who is beaten to death by the police. The novel ends with a confrontation in Hyde Park, where '[t]he workers seethe around the base of the Arch like an angry sea, and the noise comes up to the men at the top like the sound of a storm as James' flag-draped body is held up and saluted by a hundred thousand clenched fists raised in the air, a hundred thousand shouts of "Red Front"'.[59] Toynbee's work of juvenilia, *These Savage Days*, portrayed a restless and aimless young hero, Simon Lawrence, finding eventual solace and a cause in the Communist Party of Great Britain. Much of the plot is about the troubled hero, Lawrence, finding himself. The message was clear: Communism was the path of the future.[60] The events of the revolution occur late in the book and are relatively incidental. In the final pages, however, London, held by Communist insurgents, is bombed from the air by mutinous regiments from Catterick and there is fighting in the suburbs.[61] Intriguingly this novel provides brief glimpses of a post-Communist British future. Churches are fired, the distinctive stone walls of the Cotswolds are broken down to facilitate the collectivization of agriculture, and members of the British Union of Fascists and other counter-revolutionaries are interned at a camp in Hemel Hempstead.[62]

Alongside such descriptions, narratives of revolution often featured scenes of panic, desperation and flight as events in the capital spiral out of control and the city succumbs to 'the hell-broth of Bolshevism'.[63] These lurid images imported memories of the Paris Commune of 1870 into contemporary London.[64] Columns of refugees, possessions piled on handcarts, looting and the collapse of law and order were scenes familiar to a British audience from the pre-1914 Balkan Wars and the Great War itself. In John D. Mayne's *The Triumph of Socialism and How it Succeeded* from 1908, the victory of a Socialist Party at the polls in 1912 immediately leads to an exodus of the wealthy: 'We learn that the greatest agitation and alarm prevails amongst them; that every train and steamer is crammed with rich men, leaving the country with all their money and personal effects, and that every great mansion swarms with carpenters, packing up in huge cases the pictures and china and costly furniture of the proprietors, and that the roads are crammed with vans carrying them to the seaports'.[65] There's a similar rout of the wealthy and propertied as the government loses control to Communist insurgents in Dennis Wheatley's *Black August*. As the hero, Kenyon Wensleadale, makes preparations for leaving London he finds: 'A long line of cars stretched ahead of him, all bound on the same errand. Many of them were stacked high with the weirdest assortment of luggage. The great exodus from London had begun, and everybody who had a place to go to in the country was making for it'. 'London will be red to-morrow' asserts his acquaintance Bunny Cawnthorpe who is also caught up in the confusion.[66] In Addison's *The Battle of London*, well-dressed West End theatregoers are cut off by the fighting, and are cast adrift in the chaos and confusion: 'But in spite of their appearance they were all at that moment homeless, cast out on to a London which had become a tragic travesty of its old self'.[67]

The socialist and Communist threat created a trenchant vein of anti-socialist literature that answered far-Left fictions. Fear of Communist insurgency sharpened the bite of such material. It provided an unashamed antidote to the utopian novels of socialist writers. Against this background, there was often a revanchist tone about the answering literature that sought to retaliate against an apparently overmighty and insurgent socialism. Much of it explored the circumstances that led to the creation of a socialist state. As Martin Ceadel has pointed out, in the unease of the post-1919 period, fear of another war, and of the chaos and social turmoil that might accompany it, led to the creation of a new genre of 'future war' stories, highlighting the atrocities and horrors brought to human conflict by new technologies for waging destruction.[68] Much of this literature, as well as phrophesying innovations in warfare, also contemplated the chaos and social turmoil that might accompany another global conflict. Overlooked by Ceadel, anti-Bolshevism remained a strong undercurrent to works dealing with this theme. The most significant manifestation of this form was *People of the Ruins* written in 1920 by Edward Shanks. This work gained something of a cult following, featuring in other popular literature that dealt with the damaging effects of rapid and unregulated social transformation.[69] The book addressed the anxieties of a new generation who saw war and revolution leading to a new barbarism in the middle years of the twentieth century. The book begins with the ominous signs of a sudden outbreak of revolution in the capital. On his way through London to examine the prototype of an invention pioneered by his friend, the hero, Jeremy Tuft, sees the signs of social insurgency all around him. Outside Liverpool Street Station he falls afoul of a crowd 'held together apparently by an orator mounted on a broken chair who was lashing himself into a fury which he found difficult to communicate to his audience'.[70] As the first skirmishes break out, Tuft is

Figure 3.2 Bolshevik firing squad in the capital. The cover of Hugh Addison, *The Battle of London* (London: Herbert Jenkins Ltd., 1926) (Author's Collection).

magically preserved by his friend's invention, a ray that puts him into a state of suspended animation. He awakes in the year 2074 to discover a world that has reverted to Medieval conditions. Decades of war and civil strife have led to the collapse of technology and the loss of all scientific knowledge. London is a shell, in which little survives of the knowledge accumulated in the British Museum. In Regent's Park, 'every stage of desolation and decay was to be seen in that appalling tract, which had lost the trimness and prosperity of its flourishing period without acquiring the solemn and awful aspect of nobler ruins'.[71] *People of the Ruins* provided an awful prophecy of a future world blighted in the aftermath of war and disorder. It is the antithesis of the utopianism of much socialist fiction. The Medievalism society descends into is not the paradise envisaged by William Morris. Rather it provides an image of savagery and brute power, in which fanatics scheme for a restoration of the old knowledge, so that they might wage war once again. It shocked contemporaries with its bleak vision of human character, the faltering of visions of progress it represented and its apprehension that war might purge civilization altogether.[72]

V

People of the Ruins was an example of science fiction placed at the service of anti-socialism. It carried strong messages about the direction in which war and social ferment might lead. For most authors of anti-socialist and Bolshevik fictions, however, the immediate concern was not the remote future, but rather the present. The strongest sub-text to appear throughout such work was the menace posed by continental models. Popular political fictions achieved their power through their ability to imagine Britain shorn of her uniqueness and relegated to the status of just another unstable European state. The shock of much popular fiction that sought to make a point about foreign doctrines transplanted into Britain lay in its transposition of essentially alien political circumstances onto the British mainland. It was the incongruity of Bolshevism in the county towns of England that appalled the British reading public. Here conspiracies, political intrigue and plots to overthrow the government seemed out of place. Roger Taine, the hero of Geoffrey Household's *A Time to Kill*, is amused and incredulous at the thought of Bolshevik conspirators in Bournemouth plotting to undermine English agriculture by unleashing foot and mouth disease into the cattle population. He explains to his henchman, Pink: ' "I explained apologetically that it was just the idea of Bournemouth communists which I couldn't take seriously." "Why not?" he asked. "It's just so blasted full of gentility." '[73] Bolshevik firing squads in Olympia that defiled the building's purpose as a place of popular pleasure, exhibition hall and site for orderly political meetings in the *Battle for London*, or the Communist cavalry that form flying columns to defend the 'Ipswich Workers' Council' in Dennis Wheatley's *Black August*, brought the horrors of the continent to the capital, or to the sleepy backwaters of the English regions.[74] In this, they shook and violated the confident assumptions of their mainly bourgeois audiences. 'Britishness' was, in part, defined by distance from the political forms and enfeebled constitutions and regimes of the continent. In the years after the Great War, and until the relatively recent past, British exceptionalism was seen as the bedrock of the country's uniquely stable political institutions and intermittent prosperity. Movements like socialism carried continental associations and were depicted as essentially foreign theoretical doctrines. They were unsuited to a Britain whose essential moderation was expressed through her political institutions. Quentin Hogg (later Lord Hailsham) summed up this sentiment in an article on 'The Middle Way' in 1951 when he commented that respect for traditional institutions like the monarchy 'might well prevent a march on London comparable to the March on Rome'. He wondered: 'Are we on the way to make a meal of Socialism, digesting the edible matter and excreting the wholly unassimilable, or have we met at last a social and political theory which will bring our society to a full stop, or a wholly new start?'.[75] Even British Communists had their doubts, feeling that many of the party's theories, trappings and outward forms seemed continental or 'un-British' in nature. To counteract this feeling, indigenous Communists were always at pains to locate their ideas within English historical memory and precedent.[76] For writers of anti-socialist and anti-Bolshevik fictions, there were always distinctions to be drawn between foreign agitators, and decent, respectable British working-men, articulating perfectly understandable grievances and discontents. This sentiment is very marked in John Buchan's *Mr Standfast* written at the end of the Great War. The novel features a number of characters that might be seen as the honest and dependable face of working-class protest. Often manipulated and exploited by more unscrupulous foreign agitators, they were, nevertheless, justified in the stance they took. Seeking to penetrate a ring of spies and pro-German agitators who are using the pacifist movement for their own ends, Richard Hannay makes contact with a sympathizer, Andrew Amos, who, having infiltrated the movement, is his clandestine contact. Amos is an old-style border radical and Gladstonian. He remarks:

I've to keep my views to mysel', for thae young lads are all drunken-daft with their wee books about Cawpital and Collectivism and a wheen long senseless words I wouldna fyle my tongue with. Them and their socialism! There's more gumption on a page of John Stuart Mill than in all that foreign trash. But, as I say, I've got to keep a quiet sough, for the world is gettin' socialism now like measles. It all comes from a defective eddication.[77]

In a later encounter with an old Highland crofter, a veteran of the crofters' wars of the 1880s, Hannay demonstrates a romantic interest in land reform and sympathy for the plight of the crofting communities:

> He was passionate about the land. He had taken part in long-forgotten agitations, and had suffered eviction in some ancient landlords' quarrel farther north. Presently he was pouring out to me all the woes of the crofter – woes that seemed so antediluvian and forgotten that I listened as one would listen to an old song . . . I'm a Tory myself and a bit of a land reformer so we agreed well enough . . . I told him that after the war, every acre of British soil would have to be used for the men that had earned the right to it.[78]

Here, in a common image, the crofter stands for stability and historical continuity as opposed to the itinerancy and rootlessness of English rural labourers.[79] Frequently, the honest working-man was depicted as a casualty, a mere dupe of alien forces, often divided in his loyalties. In Agatha Christie's early crime novel, *The Secret Adversary*, the forces of organized Labour are resistant to the idea of a general strike: 'The more far-seeing among them realized that what they proposed might well be a death-blow to the England that at heart they loved. They shrank from the starvation and misery a general strike would entail. . . . But behind them were subtle insistent forces at work, urging the memories of old wrongs, deprecating the weakness of half and half measures, fomenting misunderstandings'.[80]

Often, such writing sought to mobilize supporters of the existing order against potential insurgency. They provided a rallying cry against revolution and appealed to bourgeois fears of political disorder and incipient social breakdown. Many envisaged a popular rising and governmental collapse with the prospect, in the words of one of Agatha Christie's Bolsheviks, of 'diamonds and pearls rolling around in the gutter for anyone to pick up'.[81] As Hans Bertens remarks about the thrillers of H.C. McNeile, author of the Bulldog Drummond stories, the narrative of such tales is rooted firmly in the experience of the 'English middle class'. Heroes are always of a resolutely burgher stock; the aristocracy, when they appear, are feckless, and liable to manipulation by suave and mannered villains.[82] John Buchan's fiction massaged the egos of the mannered 'middles', carrying explicit appeals to the virtues of a bourgeois Britain. Buchan's *Huntingtower* typifies this tendency. Set against the aftermath of the Russian Revolution, the plot revolves around a Bolshevik conspiracy to steal the ancestral fortune of a White Russian Princess incarcerated in a remote Scottish Castle. Hero of the hour is the former Glasgow grocer, Dickson McCunn, who organizes the relief of the castle and saves the Princess Saskia from abduction by the conspirators. For the Princess, McCunn is the embodiment of decent and civilized middle-class values. In Britain she sees his kind as providing an antidote to revolution and social breakdown: 'You will not find him in Russia. He is what we call the middle-class, which we who were foolish used to laugh at. But he is the stuff which above all others makes a great people. He will endure when aristocracies crack, and proletariats crumble. In our own land we have never known him, but till we create him our land will not be a nation'.[83] This was the lesson that many thriller and crime fiction authors hoped to instil.

VI

The events of the Great War loomed large over the socialist and anti-Bolshevik fictions of the inter-war years. Thriller writers like Dennis Wheatley, Peter Cheyney and Herman McNeile had served in the war; Cheyney was slightly wounded on the Somme.[84] The central characters of such literature were often veterans and former soldiers. Their role was integral to the conservatism of this genre. In essence they were militant figures. They returned from war to find their homeland undermined, or threatened, and, in most instances, pledged themselves to the moral renewal of their country, or the purging of those who threatened its stability. There is something of the 'trench mentality' about these attitudes. As George L. Mosse remarks. 'The political Right considered itself to be the inheritor of the war experience, not just in Germany but throughout Europe, and the process of brutalisation was closely linked to the spread of the Right's influence among the population'.[85] Former servicemen were occasionally seen as both vulnerable and aimless, making them prey to the blandishments of enemy powers. In Nevil Shute's *So Disdained*, an itinerant and rootless former Royal Flying Corps airman, Maurice Lenden, is bribed by the Bolshevik government to fly aerial reconnaissance missions over British coastal installations. Both he and the ex-soldier narrator, Peter Moran, rediscover their patriotism and love of country by the urgency of the fight against Communism. Seeking to account for Lenden's actions, Moran explains to his wife, Mollie: 'Just being fond of the little things you've got at home, and that you don't want to see changed. A house with a bit of garden that you can grow things in, and a dog or two, and all the little inconveniences and annoyances that you couldn't really get along without. That's your patriotism, and that's all there's in it. And that's what Lenden hadn't got'.[86]

Most often, the returned soldier sought to restore the pre-war world, or to eradicate the profiteers, Bolsheviks, plutocrats and enemy aliens that endangered it. Eric Linklater was vitriolic about profiteers and stay-at-homes who prospered whilst soldiers gave up their lives at the front: 'Gross or grim of feature, assertive in their demeanour, loud of voice, the profiteers sat at wine-laden tables, and with them were resplendent women.'[87] For many veterans, there could be no standing down. Former soldiers are very much to the fore in all the novelistic attempts to 'roll-back' Communism. In John Buchan's *Huntingtower*, veterans (most with disabilities incurred through service in the Great War) feature in the scratch army mobilized to repel a Bolshevik kidnapping attempt of a White Russian princess hidden in a remote Scottish castle.[88] The returned soldier with a conscience, eager to save his country poised on the brink, is a constant hero (or anti-hero) of this period. In Eric Linklater's picaresque comedy, *Magnus Merriman*, his bumbling and aimless protagonist attempts to give his life direction by revisiting his roots and standing as a by-election candidate for the Scottish National Party in fictional Kinluce. Despite the amiable tone of the novel, Magnus' feelings about Communism are rancorous: 'It's a damned Oriental perversion, a funk hole for weaklings, an attempt to turn the world into an ant-hill'.[89] As Michael Denning points out, the post-Great War thriller often exudes an 'authoritarian populism' particularly marked in the Bulldog Drummond series of novels by H.C. McNeile, writing under the pseudonym of 'Sapper'.[90] Emblematic of this tendency is the first Bulldog Drummond novel, which begins with the armistice of 1918.[91] Thereafter, the action turns to the exploits of Drummond himself, who, independently wealthy, and bored by the routines of civilian life, offers himself up for hire as a private troubleshooter. His advertisement in the newspaper reads: 'Demobilised officer . . . finding peace incredibly tedious, would welcome diversion. Legitimate if possible; but crime, if of a comparatively humorous description, no objection. Excitement essential. Would be prepared to consider permanent job if suitably impressed by applicant for his services'.[92] Bulldog Drummond shows himself prepared to continue the war by other means. In the successor volume, *The Black Gang*, Drummond tackles an international conspiracy of financiers, profiteers and their Bolshevik puppets. Employing vigilante methods, his 'Black Gang', which carries uncomfortable echoes of the *Freikorps*, metes out peremptory justice and sets up its own internment camp for Bolsheviks and anarchists on a small island off the coast of Mull, where discipline is enforced by an ex-sergeant major of the Guards.[93] In some instances the returned veteran is the only source of stability in a world driven mad by war. John Buchan's *The Three Hostages* is set in a weary post-war world where Richard Hannay speculates about the collapsing sanctity of the old order, and the emergence of a new morality, inured to death and conflict:

A large part of the world had gone mad, and that involved the growth of inexplicable and unpredictable crime. All the old sanctities had become weakened, and men had grown too well accustomed to death and pain. This meant that the criminal had far greater resources at his command, and, if he were an able man, could mobilize a vast army of utter recklessness and depraved ingenuity. The moral imbecile had been more or less a sport before the War, now he was a terribly common product, and throve in batches and battalions. Cruel, humourless, hard and utterly wanting in sense of proportion, but often full of a perverted poetry and drunk with rhetoric – a hideous untamed breed had been engendered. You found it among the young Bolshevik Jews, among the young entry of the wilder Communist sects, and very notably among the sullen murderous hobbledehoys in Ireland.[94]

VII

Conspiracy lay at the heart of anti-socialist fictions. Communists and Socialists assumed the form of Machiavellian schemers and plotters, employing a range of diabolical plans to further their own malign ends. Here they became composite super-villains. All-powerful, their tentacles everywhere, they are armed with a range of cunning devices, infinite resources and are able to manipulate vast armies of willing henchmen. Bolsheviks in particular fitted into this pre-existing niche in popular fiction well. Their well-known discipline, theoretical vigour, loyalty to party and dedication to abstract theory gave them a merciless quality that evoked the worst demons of pre-war penny dreadful fiction.[95] In Dennis Wheatley's *Contraband*, the renegade aristocrat Lord Gavin Fortescue uses his fortune to smuggle both lucrative goods and professional 'red' agitators into Britain in fleets of planes to foment chaos and social disorder. Wheatley's secret agent, Gregory Sallust, fears that: 'soon, when the time was ripe, agitators and saboteurs would be landing . . . from his planes to pass unsuspected into the great industrial areas where they would ferment strikes and engineer every sort of trouble. He couldn't let that happen. . .'[96]

Agatha Christie's early novel, *The Secret Adversary*, makes great play of the subtle and secretive forces at the heart of the Bolshevik conspiracy. The villain of the novel is the unidentified, shape-shifting master of disguise, 'Mr Brown'. Striking fear even into the hearts of his own followers, they speak of him in terms of awe: ' "I have seen him" said the Russian slowly. "Spoken to him face to face. I did not know it until afterwards. He was one of a crowd. I should not know him again. Who is he really? I do not know. But I know this – he is a man to fear" '.[97] Christie's Bolsheviks are utterly ruthless and unscrupulous: At a meeting with their spies and secret representatives, their leader, gloats at the duping of Britain's Labour leaders: ' "They must have no inkling that we are using them for our own ends. They are honest men – and that is their value to us. It is curious – but you cannot make a revolution without honest men. The

Figure 3.3 Images of dangerous European socialist agitators haunted the British imagination in the inter-war years. Frontispiece from a Dutch socialist songbook, *Socialistische Liederenbundel no. 3* (Amsterdam: SPD, 1922) (Author's Collection).

instinct of the populace is infallible". He paused, and then repeated, as though the phrase pleased him: "Every revolution has its honest men. They are soon disposed of afterwards" '.[98] In such fiction, Bolshevik schemes range across acts of social and criminal deviance. In McNeile's 'Black Gang' the Bolsheviks seek to suborn the young, using the tactics feared by Jesuit opponents of socialism at the beginning of the century. Socialist Sunday Schools become their instrument, teaching blasphemy, instilling hatred of capitalism, and undermining deference to the established order. Peterson, Hugh Drummond's arch-enemy, gloats: 'Blasphemy, of course – or rather what the bourgeois call blasphemy – is instilled at once. We teach them to fear no God; we drive into them each week that the so-called God is merely a weapon of the capitalist class, to keep them quiet, and that if it had not that effect they would see what a machine-gun might do . . . Get at the children has always been my motto – for they are the next generation. They can be moulded like plastic clay'.[99] Links to organized crime were also often explicit here. The captive White Russian Princess in John Buchan's *Huntingtower*, who is trying to preserve a hoard of jewels from the clutches of a pack of Bolsheviks, bemoans the fate of her beloved Russia under Bolshevism: 'Russia is mortally sick and therefore all evil is unchained, and the criminals have no one to check them. There is crime everywhere in the world, and the unfettered crime in Russia is so powerful that it stretches its hand to crime throughout the globe and there is a great mobilising everywhere of wicked men. Once you boasted that law was international and that the police of one land work with the police of another. To-day that is true of criminals.'[100]

The impetus towards clandestine and illicit dealings that recur in this type of fiction meant that specific radical and Bolshevik types are frequently present throughout the genre. The prejudices and bigotries of polite society crystallize around the image of the socialist or Bolshevik plotter. In these novels they are the forces that constitute the antithesis to intrinsic, nativist British values. Particularly marked was the presence of foreigners. The lead conspirator in Agatha Christie's *The Secret Adversary* is marked by 'the angle of the cheek bones' that 'hinted at his Slavonic ancestry'.[101] Many of these novels depict Britain as an ailing power, whose vigour is drained by a post-war pessimism directly proportionate to the number of foreigners in the country. Hugh Addison talks of a new spirit abroad in the land, 'a fatalism which was as foreign to the temperament of Old England as the pernicious doctrines which, incarnated in the persons of swarthy wide-eyed emissaries from every corner of Eastern and Central Europe, had streamed through its ports like so much evil merchandise'.[102] There were echoes of the pre-1914 associations between anarchism and foreign refugees seeking asylum in Britain in some of this material. In line with the conception of both socialism and Bolshevism as un-British, or even Asiatic, belief-systems, Bolsheviks usually carried the taint of bad blood, frequently signifying an Eastern European pedigree. As with most dime novel villains, the inner depravity of such figures is usually accompanied by an outward physical sign of their degeneracy. Seeing Zadoff, 'the emissary of terror' for the first time, Hunter, the hero of *The Battle of London* scrutinizes his face: 'As Hunter studied him now through his glasses, he could make out every detail of the features of this international Robespierre: his narrow, Mongolian, eyes, his pale sunken cheeks, drooping moustache, and the white of his chin that showed through his beard'.[103] In crime fiction, foreignness carried associations with excitability, even with a kind of political hysteria. Lack of self-control and subservience to foreign doctrines seemed to sit side by side.[104] Bolshevik characters are prone to exotic and overblown rhetoric, often delivered in a pitch of frenzy and over-excitement. In McNeile's *Bulldog Drummond*, Hugh Drummond is captured and taken to the conspirators' lair, where a Bolshevik with eyes 'burning with the fires of fanaticism' passes judgement on him:

> 'I know not what this young man has done: I care less. In Russia such trifles matter not. He has the appearance of a bourgeois, therefore he must die. Did we not kill thousands – aye, tens of thousands of his kidney before we obtained the great freedom? Are we not going to do the same in this accursed country?' His voice rose to the shrill, strident note of the typical tub-thumper. 'What is this wretched man', he continued, waving a hand wildly at Hugh, 'that he should interrupt the great work for one brief second? Kill him now – throw him in a corner, and let us proceed'.[105]

Tub-thumping and wild impromptu political oratory was a characteristic of many of the political villains of the crime fiction genre. This issue echoed concerns about the presence of radical and socialist orators on the open ground of the capital at the end of the nineteenth and beginning of the twentieth century. Anti-socialist newspapers issued dire warnings about the dangers posed by these influences. The patriotic and xenophobic newspaper *The Worker* identified a 'Red Flag Ranter' type: 'His appearance is as infinitely various as the doctrines which he preaches. At times he is hairy, foreign and unwashed, speaking English as he learnt it in the state schools of Posen or Moscow, before he fled to avoid the service of his country, or the attention of its police'.[106] In McNeile's *Bulldog Drummond*, Hugh's suspicions about the conspiracy at Peterson's mansion are aroused when the heroine Phyllis reports unsavoury visitors. She notes significantly: 'they were the sort of type one sees tub-thumping at Hyde Park'.[107] The mesmerising and exhortatory impact of such rhetoric was widely feared in the inter-war years. In Nevil Shute's *So Disdained*, the local Communist conspirators in the village of Under on the Sussex Downs are led by the street corner orator, John Nitter, from Bradford. The hero, Peter Moran, recalls: I saw him on a platform once. It was in Hyde Park and he spoke without a hat, and his hair fell down over his eyes and he kept shaking it back as he put the whole impact of his nature into his tirade. And when I heard him then, I forgot that he was a tubby little man'.[108] Novelists who drew on fantasies of the evils of elected labour governments shuddered at the prospect of such figures exercising power. The Socialist government that takes power in Bramah's *The Secret of the League* features Labour Party leaders who have graduated from Hyde Park oratory, to the cabinet.[109] Rhetoric in general was significant in most crime fiction and the thriller genre. The rhetoric of Labour denigrated and imperilled. In *The Secret of the League*, parliamentary debates begin to suffer following an influx of politicians from Labour's power base in local government. As the tone and quality of official exchanges in parliament degenerates, it becomes apparent that 'the Mother of Parliaments had sunk to the rhetorical level of a Borough Council'.[110]

The malevolent and ruthless nature of Bolshevik villains in popular fiction made them prey to particularly extreme forms of retribution. The eradication of the Bolshevik high command, in often very sadistic ways, brought a pleasing end to Bolshevik anti-conspiracy novels. A particularly dreadful fate was always reserved for the leaders of plots and conspiracies. Even in death, the fanaticism of such characters is frequently made manifest by tendencies towards self-immolation. 'Mr Brown' in Christie's *The Secret Adversary*, kills himself with his own poison. In a gesture of respect to the amateur detective Tommy, who engineers his downfall, he shouts before downing poison: "Ave Caesar! Te morituri salutant!" ', 'then his face changed, and with a long convulsive shudder, he fell forward in a crumpled heap'.[111] Abreskov, the Bolshevik arch-conspirator in Buchan's *Huntingtower*, enjoys only a brief walk-on part before being found drowned at the end of the novel. In death his body preserves an eerie beauty as his sins are washed from him.[112] The most extreme and violent end for a villain occurs however in McNeile's *The Black Gang*. Yulowski, Peterson's henchman, is the lowest of Bolshevik villains. A violent psychotic, he boasts of having battered out the brains of two members of the Tsar's family with his rifle, which he keeps as a gory trophy: ' "The last time", he said, turning on Drummond with a dreadful look of evil in his face, "that this rifle was used by me was in a cellar in Russia – on even more exalted people than you. I brought it specially with me as a momento, never thinking I should have the pleasure of using it again" '.[113] Threatening the same fate to Phyllis, Yulowski is overpowered by Drummond, and impaled by him on his own bayonet. As the Black Gang burst into Peterson's lair to free Drummond and Phyllis, they witness Yulowski's dying convulsions: 'Pinned to the wall with his own bayonet which stuck out six inches beyond his back was a red-headed, red-bearded man gibbering horribly in a strange language'.[114] This tone of gleeful vengeance is manifested even in descriptions of the incidental deaths of relatively minor Bolshevik characters. In Dennis Wheatley's *Black August*, a mutinous

Figure 3.4 Radical Demagogues in London. Socialist meeting in Victoria Park in 1893. From *The English Illustrated Magazine*, 10 (1893), p. 836. Illustration by E G. Cohen (Author's Collection).

Bolshevik seaman who attempts to foil Gregory Sallust's attempts to commandeer a British destroyer is gunned down with a frontal shot to the head: 'Arty stepped forward and Sallust stepped back. The comparatively small amount of grey matter which had constituted the brain of Leading Seaman Nobes, spilled upon the spotless deck'.[115]

Britain's enemies in popular crime fiction might also display the character-istics of the educated, liberal middle-class. Progressives, 'parlour pinks' and other misguided moral reformers were often seen as prey to the doctrines of international conspirators. Such notions arose from the generalized dislike of bohemians and their embrace of artistic and political freedom that was a marked feature of inter-war society and culture.[116] In this, crime fiction writ-ers cultivated the common British prejudice against intellectualism in all its forms.[117] For the exponents of an anti-socialist platform in Britain, the 'New Life' and back-to-the-land movements that were a marked feature of the period were a screen for more revolutionary doctrines, and presented a dis-torted and hopelessly optimistic vision of human nature that made them prey to infiltration by extreme, foreign and malign agitators. Here Bloomsburyites consorted unawares with dangerous European secret agents. In John Buchan's *Mr Standfast* written in 1919, the action begins in an English Garden Village project run on Morrisonian lines, where the ideal community has become the unwitting host for a group of idealistic, but misguided, 'militant pacifists', pre-pared to do a deal with the German government to bring the war to an end on German terms. The inhabitants are unpatriotic, foreign-orientated, preten-tious and other-wordly, proving oblivious to the spies operating in their midst. As one denizen of the community comments: 'It is one great laboratory of thought . . . It is glorious to feel that you are living among the eager, vital people who are at the head of all the newest movements, and that the intel-lectual history of England is being made in our studies and gardens. The war to us seems a remote and secondary affair. As someone has said, the great fights of the world are all fought in the mind'.[118] Throughout John Buchan's works, an interest in dilletantish and pretentious pursuits or an intellectual weakness for modernism denotes an unreliable and extremist turn of mind. In *The Island of Sheep*, Barralty's enthusiasm for art-collecting exposes him as a member of a conspiracy to expropriate the fortune of a reclusive Dane. Predictably Sandy Arbuthnot is compelled to disguise himself as 'a surrealiste' to expose his part in the plot: 'I was a French artist in a black sweater, and I hadn't washed for a day or two'.[119] Buchan was not alone in his contempt for the fashionable values of educated liberals. The adherents and followers of Toynbee Hall and other philanthropic projects to elevate the conditions of the traditional East End poor were also much criticized in British thriller and crime fiction.[120] Liberal clergymen, parsons and priests were particularly sus-pect. Exponents of Christian Socialist ideas in particular were seen as pro-viding an entrée into the church for the worst doctrines of atheistical and immoral Communism.[121] Harrington Hext's *The Thing at Their Heels* provides an extreme example of this tendency. In a series of grisly murders, the heirs to the mansion and fortune of the aristocratic seat of Kingscreet are dispatched in ingenious and cunning ways. Only the saintly Catholic father Felix Templer survives. In a startling deathbed confession, however, he reveals his guilt of all four murders. Driven to take the lives of his family by religious mania, dislike of feudalism and concern for the misuse of the unearned increment of landed wealth, he uses the fortune to invest in charitable enterprises for the poor and orphaned. To the end, he asserts his moral purity: 'Murder has surely never been approached in a spirit so pure . . . The heirs of Kingscreet were as but dust in the balance against the welfare of those thousands as yet unborn. The best that Matthew, Sir Augustine's son, would have accomplished, was to carry forward an archaic tradition and preserve the relic of a vanished feudal system until general progress and the return of the land to its rightful owners put a period to his activities'.[122] *The Thing at Their Heels* painted the most saintly and the most selfless as, paradoxically, the most fanatical.

VIII

In most anti-Bolshevik popular fiction, socialism and Communism eroded and undermined the national interest. The pacifism, internationalism and opposition to the military that were seen as intrinsic to such doctrines imperilled Britain's ability to defend herself. Many of the popular fictions about the Bolshevik threat emphasize the rapid disintegration in Britain's world position that would accompany a socialist government or a Bolshevik putsch. Most writers in this genre automatically assumed that socialism in government would hand the initiative to Britain's enemies, lead to the loss of empire, and allow Ireland to go her own way. John Buchan's *The Three Hostages*, written against the background of the first Labour government in 1924, is fixated on the loss of British prestige abroad, the emergence of colonial nationalisms and the threat posed by the Irish question. Here Ghandi shares a page with Lenin as a 'fanatic' imperilling the post-war world order.[123] Hannay's arch-rival, the villainous master of hypnotism and terrorism, Medina, is from émigré Irish stock, nurtured by his mother in the nurseries of Britain's rivals, and harbouring ancient ancestral enmities. His friend Sandy Arbuthnot explains: 'There's a far-away streak of the Latin in him, but he is mainly Irish, and that never makes a good cross. He's the deracine Irish, such as you find in America. I take it that he imbibed from that terrible old woman – I've never met her, but I see her plainly, and I know that she is terrible – he imbibed that venomous hatred of imaginary things – an imaginary England, an imaginary civilization, which they call love of country. There is no love in it.'[124] Many of the anti-socialist novels of this period speculated about the actions of Britain's enemies in the event of a Labour government. In *The Triumph of Socialism and How it Succeeded*, defence cuts and the refusal of the government to invest in new naval technologies embolden the German empire to conduct exercises in the Channel, to intimidate the population by docking at Portsmouth, and then to land an occupying army in Guernsey. With speculations about German ambitions in Egypt and the Suez Canal, the book is shot through with anxieties about a Britain reduced to the level of a German dependency.[125]

Not all anti-socialist fiction necessarily saw Britain's commercial and military enemies combining against her at the time of her greatest weakness. In *The Secret of the League*, for example, the German and French governments collaborate with British counter-revolutionaries to stockpile oil and coal, in order to help bring down a socialist government, in preference to tolerating a socialist state on their doorsteps.[126] For some authors, Bolshevism was simply a vector for other forms of conspiratorial endeavour and illegality usually involving great power rivalries. Like Chinese boxes, conspiracies opened outwards from each other. Harry Edmonds' 'The North Sea Mystery', serialized in *Chums* magazine, postulated a labyrinthine plot in which an enfeebled Bolshevism provides a cover for a darker conspiracy by Britain's rivals. Drawn into a web of intrigue by the discovery of floating submarine pens off the Frisian Islands, Naval Intelligence officer Harry Nicholls stumbles on a web of secret conspirators planning an attack on Britain's navy that would seriously undermine her world role. Ostensibly a Bolshevik conspiracy, this plan involves renegade Englishmen, anti-British Americans, the German Intelligence Service and anti-Bolshevik Russians who hope to rescue Russia from the clutches of a tottering Bolshevik government. Appealing to fears about a potential Russo-German pact, the story depicts a conspiracy of passive victims, in which the organization's cover, 'New Era Socialism', provides a screen for their activities and a flood of unsuspecting recruits. In seeking to undermine Britain's imperial position, the conspirators hope to pave the way for a single all-encompassing power bloc. Revealing the details of the conspiracy, Nicholls' superior, Mr. Budd, comments darkly:

In every part of the world where British rule exists – BOLSHEVISM HAS FAILED . . . Russia realises this. The most important boundaries of Asia are under British domination. We practically hold a circle of power around the world. So long as this circle remains unbroken it is the one great barrier against things like Bolshevism running amok, and spreading tyranny, chaos and wholesale lust and murder. Don't forget that out of two thousand million people in the old world today, only a few handfuls are really civilised.[127]

For most contemporaries, Bolshevism in particular opened the door to national enfeeblement, and, in some instances, provided a Trojan horse for the subjugation of the country to foreign powers. In *The Battle of London*, the Bolshevik rising in the capital is merely the prelude to an invasion attempt, in which a mass aerial bombardment by the German luftwaffe reduces many of the capital's finest buildings to rubble.[128] In such works, typical anti-Bolshevik fictions elided with future war phrophecies, concerns about re-armament and images of a resurgent German menace.

Not everybody viewed the advent of the Labour Party, and the emergence of Communism in such apocalyptic terms, or even as a major cause for alarm. Some saw the fears about British Communism as overly inflated. The journalist Douglas Goldring commented sceptically: 'when England goes Communist, no doubt the party in power will call itself the "Conservative Co-operative Party" and, as usual, half the government will be old Etonians'.[129] Nevertheless, in popular fiction socialism and Communism were depicted as the antithesis of the fundamental values of Britishness. They were the twin heads of the same corrosive social and political phenomenon. In the eyes of many of the authors under discussion, socialist states harboured political terrorism, hastened the loss of empire and inflamed the Irish question. Englishness, it seemed, was impervious to everything but this. Socialism was misguided and set itself against individual effort and enterprise; Communism spread the perverted doctrines of world revolution and international conspiracy. Both doctrines feature in the popular fiction of the period as forces that thrived on bureaucracy, and that stifled individual ingenuity and enterprise. The future Communist/socialist state was a conformist, lifeless institution that had little reverence or respect for hierarchy and the traditional leaders of society. In Dornford Yates' *Lower than Vermin*, a bitter attack on the politics of post-1945 Britain, the aristocratic, patriotic and self-sacrificing Ringwood family, whose only son lays down his life for his country in World War II, find themselves evicted from their ancestral land after their estates are sequestered by the Ministry of Works. They are required for re-development and the creation of one of the widely despised post-war new towns.[130] Yates was typical of a certain type of political thriller writer. Drawing on Edwardian precedents, and mired in the social and cultural conventions of the inter-war years, they located their novels and writings in the anti-conspiracy genre of popular fiction. Their influence was long-lasting, contributing to the work of later writers like Ian Fleming, and images of the villains who were the staple of post-war spy fiction. In the pivotal 1920s and 1930s, these works crystallized the vision of political and trade union agitators as somehow conspiratorial and frequently foreign. Their British heroes are bluff and uncompromising, and opposed to the secretive and covert foreign-inspired plots with which they contend. These works were an unashamed counterweight to a perceived socialist and Bolshevik threat. Shot through with patriotic views they revelled in the virtues of 'Britishness', concluded with a restoration of the established order and promoted a greater awareness of the traditional virtues Britain might potentially lose by flirting with foreign belief systems and ideas.

Chapter 4

Fascist Britain

'What I am hoping', said Vincent fervently 'is that we here, we few, can band together to make the nucleus of a group, a movement, a party, which if it does nothing else will move the British people to an awareness of the depths to which they have sunk, of the greatness they are throwing away, of the tradition and heritage which they are so carelessly denying. Let there be no mistake. The task is monumental. The whole structure of our society is worm-eaten with selfishness, rotten with laziness. We are like a great overfed animal fattening itself to be the prey of other more wily creatures. And clinging to the back of this creature, sucking and feeding on its flesh, are a host of parasites; drifters, layabouts, profiteers, immigrants. Everywhere the situation is reflected in the fits and starts of a feeble economy; the get-rich-quick tycoons squatting over money-bags; transport, a tangled and inefficient web, which will take years to unravel, a culture based on pop art. And everywhere, everywhere an apathy which stifles action, on the one hand the Conservatives posing a wild free-for-all which has largely resulted in this situation, on the other the Labourites with their watered-down Communism, that black spider threatening to poison us all. What is the answer?' He banged the table again. 'WE ARE. We must have strength and unity, We must have purpose and responsibility. We must be strong and self-sufficient and fight to bring back the greatness of our country'.[1]

'Before we broke up, Parker said a very interesting thing. Looking at the Henry Moore shelter paintings on the wall (Originals, I wonder? I felt it would be impolite to ask.), he told me "You know, Bert, during the Blitz our people went to sleep in those underground shelters, and they've just never managed to wake up. They've been sleep-walking ever since."

"They'll wake up now", Jones-Fairfield countered. "we'll see to that".[2]

Albrecht knew London. He'd walked its narrow streets, felt its buckled, broken history seaming under his feet. He knew what attacking the city would be like. It would be boiling at every turn, with resentment, with anger, with desperation. It would fall, of course, it seemed they all did in the end. Even Moscow and Stalingrad had fallen. But how many of them would it swallow first? How many of them would have to tip themselves into London's jaws before the city finally choked on their blood running in the veins and arteries of her streets?[3]

Possibilities for a Fascist Britain preoccupied the authors of popular fiction. Coups, putsches, right-wing takeovers and German invasion panics dominate the popular fiction market. By far, the largest number of novels dealing with threats to traditional British values concern a Fascist Britain, or a Britain menaced by internal Fascist insurgency. With roots in the great power rivalry of the pre-1914 period, such works mirrored fears about the frailty of British democracy, and acted as a warning about the future. For a nation preoccupied with World War II, they emphasized the importance of long-standing British liberties, closed the distance between British and continental styles of politics and demonstrated a continuing anxiety about the narrowness of British survival from the threat of Nazi invasion in 1940. In much of this material, there remained a residue of the invasion panics of the war years. Most featured explicit references to wartime preoccupations with 'fifth columnists' and internal subversion from spies, turncoats and indigenous British Fascist networks.[4] Such works occurred particularly during periods of emergent Fascism in Britain. Large numbers of these novels were produced during decades in which there were concerns about an escalation in extreme right activity. On the eve of the outbreak of World War II, a number of novels acted as warnings, revelling in the excesses that a duplicated British Nazism might import into Britain. In the 1960s and 1970s, these books kept the memory of British victory over foreign Fascism alive and warned against the potential problems posed by the National Front and other allied radical right organizations. Much of this literature was divided. Some authors divined the main threat to British democracy as emerging from invasion, others saw a threat from internal Fascist groups that, in the right circumstances, were believed to stand on the threshold of power. The presence of highly placed and respectable sympathizers was often noted. For the audience of such work, the prospects for a Fascist Britain raised the issues of collaboration and resistance. A number offered up the prospect of Fascist domination lasting many centuries, others, optimists by nature, saw Fascist victory as providing a short-term, temporary setback to the onward march of confident British democracy. In this latter group, the British state is tested, then renewed. Guided by the examples of Germany and Italy, there is often a voyeuristic feel to these novels, in which the trappings, uniforms, badges of rank and governmental forms of an alternative British Fascist state are recorded in meticulous detail. For exponents of alternative histories, the model of a divergent history in which Britain might, in the right circumstances, have made a separate peace with Germany provided grounds for legitimate speculation.[5] The notion of a Fascist Britain, then, in which a beleaguered democracy is placed in peril allowed authors to exercise their imaginations about tyranny, invasion and the 'Germanization' of nativist British political forms. For them, it was an inversion of the historical events of 1940 and a reiteration of all that Britain had to lose at the hands of totalitarians and anti-democrats that re-ignited long-standing fears about the fragility of British democracy.

I

In the manner of the anti-Red fictions of the 1920s and 1930s, Fascist panic literature spanned the genres. Narratives that envisaged a Fascist future feature in detective stories, crime writing, science fiction and political thrillers. Christened 'Hitler Wins' fiction by John Clute and Peter Nicholls, Gavriel Rosenfeld points out that such writing carried stark messages for Britain.[6] In contrast to France, which experienced occupation at first hand, and the United States, which never faced a realistic threat of invasion, Britain manufactured propaganda that bolstered morale by envisaging the consequences of defeat. Many of the early stories of Fascist governments in the United Kingdom carry echoes of these wartime warnings. Like anti-Bolshevik fiction, these stories owed something to the invasion panic novels of the pre-1914 period. William Le Queux was perhaps the strongest proponent of this form of literature. A prolific writer of sensationalist fiction, his stories captured the mood of Britain in the late Edwardian period and on the eve of the Great War. Shot through with a marked distrust of Germany's adventurism in Europe and militarist ambitions towards the wider empire, his output was enthusiastically endorsed by patriotic politicians, received generous serialization rights in the Northcliffe press and was devoured by a jingoistic public. Sensationally advertised by vendors dressed as German soldiers and lavishly illustrated with pictures of fighting in London and the suburbs, the books rapidly gained a wide readership. According to some sources they were the favourite reading matter of Queen Alexandra. Many became popular classics. His 1907 novel, *The Great Invasion of 1910*, which envisaged a German invasion of East Anglia, enjoyed a new lease of life after 1914 and is widely credited with putting the term 'Great' into the Great War.[7] Le Queux specialized in plausible and meticulously planned invasion stories. Something of a flaneur, he walked the sites of many of the imaginary battlefields where German and English armies contended on British soil for the soul of the nation's future.[8] Indeed, *The Great Invasion of 1910*, which plotted a German invasion route across East Anglia, has the feel of a travelogue and draws on Le Queux's recreational interest in hiking. For most of his readership Le Queux captured the mood of anxiety that surrounded Britain's loss of world markets and relative military and imperial decline in the Edwardian period.[9] In the pages of his novels are to be found the strongest contemporary condemnations of 'Potsdanism' and 'Prussianism'. His works set the tone for an alarmist literature that emphasized the decadence of Britain's ruling elite, the lack of national resolve to tackle imperial enemies and highlighted the absence of preparations for invasion. In Le Queux's writings, the government and polite society are riddled with spies, *agents provocateurs* and effete defeatists who welcome the coming of the Germans.[10] Unsurprisingly, his books are credited with reigniting the debate about the size of the army, conscription and the need for more rigorous military training for military recruits in the years before the Great War.[11]

The emergence of Fascism in Italy and Germany in the inter-war period fuelled concerns about the ability of British democratic institutions to withstand foreign-inspired or indigenous totalitarian movements.[12] The creation of Oswald Mosley's British Union of Fascists in 1932, which achieved some early successes and brought together many of the pre-existing Fascist organizations in Britain, concentrated popular fears around the prospect of a Fascist government.[13] The organ of the movement, *The Blackshirt*, playfully invoked the image of a Fascist Britain where Mosley's programme was inaugurated with the internment of 'Reds' on the Scilly Isles, and of financiers and plutocrats on the Faroe Islands.[14] Respectable liberal papers were in no doubt that the British Union of Fascists (BUF) would simply enact a variant of continental Fascism, marked by the sequestration of the assets of co-operatives and trades unions and the imprisonment of 'trade union officials, Labour Party secretaries, and members of co-operative management committees (women as well as men) (who) would be rounded up in their homes, beaten with wire whips, clubbed or battered; and then either left for dead, or taken to a concentration camp to be subjected to a rigorous discipline, enforced as often as not, with torture'.[15] Thereafter, periodic revivals in the fortunes of the post-war British radical right kept the issue of Fascism and the dangers it posed before the British public. From the late 1940s onwards, Oswald Mosley's return to active campaigning and attempts to reincarnate the moribund BUF in the New Union movement incited race riots against immigrants and New Commonwealth incomers in the poorer parts of the capital. The journalist James Cameron wrote: 'It has been obvious for a year that pretty soon the seedy remnants of the Blackshirt gang would crawl out of the political woodwork and here they are again, stumping East London with their shabby agitation'.[16] In 1968 Enoch Powell's peroration against immigration that envisaged a civil war shedding 'rivers of blood' lent an apocalyptic tone to debates around race and migration issues. Furthermore, the arrival of the Ugandan Asians in 1972 allowed radical right agitators to stoke the fires of racial disharmony.[17] The reconstitution of the British extremist right around issues of ethnicity and immigration in the mid to late 1970s at a time of economic downturn and industrial militancy resulted in the re-emergence of many traditional fears about the vulnerability of British democracy to a concerted Fascist threat. The formation of the National Front in 1967 gave momentum to the radical right, albeit stopping short of an out-right electoral breakthrough.[18] Comparisons between Weimar Germany and Britain's crumbling parliamentary democracy were commonplace at the time. Such notions provided comfort to members of the newly established Front, and provoked anxiety amongst journalists, politicians and anti-Fascist cam-paigners.[19] In *The Spear*, James Herbert's novel of a plot by Fascist occultists to organize a British putsch, the arms manufacturer and former Nazi, Edward Gant, raves of the comparisons between Wiemar Germany and Britain in the 1970s: 'We were strongly opposed to the Republican government in Berlin at that time because of their sinister alliance with the rabble of the land: Jews, Slavs, Marxists - these degenerates – were gradually seizing control of the state and industry, crippling the country with their demands and their greedy conniving ways, and had created a situation that is not too unlike the situa-tion in Britain today. You would agree with the similarity, wouldn't you Mr. Steadman?'[20] So engrained was this perception, that it was echoed in main-stream literature. In Margaret Drabble's novel of 1970s decline, *The Ice Age*, her cynical property-speculator, Anthony Keating, notes the similarity between the 'theatre going elite of Britain' and 'a Weimar Republic drag-show'.[21] Reflecting on such views, Andy Beckett in his recent study of the 1970s, christens the decade 'Our Wiemar.'[22]

II

For many observers, however, notions of a successful British Fascist move-ment or a German invasion were quite simply inconceivable. As with many novels of this type, incongruity is the keynote. Images of German firing squads in Oxford their bullets making 'a spattering sound' that 'rang off the Cotswold stone' strike a discordant note that imports images of occupied Europe into the British countryside.[23] British tradition, it was held, would buttress British val-ues against Fascist infiltration. The issue of national character was frequently invoked here. Many contemporaries in the 1930s saw Fascism as an alien doc-trine, undermined by its essentially Germanic character that the British were naturally resistant towards. Echoing these sentiments, visitors to Britain from the continent thought the emergence of a successful British Fascism unlikely in the extreme. The Dutch satirist, G.J. Renier, mocked 'the burlesque antics of a few misguided bank clerks who parade Hyde Park in black shirts' and concluded 'if a Communistic England is unthinkable, a Fascist England may be called highly improbable'.[24] This was a point frequently made by domestic critics and opponents of the movement. The apostate British Fascist Charles M. Dolan remarked:

> The British people are good natured and easy going, slow on the uptake, and usually bad starters, but if their history means anything, 'rule by fear' is not destined for them. Theatrical parades and 'Blood and thunder' symbols do not influence the majority, and when they realise that this sort of thing is meant seriously to plan and rule their lives for them with a big stick if they do not 'jump to attention' they will wake up and kick it damned hard, and even if it means civil war they will ultimately kill it, however strong it grows while the electorate are asleep.[25]

Others pointed out that a thick network of local government, trade unions, associational culture and co-operative societies effectively inoculated British working-class culture against a Fascist advance.[26] In the 1930s, Oswald Mosley struggled to make his message heard, and the movement's resort to physical force tactics, suggesting the vaunted importation of foreign methods into Britain, placed an even greater distance between the public and BUF supporters. Events at Olympia in 1934, when Communists and other protestors were savagely beaten by BUF stewards, cemented images of an un-British Fascism, firmly wedded to continental styles and methods of political mobilization.[27] Despite Mosley's pretensions, and the dangerous nature of his ideas, there was often ribaldry at his expense. Frequently suffused with hostility to all things continental, and specifically German, this sentiment inspired a literature that ridiculed and derided the ambitions of home-grown Hitlers. In such writing, aspiring Blackshirt and Fascist leaders (sometimes modelled on Mosley) appear as frequent guests at inter-war society gatherings. They also feature in the satirical and comic literature of the day (and even in the radical press) as outlandish or buffoonish grotesques.[28] In Aldous Huxley's *Point Counter Point*, Everard Webley, leader of the Brotherhood of British Freemen (who remains oblivious throughout to the comic potential of the shortened acronym of his organization's name) is savagely ridiculed as an obtuse and boorish 'tinpot Mussolini'.[29] Even Bertie Wooster in P.G. Wodehouse's *The Code of the Woosters* stands up to the ridiculous Roderick Spode, leader of a paramilitary militia:

> 'It is about time' I proceeded 'that some public-spirited person came along and told you where to get off. The trouble with you, Spode, is that just because you have succeeded in inducing a handful of half-wits to disfigure

the London scene by going about in black shorts, you think you're someone. You have them shouting "Heil Spode" and you imagine it is the voice of the people. This is where you make your bloomer. What the voice of the people is saying is "Look at that frightful ass Spode, swanking around in footer bags. Did you ever see in your puff such an awful perisher".[30]

George Orwell followed many of these sentiments in his well-known essay 'England, your England' in which he extolled the virtues of British hostility to militarism and totalitarian ideologies.[31] Beneath the satire, however, there were more serious concerns about the prospects for British Fascism's success. Some authors saw Britain as too complacent about her democracy. In Robin Cook's book *A State of Denmark* about an emergent British Fascist state, the political émigré, Richard Watt, who narrates the novel, comments: 'The English are desperately naïve; ironically, centuries of democracy had made them so. They thought that, however greatly the world changed, they would never have to fight for their freedom again, that the country would magically remain the same.'[32] George Orwell's anxieties about the menace posed by an indigenous British Fascism emerged in an article in *Tribune*, in which he discussed Ernest Bramah's 1907 anti-socialist novel, *The Secret of the League*. In this late Edwardian fantasy, a legitimately elected Labour government is brought low by a conspiracy of the affluent to starve the country of coal, oil and fuel reserves. For Orwell 'the tone of the book is good-natured, as it could afford to be at that date, but the trend of thought is unmistakeable'. It 'tended towards a non-parliamentary regime like Franco's'. He concluded: '*The Secret of the League* was written in 1907, when the growth of the Labour movement was beginning to terrify the middle classes who wrongly imagined that they were menaced from below, and not from above. . . . As a political forecast it is trivial, but it is of great interest for the light it casts on the mentality of the struggling middle class.'[33] As Orwell suggested, *The Secret of the League* showed a willingness to contemplate extreme methods deployed against legitimately elected governments. The resolution of the novel, in the victory of the charismatic naval hero, Captain Stobalt, adds weight to the notion of Bramah's work as a proto-Fascist text, inspired by the values of leadership, discipline, and anti-socialism. Stobalt declaims: '"Yes" he cried with a passionate vehemence that held their breath and stirred their hearts. "I am Stobalt of Salaveira, the man who brought you victory when you were trembling in despair. I saved England for you then, but that was when men loved their country, and did not think it a disgraceful thing to draw a sword and die for her. What is that to you today, you who have been taught to forget what glory means".[34]

The strategic and logistical problems surrounding a German sea borne invasion across the Channel, and the weaknesses of the British Fascist movement, meant that authors who sought to portray a credible Fascist Britain often resorted to allegory or parable.[35] Frequently these were portrayed as prophetic, or imaginary scenarios that might be rectified by sufficient application to pro-democratic and anti-Fascist activity.[36] A leap of imagination was often required to achieve this end. In Giles Cooper's *The Other Man*, for example, World War II veteran David Lewin falls asleep at a reunion of old comrades, to experience the lives they might have had if Britain had concluded an independent peace with Germany at the beginning of the war. The result is 'a terrifying novel of what could have happened in 1940'.[37] A number of works in this genre were unashamedly alarmist and pro-leftist in tone. Novels of this nature proliferated in the 1930s. Emblematic of the trend is Naomi Mitchison's *You Have Been Warned*. A Scottish writer of historical fiction for children, Mitchison was a Fabian and member of the Socialist League. Written in 1935 following Hitler's accession to power in Germany, the book follows the activities of a dedicated band of society Communists. Describing Isobel Dione's transformation from wealthy landowner's daughter, into fanatical Communist insurgent, the book concludes with two alternative glimpses of Britain's political future, brought about by the heroine's delirium during the first contractions of childbirth. In one, socialism triumphs at the ballot box, in the other the horrors of a Fascist Britain are outlined.[38] Revisiting the careers of the main characters, their fates are played out against a background of Fascist terror. Isobel's young daughter, Morag, is raped by the Secret Police Service, the Specials, and her husband and the surviving members of her Communist cell drift into collaboration or are eliminated. The climax of the novel occurs with the execution of her husband, the gentle former lecturer, Tom. Forced to watch, Isobel sees her former comrades marched out by the firing squad:

> Then Tom. With his trousers cut off at the knee and his leg bandaged. Beyond Tom two women. "Tom!' she yelled suddenly. 'Tom, we'll remember, we'll . . .' And then there was a hand over her mouth, she staggered and was shoved back, gagged. She saw Tom turn, heard him call for her agonisedly: 'Dione!' and couldn't answer him. She saw the others turn too, Stan Mason, the women beyond Tom – heard the order to the firing squad, the click of the loading – heard the beginning of the 'Red Flag', the voices rising to it raggedly – Tom's voice – and saw that the two women were the Communist mill-hands Doris and Agnes Green. 'Agnes! Tom!'[39]

Here there was an exhortation and a call to arms. The *Daily Worker* disliked the pen-portraits of society Communists and of doughty workers in the book, but was entranced by the prophetic vision of a Fascist Britain: 'The best thing in the book comes right at the end, a picture of England under Fascist terror, as seen in the semi-trance of the heroine just before she is about to give birth. There are no illusions here about the British ruling class, no pretence that they are any more gentle when they are desperate'.[40]

The prospects of a Fascist putsch in Britain, brought about by social unrest, and hostility to Communist extremism, also preoccupied those authors who sought to portray the horrors of Fascism in allegorical form or in parables. In both the 1930s, and the 1960s, the world of the fantastical seemed a more appropriate place to contemplate Fascist successes, without compromising Britain's narrative of 'standing alone' during the war years. Rex Warner, the author of a number of inter-war political fantasies, provided the strongest example of such literature in his novel, *The Aerodrome*, written in the 1930s, and only finally published in 1941.[41] *The Aerodrome* plays with Fascist and futurist images of flight and air travel as an embodiment of liberated Fascist man and as an exposition of the possibilities provided by aristocratic untrammelled aloofness standing above the common herd.[42] This was an expression of Fascism's obsession with superhuman leader figures, 'for it is the figure of the leader, the natural aristocrat whom they had thought long dead and buried in the obloquy of Whig history'.[43] Set against the background of the uneasy relationship between an RAF aerodrome and the village that adjoins it, *The Aerodrome* presents the local airmen as a closed, ascetic caste that display unyielding loyalty to the Air Vice Marshall. Gradually the traditional rural and social hierarchies in the village break down when the rector is accidently shot by an airman, and the local squire is marginalized by the machinations of the Air Vice Marshall. Thereafter, the traditional sources of rural authority are supplanted by the air base, reflecting inter-war concerns about the threats faced by village life and rural communities.[44] Following the squire's death, and the fading of his support in the village, the hero, Roy, the rector's son, drifts into the arms of the RAF and the Air Vice Marshall. For some writers, *The Aerodrome* demonstrates the beguiling nature of interwar Fascism; Roy's dilemma, accentuated by his isolation from family, home and community is an 'everyman's journey' into extremism of the type a number of young men during this period were forced to make.[45] The Air Vice-Marshall himself has something of the Fascist demagogue about him:

So for some time we waited until the lights began to grow dimmer while at the same time small bulbs, by the ashtrays in front of us, were illuminated so that, when all the lights in front of us were out, we could still see our cigarettes, knees and the table by our knees on which we had set our drinks. Two converging spotlights made a brilliant pool upon the stage. Into this pool the Air Vice-Marshall stepped and began at once to speak. He spoke somewhat quickly and without raising his voice, but with such evident command over himself and over his words that what he said seemed to need no tricks of oratory to make it emphatic.[46]

Discovering that the Air Vice-Marshall is his true father, Roy, nevertheless engineers his death in an air crash, thereby providing him with the ultimate Fascist immolation, and providing tangible hope for the future as his plans for the aerodrome posthumously unravel.[47]

III

London played a conspicuous part in narratives that envisaged a possible right-wing future for Britain. The capital was both a stage-set and backdrop for threats to British democracy. For some thriller writers, it provided a distillation of all the social forces that potentially threatened the British state and destabilized inter-war democracy more generally. The left-wing thriller writer, Eric Ambler, begins his novel *Background to Danger* with a malign meeting of city financiers, armaments manufacturers and industrialists in Northumberland Avenue where they plot to overthrow the existing government of Rumania, and to replace it with a puppet regime. The conspiracy to secure Rumania's oil supplies for use by an embargoed Italian government is an unashamed attempt to aid a Fascist power and to make profit from the turbulent political conditions in Eastern Europe. Many of the figures around the table have dubious views, and in the case of the fictionalized Lord Welterfield, an established track-record in anti-labour activity. In a Rumanian Communist newspaper quoted in the novel, he is described as 'a colliery owner and millionaire. Famous for his patronage of sport. Less well-known as the man who employed *agents provocateurs* to provoke a riot in a colliery town during a strike, and for his numerous offences against the Factory Acts'.[48] For writers of more conservative political views, London provided an example of decadence, immorality and imminent social breakdown. John Buchan's *The Three Hostages* is one of only a handful of his novels in which the action is set outside Scotland. Buchan's hero, Richard Hannay, is uncomfortable in London, echoing Buchan's view of the capital as a place of threat and social danger. This is a London of dark alleys, impoverished boarding houses, of winding staircases and of conspiracies. Dislike of metropolitan cosmopolitanism is apparent throughout. For Buchan, the metropolitan night-club circuit was a place that typified the hedonistic sexual excesses of London high society.[49] Many of these images of deprivation and decay come together around scenes in a jazz club, where Hannay is appalled by the sight of race-mixing, sexual promiscuity, implied drug-taking and jazz music performed by black musicians to a bored and burnt-out audience.

> It seemed to me a wholly rotten and funereal business. A nigger band, looking like monkeys in uniform, pounded out some kind of barbarous jingle, and sad-faced marionettes moved to it. There was no gaiety or devil in that dancing only a kind of bored perfection. Thin young men with rabbit heads and hair brushed straight back from their brows, who I suppose were professional dancing partners, held close to their breasts women of every shape and age, but all alike in having dead eyes and masks for faces, and the macabre procession moved like automats to the niggers' rhythm.[50]

Such images echoed the visions of 'alien-drug-traffickers and white-slavers, who flourish like fat slugs in the decayed body of the bourgeois' that proliferated in the ultra-right press during the inter-war years.[51] In numerous thrillers, London is represented as the conduit for the forces of migration and miscegenation that provide the preconditions for the rise of domestic Fascism. In his 1970s novel of race war and governmental collapse, *Fugue for a Darkening Island*, set in a thinly veiled future, Christopher Priest depicts London as a place of barricaded streets and segregated neighbourhoods, where black incomers fleeing nuclear war in Africa requisition houses and take charge of entire neighbourhoods.[52] Their incursions and the events that lead to a Fascist government under Prime Minister Tregarth begin with a migrant ship crashing dramatically into the structure of Tower Bridge:

> We watched them with a mixture of horror and fascination. These were men, women and children. Most, if not all, were in an advanced state of starvation. Skeletal arms and legs, distended stomachs, skull-like heads holding staring eyes; flat paper-like breasts on the women, accusing faces on them all. Most were totally naked, or nearly so. Many of the children could not walk. Those whom no one would carry were left on the ship.[53]

Fascist banners in Whitehall, military parades outside St. Paul's and SS guards in front of Buckingham Palace are part of the stage furniture of novels that envisage a Fascist Britain. As with popular fears of Communist insurgency, such images seek to shock, and to overturn our established assumptions by subverting the 'everyday'. Fascists themselves proposed plans for a remodelled London that would reflect the greatness of empire, the nation's history, and the achievements of the motherland. In the 1930s, R. Saw, writing in *The Blackshirt* looked forward to a time when 'the dreadful statues of the London squares would give place to new ones of really worthy national heroes. We are not interested in eighteenth-century statesmen and orators garbed in antique dress, not even though they appear armed with the lictor's bundle in place of an umbrella! These statues should give place to statues of the real builders of our world-empire'.[54] The German High Command planned for a wholesale 'architectural despoilation' of British cities in the event of a German victory. According to some accounts, Nelson's column was to be dismantled and re-erected in Berlin. In Owen Sheers' *Resistance*, it is 'sliced in two and tipped onto the loading platforms of a transport lorry to be taken as a trophy back to Berlin'.[55] In this novel, Hitler himself visits London to stand on Parliament Hill promising 'to bring peace at last to this nation, misguided for so long by the corrupt democracy that once sat in those shattered buildings beneath us'.[56] Depictions of an 'alien' and 'unfamiliar' London in which the great ceremonial sites are remodelled by a conquering army, or a successful British Fascist movement, are in a long tradition. In Saki's *When William Came*, the adventurer and hunter, Murray Yeovil, back from a period of illness in Eastern Europe, returns to find London under occupation by the Kaiser's army:

> The cab threaded its way swiftly along Buckingham Palace Road towards the Mall. As they passed the long front of the palace the traveller turned his head resolutely away that he might not see the alien uniforms at the gates and the eagle standard flapping in the sunlight. The taxi driver, who seemed to have combative instincts, slowed down as he was turning into the Mall, and pointed to the white pile of memorial masonry in front of the palace gates. 'Grossmutter Denkmal' he announced and resumed his journey.[57]

Much the same images occur in accounts in which an indigenous British Fascism wrests power. Guy Walters' potboiler, *The Leader*, in which Oswald Mosley inaugurates a British dictatorship begins with a reluctant work crew raising Fascist and swastika flags on the Mall to celebrate a friendly visit by Hitler to London: 'Later, much later, when they had finished, even Eric had to admit that the Mall looked magnificent. The Nazi flags and the Union Jacks were splendidly triumphant in the evening light, their colours marvellously bright in amongst the lush green of the plane trees'.[58] Similar images recur in accounts of a broken and invaded Britain, successfully occupied in 1940. In *SS-GB*, Len Deighton considers the ceremonial overhaul an invading German army would give to the capital:

> Douglas paused in the embankment corridor and looked out of the window to see the combined bands marching along the street. They looked magnificent in their dress uniforms, with dozens of brass instruments shining

in the sun, and the jingling Schellenbaum complete with horse-tails that marked its origins as the instrument of the Jannisaries. They had an imperious splendour. Artfully the Germans had used their military music to awe and pacify the conquered people of Europe. By the time Douglas got back to his office, they were playing 'Greensleeves'.[59]

Very few novels of Fascist conquest, however, portray London as an equivalent of an occupied Paris where a riotous and flamboyant pre-war social life continues under German rule.[60] Beneath the newly erected podiums, statues and street decorations lies a demoralized London in ruins where bombsites, teetering buildings and anti-Jewish notices belie the Fascist pomp that overlies and smothers it. In *SS-GB* this decrepit London provides the backdrop to the conspiracies between the Wermacht, the SS and the British Resistance over the fate of King George VI, imprisoned in the Tower of London. The book includes a sub-plot about purloined plans for a nuclear bomb: 'Hesse parked his car in the ruins of what was once the Victoria Palace Music Hall. Douglas's parents had taken him there when he was a child. Now tall weeds and flowers grew from the orchestra pit, and a row of seats tilted drunkenly from the last remaining section of the royal circle'.[61] Here London is a site of alternate imaginings, providing a counterpoint to a shattered Berlin against which many of the thrillers of the early Cold War period were set. In Cook's *A State of Denmark* London under an indigenous Fascist regime degenerates into a dirty and unkempt city of snoopers and narks: 'London is going dark and getting dirty. There's very little street-lighting at night, because of the curfew and what there is winks and flutters and doesn't work properly'.[62]

London provided the most fertile recruiting ground for British Fascism. Poor housing, bad economic conditions and intermittent employment opportunities allowed Fascism to proliferate in the most deprived parts of the East End. In the poorer districts, Mosley's BUF and post-war Union Movement profited from the presence of migrant communities and sought to muster support by stoking resentment amongst a disgruntled and resentful white working-class.[63] In an anti-Fascist leaflet of 1936, the Great Plague of 1664–5 is compared to the contemporary Fascist Plague, providing a model for Fascist depredations in the capital and a warning about potential BUF control in London: 'London – a huge and terrible graveyard – bodies lying in the streets unburied – those of the population as yet untouched by the hand of the Black Plague – the plague of death – trying feverishly to escape into the countryside, one in every five of the population dead or dying – a tragic story of a great catastrophe'.[64] Depressed inner-city environments, crumbling tenement blocks and the blasted infrastructure of post war urban planning provide the standard backdrop to many stories of a Fascist advance in Britain. In Roy Clews, *The Rise of Cromwell*

Jones, Fascism emerges in a bleak environment of fading council estates and wind-swept precincts that is never named or dated, but bears the hallmarks of South London at a time labelled: 'England – the Near Future'. This, we are to understand, is a metaphorical 'everytown'. In Clews' novel, vigilantism led by the charismatic Ivor Jones emerges in response to an escalation in crime. At the beginning of the novel, Jones surveys the degraded urban environment where the narrative is set: 'The city centre was a characterless mass of glass and concrete: cold, cheerless and inhuman. Propelled by the gusting wind, litter danced along the dirty pavements and was blown into doorways and alley-ways where homeless derelicts lay huddled in shapeless heaps beneath piled ragged coverings and cardboard tenting, snatching what uneasy sleep they could until the onset of the working day would drive them from their temporary havens'.[65] In both the 1930s, and the 1970s, British Fascism proved ambivalent about urban malaise, profiting from the economic dislocation that accompanied it, but indulging in arcadian fantasies of rustic escapism.[66] Treatments of the National Front in the 1970s, however, discerned patterns of support for Fascism outside the movement's traditional heartland in East London. Some modest successes in suburbia in local elections and in by-elections raised the profile of the National Front in these areas.[67] Michael Billig in a psychological profile of National Front members noted the presence of 'authoritarian' personalities drawn to this type of movement, who might occur anywhere. During these years there was a tendency to relocate concerns about Fascist support to the suburbs, where there were also popular fears about immigration and crime, and anxieties about declining respectability and a loss of jobs and opportunities to foreign incomers.[68] Pulp literature reflected this change of emphasis. In the heist novel, *The Ten-Tola Bars,* dealing with an attempted bullion theft from the Bank of England, a local Fascist group is manipulated into staging a riot, thereby impeding the police's ability to respond to the robbery. Posing as a well-connected American Fascist, the gang leader, William Harte, meets the Commandos for Christ ('a motley group of homosexuals, child molestors, middle-aged sado-masochists, the standard fascist fringe') in their suburban HQ: 'He'd had a thoroughly sordid afternoon. Not the least of it was an almost hour-long journey by tube out to Ruislip Gardens – almost the end of the line. And that in more ways than one. A more wretched, cold-eyed, purse-lipped little suburb he'd never seen.'[69] J.G. Ballard in *Kingdom Come,* situates British Fascism even more closely within the social and cultural context of London and its environs. His Fascism emerges against the backdrop of the soulless communities of the M25 corridor. With their senses lulled by consumerism and the entertainments on offer at the towering Metro-Centre, the giant mall becomes the focus for sports fixtures and social groups amongst the local community that rapidly mutate into a movement owing loyalty only to the Centre and its charismatic cable channel presenter, David Cruise. The sinister William Sangster is the grey eminence behind this organization. He remarks: 'This is a soft Fascism like the consumer landscape. No goose-stepping, no jackboots, but the same emotions and the same aggression. As you say, there's a strong sense of community, but it isn't based on civic rights. Forget reason. Emotion drives everything. You see it every weekend outside the Metro-Centre'.[70]

IV

In the years after World War II, there was much speculation about the social groups that might have been drawn into Fascism. Much contemporary scholarship saw Fascism as essentially a movement of the *petite bourgeoisie*, mobilized to oppose and resist Bolshevism. There was a widely held perception during these years that Fascism was a movement that appealed to and expressed the vulnerability and diminished status of the *petite bourgeoisie* in Weimar Germany. Naturally attracted by jingoism, patriotic sloganising and appeals to national security, the 'shopocracy' and 'mittelstand', it was believed, were emblematic of an ultra-conservative mindset that, in the right circumstances, could tip over into Fascism.[71] By the 1960s and 1970s, an orthodoxy had been established, which saw the lower middle class as instrumental in bringing about Fascist dictatorship in both Germany and Italy. These ideas combined with notions of 'Fascist personalities' and interest in identifying 'authoritarian types', and even psychoanalysing surviving members of the Nazi Party. In some ways, Hitler himself came to be seen as a product of the vagaries and insecurities of a lower middle class home and an unstable, petty bourgeois political environment. These notions first emerge in the literature of the 1930s, where British Fascists are often depicted as aspiring social climbers, excluded from the grandee class and extremely fragile in their social origins. Peter, the Fascist character in Patrick Hamilton's *Hangover Square*, is eaten up by 'revengeful social snobbery': 'Banished, by reason of his birth and lack of money, from the class of which he had so fanatical a desire to be a member, he had not turned in anger against that class, or thrown in his lot with any other. That would have been an admission of defeat. On the contrary, he sought to glorify it, to buttress it, to romanticise it, to make it more itself than it was already – hoping thereby, in his ambitious, twisted brain, to gain some reward from it at last'.[72] In many of the novels of Fascist takeovers in Britain, figures that typify the anxious and harassed lower middles feature strongly. The Fascist 'New Pace' movement in Cook's *A State of Denmark* attracts lower middle-class supporters and is staffed by figures like the repellent and comic Lavey (described as 'a pocket Saint Just') who gains the status and position he craves through his role in the organization. The hero, Richard Watt, comments: 'I tried to imagine his origins. It was not difficult to be reasonably accurate. His background had been the frantic struggle first to achieve, and next to cling to the outermost icy fringe of white-collar status in the howling economic void that succeeded the first world war'.[73] Albert Smith in Robert Muller's *After All, This Is England* is also a character that embodies a lower middle-class presence in Fascism. A small shopkeeper who has seen better days resident in the South Coast seaside town of Seabourne he is a petty and small-minded busybody. Tied into petty local quarrels he is neat, fastidious and consumed by envy and spite.[74] Obsessed with declining standards, juvenile delinquency, immigration and missing apostrophes from street signs, he sees evidence of national malaise and decline everywhere.[75] He is also a voyeur and repressed homosexual who lived in constant fear of exposure. Throughout the novel he is engulfed by an inner rage that leads him to seek solace in an emergent Fascist movement: the British Action Party. The organization is unashamedly a lower middle class one. The fictional equivalent of the *Daily Mail* comments: 'We are witnessing an atmosphere of national revival in our towns and villages. With the left in a state of hapless disintegration, it is becoming obvious that potentially uncommitted voters of the middle and lower middle class (shopkeepers, artisans, businessmen) are now rallying to the BAP's call for a steadfast and sturdy patriotism – encouraged no doubt by the sight of the breezy young men in uniform, who march along our high streets'.[76] Seeking approval and status, Smith gradually builds up his position within the movement. Turning his character defects to his advantage, he is able to ingratiate himself by building up a dossier of customers and locals who are untrustworthy and potential enemies of the movement. Blinding himself to the extremist tendencies apparent within the organization, and using it to settle old scores, he is perfectly positioned to take on a job as the administrator for a local concentration camp. Only at the very end of the novel is he prepared to concede that he may have made a mistake.

As with continental Fascism, British Fascism protested its adherence to the constitutional proprieties. In the 1930s, Oswald Mosley declared that the movement sought to proceed by 'legal and constitutional means'.[77] Its self-appointed role was as a bulwark against Communism and socialism. Only in the event of a threat to the king's life, it seemed, was Fascism prepared to act.[78] On the Italian model, British Fascism speculated about the possibility of stepping in to prevent a descent into lawlessness and disorder or to defend the person of the king. European parallels, however, suggested that a British Fascist government would emerge either through the imposition of a German-controlled puppet regime, or by significant failures within the electoral process and in the relations between political parties. Authors of popular fiction explored a number of routes for the emergence of a British Fascist state. In *SS-GB* the German

Figure 4.1 The 'Giant of Labour' opposing the pro-Fascist respectable classes. Cover illustration: T. Bramley, *We Are Many* (London: Communist Party of Great Britain, 1941) (Author's Collection).

military simply storm ashore at Dover, in a story told in retrospect, and install a militarized regime, subordinate to the German High Command.[79] Such possible scenarios accorded with numerous re-examinations of the military situation in 1940, and semi-fictionalized accounts of the successful unfolding of a German invasion plan.[80] In a twist to this standard plot device, Owen

Sheers' *Resistance* imagines a successful German counter-attack across the Channel following the failure of the D-Day landings in 1944.[81] In his fictionalized Fascist state, the Conservative politician, R.A. Butler, with the support of Lloyd George, becomes a national unity candidate installed in a British Vichy government at the spa town of Harrogate.[82]

Some authors, however, saw Fascism as a creeping process of accommodation with German militarism. In *The Other Man*, an Anglo-German accord emerges quite naturally in the wake of a British peace treaty with Germany negotiated on Hitler's terms in 1940. Resistance and opposition drain away as the relationship between the two powers is normalized. In a country drifting into apathy and malaise, the British state becomes an adjunct of the Reich, exercising imperial control for the German army in the broader empire and joining Fascist Germany in a crusade against Bolshevism in Russia. By the end of the novel, the British army has been relegated to the status of an imperial police force only.[83] Other authors have seen possibilities for an elected Fascism. In Robin Cook's *A State of Denmark*, the British dictator Jobling is a Mussolini figure, who tacks to the right once in power and takes advantage of flaws in the constitution. Richard Watt explains: 'He started off as a socialist and was prime minister in a legally elected Labour government. When he saw his policies were going to get him thrown out at the next election he simply announced that he was going to rule by himself. And, do you know? It turned out that there was practically nothing to stop him. The country just fell over sideways.'[84] Robert Muller's *After All, This Is England*, closely follows the precedents set by Weimar Germany. In the novel, the Fascistic British Action Party is elected as part of an anti-socialist coalition, but consolidates its hold on power by burning down the Palace of Westminster and blaming it on the Communists in a repeat of the Reichstag fire.[85] Elsewhere, the Abdication Crisis has been seen as potentially paving the way for an elected Fascist government. In Guy Walters' *The Leader*, Edward VIII refuses to abdicate, forcing an election over the issue. His actions split traditional party allegiances, allowing the formation of a King's Party, able to hold the balance of power and form a minority government in a riven parliament. Against this background, Oswald Mosley emerges as a unity candidate who is able to consolidate his hold on government through an emergency powers bill.[86]

Most often, however, fictional British Fascists simply kick their way into power. Many of the accounts of indigenous British Fascist movements produced in the 1960s and 1970s were heavily influenced by rumours of secret armies and paramilitary-style militias formed to oppose Communism and to break strikes during the period of industrial militancy that characterized Harold Wilson's failing Labour governments. Sir Walter Walker's 'Citizens' Vigilance Committee', established to oppose Communist insurgency in Wiltshire, and Colonel David Stirling's 'GB75' formed to rescue the nation from strikers and flying pickets, established a hold over the popular imagination. In the case of David Stirling, his role as former head of the SAS gave his movement some cachet, although it ultimately came to very little.[87] Both *Who Shot Enoch Powell?* and *The Chilian Club* envisage a Fascism that seeks to gain power through military means. Told from a liberal perspective, *Who Shot Enoch Powell?* issues a warning to those who might contemplate killing the politician. Beginning with the assassination of Powell, the novel charts the descent of Britain into crisis and near civil war. Behind the turmoil is the sinister war hero, Colonel Jeffrey Monckton, who employs *agents provocateurs* to inflame the trouble and dreams of establishing an extremist right-wing dictatorship. Monckton hopes that barricades in Glasgow, race riots at Wimbledon and disorder in central London will allow his organization to restore order and assume command.[88] The novel has many of the characteristics of fantasies that saw in the Britain in the 1970s the seeds of terminal drift and decline. Frederick Evans, the Home Secretary remarks: ' "What's been the pattern of public life these last few years? Student unrest – violence in every shape and form – near civil war in Ulster – this Glasgow business. The country's sick of it. Sick of permissiveness, sick of teen-age drug merchants, sick of youth worship, sick of being 'swinging'. You know what it wants? It wants a strong man – the iron fist. And you know what keeps me awake at nights?" He prodded a finger at his rumbling stomach. "The dread that it'll get one" '.[89] In contrast, in *The Chilian Club*, violence is embraced as a solution to Britain's economic and social malaise in the 1960s and 1970s. Disgusted when one of their member dies unnecessarily as a consequence of strike action and rationing, a group of retired military officers from the disgraced Sixth Hussars emerge from retirement to save Britain from communism and left-wing militancy. Led by their senior officer, General Sir Henry Mornay, they display many of the characteristics associated with those involved in private armies and counter-revolutionary militias in the 1970s. Attracting little attention as pensioners, and applying their military skills learnt in World War II, they succeed in eliminating trade union leaders, civil rights campaigners and Soviet spies.[90] This novel received numerous plaudits in the Conservative press and rapidly became a cult novel in extremist right-wing circles. The blurb on the back cover gives some idea of the constituency the book is aimed at: 'Food rationed . . . Communications disrupted . . . Race Riots . . . Commerce at a standstill . . . the answer is ASSASSINATION . . . Don't YOU, asks the Chilian Club, ever feel like shooting a Union leader?'[91]

V

Images of strongmen and aspiring Hitlers haunted the pages of popular fiction. As with European Fascism, the leader figure in British Fascism was a central component of the radical right's political platform. In the 1930s, the British Union of Fascists hoped for a new style of leader, an energetic figure who would re-energize the country, oppose the 'Old Gangs' and restore the nation's pride. In the Fascist press, Thomas Carlyle's words about the importance of 'hero-kings' were much quoted.[92] The desire for a new spirit that would bring about national regeneration provided a marked feature of inter-war fiction. Following Carlyle, John Buchan hoped for a reinvigorated aristocracy that would adopt the attributes, the dedication and the iron resolve of the Bolsheviks who threatened Britain. In his novel *John Macnab*, Sir Edward Leithen argues for a replenished and revived aristocratic and chivalric spirit that would arrest the decline of the British land-owning elites and preserve the country from assault by the enemies of order: 'Nobody in the world today has a right to anything which he can't justify. That's not politics, it's the way nature works. Whatever you've got – rank or power or fame or money – you've got to justify it, and keep on justifying it, or go under'.[93] Such sentiments were very marked on the political right. Oswald Mosley was the embodiment of the anticipated charismatic leader providing salvation and a restitution of national greatness.[94] Searching for precedents in the national past, Oliver Cromwell was often invoked as a model for such leadership and the BUF sometimes referred to themselves as 'New Ironsides'.[95] A nostalgic Cromwellianism is apparent in the literature recounting a Fascist takeover. The name of Colonel Monckton in *Who Shot Enoch Powell?* is a combination of the names of the English Civil War Cromwellian generals Ireton and Monck. In Roy Clews' *The Rise of Cromwell Jones*, the author refers explicitly to the Cromwellian precedent. His Fascist leader is a former Falklands veteran-turned-pastor, who mobilizes his community against drug-pushers, muggers, pimps and street criminals. Vigilante attitudes are apparent throughout the narrative, and the movement takes direct action against rapists and petty criminals unpunished by the law.[96] The organization he creates, christened 'the Cromwell Movement', preaches a new iron Puritanism and gives renewed hope to the demoralized, deprived and aimless followers he recruits. By the end of the novel, Jones has built a sizeable movement that is poised for national electoral success: 'Ivor Jones stood up and walked out into the hall and as he mounted the pulpit and lifted his arms in salute a thunderous roar of acclamation greeted his arrival, and the echoes of the name they bellowed reached far out from the hall and across the rooftops of the city. "CROMWELL! CROMWELL! CROMWELL! CROMWELL! CROMWELL!"'[97] Captain Wyatt who stages a coup in Peter Van Greenaway's *The Man Who Held the Queen to Ransom and Sent Parliament Packing* is surrounded by Cromwellian and Commonwealth imagery throughout. A wise and benevolent leader, he is nevertheless seen as 'Britain's self-appointed Protector', imposing military style discipline and punishments, and eliminating the old elites.[98] On the day of the seizure of power at the Palace of Westminster, Cromwell's statue looks down approvingly on Wyatt's endeavours: 'He returned to the car while Cromwell, gripping Bible and sword forever, frowned eternally on the passing world, all triviality and nothing of god'.[99]

The presence of such political strongmen who proliferate throughout these novels allows for the examination of Fascist character and motivation. A number, like Ivor Jones, have military backgrounds, reinforcing the notion of energy and action, rather than words.[100] Colonel Jeffrey Monkton in *Who Shot Enoch Powell?* is a war hero, known as 'the Panther' who distinguished himself in World War II through his use of unorthodox methods. Briggs, leader of the parliamentary opposition, storms when he hears of his appointment as Security Supremo: 'Good God! Even in war-time there was nothing to choose between his methods and those of the Gestapo! Bribery, corruption, physical violence – those are the legitimate *methods*, are they, of a peace-time democracy?'[101] Many of the popular fictions that emerge around a right-wing threat to democracy consider the personal and social characteristics of a new potential Hitler. Indeed, they display something of a fascination with the notion of a 'Hitlerian' type, and the personal circumstances that might create him. Gillian Freeman is the author who made perhaps the most imaginative attempt to portray such a figure. In her book, *The Leader*, the leader principle is inverted to show the shortcomings, rather than strengths, of aspiring leadership figures. Her book depicts a hopeful British Hitler who seeks to transcend his lonely life as a bank clerk by forging a movement to restore Britain's greatness. A contrast to the hardy physical types depicted elsewhere in literature about the radical right, Freeman's character, Vincent Pearman, is asthmatic, lazy and non-athletic. His over-protective mother, only-child status and absence of a father give him some of the characteristics of Adolf Hitler. Alone in his bed-sit, he wears uniforms and practises Fascist salutes: 'He clenched his fist, and brought his hand forward in a Communist salute. He unfolded his fingers and extended them, the fascist salute. He brought his arm close to his head, paused and thought, then bent it down from the elbow, the forearm across his forehead and clenched his fist again. He smiled. No one had thought of that'.[102] Attracting a motley collection of supporters, including 'beats' and a self-loathing Jew, Vincent sets up an organization dedicated to violence and disorder. With laughable pretensions to power, the organization plays out in miniature the history of the Nazi movement featuring purges, expulsions, and internecine rivalries. Finally Vincent is himself expelled by his most apparently loyal lieutenant. Widely read at the time of its publication, this novel captures many of the absurdities of the genuine extremist right in Britain in the 1960s.

VI

Fictionalized coups, putsches, or the imposition of a military junta in Britain raised issues of obedience or defiance, collaboration or resistance.[103] In novels written in the 1930s, the choices facing those subjugated by these regimes are made explicit. A number sought to rally resistance to European-style Fascism both at home and abroad. Storm Jameson's *In the Second Year* was an unashamed attempt to alert the public to the perils and dangers of Fascism and those social forces that might collaborate to make it victorious in Britain. Written in 1936, shortly after the dissolution of the National Government and its replacement by Stanley Baldwin's Conservatives, *In the Second Year* subscribed to the view taken by many on the political Left that Fascism could only emerge when aided by an unwitting 'social Fascism', that shared some of its agenda, but stopped short of Fascism proper. The failure of Popular Front politics in Britain, and the fragmentation of the Labour Party in 1931, Jameson believed, had paved the way for a riven Left, unable to mount a coherent threat against the rise of domestic Fascism in Britain. In the novel, there is much retrospective recrimination about the failure to prevent Hillier's government, and to resist the threat posed by his paramilitary Volunteers. The Communist and resistor, Lewis, condemns Andrew Hillier, the dictator's cousin, and liberal observer of events in the novel for the self-interest of the Labour Party, and its failure to appreciate the scale of the Fascist menace: 'You and your bloody brothers in the Labour Party, who fought nobody but the Communists . . . who worked for friendly relations with the owning classes and took their rewards, were decorated, knighted, wore silk breeches, who clothed themselves in righteousness of legality and held the door open for repression to come eagerly in'.[104] There is much of the classic leftist myth of betrayal of the working-class in this statement.[105] In the plot, only the Communists provide concerted resistance to the new regime. The heaviest Fascist repression is in Wales, where miners in Newport fight to the last under their charismatic leader, Tom Lloyd.[106] The impotence of an ineffective liberalism when faced by the determination and organization of Fascism is a theme throughout the novel. With echoes of the National Government, some of the worst members of Hillier's government are apostate labour or trade union politicians who have embraced the new order.[107] As with many narratives which consider the theme of a Fascist Britain, *In the Second Year* dwells on the plight of those opposed to Richard Hillier's right-wing dictatorship and imagines a systematic purge of intellectuals, the Left and of political opponents. As with other fictionalized accounts, the author takes the hero inside an internment camp, where he sees conditions for himself.[108]

Storm Jameson feared a contemporary Fascist putsch. Post-war accounts of a possible British Fascist state have, however, been informed by insights into the realities of the Nazi regime in Germany. Exploration of collaboration has, again, proved an enduring theme in such fiction, placing the lead characters in positions of knowing or unwitting support for a radical rightist government or German occupiers. Decisions about resistance dominate the plots of such novels.[109] In Owen Sheers' *Resistance* carefully laid plans to resist a German invasion come to very little. The novel charts 'a general slide towards collaboration': 'The Germans . . . controlled the food supplies, handed out the ration tickets, and were the only ones with cash to spend. George had seen them walking through the streets of Abergavenny, cruising the local shops jingling the loose change in their pockets.'[110] George Grant, the ambitious military officer at the heart of the narrative in *The Other Man*, is, in contrast, a naive rather than intentional collaborator with Britain's new German allies. Choosing duty and a successful career over his moral qualms he drifts further and further into the arms of the German military. Putting his doubts to one side, his moral ambivalence begins with his failure to speak up for his friend, and brother officer, David Lewin, who is evacuated with other Jewish soldiers to the Pioneers Corps in Dover.[111] On a trip through Dover, where slave labour is being used to build a Channel Tunnel, George sees a gang of slave labourers and realizes the reality of David Lewin's 'reassignment': 'George was accustomed to the sight of German uniforms, but all the same this was an odd welcome to England. These must be Russian prisoners of war, or Poles brought over to work in the docks. The line stopped moving, held up by some obstruction in front, and a face looked up at George. Haggard and hopeless, shaven-headed and filthy, there was yet a sign of recognition in it, and as the train began to move George realized that he was looking at David Lewin . . . George never told anybody what he had seen.'[112] Following the same theme of officialdom, forced to choose between duty and treachery, Len Deighton's murder detective and honest copper, Douglas Archer, in *SS-GB* seeks to preserve his career, but as the novel progresses, he is forced more and more to evaluate where he stands in relation to his family, the Resistance, his colleagues, and his German superiors. This novel carries perhaps the strongest sense of the secrecy, moral ambivalence and affected ignorance that occurred under occupation in Europe, and is repeated in Deighton's imaginary German-dominated Britain: 'Even a born and bred Londoner, such as Douglas Archer, could walk down Curzon Street with eyes half-closed [and] see little or no change from the previous year . . . And if your eyes remained half-closed you missed the signs that said "Jewish Undertaking" and effectively kept all but the boldest customers out. And in September of that year, 1941, Douglas Archer, in common with most of his compatriots was keeping his eyes half-closed.'[113] As both *The Other Man* and *SS-GB* proceed, the choices the lead characters are forced to make become more and more harrowing. Archer becomes implicated in a plot to liberate King George V from the Tower of London and to destroy the Wermacht's experimental nuclear facility, while at the same time preserving the lives of his son and his colleagues; George Grant sacrifices all his moral quibbles, and, seriously wounded, is restored to life by organs and limbs taken from Concentration Camp prisoners. His fate is the worst one of all, he is quite literally absorbed into the military and medical machine he has served so well.

For most fictional accounts of an imagined occupation of Britain, the key dilemmas relate to the adoption of guerrilla warfare in an effort to oppose occupation. The tactics to be used in the event of German occupation were widely debated in the early years of the war. Spanish Civil War veterans like Tom Wintringham and Bert 'Yank' Levy recommended irregular styles of warfare based on the mobilization of small, disciplined cells of commandos. Such tactics posed problems for military planners: bombings, assassinations, ambushes and the use of booby-traps imported terrorist methods into conventional warfare on the model of the campaigns waged by the partisans against German occupation in the USSR.[114] For some, such strategies were frankly 'un-British'. Kenneth Macksey, in his semi-fictionalized account of a German invasion, suggests that large-scale military resistance to German occupation would have been unlikely. He argues that British soldiers and civilians had little experience of guerrilla warfare. For most contemporaries, guerrilla warfare was associated with anti-colonial struggles of the kind British troops had encountered on the frontiers of empire in the inter-war period. Indeed, Macksey asserts, in the 1940s, the British public harboured a particular revulsion against asymmetrical warfare, influenced by popular memory of events in Ireland and the resistance of the Boer Commandos during the Boer War.[115] For Levy, guerrilla warfare was far more a recurrent feature of British history, and one embraced by previous resistance movements to foreign occupation. In his writings, he sought to remind the British of their heroic tradition of opposition to foreign rule. His model to inspire a new generation of British guerrillas was Hereward, the Wake: 'England had been conquered. The heavily armoured forces of the enemy, more mobile and equipped with better weapons than the defending forces, had broken every element of resistance throughout the country. Then in the fens and marshes of East Anglia an outlaw raised rebellion. He did not try to make an army that could stand against the overwhelming force of the enemy. He raised guerrilla bands to harry them.'[116] Most novels of an imagined German occupation grapple with the moral dilemmas associated with the use of irregular methods of warfare. In Gordon Stevens' *And All the King's Men*, resistance ranges from minor sabotage to roadside bombings and assassination: all, however, come at a heavy price. In the German-occupied south of the country, civilians are interned and there are brutal acts of reprisal and indiscriminate torture of civilians. The resistance, in turn, embraces the terror tactics of the French *maquis*. Under the command of the shadowy 'Watchman' collaborators, spies and double-agents are shot, and their bodies placed on public display as a warning to traitors, their faces daubed by a crudely drawn Cross of St. George. The 'Watchman' orders: 'Tonight, when it's dark, put him in the square where the mayor and his people were to have been shot. Make sure that nobody sees you, but make sure that everybody sees him in the morning before he's taken away'.[117]

Imaginative studies of potential British Fascist movements dominate the popular pulp market. Fascism provided the model for an anti-Britain that contradicted the positive virtues of the Westminster system of government, and negated Britain's reputation for freedom and tolerance. For some authors, the idea of a Fascist Britain was so remote from everyday reality that it could only be the stuff of fantasy. The Labour historian H.N. Brailsford imagined a British Fascism so mediated through the constitutional proprieties and essence of British character that 'when our Labour leaders are interned they will not beat them: they will play cricket with them on Saturday afternoons'.[118] Only truly apocalyptic circumstances, it seemed, could deliver a truly continental-style Fascism. In James Herbert's '48 death-dealing rockets fired by the German High Command in the final days of the war destroy most of the population in a terrible 'blood-plague', allowing ailing Fascists to establish a dictatorship under an Oswald Mosley-style leader called Max Hubble: 'Hubble had never been handsome, but I guess he had that arrogance of features that had some allure for the weak-minded. Pencil-thin moustache, beaky nose, he could have been a shorter version of his own hero, Oswald Mosley, the leader of England's very own Fascist Party, a megalomaniac who spent most of the war years locked away in Holloway Prison'.[119] A Nazi Gothic style has increasingly placed the notion of a successful British Fascism at one remove, in the realm of witchcraft and horror fiction.[120] As one reviewer commented, in some ways novels like Gillian Freeman's *The Leader*, written in the 1960s, fall into the same trap as the inter-war novels that ridiculed aspiring British Fascists. By so doing, they minimizes the repellent and reprehensible nature of the doctrines that such individuals expound: 'The impression remains that somehow this is not quite serious enough, just the least bit glib, as an imaginative reconstruction of how a new Hitler might arise; the prototype was never quite so obviously a sick little psychological mess as this, or millions would not have been murdered in his name'.[121]

Chapter 5

Revolution and Counter-Revolution in London in the 1960s and 1970s

There is a smell of murder about England nowadays. As soon as people begin to feel these things threatened, they will see naked murder committed rather than lose any of their comforts. They will encourage tyranny and massacre, rather than lose an ounce of butter from their regular grocery order.[1]

It would be good to get back. Or would it? Was England still that dangerous, violent place she had left, where each step could mean death? She could not help hoping that everything would have changed, during her brief absence, for the better. It was too much to hope that all the problems hanging round the neck of the government – Ireland, unemployment, inflation – would have sorted themselves out, but surely things could not be quite so bad as they had been when she had left?[2]

The most lurid depictions of terrorism and political outrage occurred during the 1960s and 1970s. These were periods of rapid social change marked by dramatic political events both at home and abroad. Against this background, narratives of 'declinism' became the overarching theme of the late 1970s in particular.[3] The domestic turmoil and volatile political landscape of these decades laid themselves open to scrutiny by authors of fiction that engaged with flux, rather than stasis. Ailing governments, industrial militancy, ultra-left insurgency, the 1973 oil crisis and bombing campaigns by the Irish Republican Army created ready sources of anxiety, drawn upon by pulp writers, allowing their imagination free rein to speculate about alternative politics, or apocalyptic scenarios of military takeover and national collapse. During the period from 1960 to 1980, the popular fiction novel reached its apogee and achieved a recognizably modern format. Cheaply available, featuring garish and sensationalist cover illustrations, these novels were produced in large numbers by pulp publishing houses like Pan and the New English Library. During these years pulp was ubiquitous. Easily available at numerous retail outlets, the novel of political fiction featuring unstable governments, conspiracies, coups and insurgent Communist takeovers became a feature of airport lounges, corner shops and long-running serializations in the popular press. Part of the cultural and social fabric of the period, these novels fed concerns about post-imperial decay and heightened fears about incipient social and political collapse.[4] For cultural commentators, such writings are perceived as a barometer, measuring the political health of the period.[5] For some, they were themselves part of the moral malaise of these years. In recognition of their irreverence and universality, some pulp authors mocked their own genre, or saw it as highlighting the hypocrisies of the period. In *The Prime Minister's Daughter*, by the Labour MP for Coventry North-West, Maurice Edelman, the fictional PM, Richard Melville, opens his morning newspaper to be confronted by a serial shocker: 'Melville turned the page to the serial story by Alvin Long, a writer described as the greatest thriller writer since Buchan. Under the drawing of a monstrous bespectacled scientist bending against a background of retorts over a terrified, big-breasted girl in a bikini, he read 'Chort looked at her fingernails, and said, "Pliers, I think"'.[6] Breaking the pattern of previous sections of this book, in this chapter, popular fiction is located in a chronological context and examined against a situation of extreme social and political volatility.

I

Following the optimism of the 1960s, the mood in Britain darkened in the subsequent decade. Dominated by images of 'declinism' the period from the late 1960s through the 1970s is often judged as a period of failure and governmental collapse. Many of the popular images applied to Britain in this period focussed around decay and disintegration in studies that overlooked the very considerable social mobility and egalitarianism of these years. In his analysis of 'The Seventies' Christopher Booker commented: 'We may, in short, remember the seventies as a kind of long, rather dispiriting interlude: a time when in politics, in the arts or in any other field one considers, the prevailing mood was one of a somewhat weary, increasingly conservative, increasingly apprehensive disenchantment'.[7] An underperforming economy, inflation, devaluation of the pound and failures in essential services were augmented by a loss of national self-confidence, status and world role. For some, the 1970s was a decade of near despair. An ossified Labour Party under Harold Wilson and Jim Callaghan and a revival in trade union militancy led to fears about the power of the trades unions and the 'ungovernability' of the United Kingdom.[8] In 1979, the mood of the period was captured by the sequence of essays in the academic volume *Is Britain Dying?*[9] In the face of a calcified Labour Party, political energy seemed to be migrating to the extremes. The language of instability, coups and political takeovers transposed narratives from more unstable political environments and fed into descriptions of Britain as a 'banana republic' or 'a third world economy'.[10] In 1967–8 and the mid-1970s there was much talk of a 'business government' or an 'emergency government' to stave off national disintegration.[11] Public pronouncements about a decrepit and ailing Britain fuelled the public mood of despondency. In 1975 the newly installed Archbishop of Canterbury, Donald Coggan, talked about 'a drift towards chaos'.[12] Such sentiments are echoed in the memoirs and reminiscences of leading political figures of the day. The Liberal MP Cyril Smith claimed in 1977 that 'for the last three years, ever since the miners brought down Ted Heath there have been long and passionate discussions in all the rooms of Westminster, except the Chamber of the House of Commons, in the bars, in the restaurants, even in the splendid marble halls of the toilets, about the possibility of revolution in this country. I am by no means the only MP who thinks that it is not only possible, but, in fact, quite likely *if* the present situation is allowed to drift'.[13] The mid-1970s marked the high point for these kinds of sentiments. In 1975 Lord Plowden was adamant that the end of the year 'would see some kind of authoritarian government of the left or the right . . . the latter is more likely and Enoch (Powell) may well lead it'.[14] Inflammatory and uncompromising language fanned these fears and demonstrated a marked polarization of politics. Paul Johnson's *Enemies of Society* captures the tempo of the times, not least in his description of militant trades unionists as 'Red Fascists'.[15] As G.R. Searle points out, the violence of such language on both left and right made the expedient of a government of national unity and salvation highly unlikely.[16]

The climate of moral panic that characterized the period led to a revival in popular fiction that foretold national danger or envisaged circumstances of political and social turmoil, the better to bolster national resolve. Updating some traditional preoccupations, a number of these popular novels of the 1960s and 1970s carried undertones of an older tradition of invasion-panic fiction. During these years, pulp itself became aware of its own importance in guiding the national debate. Its voluminous output celebrated its centrality in charting the state of the nation or in warning about potential dangers. The *Times Literary Supplement*'s review of Constantine Fitzgibbon's novel of a Soviet subversion of Britain, *When the Kissing had to Stop* noted: 'The "kissing" in the title is Mr Fitzgibbon's warning to those whom he clearly views as unreliable idealists, misguided into co-operation for humanity's sake. His political stance is uncompromising: let us keep the bomb, the Americans and a very sharp and wary eye turned to the east'.[17] Harking back to the 1870s and 1880s, a number of these narratives revived fears about internal and external threats. In Paul Bryers' thriller about the oil industry, *Hollow Target*, the book speculates about the vulnerability of the new North Sea Oil platforms to attack, using images from Britain's embattled island past: 'The North Sea discoveries with all their benefits for Britain brought a new vulnerability. A fear of attack almost as profound and as paranoic as the invasion scares of the past. But there were no wooden walls, no Martello towers that could deter an attack by terrorists on this fragile life-line'.[18] The decision to investigate the viability of a Channel Tunnel project in 1975 constituted one such possible area of concern, reviving the invasion-panic narratives of the 1880s.[19] Closer proximity to Europe, it was argued, raised the spectre of potential invasion and created an easy target for terrorists. Robert Byrne's *The Tunnel*, written at the time of these speculations about a possible fixed link to the continent, brought all these notions together. A civil engineer with a long-standing interest in Channel Tunnel projects, Byrne envisaged the consequences of a successful terrorist attack on the Tunnel by an Irish Republican Army (IRA) splinter group. Replete with period details and a close personal knowledge of previous abandoned Channel Tunnel projects in the area, the novel imagined terrorists gaining access to the old tunnel workings set up by Colonel Frederick Beaumont in 1881. Using them as a base, they excavate under the new tunnel to detonate a bomb with deadly effect. The book rehearses many of the traditional concerns about the possibilities for invasion opened up by this engineering project. In Byrne's novel, the debate in the House of Commons about the Tunnel echoes General Wolseley's concerns of the 1880s.[20] Caldwell Morestock, the fictional MP for Plymouth and Devonport, comments:

> The main reason why I am opposed to the project relates to national defence . . . With the existence of the tunnel our main natural defence will be breached. It would be feasible for a force of parachutists and commandos to seize the tunnel head and hold it for a long enough period for an invader to pass through and thus completely bypass the barrier that has protected us for thousands of years. I ask the hon. Members not to treat this matter lightly. History offers a plethora of examples of successful lightening strikes – Rotterdam, Nijmegen, and Corinth from the last war alone.[21]

Evoking the notion of subterranean fears re-emerging, and responding to the decade's obsession with nostalgia for Victoriana, a number of the novels of this period traded in underground imagery and themes deriving from the nineteenth century. In *The Weatherman Guy*, the journalist John Burmeister envisaged a conspiracy by contemporary terrorists to assassinate members of the British cabinet and the queen. In his book, a member of the American Weathermen Underground teams up with a renegade British historian and expert on the Palace of Westminster to blow up the House of Commons during the state opening of parliament. The plot carried obvious undertones of

Guy Fawkes' 1605 conspiracy in it title, but also harked back to the bombing campaigns in London by Irish republicans in the 1880s. The plotters build
their plans around a still-intact tunnel excavated by Fenians under the House
of Lords in 1885. Karen Einsbach, the leader of the conspiracy, explains to
Rodney Watkinson-Hughes, the turn-coat historian:

> 'I know there is an old tunnel running under the Palace of Westminster
> to a point directly under the House of Lords. It was built by the Fenian
> Brotherhood between 1884 and 1885, and is packed with explosive dating
> from the time. Even the fuse is laid. The Fenians' object was to destroy the
> House of Lords, but their leader died and the group broke up before the
> plan could be put into operation . . . Once you are satisfied with our effec-
> tiveness you will disclose the entrance to us. Then on the day the Queen
> opens parliament, with the coming together of both Houses, and most of
> the royal family, then, Rodney' – a still look settled on her face and she
> reached out and gripped him tightly about the arm – 'then down will come
> baby, cradle and all'.[22]

For many writers of popular fiction, however, the old worries about invasion
were supplanted by concerns about the erosion of traditional and long-standing
British institutions. Against the background of the tensions of the decade, popular fiction was characterized by a sense of Britain's loss of direction. Many of
the novels of the period that deal with Britain's changing world role, or of the
import of extremist and unfamiliar politics into the United Kingdom, increasingly placed an emphasis on a declining and conflicted sense of national identity. In the late 1970s, these ideas migrated into more mainstream fiction. In
Margaret Drabble's novel of property speculation and British decline, *The Ice
Age*, Britons feel nothing but contempt for their decrepit country: 'England,
sliding, slinking, shabby, dirty, lazy, inefficient, dangerous, in its death throes,
worn out, clapped out, occasionally lashing out'.[23] In Paul Bailey's *Old Soldiers*,
dealing with the traumas of two Great War veterans in London, the emphasis
is on the outworn, the illusory and the sheer stultifying weight of the national
past.[24] Similar notions proliferated in the popular fiction market. In Donald
Seaman's *The Committee*, a jaded, introspective and enfeebled Britain becomes
the perfect target for a terrorist cell intent on planting atomic bombs in the
major cities. Their leader explains:

> It's run-down and disillusioned, and industrially sick, a nation which has
> lost its way. And as a result, the moral fibre of its leaders has been eroded
> to a degree where all seek the easiest way out of each ensuing crisis. Yet at
> the same time it is a country which has an uncensored and highly efficient

Press and broadcasting system, so that any threat to the public safety must be given maximum publicity in a matter of hours. Those two factors make it the ideal country to attack.[25]

Many popular novels focussed on Britain's loss of autonomy. As Christopher Booker comments, by the mid-1970s, with the exception of Rhodesia and Hong Kong, British decolonization was complete, considerably reducing Britain's role in the world.[26] Fears about integration into Europe and of the impact of an unrestrained 'Americanization' of popular culture are particularly evident here. Some explicitly stated the threat posed by former war-time allies, now strengthened by a post-war prosperity from which Britain was excluded.[27] Closing the gap with Europe through membership of the Common Market reinforced fears that an ailing Britain might take on some of the more unstable features of her near European neighbours. In Peter van Greenaway's novel about a British coup, *The Man Who Held the Queen to Ransom and Sent Parliament Packing*, a weary police sergeant comments: 'It's all these holidays abroad. Too many people go over there these days, bring back Continental ideas – you wait, once we're in the Common Market they'll be revolutions every other Sunday'.[28] At the beginning of the 1960s, Angus Wilson restated Britain's vulnerability to incursions from the continent in terms of hostility to the emergence of the Common Market and integrated European institutions. In his *The Old Men at the Zoo*, Wilson portrayed the consequences of a power struggle between Britain and Europe, framed against the background of the imagined tensions within the administration of London Zoo. In this parable of national decline and disintegration, the Zoo stands for England, nostalgic and in disarray, and incapable of dealing with the realities of the rise of a Uni-European movement from which it is expelled, both by choice and by history. In the narrative, the zoo is a living homage to lost glories, fixed and unchanging, and paying obeisance to its Victorian past. In attempts to widen the appeal of the zoo, the only recourse available to its administrators is the strategy of increasing this nostalgic dimension to its exhibits and displays. At the grand opening, the Victorian ballad 'Home, Sweet Home' is performed, overwhelming the narrator: 'Everything that was absurd about Victorian England seemed to come from that genteel, sugary drawing room-parlour voice, and yet it filled me with deep nostalgia, a willingness to surrender myself to the pettiness and to die'.[29] Easily defeated in a war with the armies of Uni-Europe, Britain surrenders and the zoo animals are decimated. Under Uni-European control, Britain gives up much of her traditional culture and becomes a more 'Mediterranean' country, ruled by a Bonapartist-style European dictatorship.[30]

Images of Britain as a theme park or a museum exhibit resurface in Daphne Du Maurier's *Rule Britannia* published in 1972. A jeremiad, written at the end of her life, it sits uneasily alongside the rest of Du Maurier's work. A bitter attack on the increasing 'Americanization' of the United Kingdom, the book imagines an invasion by American forces to reduce Britain to the level of a colony. As with similar anti-American polemics of this nature, the book reflects concerns about the American presence in Europe, highlights her apparent contempt for her allies and exposes her as a de facto imperial power. It this, it mirrors the tensions evident in Britain's relationship with the United States since the early 1950s.[31] In the novel, under the American-backed puppet government (USUK), there is a crackdown on resistors and a programme of internment for potential insurgents that recalls American policies in South Vietnam.[32] Throughout the book, the contempt for the superficiality and coarseness of American popular culture that transcended left/right divides is on show. Under this new order, and mirroring Britain's diminished status in the 1970s, Britain faces relegation to a tourist theme park for American visitors: 'There is not a county in England or Wales', wrote an enthusiastic supporter of the scheme [in the novel], 'that is not steeped in history. King John signing the Magna Carta at Runnymede . . . Richard III losing his crown at Bosworth Field . . . the Wars of the Roses . . . all these scenes and countless others could be enacted for our visitors. Hotels and restaurants could be transformed into old coaching inns as a further attraction. Bear-baiting, cock-fighting, jousting, duelling, masked highway men on horseback – the tourist could watch them all from the comfort of a roofed-in stadium, or even from his car'.[33] Du Maurier envisages a more positive outcome to the conflict than Wilson. At the conclusion of the book, Cornwall becomes ungovernable, and the writer sees the salvation of the nation as lying in an appeal to history and the traditional doughty values of West Country farming folk.[34] Here her ideas were congruent with a much broader retreat into the certainties of the English rustic past in the 1970s that provided an antidote to notions of urban decline, flyover culture and industrial decline in the present.[35]

II

For many popular fiction writers, Britain was slowly sinking into a decadence that undermined her will to resist the power and expansionism of her international global rivals. Constantine Fitz Gibbon's *When the Kissing Had to Stop* typified this trend. Written in 1960, but republished throughout the 1970s, the book was a final homage to the nineteenth and early twentieth century genre of the invasion-panic novel.[36] Envisaging the landslide election of an ultra-left Labour government dominated by unilateralist sentiment, the plot centres around the steady erosion of Britain's ability to resist the machinations of

Moscow and the role of unwitting collaborators in furthering the Soviet Union's ends. Events in the novel mirror the fantasies of those who saw the Labour Party as in thrall to a 'power-mad socialism, inspired by the Communist variety of hate for any successful individual'.[37] For Fitz Gibbon, the Labour government, which drifts steadily out of control under the 'socialist megalomaniac', Rupert Page-Gorman, represents a culmination of all that is deviant and erratic about the British political left.[38] Defeatist, introspective and anti-patriotic, the Labour government under its new leader reneges on its commitments to its American allies, expels the personnel of American bases from the country and opens the way for a Russian trade delegation, which is, in fact, the front for a Soviet invasion of Britain.[39] The Soviet invasion is aided throughout by the apathy and indifference of the public, described as 'a passive fifth column' in one review of the work.[40] Chief culprits throughout are British pacifists, misguided liberals and youthful idealists, who underestimate the duplicity of the nation's enemies. The narrator of the novel, Patrick, the sixth Earl of Clonard, remarks in an exchange with his American business partner Cuthbertson about the 'Ban the Bomb' movement that exercises control over the new Labour government:

'Just kids, eh?'

'Not altogether, of course. You mustn't forget that there is a long tradition of radical pacifism in this country, dating from at least to the time of the Little Englanders during the Boer War period and the conchies of World War I. And remember how strong pacifism was between the wars. Lansbury, the Peace Pledge Union and all that. This fits into that same tradition.'

'I guess I'm not up on British history as I should be. But it smells awfully strong of Communism to me'.[41]

The novel casts itself firmly in the tradition of a warning. It ranges itself against youthful exuberance, crime, homosexuality, the leftist press, post-war new towns and fashionable theatrical types. All are seen as symptoms of moral and political decline. Lenin's dictum, quoted at the beginning of the novel that 'the soundest strategy in war is to postpone operations until the moral disintegration of the enemy renders the mortal blow both possible and easy' provides a wake-up call and a rallying cry to Britain.[42] At the end of the novel, most of the key characters die either through political assassination, crushing by tanks in forced labour camps, or as partisans in a hopeless war against the Soviet occupiers. Only the aimless social climber, Felix Seligman, finds a new lease of life as an anti-government guerrilla and offers a faint gleam of hope in broadcasts from his 'Radio Free Britain' transmitted from the Welsh mountains to a Midlands audience.[43] In other novels of this nature, there is no Soviet invasion of Britain, rather the country slides slowly but decisively into totalitarianism.

In Wilfred Greatorex's thriller *1990* based on the television series starring Edward Woodward, the Britain of the 1990s is an ersatz Eastern European state. The country is supervised by a grey bureaucracy and state subsidies for political parties have transformed them into arms of the state apparatus.[44] In echoes of the methods used by the Soviet Union to quell internal dissent, there is constant political surveillance, enemies of the government are interned in state-run Rehabilitation Centres for mind-control experiments, and there are strict penalties for attempts to emigrate or to flee the country.[45] In a visit to New York, Charles Wainwright, General Secretary of the Metalturners' Union, inveighs against conditions in Britain: 'I live in a country where freedom's just a word in a dictionary – like sewage. I live in a sceptred isle surrounded by barbed wire, where a British Parliament of 400 put in by the 20 per cent of the electorate who bother to vote, is a rubber stamp for a faceless Civil Service with the sort of power Genghiz Khan would have envied. I live in a country where, if you don't hold a union card, you starve: where jobs, food and housing are rationed'.[46] The role of key trades union figures in the government show that this is a Labour Party oligarchy, run in tandem with overmighty trades unions. Indeed in a direct reference to the dying days of Harold Wilson's government in the 1970s, the words 'social contract' have passed into everyday language 'as a mild obscenity'.[47] Here the forces of organized Labour are triumphant, able to create a state in which all civil society is subservient to government. In a conversation with the Prime Minister, ex-trades union boss, Dan Mellor, Charles Wainwright seeks to justify his position:

> 'We were the dissenters once, Jim. The lodge banners at the Durham Miners' Gala, the picket lines, the negotiations, the belief. We were both there.'
>
> Mellor hunched largely over his desk. 'And we won. We sit on every company board. We own 40 per cent of Parliament' he asserted forcibly. 'I was a trade union MP myself'.[48]

III

For some authors, the auguries pointed towards the emergence of a trade union state in Britain, dominated by the ethos of strikers, trade union barons and the notion of permanent industrial action. In the fictionalized scenario for British decline painted by Robert Moss, a general strike has reduced Britain to the level of a 'demobilised society' in which all decisions are in the hands of 'The Working People's Government' dominated by the unions. The army has eroded to a level comparable with Iceland, inflation is rampant, nationalization is entrenched, and Britain has become a truncated republic, weakened by the secession of Scotland and Northern Ireland. Under trade union rule, there is rationing and censorship of the press. Following a retreat into protectionism, Britain is a pariah state; the only vibrancy remaining in British culture is located in the dispossessed *émigré* circles of Scotland and the United States.[49] Anthony Burgess took this conceit of a British 'Tucland' and applied it to the imagined 'syndicalist' state he envisaged in his novella *1985*. Drawing on the model provided by Orwell's *1984*, Burgess envisaged a society disfigured by the prevalence of strikes and an institutionalized ethos of striking. At the start of the novel the anti-hero, Bev Jones, experiences the worst aspects of 'Tucland' when a fire in a hospital, ignored by striking firemen, leads to the death of his wife. Thereafter he enters a spiral of decline in which he increasingly opposes the trade union state embodied by 'Bill the Symbolic Worker'.[50] Seeking to break a strike at the local confectionary factory where he works, he falls foul of the closed shop arrangements that underpin life in Tucland.[51] On the run and roaming a twilight world of those eking out a living on the fringes of society, Bev begins to understand the principles that characterize the Tuc state:

> With a socialist state you don't strictly need unions any more. Why not? Because the workers are officially in power, and who do they have to defend themselves against? East European Socialism has no unions, and that's logical. But British syndicalism, once started, has to go on existing. It needs its opposite still. Of course, there are still a few private bosses around, but the State is the main employer. You still have the old dichotomy of employer and employee. The workers have to regard their own political executive not as an aspect of themselves but as an entity they have to oppose. They oppose and the opposition has to give in, because it's not a true opposition. Hence all wage demands are met and inflation flourishes.[52]

1985 expresses many of the themes that are characteristic of Burgess' work. A decline in education, youth deviance and crime, and a general coarsening of society and civic culture are apparent throughout.[53] Very marked in the novel is the decline in civic amenities that became a feature of life in the 1970s: 'Hunger, chaos, thawed mud everywhere, uncollected debris, water pipes bursting, unofficial warnings of tainted water supplies, gas explosions.'[54] In many ways, the book is representative of the fears that emerged about trades unionism in the late 1970s and may be seen as a straw in the wind for the emergence of Thatcherism at the end of the decade.

IV

Much of the popular fiction of the 1970s, however, focused on the new threats posed by politically inspired terrorism. Following the foundation of the New Left in the late 1960s, the traditional forces of organized labour began to break down, encouraging the formation of extra-parliamentary political groupings that saw the Labour Party as merely ameliorating, rather than challenging, the worst excesses of capitalism. Connecting up with the youth movements spawned by the 1960s, the New Left saw possibilities for organization and political activity existing outside mainstream politics in the workplace, in communities and in universities.[55] Some members of the militant wing of the 'new politics' moved into political extremism, embracing the tactics of the peasant fighters that fought against American interventionism in South Vietnam. The figure of the 'urban guerrilla' was a construct of this period, and featured in a number of possible scenarios for paramilitary activity in urban centres.[56] The Red Brigades in Italy and the Baader-Meinhof gang in the German Federal Republic provided a model for Leftism that moved beyond democratic methods to take up arms against the state. In the 1970s, their activities generated fears about an international terrorist underground. Against the background of a number of notorious atrocities, they became the subject matter of a series of lurid paperback exposures of their activities.[57] In Britain, the Angry Brigade bombing campaign of 1970–1 revived nineteenth-century fears of alienated individuals exacting retribution against prominent public figures and governments. Picking targets that ranged from Cabinet ministers to the Biba fashion chain, the Angry Brigade provided the example of a radical splinter group gestated in the ranks of the post-1968 Left that brought direct action methods and tactics to the British mainland.[58] Some sympathetic contemporaries saw the Angry Brigade as a harbinger of a revival of the anarchist terror of the 1880s and 1890s.[59] Rooted in the numerous terrorist cases of the decade, many of the popular fiction novels of the 1970s depicted a soured student radicalism that had splintered and curdled since the optimism and utopianism of the 1960s, and now sanctioned a resort to physical force extremism. Many of the fictional terrorist cells that feature in popular fiction are made up of former student radicals and activists. The roots of Paul Bryers' militant ex-student cell in *Hollow Target* lie in their student experiences:

> They were an unlikely set of companions – hardly to be called friends, since the only interest they shared was revolution. It had started at Cambridge, where Tennant had been a research fellow in higher mathematics, Duggan had been reading political economy and the two Americans were doing post-graduate work. It was all a bit of a game then. The student revolt. Vietnam.

The left-wing ginger groups. Caine often marvelled at their progress since then.[60]

Similarly, John Burmeister's *The Weatherman Guy* also takes place against a background of student radical unrest. Discussing descriptions of a suspected female bomber, Commander David Linnet of the MET and Assistant Commissioner Ian Knock confer:

'God, how nearly we had her!' The assistant commissioner rocked reflectively on the edge of the kerb. 'What motivates a person like this, David? She's beautiful, and obviously highly intelligent. She is used to money and good things. There is no personal gain involved. Yet she has voluntarily chosen to put herself outside the law, which calls for tremendous dedication and fanaticism. Why?'

'I don't understand the revolutionary mind' Linnet said. 'I know what motivates her. She wants to change the world with T.N.T. What I don't understand is how she got like that'.

'Mostly it happens at university'.

'Yes. And then they convey bombs in Jaguars'.[61]

The 1970s provided new targets for such guerrilla cells in popular fiction. New technologies for destruction, expanded international terrorist rings and innovations in British energy production fuelled concerns about Britain's position as a terrorist target. The rapid expansion of the North Sea oil fields in the early part of the decade in particular encouraged fears about the vulnerability of isolated rigs to a terrorist atrocity. In Hammond Innes' *North Star*, a former extremist finds it impossible to escape from his militant past. Hired to patrol an oil rig, the 'North Star', in his trawler, his former comrades exert pressure on him to allow security to drop, exposing the rig to attack. The militants hope for disruption of oil production, a 'wildcat' strike amongst the workforce on the oil platform or, even worse, an oil spillage that will cause a major environmental disaster and discredit the industry.[62] Oil spillages and the resultant pollution drew on fears of a repeat of the Torrey Canyon disaster of 1967 that ruined miles of West Country beaches.[63] The new North Sea oil industry of the 1970s was seen as careless and indifferent to the environmental consequences of its activities. In the novel, Vic Villiers is the acceptable face of hard-nosed entrepreneurial exploitation in this new 'Wild West'. Bringing together the environmental concerns of the 1970s, suspicions of buccaneering capitalism in the North Sea, as well as popular fears about terrorism, the novel envisaged a hardened and ruthless terrorist ring, indifferent to the possible victims of an

Figure 5.1 Anarchist guerrilla manual for the formation of people's militias at the end of the 1970s. Front Cover of *Towards a Citizens' Militia: Anarchist Alternatives to Nato and the Warsaw Pact* (Cienfuegos Publishing, Orkney, 1980) (With the permission of Stuart Christie).

oil spill in the Shetlands.[64] 'Mr. Stevens', leader of the terrorists, with the classic disfigurement of pulp villains, in this case a cast in his eye, tells the hero, Mike Randall, of his plans:

> He was watching me, and now the squint had a strangely menacing quality, so that I had a feeling that it was this slight physical disability – and it was only slight – that had warped him mentally. 'A pay dispute, a halt to operations – that would focus attention on the rig. And if we can involve Villiers directly, so much the better. Then, if the rig drags at the moment they strike oil . . . Then we would have a major environmental disaster and Villiers would be branded as a man intent on making millions by cashing in on oil without any regard to the environment, or to the fishermen who make a living by the sea.'[65]

Paul Bryers uses some elements of this plot device of environmental terrorism in the *Hollow Man*. His terrorists sabotage an oil refinery at Milford Haven and conspire to counter attempts by the oil giant, Plutex, to manipulate domestic politics in Angola. In a bid to escape, his terrorist ring takes an oil tanker hostage, threatening to dump her cargo of oil on the beaches around Torbay. In the book, the threat is depicted as the unacceptable face of militant extremism. The Defence Secretary ruminates:

> There had been a certain amount of sympathy for the extremists from the Left of British politics – engendered no doubt by the extreme measures needed to deal with them. This particular group, if they were who they said they were, had picked a popular target. Their attacks on Plutex had tapped a latent antagonism towards the multinationals – especially the major oil companies who were felt to be milking the country dry. But no idealist could possibly countenance their latest move – an attack on the environment. It was the worst thing they could have done.[66]

V

During this period, popular fiction also speculated about coups, putsches and political challenges from the army and other entrenched sources of authority. Many of these anxieties were fuelled by the overthrow of President Allende's socialist regime by a military coup in Chile in 1973.[67] Stories about the foundation of private armies and political militias abounded during the late 1960s and the mid-1970s. The role of such organizations mirrored the deep sense of public unease about the radicalization of the Labour Party, the emergence of the extreme Left and the spread of trade union militancy, frequently articulated by business leaders and opinion formers. The business mogul, Frederick Robinson, comments in *A Bed of Flowers* Auberon Waugh's satire on the counter-culture of the late 1960s and early 1970s: 'I sometimes think that the businessman is the only person left in our society who is completely sane. He has his priorities worked out, of course. It is a sad prospect for the world . . . if I am right. Somehow, we people in business – and in politics, perhaps – must keep the rest afloat. What is it, do you think, which has suddenly afflicted the whole of our society with insanity?'[68] Rumours circulated around a number of prominent public figures, suggesting their involvement in plots to destabilize civil government and to pave the way for a British military junta. Earl Mountbatten is frequently named as the preferred choice for leader of an interim government. Other rumours saw the right-wing publisher of the *Daily Mirror*, Cecil King, as in league with the security services to destabilize Harold Wilson's 1966 government. In 1968 King held private meetings with Mountbatten in which he talked about national collapse and 'bloodshed in the streets'.[69] The renegade intelligence operative Peter Wright alleged plots by members of MI5 to smear Wilson and his cabinet during the first general election of 1974 with material planted in the press: 'it was a carbon copy of the Zinoviev Letter, which had done so much to destroy the first Ramsay MacDonald government of 1924'.[70] Wilder and more unsubstantiated rumours revealed plans to use the luxury liner, the Queen Elizabeth II, as a place of confinement for the deposed cabinet.[71] Resonances of the political polarities of the 1920s also recur elsewhere. In his account of the Grunwick dispute of 1976–7, Joe Rogaly describes Ross McWhirter's National Association for Freedom as having some of the characteristics of a private militia mobilized to break the strike at the Grunwick Plant. Despite the attempts of the organization to distance itself from 'some of the outer fringe groups that sprang up in 1975 looking very like "private armies"', Rogaly noted eyewitness accounts of 'City types' who came to rescue the mailbags 'the kind whose earlier incarnations so joyously drove buses in the general strike'.[72] A prevalent literature on mercenaries and military adventurers planning coups and insurgencies abroad reflected this apparent militarization of British society and demonstrated a drift away from moderation and the political centre.[73]

Popular fiction was re-energized by these developments. The plot of Peter Van Greenaway's *The Man who Held the Queen to Ransom and Sent Parliament Packing* grew out of this milieu. Published in 1968 at the highpoint of the rumours about attempts to depose Harold Wilson, the novel deals with the benign dictatorship of Captain Wyatt who sets himself up as a military ruler. The novel inveighs against a corrupt establishment, moribund and self-interested politicians and their political parties, the establishment, broadly defined, the court, the civil service and the arrogance of Britain's governing institutions in general.[74] In this, and recalling the celebrated scandals of the 1960s, it is in line with much contemporary popular fiction that traded in images of an empty and morally bankrupt, ruling elite.[75] Wyatt deposes the monarchy, holds the royal family hostage and takes control of parliament with a hand-picked group of followers. His aim is nothing less than a cleansing of existing institutions and a re-negotiation of Britain's wider relationship with her allies. Wyatt's dictatorship provides a populist programme for government. Criminals are displayed naked in zoo cages, inherited peerages are abolished, Britain distances herself from her American allies and steps are taken to topple Ian Smith's white minority regime in Rhodesia. Sensing his tenuous grip on power, he prepares for a counter-coup from the forces of reaction he despises: 'We don't need to worry about the corridors of power – corridors are for the couriers, the satellites, minions, and twopenny mandarins. The men who matter, our real opponents, are elsewhere, cliques in club-rooms and discreet gatherings in country houses – an "old boy" network in gilded sewers'.[76] Overthrown, Wyatt's aborted coup and well-intentioned attempt to arrest national decline paves the way for a restoration of the monarchy and an authoritarian government of the political right.[77] The MP Chris Mullin's novel, *A Very British Coup*, pursued this theme of counter-revolution into the early 1980s. Mullin wrote the novel at a time of the emergence of the extreme Left and during a phase of Trotskyite 'entryism' into the Labour Party, to illustrate the impotence of a programmatically left-wing government in the face of the forces of conservatism within the establishment.[78] In his vision of the future, a radical left-wing Labour government, under the former steel-worker Harold Perkins, is swept to power with a mandate for nuclear disarmament. Forces hostile to the government, including press barons, senior civil servants, the American government and the security services, rapidly mobilize to undermine the ministry. The Prime Minister recognizes his enemies and the fragility of his position. He greets his election victory cautiously with the words:

> All we have won tonight is political power. By itself that is not enough. Real power in this country resides not in parliament, but in the boardrooms of the City of London; in the darkest recesses of the Whitehall bureaucracy and in the editorial offices of our national newspapers. To win real power we have first to break the stranglehold exerted by the ruling class on all the important institutions of our country.[79]

At the conclusion of the novel, a mixture of political scandal, diplomatic pressure, intrusive investigations by the media and intervention by the intelligence community forces Perkins from office. The coup of the title is a bloodless one,

Figure 5.2 Racial violence in London in the late 1970s added to the fear of violence and social breakdown. Front cover, *Blood on the Streets* (Bethnal Green and Stepney Trades Council, 1978) (Author's Collection).

in which the entrenched forces of the British establishment reassert their control. As the chief conspirator, Sir Peregrine Craddock comments at the end of the novel: ' "there had been no tanks in the street. No one had gone to the firing squad. Apart from the odd demonstrator on the receiving end of a police baton, no one had even been injured." In fact, he said with a wan smile "It had been a very British coup" '.[80]

VI

London provided the arena for most of the terrorist outrages of the 1970s. Images of London as a city in the throes of post-imperial malaise recur in such literature. Seedy and in decline, the London described in both popular and mainstream fiction was a demoralized city on the brink of disintegration. Margaret Drabble in *The Ice Age* wrote of the crowds in St Pancras Station exuding 'a fear and sadness': 'old ladies with bags, a black man with a brush and bin, pallid girls in jeans, an Indian with a tea trolley, a big fat man with a carrier bag, they all looked around themselves shiftily, uneasily, eyeing abandoned packages, kicking dirty blowing plastic bags from their ankles, expecting explosions.'[81] Kramer, the instigator and 'inside man' of the terrorist conspiracy against Plutex Oil in *Hollow Target*, expressed the weariness many contemporaries felt about the capital following its decline from its hey-day as 'Swinging London': 'Kramer had grown tired of the mindless chore of being a charmer. Tired of London which was no longer the swinging city of the sixties. All the best people had gone. Heading for the next fashionable hot spot. London, and indeed the whole of England was on the scrapheap. It reminded him of Eastern Europe. Creeping socialism, high taxes, austerity, cold porridge and power cuts.'[82] The London of the 1970s was again a place of confrontation and disorder. Fictional terrorism in London placed the capital on alert, increasing its resemblance to a European City under threat. In Bryers' *Hollow Target*, the scale of the police manhunt for a terrorist cell makes the city 'more like Paris during the Algerian emergency than the London Havelock knew'.[83] Ceremonial and diplomatic London was often the scene for fictional clashes between demonstrators and the police based on some of the civil disorders instigated by anti-Vietnam War protestors outside the American Embassy in Grosvenor Square in 1968.[84] Peter Van Greenaway's *The Man Who Held the Queen to Ransom and Sent Parliament Packing* juxtaposes images of armed soldiers and military men alongside traditional images of the Palace of Westminster as a sanctuary of democracy in order to convey the shock of a military coup in the capital.[85] This was a turbulent London, in thrall to the mob and the unruly young. In John Burmeister's *The Weatherman Guy*, both the extreme left and the extreme right seek to manipulate a demonstration in Grosvenor Square for their own ends. Attempting to provoke anarchy in the heart of London both the youthful mob and the police are incited to further violence by *agents provocateurs* and a bomb explosion in the crowd:

> There is a limit to the restraint imposed by discipline and training. Those [police] nearest the North Audley Street corner, seeing some of their number

knocked off their feet by the force of the blast presumed that they were about to be massacred. For those further away the effect was more confusing and probably worse. In any event, the long line of blue-clad men reacted as the revolutionary text-books tell you they will do. Pressed beyond the point of further control, they over-reacted. As one the police leapt after the churning, retreating mob, their truncheons swinging in vicious unison.[86]

The volatility and uncertainty of popular crowd politics in London is a marked theme throughout such literature. In Van Greenaway's account of a British coup, crowds of sightseers gather in Parliament Square to see events unfold for themselves, much to the consternation of the police. His book captures the sense of national paralysis as government is suspended and ironically subverts iconic images of London itself: 'The police, uncertain of their role in the changing circumstances, lacking precise orders from above, stayed passively alert. They found it beyond their powers to gauge the general mood of the people, and if the news of revolt was more than rumour, if the sudden crowds were on their way to a popular rising, buses might well turn into tumbrels and heads, their heads, could be among the first to be paraded down the Strand on the sharp end of a businessman's furled umbrella'.[87] With specific reference back to the anarchist fiction of the 1890s, London during this period was a place of danger, terrorist cells, and dark, dangerous and insurgent forces. The metropolis of the 1970s provided camouflage and a cover for militant terrorist groups. Radicals and militants were able to conceal themselves within its immensity. Chief Inspector Desmond Havelock in *Hollow Target* cynically surveys the anonymous commuter crowds of the city that he sees as cloaking their activities: 'Anonymity was the name of the game. The key weapon in a war that had moved out into the streets, to become almost an accepted fact of urban life. Something that you took in your stride, like the shopping. Yet the police and guerrillas were stalking each other in this fish tank of concrete and glass, often not knowing each other when they met, for the killer fish looked the same as the most innocent tiddlers'.[88]

Popular fiction saw these terrorist cells emerging from the counter-cultural networks of alternative London. Moral panics demonized the inhabitants of the communes, squats and radical bookshops that some believed furnished the infrastructure of terrorism. Squatters haunt the imagination of Anthony Keating, the troubled metropolian property speculator in Margaret Drabble's *The Ice Age*.[89] Keating's fantasies roam across a historical landscape inhabited by the seventeenth century Diggers, free housing, and charities like Shelter working for the homeless.[90] In 1974, London was home to nearly 30,000 squatters whose spaces of communal living were frequently depicted as places in which terrorism was incubated. In his fictionalized re-creation of the British revolutionary underground in the 1970s, Hari Kunzru describes Notting Hill as 'a couple of square miles of rotten ghetto housing cut through by a half-built flyover, but it supported a ramshackle counter-culture made up of hundreds of cliques and groups and communes, little magazines, support groups, co-ops, bands', it was 'an anti-city of bed-sitters and bookshops, rehearsal rooms and cramped offices'.[91] Something of this squatting issue lingers in *The Man Who Held the Queen to Ransom* in which London's poor, indigent and homeless are moved into the royal palaces vacated by the queen.[92] Communes with their distrust of family life, alternative moralities and connection with the drug underground revived popular fears about free love and their anarchist inclined inhabitants.[93] This was the 'lifestyle politics' that gave form to many of the 'DiY' 'avoidance' cultures of the 1980s and 1990s.[94] Some of these preoccupations spilled over into more conventional literature. Doris Lessing's *The Good Terrorist* charts the activities of a group of egotistical, self-absorbed and naïve inhabitants of a London commune who find themselves drawn into an IRA bomb plot. The commune's members are shallow and hopelessly idealistic, holding over-inflated views of their own importance. The mother of the house, Alice, speculates about the significance of her own squat within the revolutionary network: 'everywhere in fact was this network, and even in little unimportant places like these two houses, Nos 43 and 45, just ordinary squats and communes. Nothing was too small to be overlooked, everyone with any sort of potential was noticed, observed, treasured . . . It gave her a safe, comfortable feeling'.[95] Auberon Waugh was less impressed by the danger posed by communes and squats. He dismissed them derisively as places of pretension and eccentricity. In his *Bed of Flowers*, a West Country commune attracts eccentrics, drop-outs, drug addicts and seekers after the Holy Grail. John Robinson, the wealthy patron of the Somerset commune, comments pretentiously: 'Don't compare us to a kibbutz so much as to one of those monasteries which helped to keep the Christian faith and also the benefits of Greek and Roman civilisation alive throughout the Dark Ages, while barbarian hordes roamed at will over the face of the earth'.[96]

VII

The public mood of the 1970s was coarsened by the reality of terrorist outrages on the British mainland. For the IRA, one successful bomb in London drew far more attention to the cause than numerous acts of terrorism in Northern Ireland. In the 1970s IRA terrorism became part of the accepted background noise to politics. Margaret Drabble's *The Ice Age* begins with the account of an IRA bomb blast in a Mayfair restaurant that kills one character, and maims a second.[97] In Paul Bryers' *Hollow Target*, old headlines on a newsstand show an indifferent acceptance of bomb outrages: '"Big Arms Find" – "Bomb Victim Dies" – the old headlines continued to scream, unnoticed. Unremarkable news even when it was fresh'.[98] IRA bombing campaigns in London and the governmental response to the situation in Northern Ireland conjured up images of a society slipping steadily out of control. Counter-measures by the state in the form of internment and the H-Blocks fed the notion that the weak governments of the period were prepared to consider extreme measures in domestic politics. The reality of IRA pub bombings, and negative images of Irish republicanism mediated through a condemnatory media, meant that that there were far fewer imagined scenarios in popular literature of Irish terrorist activity in Britain's towns and cities. The fiction of the period that dealt with Irish republicanism tended to confine itself to tales of intrigue, honour killings, militant loyalism and counter-insurgency in Belfast or in Derry.[99] Where republican terrorism did feature, it usually implied an incremental slide into anarchy and disorder.[100] In Hammond Innes' *North Star*, repeated references to the Troubles demonstrate the severity of the menace posed by an extremist left with strong links to the situation in Ulster. Confronted by his ex-wife, Fiona, who is still involved in terrorist circles, the apostate militant Mike Randall is appalled by her verdict on the use of physical force: 'You must understand Mike, it's like Ireland. Nobody listens to reason unless you make them. Stormont, the "B" Specials, all the everlasting persecution of Catholics . . . Nobody likes bombs, but without bombs nothing would have changed'.[101] A number of authors suggested a link between the various forces of international terrorism. In such books, a united front promoting revolutionary activity with strong international links in the Middle East and North America is implied. In most pulp treatments of the situation in Northern Ireland, the context of the troubles is seen as a form of nursery, incubating and training fanatical terrorists with little regard for the rule of law. Terrorists schooled in the politics of Northern Irish sectarianism occupy walk-on parts in much of the popular fiction of the period. Duggan in *Hollow Target* is a veteran of all the major political protests of the late 1960s and early 1970s, graduating from the '*eventments*' in Paris in 1968, through the Grosvenor Square protests to the Civil Rights agitation in Northern Ireland:

> He had been in the Bogside when the B Specials charged the barricades and the students of People's Democracy who later became the Provo zealots, hurled petrol bombs down from the new tower blocks. He had been there when the British army arrived as friends and stayed as enemies. He had been with Joe McCann in the Markets area of Belfast, hiding from the army and organising the Official IRA in the city until Joe the Pastrycook was gunned down by a para patrol at the back of the City Hall.[102]

A veteran of violence, it is Duggan who finally blows up the oil tanker at the end of the novel. Where they are depicted at all, Irish Republicans are usually represented as little better than gangsters. Vicious, uncaring and inured to pain and suffering, they live in a twilight world of betrayal and personal vendettas. The IRA conspiracy in *The Tunnel* grows out of a schism within the movement and a struggle to topple the old leadership. An extremist splinter group, led by the ambitious Jamie Quinn, seeks to make a bid for leadership of the Provos through a daring and audacious bomb conspiracy that will show up the timidity of the Army Council. Here the image of the megalomaniac bomber and lone fanatic that has a long provenance within such fiction is revived: 'Quinn wasn't listening. He was telling himself that the reason the Irish revolution had accomplished so little was that its leadership lacked imagination. Men too small to think big. Men who didn't know how to get headlines and influence world opinion. He would show them. In one grand move he, James L. Quinn, would erase fifty years of IRA futility'.[103] In *The Tunnel*, most of these traditional images of violent and fanatical IRA men are apparent. The IRA gunmen are fratricidal and untrustworthy, indifferent to bonds of loyalty. Quinn speculates about ditching members of his dysfunctional team once the job is completed: 'When the crisis came Eagan was likely to be in a pub singing Irish songs about the Easter Rising of 1916. He was tough and fearless, yes, but not a man you would trust with your life if you had any choice. Quinn wondered if he might be better off leaving Eagan behind when the rough stuff was over, to simplify the escape. There were a thousand like him in Belfast'.[104] In many of these novels, there is a sense that the mere act of conspiracy, rather than any definable outcome, is the end in itself. This confirmed the belief as the 1970s progressed that the Irish republican movement had lost its way in a maze of violence from which it was unable to extricate itself. In Paul Theroux's *London Arsenal*, an updating of Henry James's novel about anarchism *The Princess Casamassima* to South London in the early 1970s, the Irish republican terrorists are inveterate plotters, fixated on conspiracy and comparable to dependant drug addicts: 'Their opiates were plans, plots, counterplots, circular stratagems, this drugged sentry duty to which they attached importance. Threat and plot replaced action, the motions of militant bureaucracy blinded them to the fact they had no power. But they were satisfied with the self-flattery of their secrets, like addicts sucking a pipe of smoking promises'.[105]

For most popular fiction writers, the strengthening of support for Celtic nationalist parties in Scotland and Wales opened up possibilities for another Northern Ireland on the British mainland. Terrorism and physical force violence in Wales surrounding the Investiture of the Prince of Wales in 1969 predated bombing campaigns by the IRA on the British mainland in the 1970s. Richard Weight argues that the campaign for autonomy in Wales in the

1960s and 1970s had more in common with the situation in Northern Ireland than the more high-profile agitation surrounding Scottish separatism.[106] The revival of the Scottish National Party and Plaid Cymru in the late 1960s and campaigns for devolution in the 1970s implied a splintering of British identity, and the collapse of national government.[107] Pan-Celticist fantasies and images of a militant Welsh nationalism are depicted in John Summers' semi-autobiographical novel, *The Disaster*, which includes a description of a raid by extremists on a water pipeline taking water from Welsh reservoirs to Birmingham, and a sketch of the headquarters of the extremist Free Wales Army:

> A large Red Dragon of Wales flag was flapping in the fierce breeze where it was hitched forty feet high on a tree with lopped branches and slapped with whitewash to make it a flagpole. Outside in the drive, and before the big oak double doors of his mansion house, Lt Col Sir Owen Tudor and some violently vivid farmers in green uniforms were being interviewed by newspapermen . . . *'Oh, bydded yr hen iath parhau'* said Sir Cenlais Owen Tudor. 'And that means, we will be fighting for the preservation of our language and our ancient land. We'll be prepared to make martyrs of ourselves if necessary – die for the sake of Wales . . . save the nation from extinction.'[108]

Fantastical suspicions about the IRA working in tandem with militant Celtic cells in Britain were a feature of the period. They occur in *Merlin's Web* by the Canadian author, Susan Mayse, published in the 1980s, but preserving many of the popular panics of the 1970s intact. Here the Provos mount a diversion whilst Welsh nationalists kidnap Pip, the heir to the throne. Hard-bitten newsman Peter Holt muses: 'The Provisional IRA had already taken responsibility for the car bomb that had devastated Grosvenor Square. Provos co-operating with the Welsh? It was definitely an escalation from their occasional pan-Celtic fantasies. Police were rounding up all London's known Welsh nationalists for questioning. Peter heard the reports. Believing them was another matter.'[109] Groups like the Free Wales Army, which gained notoriety in the late 1960s, provide the inspiration for the militants in Mayse's *Merlin's Web*. Pip's nanny, Jean Douglass, kidnapped with the heir to the throne, demands to know the aims of the Welsh extremists: ' "Self-government for the Nation of Cymru" Gwyn said. He seemed to have said this several thousand times. "A fraction of the English profits taken from our coal valleys and slate quarries, to do something about unemployment and industry. A Welsh television channel" '.[110] As with similar depictions of Northern Irish militancy, the book echoes contemporary fears about a fused international paramilitary platform, with links to Colonel Gaddafi in Libya, Euskadi Ta Askatasuna (ETA), the Palestine Liberation Organization (PLO), Breton extremists and the Red Brigades that could bring terrorist bombing campaigns to Welsh seaside resorts.[111]

In Scotland in particular, there was a long tradition of novels that speculated about a Scottish struggle for freedom and independence. These were indicative of the post-war popularity of the Scottish National Party, which returned its first MP in 1945. Much of this literature reflected the emergence of young nationalist groups that flirted with civil disobedience in the early 1950s.[112] Nigel Tranter's *The Freebooters* imagined a group of young militants taking to the heather and dedicating themselves to the cause of an independent Scotland. Through a number of daring escapades that involve rustling cattle to feed the people of Glasgow and aiding impoverished crofters, the group re-ignite a debate about Scottish nationhood. By the end of the novel, the country has found its pride again. The model for their actions is the celebrated Highland outlaw Rob Roy Macgregor. In the early stages of the campaign, the group finds its natural leader in the form of a distant descendant of the outlaw, Roderick Macgregor. Adrian Hope, the instigator of the group, inspires Roderick to act with the words: 'In time, he could set this country into a ferment such as it hasn't been in since the 'Forty-Five. But first he'd have to set the heather on fire – like Rob Roy did. He wouldn't have to ambush troops, and levy blackmail, and set men to burning each other's houses, but he *would* have to defy authority, and what's worse, the cramping, weary inertia of an over-governed, official-ridden, spirit-stifled people'.[113] Tranter's novel gave inspiration to later fiction about militancy in the cause of Scottish independence, and, in one brief casual reference, is widely credited with inspiring the idea for the theft of the Stone of Scone by Scottish militants in 1950.[114] Thereafter fictional accounts of Scottish national revival moved away from romanticized representations of the Scottish past to consider the role of the Scottish urban guerrilla, on the model of the IRA. In Douglas Hurd and Andrew Osmond's *Scotch on the Rocks*, a Scottish Liberation Army emerges against the background of a constitutional crisis in Scotland. Uniting Glasgow razor gangs, with traditional campaigners for the Gaelic language, Clydeside socialists and paramilitaries, the SLA commits bomb atrocities, blows up the statue of Queen Victoria and the Prince Consort in Glasgow, and takes control of Fort William in the Highlands.[115] In high-level cabinet meetings, Richard Anstruther, Chief of Defence staff, outlines the SLA's strategy based on guerrilla tactics borrowed from the Vietcong: 'You see, Prime Minister, they've now moved into what we call the Second Phase of Insurrection . . . In the First Phase you operate from the mountains using secret headquarters; holding territory is not important, and you avoid towns. But in the Second Phase you seize a town, in this case, Fort William, and use it as a base to dominate quickly as much territory as you can, at the same time mounting your maximum political effort. The Third phase is of course the capture of the main cities'.[116]

VIII

A legacy of the 1960s, the decade of the 1970s was also characterized by the emergence of new social forces that threatened the status quo on gender issues. Many of the popular novels of the period expressed unease about the potential threats posed by the new wave feminist movement of the early years of the decade. Visions of a society in which the 'normal' gender hierarchies were inverted by dominant women who exercised control over feminized and feeble men was nothing new. In the nineteenth century, the campaign for female enfranchisement had provoked an answering literature that imagined reversed gender roles and evoked fears of 'petticoat rule'. Such notions emerged from the popular fears surrounding the establishment of pressure groups for female enfranchisement. Walter Besant's *The Revolt of Men* described a society ruled entirely by women, but highlighted the drawbacks provided by female rule and the contrasting advantages and benefits of the benevolent paternalism of males.[117] Visions of the potential power and strength wielded by women took on a new urgency in the middle years of the twentieth century. Often presented in somewhat comic vein, there was, nevertheless, a greater consideration given to the potential role of women in the public sphere. Eric Linklater's *The Impregnable Women*, for example, showed women in revolt against a destructive and unnecessary war between Britain and France, and taking a key role in bringing the conflict to an end.[118] Most popular fiction in the 1970s, however, emphasized the drawbacks rather than positive aspects to the emergence of movements dedicated to the rights of women.[119] Particular targets of the novel are the 'strident' feminist leaders of the 1970s who were much reviled in the popular press of the period.[120] All this genre of novels feature self-aggrandising feminist leaders with unconcealed designs on power and influence. Pamela Kettle's *The Day of the Women* imagined the circumstances in which a Women's Party christened 'Impulse' gains power and establishes a stranglehold on Britain's democracy. Its ambitious leader, Diana Druce, aims initially to redress gender inequalities, to galvanize the female vote and to feminize government and society. She declares at a rally during an imaginary general election in 1974: 'Governments are manmade because many women are too lazy to use their vote. Others vote under the influence of husbands, or even current boy-friends. In this way our sex has opted out of the responsibility of the franchise. We have left it to men to make the government of our country and they have made it in their own image, not yours, not mine'.[121] Thereafter, following its victory at the polls, there is a steady descent into extremism. In keeping with much of the dystopic fiction of the decade, 'Impulse' has many of the characteristics of a prototype Fascist Party. Druce seeks to relegate men to a subordinate role in British society. Those who dislike the new order are required to leave the country, women are placed in key management jobs and 'The Mother' nurtures other female-orientated parties abroad to create an international female-dominated power bloc. With the movement's uniforms, salutes, and Druce's paranoia, love of astrology and pure breeding experiments she is clearly a feminist Hitler, and the movement she leads is aptly described as 'high-heeled Fascism'.[122] The novel concludes with a Nazi-style rally addressed by Druce from the balcony of Buckingham Palace, which has been vacated by the royal family, now resident abroad: 'Diana stood on the balcony of Buckingham Palace and looked down at the crowd, which pressed up to the very walls of the building, cramming the forecourt within the railings and stretching away down the Mall and in every direction as far as the eye could see. Yet there was no confusion. The ranks of women were orderly. Even their cheering was rhythmic, like a pulse on the still summer air'.[123] Similar stereotypes recur in other contemporary anti-feminist fiction of the 1970s. A female demagogue also features in W.I.T.C.H, an account of the emergence of a militant feminist party that resorts to terrorism to achieve its ends. Led by the redoubtable American Feminist, Ophelia Stanway, the group's avowed aim (and the Source of the acronym of its title) is: 'We Intend To Create Havoc'. The book written by Terry Harknett (better known as the Western writer, George G. Gilman) evokes many of the traditional fears of an inverted carnivalesque world in which women ogle men at strip-clubs, roving feminists castrate men and feminist biker gangs raid seaside resorts on the South Coast.[124] It draws on many of the popular moral panics of the period about feminism and reduces the movement to a series of stereotypes. At the conclusion of the novel, common sense prevails, and the ordinary women of England revolt to put an end to Feminist-inspired anarchy.[125] An apostate member of W.I.T.C.H, Daphne Mainwaring, leads the counter-revolution with the words: 'I am no longer associated with the movement and in almost every respect I am sorry and ashamed of ever having been connected with it. What I am not sorry and ashamed about is having proved the power of women . . . Not your sort of power. Not the power of the mob to hate and lust and run wild in the streets. But the power of these marvellous women behind me. Women who have done what no men could have – stop you'.[126]

The volatility and instability of the 1970s is mirrored in the political fiction produced during the decade. The narrative of the period was one in which traditional institutions apparently calcified, and political energies migrated to the extremes. In a decade dominated by talk of crisis, it is unsurprising that there is an apocalyptic feel to much of this writing. The idea of a Britain toppled from her former greatness and losing her position and role in the wider world is very marked here. The pulp novels of the period reflected Britain's perceived loss of direction, and the sense that political leadership itself was morally bankrupt. 'I am not mad' raves the right-wing occultist Edward Gant in James Herbert's *The Spear*, 'it's the leaders of this country who are mad, allowing it to sink to these depths'.[127] Such notions fed into the belief that the post-war welfare consensus was played out and that the direction taken by Britain needed recalibration. In many ways the popular fiction of these years demonstrated the unease and anxieties of its readership. Buffeted by strikes, let down by their leaders, struggling with a rising cost of living, and left diminished and ashamed by the break-up of empire, pulp fiction provided the perfect fodder for their fears. Unsurprisingly, Margaret Thatcher was a great devotee of such fiction, declaring her enthusiasm for Frederick Forsyth (which she liked to re-read) and 'books about the horrors of Marxism'. Such material struck the correct populist note for a contemporary Conservative.[128] Thatcherism's role as the faith of the lower middle-class is strongly informed by the images of decay, defeat and destruction that recurred in such fiction. In this sense, the pulp literature of the period may best be seen as a seed-bed and harbinger of Thatcherism itself. For Conservatives, such works drew an image of the country stalled on the edge of a precipice, and urgently in need of rescue. Given the tensions of the period, it is unsurprising that such books mirrored the lurch towards political Conservatism at the end of the decade of the 1970s.

Chapter 6

Post 9/11: Radical Islamism in Recent Metropolitan Fiction

'A lot of noise. A lot of wild movement. The neat rows of domed umbrellas suddenly breaking apart as their owners struggled to escape. Some of the umbrellas being whipped by the winds and shooting free like parachutes into the air. Others getting their sharp spokes entangled in clothes and flesh. The nearer crowds retreating in fear, the further ones being sucked inwards by curiosity. Collision. Confusion. Panic. For a second Danny Boyce was the centre of London.'[1]

'The way they live in the shadows, live willingly with death. The way they hate many of the things you hate. Their discipline and cunning. The coherence of their lives. The way they excite, they *excite* admiration. In societies reduced to blur and glut, terror is the only meaningful act.'[2]

The 9/11 attack on New York changed the frame of reference for terrorism. From a fantastical possibility dealt with only in speculative fiction, terrorist attacks on first world urban centres became a reality that superseded the hitherto imaginative possibilities of popular literature. In the United States in particular, the events of 9/11 connected up with imagined destructions of New York, derived from the popular anxieties of the Cold War period and commonly expressed both in film and in pulp writing.[3] In the days after the attack, commentators discussed the gap between reality and imagination that coloured many responses to the destruction of the Twin Towers. The record of the events of 9/11 was often mediated through this gap between fictional imaginings and the reality of the experience. There was a persistent dream-like quality to this event. Numerous witnesses who saw the planes crash live into the World Trade Center on television commented that it seemed unreal, like a sequence from an action film. Thereafter, with the scale of the experience often too difficult to face, some of the most imaginative attempts to make sense of 9/11 occurred in fictions that were grounded in the events of that day. In writing that combined the themes of a loss of innocence and images of the apocalypse, a number of imagined futures, informed by the collapse of the Twin Towers, were played out in bleak, blasted and pessimistic dystopias.[4]

In Cormac McCarthy's *The Road*, which explored the sufferings of survivors from an environmental disaster, the cities of North America were depicted as places of confusion, panic, urban destruction and social disintegration 'held by cores of blackened looters who tunnelled through the ruins and crawled from the rubble white of tooth and eye carrying charred and anonymous tins of food in nylon nets like shoppers in the commissaries of hell'.[5] Rather than diminishing the relevance of fictional representations of urban destruction, therefore, the events of 9/11 created fresh possibilities for a literature that brought together themes of terrorism, external threat, destruction of the metropolis and conspiracies of the disaffected. Both in Britain and the United States, a 'literature of terror' has flourished in the first decade of the twenty-first century that considers the threat posed by Islamist extremism and examines the possibilities and opportunities for further terrorist strikes. The remainder of this chapter considers these themes against the backdrop of anxieties about the imminence of a terrorist threat against London.

I

The potent image of 9/11 cast a long shadow that hung over representations of subsequent terrorist attacks in London and elsewhere. The Madrid bombings of 2004 and a premeditated explosion by suicide bombers on the London underground in July 2005 evoked inevitable comparisons with the attacks on New York. Responses to the 7/7 attacks on the London underground echoed many of the fears and anxieties expressed in the aftermath of 9/11.[6] In both the United States and in Britain, a close relationship emerged between the writers of fiction and the events of 7/7 itself. In the United States in particular, a literature developed amongst established writers that, in a long tradition, saw terrorism as a product of the rejection of American values and culture, and a reaction against the enhanced world role of the United States following the collapse of the Soviet Union. The views of Sayyid Qutb, inspiration for the Muslim Brotherhood and highpriest of the modern Islamic revivalist movement, who formed many of his opinions during a long stay in the United States in the 1940s, was seen as central to this outlook.[7] John Updike in particular represented the origins of domestic Islamist movements in an exhaustion of American values, economic retreat and a collapse of the American dream. Ahmad Ashmawy, the disaffected teenager in his novel, *The Terrorist* is in revolt against the superficiality of American popular culture:

> He had taken to searching television for traces of God in this infidel society. He watches beauty pageants where luminous-skinned and white-toothed

girls, along with one or two token entrants of color, compete in charming the master of ceremonies with their singing or dancing talents and their frequent if hasty expressions of gratitude to the Lord for their blessings, which they intend to devote, when their singing days in bathing suits are done, to their fellow-man in the form of such lofty vocations as doctor, educator, agronomist, or, holiest calling of all, homemaker.[8]

Others volumes of this nature explored the internal conflict of Muslims working or resident in the United States and their ambivalent relationship with American financial institutions and values.[9] For most writers in the United States, explorations of domestic Muslim identity focussed on their embrace or rejection of Americanism. In Britain, by contrast, the key themes in such fictions are about the origins of British Islamism, and its receptivity to more violent and extreme ideas about an Islamic revival in the broader Muslim and secular Middle Eastern world. Here Islamism provided a reformist gateway for the import of terrorist creeds into Britain.[10] Many of these violent cults in a number of assessments were felt to bear comparison with other movements of violent political dissent in the British political past.

In most popular fiction, Islamist terrorism filled the gap left by the beginning of the Irish peace process in the 1990s and the suspension of attacks by the Irish Republican Army (IRA) on targets in London and the British mainland. Many fictional accounts of IRA operations now dealt with the consequences of the peace process for former republican militants and the compromises that turned comrade against comrade, and undermined the will to continue bombing campaigns towards the aim of a united Ireland. Tensions and betrayal between former comrades colour much of this fiction. Riven by informers, turn-coats and personal animosities, the IRA cells of this late phase in the history of fictional terrorism about the armed struggle in Ireland were ineffective and rapidly suborned. In James Kennedy's *Armed and Dangerous*, a group of IRA escapees are hunted down both by the security forces and IRA commanders loyal to the ceasefire. Intent on destroying the control tower of the Thames Barrier during a high tide in order to flood London, the group is gradually whittled down by its own internal animosities, internecine hatreds and lack of enthusiasm for continuing violence. The IRA militant fanatic, McDiad, who plans the attack represents the unrepentant, unreformed wing of Irish militancy, impervious to negotiation and compromise: 'To argue is to lose strength he told himself. Discussion and dialogue are weakness. Nobody fears you when they only have to listen to you. Open your mouth and you eventually talk yourself into a ceasefire.'[11] Shot down whilst unsuccessfully attempting to arm his explosive device, McDiad symbolizes the fruitless impotence of continuing terrorist violence during a period of peaceful political progress and constitutional reform in Northern Ireland.

With the threat from Irish republican terrorism blunted, London gained a central place in the arguments about Islamic extremism in Britain. In most popular fiction, the city acted as a target, the home of extremist terrorist cells or as a point of counter-operations against Islamic militancy. Some novels drew strongly on the notion of a tourist trail London, where visitor attractions and well-known local landmarks became targets of attack, amid scenes of mayhem and violence. In Don Delillo's novel *Mao II*, about a reclusive novelist's engagement with terrorism, London is 'a dream locus', expressing 'a doubleness, that famous places share, making them seem remote and unreceptive, but at the same time, intimately familiar, an experience you've been carrying forever'.[12] A number of fictions saw London as one stop amongst many international locations that helped emphasize the fast-moving and cosmopolitan nature of the plot lines unfolding in the book. Some specialize in a deep understanding of the geography and topography of the city to add authenticity to the situations developed in the plot. In Daniel Silva's *The Secret Servant*, dealing with the kidnap of the US ambassador's daughter by Islamic militants, the terrain of the kidnap in Hyde Park during a routine jog with embassy bodyguards is plotted precisely:

They had entered the park through Brook Gate, headed south along Broad Walk to Hyde Park Corner, then westward along Rotten Row, past the Rose Garden and the Dell. Elizabeth Halton moved to the front of the park when they reached the Albert Memorial; then, with a DS at her side, she steadily increased the pace as they headed north up Lancaster Walk to Bayswater Road. Jack Hammond, the embassy spokesman, slipped past Elizabeth, and pushed the pace hard to Victoria Gate, then down the West Carriage Drive to the shore of the Serpentine.[13]

Others depict the statuery, street furniture and monuments of ceremonial London under threat. Colin Forbes in his novel *The Cell*, about an al-Qaeda attack on the commuter bridges across the Thames, depicts a pitched battle between SAS operatives and terrorists around the monumental sculpture of the Embankment. Here the attack by terrorists is represented as an attack on the deep history of the city itself and the very traditions of the British state: 'Beaurain was crouched behind the statue, which loomed above them. For the first time, Paula wondered who had merited the honour of the stone figure on horseback. Some general who had commanded in some long-ago war. Now he was hardly noticed. Pass beyond your time and you became a footnote in history'.[14] Social and cultural life in the city is often seen as one potential casualty of a terrorist strike. Chris Cleave in his book, *Incendiary*, written on the eve of the 7/7 attacks on the capital, feared the consequences of a terrorist attack in London on the everyday life of the city. In the aftermath of his fictional attack on Wembley Stadium, London turns in on itself. The security services impose curfews, cultural life is abandoned and the city becomes an armed camp: 'First they stopped boats using the river. All those boat buses, and disco ships and sightseeing barges. Well they just stopped them. They did it so you couldn't blow up the Houses of Parliament, Osama. With some horrible floating disco full of Semtex and Dexy's Midnight Runners. They drained the life out of the river till it was just an empty vein with police boats drifting up and down it like white blood cells.'[15]

In contrast to the popular fiction of the late 1980s and 1990s, which tended to depict Muslim incomers as the innocent victims of the extreme right and of delinquent white youth gangs, popular fiction now places the Muslim Islamist at centre stage, seeing this figure as one that channels the anxieties and popular fears of the post 9/11 years.[16] Depictions of terrorism in British popular fiction gained a renewed momentum from 7/7. Following the arguments of Don Delillo in *Mao II*, written during the period of a number of prominent hostage situations in Beirut at the beginning of the 1990s, this literature reflects a future in which the terrorist has established a strong presence in popular culture. His novelist anti-hero, Bill Gray, comments: 'Years ago I used to think that it was possible for a novelist to alter the inner life of the culture. Now bombmakers and gunmen have taken that territory. They make raids on human consciousness.'[17] Trying to make sense of the experience of radical 'Islamist terrorism', numerous studies have emphasized the affinities between Islamic militants and previous movements that had posed a threat to British constitutional liberties. Drawing on the established traditions of popular fiction and the thriller genre, a favourite point of comparison is with the anarchist agitators and bombers who clustered in London and were objects of popular alarm at the end of the nineteenth century. Nineteenth-century anarchism offered an apparent template for organizations like al-Qaida in which 'propaganda by deed', and fears of highly advanced (and sometimes nuclear) terrorist weaponry created a climate of fear that fomented a backlash against those wrongly suspected of sympathy with militants.[18] As in the nineteenth century, 'moral panics' about terrorism dominated a sensationalist news media and provided the rationale for secret conferences of world leaders and specialist units dedicated to a 'War Against Terror'. In the aftermath of the Cold War, there was a pronounced move away from the ready acceptance of refugees as emblems of the openness and economic success of the West, towards a vision of the Islamic community as unreliable strangers, retaining outside links and loyalties.[19] Echoing the popular fears of the 1900s, Britain's benign tradition of receiving political and economic exiles was represented as a vulnerability, opening up the country to penetration by extra-European militants seeking refuge behind its comparatively open borders. These preoccupations have fomented fears that London is a natural magnet and target for Islamic extremists, in a series of panics and media *exposés* around London depicted as 'Londinistan'.[20]

II

Like anarchism, in many accounts, radical Islamism appears a fanatical and intolerant creed that breeds merciless and steely eyed enemies of society. Affinities and overlaps with this older tradition of anarchist atrocities in London are frequently noted in the media and by academics. An anarchist bomb attack on the underground in 1896, an attempt to blow up Greenwich Observatory in 1894 and the Siege of Sidney Street in 1911 in which the police and troops exchanged fire with East European anarchists besieged in an East End tenement, have all been all cited as precedents and models for the new terrorist wave of the early twenty-first century.[21] As writers like James Gelvin have demonstrated, Islamist extremism replicates key characteristics of anarchism that in some contexts enable it to substitute for this earlier agitation in the popular imagination.[22] Sharing with its predecessor a devolved and localized structure, and with left politics more generally, notions of an educated and informed 'vanguard' established to incite and mobilize others, militant Islamism deals in 'propaganda by deed' designed to attract world attention. Islamism's contempt for Western decadence, celebration of violence, pronounced culture of martyrdom and the youthful age profile of those attracted into its ranks (many of whom might once have been enticed into movements of the political left) show that radical Islamic organizations occupy a space within a spectrum of dissent, drawing on the traditions both of the left and of the right. It also shares with movements of the political left, the ability to mobilize a wide variety of social groups and political grievances.[23] As the apostate Islamist and member of the British extremist *Hizb-ut-Tahrir* organization Ed Husain notes, some Islamic extremists have a history of involvement in socialist organizations and utilize the vocabulary of the left: 'we replaced "workers" with "Muslims", and swapped "Islam" for the "social" in "socialism"'.[24] For Paul Berman, the presence of a Western university-educated elite at the core of the movement indicates that Islamism draws as much from the Western traditions of youthful rebellion, morbid political introspection, disillusionment with democracy and impatience at the restraint imposed by established societal values, as from anti-colonialism and the ideas of the Muslim Brotherhood.[25] Read in this way, Wahabist fundamentalism and appeals for the restoration of a Golden Age

Caliphate carry echoes of the asceticism and self-denial that typified anarchism and the return to simpler, ruralist certainties it advocated.[26] For some, Islamism is more properly a kind of nihilism in a long tradition in Europe, fixated by Western immorality, and the metropolitan 'binge drinkers', 'football hooligans' and 'slags in nighclubs' that for militant Islamists symbolize the sybaritic outlook of modern European popular culture.[27] Reflecting these aspects of previous subversive and terrorist movements, al-Qaida and its supporters often occupy the place in popular fiction previously reserved for Bolsheviks and Soviet agents. The fiction that deals with al-Qaida frequently draws on the established plot-lines of internal subversion, spying, political subterfuge, rogue agents and surveillance by the security services that characterized the thrillers of the Cold War period. These themes provide the established plot devices in a new wave of pulp fiction preoccupied by the menace posed by Islam in the aftermath of the collapse of the Twin Towers.

Following on from the comparison between Islamic militancy and anarchism, for some cultural commentators, the real insights into the worlds of conspiracy and intrigue they both share are to be found in Western literature that assesses the origins of terrorism. Searching for points of comparison, writers are often drawn to an analysis that revisits established fiction dealing with the anarchist impulse in late nineteenth-century Europe. A number of novels about terrorism traditionally drew on anarchist precedents even before 9/11. In Eric Ambler's early nineteen-eighties novel, *The Care of Time*, a hack writer, Robert Halliday, is lured into a terrorist plot by a research project on a missing manuscript by the nineteenth-century anarchist and confidante of Bakunin, Sergei Nechaev. In the novel, the anarchist movement of the 1870s is depicted as 'the first great terrorist wave' whose 'real power lies with those who have the catalytic ability to provoke over-reaction'.[28] Post 9/11, Joseph Conrad's *The Secret Agent*, about *émigré* anarchists in London, remains a popular point of reference. For some, the gleeful celebration of indiscriminate violence involved in the attacks on New York and the 'hideous futility' of the destruction of the Twin Towers carries echoes of the attitudes displayed by the anarchists described in the novel and in Conrad's other writings.[29] Emerging alongside this view is an attitude that all terrorism shares the same poisoned tap-root that causes it to embrace violence as an end in itself.[30] Writing soon after 9/11, Niall Ferguson saw close parallels between the outlook of the Russian ambassador Vladimir in *The Secret Agent*, who seeks to sponsor a terrorist attack in London that has 'all the shocking senselessness of gratuitous blasphemy', and the 9/11 suicide bombers, who had no immediate demands, and no broader programme for action.[31] For others, the tolerance by the authorities of exile communities in Britain displayed in the novel is a weakness of the political system in the country, allowing extremists to plot unhindered on UK soil, and incubating terrorist cells that might strike against domestic targets. As the diplomat Vladimir comments in *The Secret Agent*: 'the general leniency of the judicial procedure here, and the utter absence of all repressive measures, are a scandal to Europe'.[32] Much commentary has settled around the presence of a marginalized and discontented youthful group within Islam that provides a reservoir of support for Islamic extremism. As Jason Burke has remarked, home-grown terrorism rooted in these new terrorist networks allows British Islamism to evolve from a base facilitating operations abroad, to one that strikes at targets in Britain itself.[33] Here there has been speculation about the model for such recruits provided by Dostoevsky's dislocated and defiant 'underground man' on the margins of urban society and present as the core of his Russian anarchist cell in *The Devils*.[34] The significance of this book for those who write about terrorism was compounded by George W. Bush's unwitting reference to the work in 2006, when he mistakenly quoted its most famous line 'a fire in the minds of men' (a reference to anarchism) in relation to the emergence of democracy in Eastern Europe.[35] As with recent statements about young Muslim men, the 'alienated', 'disaffected' and 'un-integrated' in the nineteenth century were said to provide a recruiting ground for anarchism. Such notions often reflected contemporary concerns about the breakdown of the family. Orphans, those from broken homes and the illegitimate, were all believed to be potential anarchists in the 1890s (see Chapter 2). For some commentators, unconventional family backgrounds and ruptured familial relations tend to be a feature of migrant communities. For this reason, the Muslim families of East London and the northern urban centres are often seen as replicating the features of dislocated Jewish migrant families of the East End, which in the nineteenth century were depicted as breeding and proliferating an anarchism grounded in youthful rebellion. Using this model, commentators claim to discern a landscape of Islamist terrorism, rooted in the associational and educational life of the British Muslim community that echoes Dostoevsky's concerns about youthful malcontents in Tsarist Russia. Here, in many accounts, there is a terrain of terrorism, particularly in London, similar to the landscape and social networks of anarchism in the later nineteenth century that evolved around particular meeting places and areas of the city. Particular mosques have gained notoriety as places of recruitment for young, confused, uncertain men from difficult backgrounds, seeking a cause and a surrogate family. In most accounts, the recruiters of the young into Islamic terrorism are charismatic prophets and preachers like Abu Hamza at Finsbury Park Mosque. This vision is reinforced by the reminiscences of apostate Islamists and government informers who have penetrated the congregations of rootless young men that cluster around the Finsbury Park Mosque in particular. In a number of accounts, this confessional literature exposes a world of predatory and violent extremist recruiters.

The secret intelligence operative Omar Nahiri notes in his recollections that under the preacher Abu Hamza, 'different people came to Finsbury Park after the takeover. People who were younger, less settled in their lives.'[36] Here there is a refusal to conform that in its renunciation of parents and elders, and the more mainstream conservative side of Islam constitutes a 'teenage rebellion' against the traditions of the community.[37] Drawing these themes together, Ed Husain in his autobiography of a former Islamic militant is keen to stress that as a young Islamist, he was 'made in Britain'.[38]

The origins of popular fiction that deals with an Islamic menace lies in the inter-war period. Rooted in Enlightenment notions of Islam as a threat to Western values, fiction proliferated during these years that linked together a resurgent Islam and the decline of the West.[39] The inter-war period saw a marked emphasis on introspective and introverted examinations of Western culture poised on the brink of disintegration. This tone of anxiety about the future of the West grew out of the upheaval following the Great War, a loss of optimism about democratic values and the contraction of the inter-war economy. Influenced by classical precedents, writers as diverse as H.G. Wells, Leonard Woolf and Lewis Mumford believed the West to be exhausted. New departures in archaeology deriving from pre-war studies of past Middle Eastern civilizations apparently confirmed that there was a life-cycle to dominant cultures that either renewed themselves or were eradicated entirely.[40] In a number of studies, the West was represented as reaching the end of a pinnacle of influence and was now portrayed as adrift under the shadow of imminent disintegration and collapse.[41] In line with this view, numerous mysteries and thrillers increasingly took on a 'clash of civilizations' theme between a decadent West and a volatile but emergent Middle East. Ruins and collapsed cultures featured in a number of novels, notably those of Agatha Christie, drawing on the work of her archaeologist husband, Max Mallowan, who she met on a dig during a tour of the Middle East.[42] Her novel, *They Came to Baghdad*, written on the site of an archaeological excavation in Iraq, included a plot line that revolved around an archaeological excavation in the Middle East.[43] Sifting amongst the ruins of a past civilization, her heroine, Victoria Jones, is unaware that her lover, Edward Goring, is intent on creating a new dictatorship mediated between the tensions of a Communist East and a free market West.[44]

Elsewhere, in other fiction, sterner and more united faiths and movements like militant Islam, which had the ability to draw on anti-colonial sentiments, were depicted as new barbarians, capable of sweeping away a decadent and divided West in the manner of the Roman empire. In the early twentieth century, the incompatibilities between Eastern influences and the West had already been explored in novels like M.P. Shiel's novel of global catastrophe, *The Purple Cloud* written in 1901. In the aftermath of a poisoned gas cloud that wipes out almost all humanity, one of the few survivors sees evidence of foreign tribes and cultures fleeing before the oncoming death, but looking out of place amongst the corpses of Londoners and metropolitan natives in the capital. He paints a picture of the West, overwhelmed in its dying days, by an incursion from the Orient. At Dover, gateway to England, he becomes sickened by the ethnic mix of the corpses he encounters of:

> spahi, and bashi-bazouk, of Greek and Catalan, of Russian 'pope' and Coptic abuna, of drogoman and Calmuck, of Egyptian maulawi and Afghan mullahs, Neapolitan and sheik, and the nighmare of wild poses, colours, stuffs and garbs, yellow-green kefies of the Bedouin, shawl-turbans of Baghdad, the red tarboosh, the voluminous rose-silk tob of women, and face veils, the labourer's corduroy, and stark distorted nakedness, and sashes of figured muslin.[45]

Throughout, the novel reflects an abhorrence of race-mixing and extra-European migration from the former colonies of settlement in which the exceptionalism of the West is steadily diluted and undermined. Explorations of this theme reached their peak in the popular fiction printed in the closing stages of the Great War. In John Buchan's novel *Greenmantle*, which dealt with espionage in the Turkish empire, the Islamic prophet Greenmantle represents the first fictional appearance of the charismatic and devout Islamist, able to mobilize the excluded millions of the Middle East to overturn Western influences in the region. Richard Hannay's colleague at the Foreign Office, Bullivant, comments: 'Islam is a fighting creed, and the mullah still stands in the pulpit with the Koran in one hand, and a drawn sword in the other. Supposing there is some Ark of the Covenant which will madden the remotest Moslem peasant with dreams of paradise? Where then my friend?[46] In a debased form, Sax Rohmer's *The Mask of Fu Manchu* from 1932 continued much the same themes. Here the oriental arch-super villain, Dr Fu Manchu, plunders relics from the tomb of the prophet, Mokanna, to incite a holy crusade against the West. Captain Woodville, a British intelligence officer, comments grimly to the archaeologist, Sir Lionel Barton:

> A certain fanatical iman took upon himself the duties of a sort of Eastern Peter the Hermit . . . He declared that the Masked prophet had been reborn and that with the Sword of God he would carry the New Creed throughout the East, sweeping the Infidel before him. That movement is gathering strength, Sir Lionel, and I need not tell you what such a movement means to the Indian government, and what it may come to mean for Arabia, Palestine, and possibly Egypt, unless it can be checked.[47]

In R.C. Sherriff's *The Cataclysm* published on the eve of World War II, these threats are brought closer to home. Postulating a future in which the moon has crashed into the earth, provoking a war between the Western powers over its rich raw materials, Sherriff shows the weakened West as petulant and divided in its response to global catastrophe. Unable to co-ordinate a united front against attacks from the former colonies, the European powers collapse in the face of an onslaught from the Persian demagogue, Selim. Under Selim, former colonies and the untamed East embrace a doctrine of renunciation of the West. Described as 'a revolutionary – possibly an anarchist . . . he [preaches] against the exploitation and oppression of the Eastern peoples by the nations of the West'.[48] Here Selim acts as a nemesis against the arrogance of an overbearing, colonising Westernization. In a gloomy depiction of the closing days of Western colonial supremacy that sums up the pessimism of the period, Sherriff shows survivors of the war eking out their final days in the ruins of a devastated London as the darkness falls on Western urban culture: 'It is long past midnight and I am very tired. From the blackness of the city comes one solitary, flickering light, one fitful little gleam from a house in Ladbroke Square . . . I wonder who it is?'[49] For Sherriff, the key to the survival of the West lay in its ability to consolidate itself, or repel its enemies in an era of European and extra-European turbulence.

III

In more recent popular fiction, authors have explored the menace from the East through the literal ownership of the West by Eastern potentates and Arab millionaires. Many of these moral panics about an influx of wealthy Arab princes buying up England have their origins in the oil crisis of 1973, which alerted the public to the power and wealth wielded by Arab dynasties and families. In contemporary revelations about these events, the popular press was alarmed by the covert power of oil billionaires that monopolized and exploited the dependency of Western governments on this key commodity. The first representations of urban sheiks establishing themselves in London date from this period. Images of wealthy Arabs buying up exclusive properties in London and the loss of traditional British businesses and brands to Middle Eastern cartels are a feature of these years. The purchase of Harrods by the Al-Fayed brothers in 1985 came to symbolize this process.[50] As Jerry White comments, London can still lay claim to the title of 'intellectual and political capital of the Arab world'.[51] Creating communities in the West End, around Bayswater ('Beirut-on-Thames') and Marylebone, restless Arab princelings often appear in fiction from the 1970s as property speculators and one of the generic threats to the stability of Britain during this period. In Paul Bailey's novel of British exhaustion marking the end of the decade, the war veteran Captain Standish warns the naïve Victor Harker about the Arab community 'besieging' the capital city: ' "You'll see them. Before the week's over, you'll see them. You'll see the buggers everywhere. You'll begin to think that we're in a suburb of Port Said," he said menacingly, "we'll soon be outnumbered by burnouses" '.[52] In Margaret Drabble's *The Ice Age*, Arab businessmen feature alongside other period fears as emblems of things going wrong: 'the trade unions, the present government, the miners, the car workers, the seamen, the Arabs, the Irish, their own husbands, their own wives, their own idle, good-for-nothing offspring, comprehensive education. Nobody knew whose fault it really was, but most people managed to complain fairly forcefully about somebody'.[53] Anthony Burgess in his ironic novel of a dystopian future, *1985*, depicted an ailing Britain entirely dependant on Arab subsidies to pay off debts to the International Money Fund in which North Sea oil revenue is mortgaged off to reimburse Middle Eastern creditors. In his image of Britain, 'crescent moon banners waved from the chilly derricks' in the North Sea.[54] In Burgess' London, the construction of the Great Mosque at Regent's Park in 1978 came to stand for a creeping influence that reduced the capital to the level of an Arab satellite: 'The Arabs were in Britain to stay. They owned Al-Dorchester, Al-Claridges, Al-Browns, various Al-Hiltons, and Al-Holiday Inns, with soft drinks in the bars, and no bacon for breakfast. They owned things that people did not even know they owned, including distilleries and breweries, and, in Great Smith Street, soon would stand the symbol of their strength – the Masjid-ul-Haram or Great Mosque of London.'[55] In the conclusion of his novel, riots and civil disorder surround the work performed on the mosque and the role of influential Arab princelings in its construction.[56] In more recent fiction this image of an 'Orientalised' London persists. In James Patterson's *London Bridges*, Colonel Geoffrey Schafer, a misanthropic army veteran who is co-opted into plans to attack London by the sinister ex-KGB agent, the Wolf, feels alienated in his own city: 'The streets were filled with Middle Eastern coffee shops and restaurants and grocers. The aromas of ethnic cuisine were thick in the air that morning – tabbouleh, strong coffee and lentil soup, mixed with the fragrance of pastilla. In front of the newsagent's two elderly men smoked tobacco through a water-filtered hookah. *Bloody Hell! What the fuck has happened to my country?*'[57]

Many of the precedents for recent thrillers that explore Islamic extremism in fiction derive from a previous genre that dealt with the threats posed by Palestine Liberation Organization (PLO) operations in Britain. After its foundation in 1964, the PLO established an international network of sympathizers and helpers rooted in the displaced Palestinian community. Specialising in assassinations, hostage taking and high-profile acts of air piracy, the PLO operated outside the borders of the Middle Eastern states, often with the tacit support of Arab governments. In both Jordan and the Lebanon, they were responsible for robberies and kidnappings that further destabilized these states in a volatile region. In Europe, they established strong connections with the militant political left and provided a model for their operations.[58] The reach of the PLO conjured up fears of an armed and well-supplied terrorist international, operating with impunity on European soil and dedicated to striking directly against known supporters of Israel. In Eric Ambler's novel, *The Care of Time*, a plot is uncovered when the writer Robert Halliday is lured into a conspiracy around a rogue PLO faction. In Ambler's book, the European branch of the organization has criminalized, diversifying into illegal activities and mafia-style operations. His Rasd organization, incubated in the Gaza refugee camps and drawing on national resentment at the treatment of the Palestinian people, becomes a breakaway faction that adopts mafia-style organization and reprisals. This enables the remainder of Ambler's novel to settle into the routine of a crime drama plotted around themes of racketeering, revenge and extortion: 'Quite logically, Rasd took itself to fund-raising. Ultimately, it . . . became corrupt. It bought into nighclubs, gambling casinos and brothels. All in the decadent west, you understand. Soon it was making huge profits, and spending them on high living.'[59] In Peter Nieswand's *The Underground Connection*, PLO terrorism emerges as a direct threat to Britain for the first time. This novel is the first to link PLO violence with a planned act of reprisal in London. Placing an unwitting female accomplice and her baby as a human bomb on the London underground, this novel speculates grimly about the carnage to commuters that would ensue after an explosion in a confined space on the metro.[60] The novel conjures up a seedy world of conspirators and professional terrorist operatives living in bed-sits and council accommodation in London where they day-dream of the secret power they wield and the god-like status it bestows on them. Considering the female dupe and her child he has recruited for the mission, the terrorist Ziad 'did not feel he was in the same room. It was as if he was detached from them and invisible, not linked by blood or emotion, a kind of god who could use people for his own purposes, who held destinies in his hand. The fact that they did not know his power increased his excitement'.[61] Subsequently, the imaginings of such bed-sit martyrs have become familiar in standard accounts of al-Qaeda conspiracies and operations on the mainland of the United Kingdom.

IV

In many popular thrillers, al-Qaeda operations substituted for other prior menaces to the state and to the British people themselves. Most recent novels in this area imagine the Islamic terrorist as symptomatic of the nation under threat. Such fears are in a long tradition, having deep roots in the invasion panic novels of the Edwardian era and beyond (see Chapter 3). Most such works trade heavily in images of Englishness under siege. In Stella Rimington's novel *At Risk*, dealing with MI5 counter-terrorism operations, the al-Qaeda agents stalked by her hardened intelligence operatives enter the country concealed among a convoy of asylum seekers landed on the north Norfolk coast.[62] Representative of a 'deep' England, and the county that William Le Queux always feared would be invaded by Germany, East Anglia is the site of a planned terrorist atrocity against a wedding party in the cricket club of the small village community of West Ford. Here a tit-for-tat reprisal is to be enacted by an al-Qaeda squad for the accidental destruction of a wedding party in Iraq during US bombing raids. Their operations are designed to bring home to the British public the cost of Western intervention in Iraq and Afghanistan. Rimington's female terrorist, Asimat, justifies her actions as a warning against Western governments in their actions against Muslim innocents: 'The action she was taking today would save lives. It would make the West think twice before raining bombs and bullets on those they considered faceless and of no consequence. The cascading triple detonation in which the British family would die would serve as the scream of those countless others across the world who had died without a voice'.[63] Other popular novels embrace a similar theme of village England under direct attack or as a place of subversion and conspiracy. In Colin Forbes' novel of treachery within MI5 based around an al-Qaeda attack on London, component parts of the torpedo boats used to destroy the bridges across the Thames are smuggled into the capital in milk churns from a secret rural base in Berkshire.[64] The plot of the novel turns around events in the sinister village of Carpford, which has become an operational cell for al-Qaeda under the direction of a rogue MI5 officer. A modernist fantasy build by an innovative development company, the village of Carpford has lost its traditional village character and assumes many of the features of the isolated villages and communities that harboured deviant bohemians and Bolsheviks in the inter-war years. Paula, Inspector Tweed's assistant, views the resulting community and mismatched buildings of Italianate design with horror: 'Well-spaced out and near the edge of the silent lake was the oddest collection of dwellings Paula had ever seen. The nearest to where they were stood was a distance back from the lake, perched on a small hill. It had a massive tower at one corner with a mosaic-decorated roof rising high above the three floors below. Attached to it were lower floors with tall narrow windows. At the far end was a smaller tower with a peaked roof'.[65] For many authors of popular fiction, al-Qaeda terrorist plots and operations in Britain provided the opportunity for meditations on the state of the nation and of Englishness more generally. Some of this fiction questioned the direction taken by governments in their attempts to tackle terrorism, and the sacrifices demanded of the population and the armed services in the pursuit of victory. Many of these novels became barometers of the national mood. In Ken Macleod's novel of an alternative future, Britain is losing the War against Terror and drifting steadily into chaos. Reflecting disillusionment with government for the support accorded to the United States in the wars in Afghanistan and Iraq, and the increasing governmental disregard for civil liberties, Travis detects a sense of national malaise and loss of direction: 'At some point England had simply failed itself. In his own mind he had connected it with the times when it had failed him: the incompetence and lack of preparation for the pandemic that had killed his wife and half a million others, the hollow justifications for the attack on Iran, which he'd been so sure the commons would see through. But they hadn't and the war had been bounced through on a snap division. And the people who hadn't filled the streets as a consequence.'[66]

In the aftermath of the 7/7 bombings, responses to the terrorist attack on the London underground were also believed to reflect national character and identity. In contrast to the United States, however, where incidents of terrorism and attacks on domestic soil were unusual, an unpanicked popular co-existence with terrorist violence was frequently stated to characterize public reactions to terrorism in the United Kingdom. Journalists lauded the ability of Londoners to simply carry on, even in the face of imminent terrorist threats. One year on from the 7/7 suicide bombs, commentators discerned evidence of rapid recovery from the trauma of the attack. Memories of wartime, it was argued, provided opportunities to demonstrate the phlegmatic outlook and 'stoic fatalism born of grim experience' that had stiffened the city's morale at the height of the Blitz. Sir Ian Blair, Metropolitan Police Commissioner, invoked the vision of 'this wonderful, diverse city' as 'one united community against atrocity'.[67] Many writers sought to puncture the image of metropolitan insouciance in the face of terrorist conspiracies. In Chris Cleave's imaginative description of mourning and loss in the aftermath of a terrorist bomb attack on Wembley Stadium, the response to the bombing is chaos and disarray on the part of the emergency services and the mass of the population of the capital.[68] In a jaundiced depiction of governmental unpreparedness against the threat of terrorism, this novel depicts a city quite unable to cope with the pressures of crowd panic and the determination of terrorist bombers. Beneath the façade of governmental anti-terrorist control lurks a barely suppressed and palpable crowd violence, which erupts in violence and hysteria during a bomb hoax in Parliament Square towards the end of the novel. Swallowed up by the crowd in Victoria Square Gardens, Cleave's East End heroine is trampled by office workers running from the city in panic: 'I was in the middle of all those young blokes in office suits and they were shouting and barging everyone out of their way so I just had to run with them. Then I couldn't keep up anymore and I fell. I lay on the streaming wet tarmac and they all ran over me in their hard leather shoes. I curled up into a ball and when it was finished I got up and walked on down towards Lambeth Bridge'.[69] A number of novels explore the impact of Islamic extremism as a threat that divides and fragments communities, rather than bringing them together in defiance of terrorism. In Cleave's novel, Muslims are suspended from their jobs as a potential threat to national security.[70] Other books of this type imagined riots and civil disorder directed against the Muslim community in the aftermath of terrorist atrocities. In Macleod's *The Execution Channel*, the government struggles to restore order after pogroms break out against Muslim shop-keepers in London. In Wood Green, '[t]he sky was pink, with black clouds. The pavements of Wood Green's Main Streets seemed to reflect the colours: pink with cherry blossom, black with ash. Roisin and Maxine crunched over broken glass and past boarded-up houses. Several days of an unnatural alliance between white and Afro-Caribbean mobs had left most of the Asian-owned shops trashed'.[71] In Macleod's novel, British Muslims are expelled from the country altogether and given refuge by the French government.[72] Ultimately, most of the popular fiction dealing with Islamic terrorism betrays a profound pessimism about the future and about relations between communities and religious faiths in the United Kingdom. Macleod's hero, Travis, records the words of his wife, long dead from an imagined flu epidemic: 'He remembered Deborah, years back, looking away from the first confused coverage of the 7 July bombings, three days after she'd come back from a Make Poverty History march. "We'll be in this shit till we die" she'd said'.[73] Travis hopes that what was true for her wouldn't necessarily be true for him.

Al-Qaeda operatives are now stock features of plot devices in much Western popular fiction. Fears about terrorism in twenty-first century Britain, however, are in a long tradition. Mediated through images of terrorist activity familiar from popular literature, Islamist-inspired militancy has come to assume many of the characteristics established by previous generations of dynamitards and incendiarists. The long-forgotten campaigns organized by anarchists and Irish republicans on British soil provide strong parallels with recent concerns about Islamic terrorism in the United Kingdom. Moral panics about al-Qaeda sleeper cells and disaffected Muslim youth, fallen prey to recruiters for militant Islamic organizations, echo fears about the international power and reach of the anarchist movement in the nineteenth century and its appeal to the marginal, the ill-informed and the naïve. Moreover, nineteenth-century anarchism set the tone for all subsequent governmental responses to terrorism and the threats posed to Britain's traditional civil liberties, both by terrorism and by government itself. In the early twentieth century, fears of terrorist atrocities led the government to embrace legislation to exclude suspected bomb-makers from the country, causing a backlash from those who sought to maintain Britain's traditions of welcome and openness to those who were the victims of oppressive regimes. In 1905, as in 2005, government stood accused of dismantling the country's traditional legislative safeguards for asylum seekers and of eroding traditions of tolerance and of 'fair play'.

Conclusions

The image of catastrophe is integral to the image of London. Failure and success are intertwined in the image of the city. For that reason, depictions of a 'London under siege' feature significantly in novels of political collapse and British decline. Drawing on images of political destruction and cultural failure familiar from other urban contexts, the political disintegration of the capital and the implications of such events for the rest of Britain are recurrent themes of popular fiction. Ranging across acts of terrorism, putsches, Communist uprisings and acts of internal subversion, in these texts, the collapse of the kingdom is predicated on the collapse of the capital itself. For many authors, the symbolic destruction of the Palace of Westminster, or the vandalism of Buckingham Palace by insurgents, presented a broader image of British democracy in crisis and undermined prevailing visions of British exceptionalism and centuries-old stability. Authors who speculated about alternative political futures or presented narratives of national collapse and disarray dared to imagine a Britain politically changed, and brought much more into line with the democratic crises and unstable governmental forms characteristic of her continental neighbours. Here London took on the form, outward appearance and appurtenances of other European cities, in a manner that recalled the comparisons and similarities with other urban contexts that featured heavily in guidebooks and travelogues of London from the eighteenth century onwards.

Conventional images of London remain fixed by memories of the blitz, when Londoners stood shoulder to shoulder in defiance of German heavy bombers. A patina of nostalgia and popular memory has made this episode impervious to reassessment, despite the evidence of fractured social and ethnic relations in the capital at the height of the bombardment.

As Robert Colls has commented, 'London entered the twentieth century as the world's greatest city, but as England's greatest problem'.[1] Always depicted as a city in crisis, the capital's unprecedented urban growth, extremes of poverty and wealth, the restive rootlessness of her population, and deep spiritual malaise deriving from the capital's legendary 'godlessness' made the city an object of wonder, but also of popular dismay. From Social Darwinists who saw it as the graveyard of the race, through municipal reformers who believed the

Figure C.1 Propaganda by the Communist Party of Great Britain highlighting the inadequacies of air-raid shelter provision for the poor on the eve of the blitz. *ARP: The Practical Air Raid Protection Britain Needs* (London: Communist Party of Great Britain, 1939), p. 9. (Author's Collection.)

city resistant to order and control, and imperialists who saw its decline as heralding the retreat of empire, London was a city that provoked anxieties.[2] Here new forms and styles of dance and music opened up the image of an unbridled cosmopolitanism that took the capital away from its indigenous English roots. London's yearning for a ruralist past and attempts to remedy the capital's creeping urban decay by returning the city to its rural and village origins were always destined to fail in the face of the city's unrelenting expansion, internationalism and increasing poverty and squalor in the nineteenth century.[3] Most writers of popular fiction hoped in their imaginings to restore order to this formless, inchoate and chaotic capital of the empire.

Popular fiction about Britain's collapse or occupation by foreign powers is in part warning, in part prophecy and revels in the orderliness and stability of pre-existing British institutions. This volume has tried to locate such works within a broader narrative about Britain's success and the political fears that sought to warn against the fragility of that settlement and the dangers of London's unregulated growth. Images of 'foreignness', 'difference' and 'alien' imported forms, customs and populations are integral to images of the capital in dissolution. Popular fiction fitted effectively into these narratives. In a deeply anglophone tradition of highlighting impending political decline and disarray via the novel of alternative political futures, these volumes accentuated the features of Britain that might drag the city down into destruction.[4] In such accounts, London is characterized by semi-criminalized sub-cultures, corrupt politicians and a restive crowd politics. The East End, which figures largely in such fiction, was always depicted as a place of darkness and migrant disorder, characterized by imported customs of violence and aggressive physical force action. Bringing with them un-English customs and attitudes, foreign populations were often seen as the first step towards the alien occupation of the capital itself. In the absence of the populations of dangerous agitators and radical emigres that feature significantly in nineteenth- and early twentieth-century novels, the focus of these accounts of dangerous outsider presences has shifted towards mobile capital and rootless financial institutions. In recent fiction, wealthy Russian oligarchs have replaced exile radicals as the locus for ancestral vendettas imported from Old Europe into the capital. Reggie Nadelson's recent *Londongrad* is in a long tradition in this respect. Dealing with acts of assassination initiated by exile Russian mobsters, it sees London as in thrall to wealthy emigrant Russians: ' "For Russians, London is the bank, the offshore island, the money, and where is money, is killing, where people are rich, criminals come, more and more and more" said Tolya. "I did some bad deals, Artemy, I took too much" '.[5]

Fiction that considers London's problems follows specific patterns. Shifting crowds are always central to such narratives, either as threat or as a place of sanctuary and concealment. William Boyd's *Ordinary Thunderstorms* in which a climatologist becomes unintentionally embroiled in a conspiracy by a prominent pharmaceuticals company is again in a long tradition in its image of an anonymous London, concealing the fugitive, refugee and the vagrant: 'There was something about London that he needed, he realized, something basic and fundamental: he needed its size, its great sprawling scale, its millions of denizens, the utter and protective anonymity it provided. He thought about the 600 people a week that went missing in the country . . . Only London was big and heartless enough to contain those lost multitudes, the vanished population of the United Kingdom – only London could swallow them up without a qualm, without demur.'[6] In these imaginings London is a dislocated modernist society, lacking the restraints of community, convention, tradition, and authority and impervious to governmental control. For this reason, much of the popular fiction that concerns itself with rapid political change or threat begins with crowd violence. Mobs were about transition. Crowds in London postulate threat and pose the menace of unbridled displays of disorder and defiance of government. Images of 'the mob' or the crowd were central to depictions of London. In their depredations they posed the possibility for change and the imminence of alternative power structures. The London they envisaged was essentially a 'republic of the streets'. Moreover, these demonstrations highlighted the long-standing polarization of London, and its segmentation into quarters of relative dispossession and of affluence.

Much of this book has focussed on a London in decline. The authors who wrote about a London in disarray were in thrall to a particular model of London that emphasized its negative elements, and its imminent disintegration. Fixated on the thrill of decline, such novels highlighted the failure to impose order on London, the inability of the city to govern the temper of its crowd politics or to control its urban spaces effectively. Rooted in anxiety, fear, apprehension and visions of imminent societal or governmental collapse, popular fiction always imagined not the life, but the death of a great city.

Notes

Notes to Introduction

1 I. Fleming, *Moonraker* (London: Penguin, 2004), p. 241.

2 See D. Cannadine, *In Churchill's Shadow: Confronting the Past in Modern Britain* (London: Allen Lane, 2002), pp. 286–308.

3 See A. Taylor, '"And I am the god of destruction!": Fu Manchu and the construction of Asiatic evil in the novels of Arthur Sarsfield Ward', in T. Crook, R. Gill and B. Taithe (eds), *Evil, Barbarism and Empire: Britain and Abroad, c.1830–c.2000* (London: Palgrave-Macmillan, 2011), 73–95.

4 See M. Ignatieff, *The Lesser Evil: Political Ethics in an Age of Terror* (New Jersey: Princeton University Press, 2004), ch. 5, P. Berman, *Terror and Liberalism* (New York: W.W. Norton and Company, 2003), ch. 5 and J. Gray, *Al-Qaeda and What it Means to be Modern* (London: Faber, 2003).

5 See for one such appreciation, P. Baker, *The Devil is a Gentleman: The Life and Times of Dennis Wheatley* (Cambridge: Dedalus, 2010), chs. 48 and 49.

6 For a major attempt to understand this material in the context of film, fiction and other aspects of popular culture, see W. Webster, *Englishness and Empire, 1939–1965* (Oxford: Oxford University Press, 2005), ch. 5.

7 For a timely meditation on some of these themes from a historian's point of view, see J. Baxendale, *Priestley's England: J.B. Priestley and English Culture* (Manchester: Manchester University Press, 2007), pp. 15–21.

8 P. Waller, *Writing, Reading and Reputations: Literary Life in Britain, 1870–1914* (Oxford, 2006), chs. 2, 3.

9 I. Haywood, *The Revolution in Popular Literature: Print, Politics and the People, 1790–1860* (Cambridge: Cambridge University Press, 2004), ch. 9.

10 See W. Laqueur, *The New Terrorism: Fanaticism and the Arms of Mass Destruction* (London: Phoenix Press, 2001), pp. 8–48.

11 Ibid., 105–26.

12 W. Laqueur, 'Interpretation of Terrorism: Fact, Fiction and Political Sense', *Journal of Contemporary History*, 12 (1977), p. 11.

13 See in particular, D. Pike, *Subterranean Cities: The World Beneath Paris and London, 1800–1945* (New York: Cornell University Press, 2005) and L. Nead, *Victorian Babylon: People, Streets and Images in Nineteenth Century London* (London: Yale University Press, 2000).

14 See A. Hepburn, *Intrigue: Espionage and Culture* (London: Yale University Press, 2005), pp. 10–18.

15 See M. Denning, *Cover Stories: Narrative and Ideology in the British Spy Thriller* (London: Routledge and Kegan Paul, 1987).

16 K. Foster, 'National fictions and the spycatcher trial', in I. Craven (ed.), *Australian Popular Culture* (Cambridge: Cambridge University Press, 1994), p. 124.

17 D.L. Sayers, 'Introduction', in Sayers (ed.), *Great Short Stories of Detection, Mystery and Horror* (London: Odhams Press Ltd., 1928), p. 19.

18 Quoted in Waller, *Writing, Reading and Reputations*, p. 675.

19 B. Diemert, *Graham Greene's Thrillers and the 1930s* (Belfast: McGill-Queen's University Press, 1996), pp. 14–22.

20 J. Rose, *The Intellectual Life of the British Working Classes* (New Haven, CT: Yale University Press, 2001), especially pp. 224–53 and 331–4.

21 B. Crick, *George Orwell: A Life* (London: Penguin, 1980), pp. 249–50.

22 R. Hoggart, *The Uses of Literacy* (London: Penguin, 1962), p. 257.

23 See C. Hilliard, *To Exercise Our Talents: The Democratisation of Writing in Britain* (Cambridge, MA: Harvard University Press, 2006), especially chs. 1, 7 and 8. For the travails faced by new working-class writers in particular, see idem, 'Producers by hand and by brain: working-class writers and left-wing publishers in 1930s Britain', *The Journal of Modern History*, 78 (2006), 37–64.

24 Hilliard, *To Exercise Our Talents*, pp. 8–9.

25 For European rejection of American influences in the inter-war and post-war period, see J. Caesar, 'The philosophical origins of anti-Americanism in Europe', in P. Hollander (ed.), *Understanding Anti-Americanism: Its Origins and Impact* (Chicago, IL: Ivan R. Dee, 2004), pp. 51–70.

26 D. Hajdu, *The Ten-Cent Plague: The Great Comic Book Scare and How It Changed America* (New York: Farrar, Straus and Giroux , 2008), chs. 1, 2 and 16.

27 See the afterword in Philip Roth's account of a fictionalized quasi-Fascist presidency by Charles Lindbergh in his *The Plot Against America* (London: Vintage, 2005), pp. 364–91. This book carries strong resonances of works of popular science fiction that imagined a German and Japanese victory in World War II, notably P.K. Dick, *The Man in the High Castle* (London: Penguin, 2001).

28 Hoggart, *The Uses of Literacy*, pp. 259–64. Crime writers like Peter Cheyney were strongly influenced by this American model; see M. Harrison, *Peter Cheyney: Prince of Hokum* (London: Neville Spearman, 1954).

29 E. Ambler, *The Dark Frontier* (London: Hodder and Stoughton, 1959), pp. 28 and 29–34.

30 C. Bloom, *Cult Fiction: Popular Reading and Pulp Theory* (London: Macmillan, 1996), ch. 1.

31 Ibid., p. 226.

32 Ibid., p. 152.

33 H. C. O'Neill, *Can Britain be Invaded?* (London: Dent, 1941), p. 62.

34 M. Allingham, *The Tiger in the Smoke* (London: Penguin, 1957), p. 25.

35 P. Cheyney, *The Urgent Hangman* (London: Penguin, 1938), p. 97.

36 A.J. Weitzman, 'Eighteenth century London: urban paradise or fallen city?', *Journal of the History of Ideas*, 36 (1975), 469–80. William Morris still uses the term 'modern Babylon' to describe nineteenth-century London in *News From Nowhere*; see Morris, *News from Nowhere* (London: Penguin, 1993), p. 99.

37 Nead, *Victorian Babylon*, p. 212.

38 Ibid., pp. 212–15 and R. Belich, *Making Peoples: A History of the New Zealanders* (Rosedale: Penguin, 1996), pp. 297–9.

39 R. Dingley, 'The ruins of the future: Macaulay's New Zealander and the spirit of the age', in A. Sanderson and R. Dingley (eds), *Histories of the Future: Studies in Fact, Fantasy and Science Fiction* (London: Palgrave, 2005), pp. 15–33.

40 P. Wright, *A Journey Through Ruins: The Last Days of London* (London: Radius, 1991), pp. 160–5.

41 A. Lees, *Cities Perceived: Urban Society in European and North American Thought* (Manchester: Manchester University Press, 1985), pp. 276–9. Throughout his study Lees focuses on critics of urban growth, arguing that in the great urban expansions of the high nineteenth century, 'critics of cities set the prevailing tone of urban consciousness' (p. 311).

42 R. Colls, *Identity of England* (Oxford: Oxford University Press, 2002), pp. 213–15.

43 M. Page, *The City's End: Two Centuries of Fantasies, Fears, and Premonitions of New York's Destruction* (New Haven, CT: Yale University Press, 2008), chs. 1 and 2.

44 Ibid., pp. 26–8.

45 See J. Schneer, *London 1900: The Imperial Metropolis* (New Haven, CT: Yale University Press, 1999), pp. 3–36, idem, 'London's docks in 1900: nexus of empire', *Labour History Review*, 59 (1994), 20–33, T. Smith, 'A grand work of noble conception: the Victoria Memorial and imperial London', in F. Driver and D. Gilbert (eds), *Imperial Cities* (Manchester: Manchester University Press, 1999), pp. 21–39. So central were imperial concerns to London that its politics were often defined by them; see A. Windscheffel, '"In darkest Lambeth": Henry Morton Stanley and the imperial politics of London unionism', in M. Cragoe and A. Taylor (eds), *London Politics, 1760–1914* (London: Palgrave, 2005), pp. 191–210 and idem, *Popular Conservatism in Imperial London, 1868–1906* (Woodbridge: Boydell and Brewer, 2007), chs 3 and 7.

46 R.F. Betts, 'The allusion to Rome in British imperialist thought of the late nineteenth and early twentieth centuries', *Victorian Studies*, 15 (1971), 149–59.

47 J.A. Froude, *Oceana* (London: Longmans, Green and Co., 1886), pp. 8–9. See for these themes in the White Settler dominions, R. White, *Inventing Australia: Images and Identity, 1688–1980* (St. Leonards: Allen and Unwin, 1981), ch. 5 and J. Phillips, *A Man's Country: The Image of the Pakeha Male* (Auckland: Penguin, 1987), chs. 1–3.

48 G. Davison, *The Rise and Fall of Marvellous Melbourne* (Carlton: Melbourne University Press, 2004), pp. 166–8 and ch. 10.

49 In this sense they provide a counter-point to the popular literature of empire that abounded in the late Victorian, and early Edwardian period. See J.S. Bratton, 'Of England, home and duty: the image of England in Victorian and Edwardian juvenile fiction', in J.M. Mackenzie (ed), *Imperialism and Popular Culture* (Manchester: Manchester University Press, 1986), pp. 73–93. See for post-war juvenile fiction relating to empire, K. Castle, 'Imperial legacies, new frontiers: children's popular literature and the demise of empire', in S. Ward (ed), *British Culture and the End of Empire* (Manchester: Manchester University Press, 2001), pp. 145–62.

50 See J. Thompson, *Fiction, Crime and Empire: Clues to Modernity and Postmodernism* (Chicago, IL: University of Illinois Press, 1993), pp. 122–33 and S. Ward, 'Introduction' to Ward (ed), *British Culture and the End of Empire*, p. 17.

51 N. Shute, *In the Wet* (New York: Permabooks, 1957), p. 69.

52 Morris, *News from Nowhere*, pp. 132–58. G.D.H. Cole was amongst those converted to 'the passionate and consuming faith of socialism' by *News from Nowhere*. See Kingsley Martin's obituary of him in the *New Statesman*, 17 January 1959, p. 63.

53 Morris, *News from Nowhere*, pp. 77–8 and 99–100.

54 M. Beaumont, *Utopia Ltd.: Ideologies of Social Dreaming in England 1870–1900* (New York: Haymarket Books, 2005), ch. 4.

55 Quoted in R. Harrison, *The English Defence of the Commune (1871)* (London: Merlin Press Ltd., 1971), p. 161.

56 Beaumont, *Utopia Ltd.*, p. 147.

57 Ibid., pp. 159–60 and W.D. Hay, *The Doom of the Great City* (London: Newman and Co., 1880).

58 J. Christopher, *The Death of Grass* (London: Penguin, 2009), pp. 93–4. Christopher always denied that his novel was science fiction, and it has apparent political implications. In it, as in other works dealing with post-apocalyptic scenarios, there are discussions of the most appropriate governmental forms for the new society. The survivors eventually settle on feudalism (ch. 10).

59 Quoted in A. Wilson, *The Search for Ernest Bramah* (London: Creighton and Reed, 2007), p. 233. Bramah's dislike of radicalism stemmed from the failure of his attempts to establish a farm in the 1880s, which he attributed to political agitators inspired by his neighbour, Joseph Arch (p. 25).

60 E. Ambler, *Here Lies: An Autobiography* (London: Harper Collins, 1985), pp. 120–1. Ambler transposed these traits from his heroes, onto his villains. See the truncheon-wielding Captain Mailler in *Background to Danger*, described as an ex-Black and Tan who 'was also, at one time, the only professional strike-breaker in America with a public school education.' See Ambler, *Background to Danger* (New York: Dell Publishing Co, 1965), p. 65.

61 See D.L. Smith, 'Mirrors of Inscrutability: British Textual Representations of China and the Chinese, 1880–1940' (PhD, University of Birmingham, 1998), p. 178.

62 A. Light, *Forever England: Femininity, Literature and Conservatism between the Wars* (London: Routledge, 1990), p. 83 and ch. 2.

63 Bloom, *Cult Fiction*, p. 133.

64 See E. Laclau, *On Populist Reason* (London: Verso, 2005), chs. 4 and 7.

65 A. Calder, *The Myth of the Blitz* (London: Jonathan Cape, 1991), p. 250.

66 Ibid., pp. 195–7.

67 Lewis also used the image of a London in ruins and subject to a creeping dry rot as an indictment of Labour state planning: 'Every district has its quota of gaps or of ruins, and these wet, draughty weed-gardens – rain filled cavities of cellars that have lost their houses – serve I think, to prolong the rot. Many of the gaps and ruins we know will remain. The present rulers are in no hurry to reconstitute London as it was: they have not much love, in fact, for Dick Whittington's city. If actually it did drop to bits, it would not break their hearts. So there it is, a monstrous derelict of a city . . . Wyndham Lewis, *Rotting Hill* (Santa Barbara: Black Sparrow Press), p. 96.

68 Of the alternative histories outlined in one recent volume, fifteen of the twenty-five essays deal with 'great men' figures. Women figure only tangentially in a study of Anthony and Cleopatra; see J. Ober, 'The Triumph of Anthony and Cleopatra at Actium in 31 BC',

in R. Cowley (ed.), *More What If? Eminent Historians Imagine What Might Have Been* (London: Macmillan, 2001), pp. 23–47.

69　N. Ferguson, 'Introduction' to Ferguson (ed), Virtual History: Alternatives and Counterfactuals (London: Macmillan, 1997), pp. 7–8.

Notes to Chapter 1: Wat Tyler, Jack Cade and the Threat of Peasant Revolt in Nineteenth-Century London

1　T. Cooper, 'A Chartist Song' from Cooper, *Poetical Works* (London: Hodder and Stoughton, 1877), p. 285.

2　*The Labour Prophet*, 1 March 1892, p. 19.

3　An exception to this rule is R.B. Dobson, 'Remembering the Peasants' Revolt', in W. H. Liddell and R. G. E. Wood (eds), *Essex and the Great Revolt of 1381: Lectures Celebrating the Sixth Hundreth Anniversary* (Chelmsford: Essex Record Office, 1982), pp. 1–15.

4　R.H. Mottram, *Bowler Hat: A Last Glance at the Old Country Banking* (London: Hutchinson, 1940), pp. 159–60.

5　A. White, 'England and America: Strangers Yet', *Anglo-Saxon Review*, 7 (1900), 11.

6　*Daily Mirror*, 15 February 1934, p. 13.

7　See for this debate, *The London News*, 1 June 1934, p. 7 and 1 May 1934, p. 8. The name was eventually accepted, and today Lewisham duly has a 'Wat Tyler Road'.

8　J. M. Davidson, *Annals of Toil: Labour History Outlines, Roman and British* (London: William Reeves, 1899), pp. 134–5. The Owenite socialist, Patrick Lloyd Jones, blamed the records kept by partisan chroniclers like Froissart for the distorted images of Tyler and Cade passed down to posterity. See the *Newcastle Weekly Chronicle*, 22 March 1884, p. 4.

9　See for incarnations of Tyler in relation to Jack Jones and José Bové, *The Guardian*, 22 September 2000, p. 19 and 13 June 2001, p. 8. Bové's career is described in K. Ross, *May '68 and its Afterlives* (Chicago: Chicago University Press, 2002).

10　The appeal made by motorway protestors and New Age culture to peasant revolt and the Medieval brigand tradition is recorded in G. McKay, *Senseless Acts of Beauty: Cultures of Resistance since the Sixties* (London: Verso, 1996), pp. 45–71 and 179. There is a tribute to Heathcote Williams in *The Guardian*, 19 July 1996, p. 3.

11　*Poll-Tax Riot: Ten Hours that Shook Trafalgar Square* (London: Acab Press, 1990), pp. 18–20, 27 and cover blurb.

12　See F. Williams, *Fifty Years March: The Rise of the Labour Party* (London: Odhams Press Ltd., 1950), pp. 111–12.

13　A.L. Morton, *When the People Arose: The Peasants Revolt of 1381* (London: CPGB, 1981), p. 1; A. Prescott, 'Writing about rebellion: using the records of the peasant revolt of 1381', *History Workshop Journal*, no. 45 (1998), 1–29 and for a commemoration of the events of 1381 at Blackheath addressed by Tony Benn, "Wat every revolutionary should know now', *The Guardian*, 5 May 1981, p. 4. Patrick Wright sees Benn's exhortations to remember the peasant revolt as symptomatic of what he terms the 'Blue Plaque' tradition within the British Labour movement; see P. Wright, *On Living in An Old Country* (London: Verso, 1985), p. 156. For Benn's own views on peasant revolt, see T. Benn, *Fighting Back: Speaking Our for Socialism in the Eighties* (London: Hutchinson, 1988), pp. 38–9.

14   *Labour Leader*, 3 November 1911, p. 700.

15   *Justice*, 14 June 1884, p. 1, E.A. Vizetelly, *The Anarchists: Their Faith and Their Record* (Edinburgh: Turnbull and Spears Printers, 1911), pp. 1–5, J. Wakeman, *Anarchism and Democracy* (London: Freedom Press, 1920), p. 8 and *Freedom*, 1 July 1913, p. 56, and 1 October 1913, p. 79. Anarchist views of Tyler and the anarchist appeal to the peasant revolt tradition are also articulated in F.A. Ridley, 'The technique of armed insurrection', *War Commentary*, 1 March 1941, p. 7, and idem, *The Revolutionary Tradition in England* (London: National Labour Press, 1948), pp. 43–53 and more recently in P. Marshall, *Demanding the Impossible: A History of Anarchism* (London: Fontana, 1992), pp. 89–92. For republican interpretations of the events of 1381 see Jane Cowen (daughter of the prominent nineteenth-century republican Joseph Cowen), *Tales of Revolution and of Patriotism* (London: Walter Scott, 1884), pp. 16–17 and *Tribune*, 21 May 1937, p. 15. Radicals even detected a freethought connection in the sixteenth-century peasant revolts. In 1588, a relative of the Norwich rebel, Robert Ket, was burnt at Norwich Castle 'for divers detestable opinions against Christ our saviour' enabling his inclusion in J.M. Wheeler, *A Biographical Dictionary of Freethinkers of all Ages and Nations* (London: Progressive Publishing Company, 1889), p. 191. Following this tradition, the secularist Joseph Symes gave a talk to Leeds Secular Society on the 'Wat Tyler Rebellion', see the *National Reformer*, 5 May 1878, pp. 12–14.

16   See T. Hodgkinson, *How to be Idle* (London: Penguin, 2004), p. 166.

17   J. Cleveland, *The Rustick Rampant, or Rural Anarchy Affronting Monarch in the Insurrection of Wat Tyler: An Edition of the Idol of the Clownes* (London: John Cleveland, 1658).

18   *A Dialogue between Wat Tyler, Mischevous Tom and an English Farmer* (London: John Stockdale, 1793), pp. 11–12.

19   *The Rebellion of Norwich in 1549, A Drama Interspersed with Music First Acted on Monday April 17 1815 at the Theatre Royale, Norwich: With Notes, Historical and Explanatory by George P. Bromley* (Norwich: Bacon, Kinnebrook and Co., 1815), v–viii.

20   Charles Dickens, *Bleak House* (Oxford: Oxford World's Classics, 1996), p. 22. Dickens had some sympathy for Tyler, writing: 'Wat was a hard-working man who had suffered much, and had been foully outraged; and it is probable that he was a man of a much higher nature and a much braver spirit than any of the parasites who exulted then, or have exulted since, over his defeat': see Dickens, *A Child's History of England* (London: Thomas Nelson and Sons, 1900), p. 178.

21   For Arch as Jack Cade see *The Bee-Hive*, 24 May 1874, p. 7, for the Tolpuddle Martyrs as Cades and Tylers see J. Marlowe, *The Tolpuddle Martyrs* (London: Deutsch, 1971), p. 239, for John Burns as Cade see W. Kent, *John Burns: Labour's Lost Leader* (London: Williams and Norgate Ltd., 1950), p. 25, for the Fenians (rather perversely) as Cades, N. Rance, *The Historical Novel and Popular Politics in Nineteenth-Century Britain* (London: Vision, 1975), pp. 68–9 and for David Lloyd George as 'a second-rate Jack Cade', *Our Land*, 1 September 1909, pp. 25–9.

22   The Wilkeite reform movement was accused of emulating both Cade and Tyler: P.D.G. Thomas, *John Wilkes: A Friend to Liberty* (Oxford: Oxford University Press, 1996). p. 197. For the Gordon Riots see P. Linebaugh, *The London Hanged: Crime and Civil Society in the Eighteenth Century* (London: Penguin, 1991) p. 347.

23 J. Wheelwright, *Landlordism: Its Origin and Growth* (London: English Land Restoration League, 1896), pp. 11–12.

24 J. Clayton, *Leaders of the People: Studies in Democratic History* (London: Martin Secker, 1910), p. 335. Also see for the connections between land reform and peasant revolt, H. Cox, *Land Nationalisation* (London: Land Nationalisation Society, 1892), p. 28, R. Heath, *The English Peasant; Studies, Historical, Local and Biographic* (London: T. Fisher Unwin, 1893), pp. 4–27, C. Turner, *Land Problems and National Welfare* (London: John Lane, 1911), pp. 116–17 and W. Webster, 'The Land and the People', *The Radical*, 2 July 1881, p. 2.

25 *Commonweal*, 13 November 1886 to 22 January 1887.

26 Quoted in Morris, *News from Nowhere and Other Writings*, xxxiii.

27 *Freedom*, 1 February 1927, p. 12.

28 J. Bruce Glasier, *William Morris and the Early Days of the Socialist Movement* (London: Longmans, Green and Co, 1921), pp. 68–9. Harold Laski claimed to have found copies of *The Dream of John Ball* in the houses of impoverished Northumberland miners during the Great Slump; see F. MacCarthy, *William Morris: A Life for Our Time* (London: Faber and Faber, 1994), p. 548. The journal *Freedom* stated that the work enables 'us to realise what men can be when for a little while they have thrown from them the yoke of despotism and are able to live according to the fullness of their own nature'. See *Freedom*, 1 June 1888, p. 83.

29 See for a serialization of the novella in a socialist paper produced in Christchurch, New Zealand, *The Socialist*, 1 August 1897, p. 4.

30 J. Kellett, 'William Lane and "New Australia": a reassessment', *Labour History* (Australia), 72 (1997), 19–34. 'John Miller' was the fictional name appended to the ballads produced during the revolt; see Davidson, *Annals of Toil*, p. 121. The name located the heroes of the revolt within the folkloric archetypes of popular culture like 'John Nameless' and the hated tax-gatherer, 'Hobb the Robber'; see A.L. Lloyd, *Folk Song in England* (London: Panther, 1967), p. 96. William Lane's brother, Ernest, wrote under the pseudonym 'Jack Cade', in Australian labor periodicals like the *Daily Standard* during the Great War; see G. Souter, *A Peculiar People: The Australians in Paraguay* (Sydney: Angus and Robertson Ltd., 1968), p. 249.

31 H. Hyndman, *The Historical Basis of Socialism in England* (London: Kegan Paul, 1883), pp. 3–4, and H. Broadbridge, 'The turning of the worm', in *Fifty Mutinies, Rebellions and Revolutions* (London: Odhams Press Ltd., 1933), pp. 371–84. For an account of Britain's last peasant rising, the 1607 Midland Rising, and its significance for the history of the Labour Party, see *The Labour Pioneer and Yorkshire Factory Times*, 18 August 1921, p. 2. The Midland Rising is also discussed in Communist Party sources; see Jack Lindsay and E. Rickword, *A Handbook of Freedom: A Record of English Democracy through Twelve Centuries* (London: Lawrence and Wishart, 1939), pp. 98–100.

32 M. Gilliland, 'The idea of equality', *Seed Time*, 1 April 1897, pp. 2–4.

33 P. Ward, *Red Flag and Union Jack: Englishness, Patriotism and the British Left, 1881–1924* (Woodbridge: Boydell and Brewer, 1998), pp. 26–36.

34 There is a brief autobiography of Joseph Clayton in his *The Rise and Decline of Socialism in Great Britain 1884–1924* (London: Faber and Gwyer, 1926), viii–x. Other studies by him include: *Wat Tyler and the Great Uprising* (London: Francis Griffiths, 1909); *The True Story of Jack Cade, Captain of Kent A.D. 1450: A Vindication* (London: Frank Palmer, 1909) and *Robert Ket and the Norfolk Rising* (London: Martin Secker, 1912). For his Christian Socialism

see his admiring sketch, *Father Stanton of St. Albans, Holborn: A Memoir* (London: Wells, Gardner, Darton and Co., 1913), pp. 79–80 and for reviews of his work the *Labour Leader*, 4 February 1910, p. 67 and 6 January 1911, p. 3.

35 B. Jarrett, *Medieval Socialism* (London: Burns Oates and Washbourne Ltd., 1913), p. 32.

36 C. Noel, *Autobiography* (London: J.M. Dent and Sons Ltd., 1945), xi, pp. 90 and 127 and 'A Twopenny Guide to Thaxted Church' c. 1945, tipped into my edition of the above. The veneration of Ball at Thaxted was continued by Noel's successor, Jack Putterill, whose pamphlet on Ball was still for sale in the church in the 1980s; see for Wyndham Lewis' visit to the church, *Rotting Hill*, pp. 241–3 and 335–6.

37 Ruskin History Workshop Students Collective, 'Worker-historians in the 1920s', in Raphael Samuel (ed), *People's History and Socialist Theory* (History Workshop, 1981), pp. 17–20 and R. Samuel, 'British Marxist Historians, 1880–1980', *New Left Review*, I (1980), especially pp. 38–41. WEA and University Extension courses also followed this narrative: see H.D. de. Gibbins, *English Social Reformers* (London: Methuen and Co., 1892), p. 14.

38 J. Keir Hardie, *From Serfdom to Socialism* (London: Gorge Allen, 1907), pp. 40–1 and 48.

39 J.E. Thorold Rogers, *Six Centuries of Work and Wages: The History of English Labour* (London: T. Fisher and Unwin, 1903), pp. 254–63. Rogers' popular history spawned a host of imitators, most of which dealt with the Wat Tyler rising, see W.G. Wilkins, *The Penny History of the Poor People of England: The Rise and Progress of Poverty in England from the Norman Conquest to Modern Times* (London: Headley Brothers, 1911), pp. 5–6 and *The Weekly Tribune*, 28 May 1904, pp. 1–2.

40 In 1861 Richard Cobden wanted to know why it was that British workmen had no Spartacus 'to head a revolt of the slave class against their political tormentors?': D. Read, *Cobden and Bright: A Victorian Political Partnership* (London: Edward Arnold Ltd., 1967), pp. 159–60. For the Spartacus tradition more broadly see T. Urbainczyk, *Spartacus* (Bristol: Bristol University Press, 2004), pp. 9–11 and the *Labour Leader*, 27 October 1911, p. 683. Reformers on the continent also embraced a pan-European tradition of peasant revolt including the German peasant wars of the 1520s and the Czech Hussites; see M. Beer, *Social Struggles and Socialist Forerunners* (London: Leonard Parsons, 1924), chs. 3 and 4, and pp. 44–54 for the 1381 English peasant revolt.

41 See discussion of this point in *The Commonweal*, 27 April 1889, p. 129.

42 *Justice*, 24 January 1885, p. 3. See on this theme R. Hall, 'Creating a people's history: political identity and history in Chartism, 1832–1848', in O. Ashton, R. Fyson and S. Roberts (eds), *The Chartist Legacy* (Woodbridge: Merlin, 1999), pp. 255–85, C.V.J. Griffiths, *Labour and the Countryside: The Politics of Rural Britain, 1919–1939* (Oxford: Oxford University Press, 2007), pp. 44–8, P. Karsten, *Patriot-Heroes in England and America: Political Symbolism and Changing Values over Three Centuries* (Madison: University of Wisconsin Press, 1978), chs. 2–3 and 6, P. Readman, 'The place of the past in English culture c.1890–1914', *Past and Present* no. 186 (2005), 147–99 and idem, *Land and Nation in Britain: Patriotism, National Identity, and the Politics of Land, 1880–1914* (Woodbridge: Boydell and Brewer, 2008), pp. 185–6.

43 *Labour Leader*, 21 February 1908, p. 118. Rodney Hilton, the most famous historian of the 1381 revolt, grew up in a strongly ILP family in Middleton, in Lancashire. See his obituary in *The Guardian*, 10 June 2002, p. 20.

44 For the interest of Scottish radicals in William Wallace, see the career of John McAdam, a campaigner for the 1832 reform act, a former Chartist, and one of the moving spirits behind the monument to Wallace outside Stirling in the 1860s: J. Fyfe (ed), *Autobiography of John McAdam (1806-1883)* (Edinburgh: Clark Constable Ltd., 1980), x–xxi and pp. 79–81. English peasant rebels were not, however, entirely absent from Celtic narratives of political reform. Tyler and Cade feature in the mixed list of Scottish, English and continental freedom fighters listed by the Aberdeen radical, W.C. Anderson, in 'Once More unto the Breach', *Labour Leader*, 29 April 1910, p. 7, and Tyler, Ball and Cade are mentioned in D. Thomas, *Y Werin a'i Theyrnas* (*The Common People and their Kingdom*) (Caernarfon: Cyhoeddwyd gan yr Awdur, 1910), pp. 74–5. Thomas was an ILP pioneer in North Wales, his book becoming a manifesto for militant quarrymen in the 1900s. My thanks to Wil Griffiths for this reference.

45 Samuel, 'British Marxist Historians', p. 41. Henry Pelling's history of the British Communist Party begins with a commentary on this fictional radical pedigree; see H. Pelling, *The British Communist Party: A Historical Profile* (London: Adam and Charles Black, 1958), p. 1. For the full family tree of British radicalism in the 1930s linking John Ball, the Levellers, the Chartists and the CPGB see E. Rickword, 'Culture, progress and English tradition', in C. Day Lewis (ed), *The Mind in Chains: Socialism and the Cultural Revolution* (London: Frederick Muller, 1937), pp. 237–56. The definitive statement of a Popular Front position on the 'people's history' is A.L. Morton, *A People's History of England* (London: Lawrence and Wishart, 1986), ch. 4 and there remain echoes of this project in W. Gallacher, *The Case for Communism* (London: Penguin, 1948), pp. 49–53.

46 'The March of English History: A Message to you from the Communist Party', p. 4. Flyer, Marx Memorial Library, 1936, Communist Party Ephemera. My thanks to John Baxendale for this reference.

47 There is heated, contradictory correspondence in *The Times* about the exact circumstances in which 'Wat Tyler' found its way into the hands of radicals for publication. See *The Times*, 12 and 25 January 1822. For an account of the same events see the *National Reformer*, 10 February 1879, p. 102. Literary radicals were appalled by the degree to which Southey had reneged on the principles of his youth; see Byron's *The Vision of Judgement by Quevedo Redivivus suggested by the Composition so Entitled by the Author of Wat Tyler* (London: L. Hunt, 1824), pp. 4, 17–18 and 22–3.

48 This episode is widely discussed by the biographers of Southey: see W.A. Speck, *Robert Southey: Entire Man of Letters* (New Haven, CT: Yale University Press, 2006), pp. 171–3 and M. Storey, *Robert Southey: A Life* (Oxford, 1997), pp. 67–70; 253–62. Southey's decision to renege on the ideas of his youth is satirized in W. Hone, *The Political "A, Apple-Pie"; or the Extraordinary Red Book Versified* (London: Adams and Dart, 1971), p. 160.

49 W. St. Clair, *The Reading Nation in the Romantic Period* (Cambridge: Cambridge University Press, 2004).

50 J. Epstein, *Radical Expression: Political Language, Ritual, and Symbolism in England, 1790-1850* (Oxford: Oxford University Press, 1994), p. 103 and James Finlen, 'The English Press', in the *People's Paper*, 30 April 1853, p. 2.

51 See *Sherwin's Political Register*, 22 March 1817, pp. 2–15 and R. Poole, 'French revolution or peasants' revolt?: petitioners and rebels in England from the blanketeers to the Chartists', *Labour History Review*, 74 (2009), 6–26.

52   A.R. Schoyen, *The Chartist Challenge: A Portrait of George Julian Harney* (London: Heinemann, 1958), p. 8 and F.B. Smith, *Radical Artisan: William James Linton, 1812–97* (Manchester: Manchester University Press, 1973), p. 6.

53   *English Chartist Circular*, vol. 1, no. 14 (1841), p. 56. Also see 'Hymns to be Sung at the Sheffield and Barnsley Chartist Camp-Meeting, on Sunday, Sep. 22nd, 1839', ballad in Sheffield Local Studies Collection, Sheffield Central Library.

54   See *Freedom*, 1 June 1923, p. 29.

55   J. Collings, *Land Reform: Occupying Ownership, Peasant Proprietorship and Rural Education* (London: Longmans, 1906), xvi–xvii.

56   Especially, *Wat Tyler and Jack Straw, or the Mob Reformers, a Dramatic Entertainment as it is Perform'd at Pinkethman's and Giffard's Great Theatrical Booth in Bartholomew Fair* (London: J. W., 1730).

57   Dobson, 'Remembering the Peasant's Revolt', p. 11. Both Tyler and Cade were strongly enmeshed with the history of the City Corporation: see A.J. Glasspool, *The Corporation of the City of London: Its Ceremonies and Importance* (London: Effingham Wilson, 1924), pp. 50–1, and 91. The centrality of popular pageantry and historical re-enactments for the public image of the City Corporation is outlined in T.B. Smith, 'In defence of privilege: the City of London and the challenge of municipal reform, 1875–1890', *Journal of Social History*, 27 (1993), 59–83 and A. Fahrmeir, 'The London Lord Mayor's Show in the Nineteenth Century: Celebrating Achievement or Glorifying Tradition', in J. Neuheiser and M. Schaich (eds), *Political Rituals in Great Britain, 1700–2000* (Augsburg: *Arbeitskreis Deutsche England-Forschung*, 2006), pp. 55–73.

58   *Justice*, 15 November 1884, p. 2.

59   See Dobson, 'Remembering the Peasants' Revolt', p. 12 and R.H.H. Evans (ed), *Thomas Evans, Old Ballads, Historical and Narrative* (London: R.H.H. Evans, 1810), pp. 311–15.

60   Anon, *Robert Ket, The Wyndham Tanner: A Poem* (London: A. Brown, 1869), pp. 6 and 64. Also see F.W. Russell, *Ket's Rebellion* (London: Longman, Brown and Green, 1859) and Cowen, *Tales of Revolution and Patriotism*, pp. 32–47. In this work Ket rubs shoulders with the leaders of the Ghent rebellion in the Low Countries, Russian peasant revolt leader Pugachev, the Latin American revolutionary Simon Bolivar, and the Polish nationalist leader, Kosciuszko. See for a novelistic treatment of Ket's rebellion, F.C. Tansley, *For Kett and Countryside* (London: Jarrold and Sons, 1910), especially pp. 399–402.

61   For a few random examples amongst many, see *The Commonwealth*, 20 October 1866, p. 1, *The Gauntlet*, 16 February 1834, p. 857, Justice, 30 April 1892, p. 5, *Reynolds's Political Instructor*, 19 January 1850, p. 82, *The Sunday World*, 14 February 1891, p. 15, 'Wat Tyler', *Two Essays: The Earth Question or Landlords and People, and the Capital Question or Employers and Workers* (Belfast: Reid, 1889), the *Labour Leader*, 14 March 1918, p. 6 and B. Worden, *Roundhead Reputations: The English Civil War and the Passions of Posterity* (London: Penguin, 2001), p. 246.

62   In Stoke, the Chartist radical Joseph Capper was compared to John Ball; see C. Shaw, *When I Was a Child* (London: Caliban Books, 1983), p. 148. For Wat Tyler as John Burns, see *The Sunday World*, 17 January 1891, p. 12.

63   See J.M. Davidson, *Eminent Radicals In and Out of Parliament* (London: W. Stewart and Co., 1880), p. 20.

64   *Northern Star*, 26 February 1848, p. 5.

65   See for the text of amateur theatricals about Robert Kett in Norwich, G. Colman Green, 'Ket the Tanner,' ms play by the Norwich Bohemian Art Club, 1921, in materials relating to Robert Ket, Norwich Public Library.

66   H. Glover, *Wat Tyler: A Play in Three Acts* (London: Kegan Paul, Trench, Trubner, 1925), p. 72. For the nineteenth century emphasis on the chivalric tradition which the Tyler myth subverted, see M. Girouard, *The Return to Camelot: Chivalry and the English Gentleman* (New Haven, CT: Yale University Press, 1981), chs. 4, 5, 6 and 7.

67   *People's Paper*, 11 February 1854, p. 4 and for a poetic description of Wat Tyler as 'The Lord o' the Anvil', *The Odd Fellow*, 18 April 1840, p. 4.

68   *Freedom*, September–October 1927, pp. 45–6.

69   H. Spring, *Fame is the Spur* (London: Fontana/Collins 1982), p. 328. Tyler and Ball are also cited as part of the radical canon (alongside Shelley, Heinrich Heine, Ernest Jones, Robert Owen and William Morris) in the novel by Ethel Carnie, *This Slavery* (London: Labour Publishing Co., 1925). The work is discussed in H.G. Klaus (ed), *The Socialist Novel in Britain* (Hassocks: Harvester, 1982), p. 94.

70   T. Paine, *The Rights of Man* (London: Penguin, 1979), p. 254. The agitator Martin Boon lamented the absence of a statue to Tyler at a meeting of the Working Men's National Reform League on Whitechapel Road in 1869; see the *National Reformer*, 5 December 1869, p. 365.

71   *Lansbury's Labour Weekly*, 5 September 1925, p. 6.

72   Ibid., 11 December 1926, p. 10. Joseph Clayton wrote of Ket's body hanging from the wall of Norwich Castle, that 'there were some who could not look upon that poor body, waving on high above the castle, and not see in it a pennon of the good cause, a torn banner of the fight for freedom, and gaze on it with reverence as upon the tattered flag of a famous regiment hanging, when its work is done, in the quiet of a great church'. See Clayton, *Robert Kett*, p. 243.

73   Ibid., p. 6.

74   R.F. Foster, *Lord Randolph Churchill* (Oxford: Clarendon Press, 1981), p. 78. For the dubious origins of the connection between Jack Straw's Castle and the events of 1381, see J. Larwood and J.C. Hotten, *English Inn Signs* (London: Chatto and Windus, 1951), pp. 45, 246 and 282.

75   A. Wood, *The 1549 Rebellions and the Making of Early Modern England* (Cambridge: Cambridge University Press, 2007), pp. 262–3.

76   *Eastern Daily Post*, 18 July 1949, p. 5.

77   For Samuel Holberry's funeral and the Sheffield Chartist Club see R.G. Gammage, *History of the Chartist Movement* (London: Merlin Press, 1976), pp. 215–16, and Schoyen, *The Chartist Challenge*, p. 123. For Isaac Jefferson, see the *Northern Star*, 22 July 1848, p. 4, E. Royle, *Revolutionary Britannia? Reflections on the Threat of Revolution in Britain 1789–1848* (Manchester: Manchester University Press, 2000), pp. 131–2 and D. Thompson, *Popular Politics in the Industrial Revolution* (Aldershot: Wildwood House Ltd., 1984), p. 198.

78   *Reynolds's Newspaper*, 9 May 1858, p. 7.

79   Dobson, 'Essex and the great revolt of 1381', p. 14 and the *Northern Star*, 30 September 1848, p. 7.

80   *The Commonwealth*, 12 January 1867, p. 5.

81   J. Breuilly, G. Niedhart and A. Taylor (eds), *The Era of the Reform League: English Labour and Radical Politics 1857–1872: Documents Selected by Gustav Mayer* (Mannheim: Mannheimer Historische Forschungen, 1995), p. 241.

82 This was the title of an article by De Morgan on the 1381 insurrection, entitled: '"Kentish Fire". Or episodes in the history of Kent', *De Morgan's Monthly*, 1 September 1876, pp. 3–4. Fred Hammell, a devout follower of de Morgan, who went on to become a Labour parliamentary candidate for Newcastle-on-Tyne, still felt it necessary to recall Wat Tyler's revolt in his election address; see the *Labour Prophet*, 1 December 1893, p. 117.

83 *Kentish Mercury*, 15 July 1876, p. 3. For public access struggles in London and its environs in the nineteenth century, see A. Taylor, '"Commons-stealers", "land-grabbers" and "jerry-builders": space, popular radicalism and the politics of public access in London, 1848–1880', *International Review of Social History*, 40 (1995), 383–407 and R. McWilliam, *The Tichborne Claimant: A Victorian Sensation* (London: Hambledon Continuum Press, 2007), pp. 159–65.

84 'Fagin', *'Reds on the Green': A Short Tour of Clerkenwell Radicalism* (London: South London Radical History Group, 2005). Blackheath was one of a series of iconic meeting place that stirred memories of popular revolt: 'Blackheath, and Copenhagen Fields, the moors of Lancashire and Yorkshire, Glasgow Green and our own Moor are famous places in the popular history of Britain'; see the *Newcastle Weekly Chronicle*, 7 July 1866, p. 4. For Gladstone's set-piece speeches at Blackheath during the Eastern Question agitation which caused W.T. Stead 'on his first political pilgrimage' to recall popular heroes like Hereward the Wake and Cromwell, see R. Shannon, *Gladstone and the Bulgarian Agitation, 1876* (London: Hamish Hamilton, 1963), pp. 115–16. There is a description of Gladstone speaking at Blackheath on the Eastern Question in *Reynolds's Newspaper*, 10 September 1876, p. 5. Anti-globalization protestors mobilized at Blackheath in memory of Tyler in 2009: see *The Guardian*, 27 August 2009, p. 9.

85 See the poem 'Wat Tyler' by Leonard Wells, commemorating Tyler 'murdered 16 June 1381', in ibid, 17 June 1888, p. 2.

86 T. Cooper, *Captain Cobler or the Lincolnshire Rebellion: An Historical Romance of the Reign of Henry VIII* (London: J. Watson, 1850). There are echoes of the 1536 'Pilgrimage of Grace', in Tory radical Richard Oastler's 'Pilgrimage to York', in 1832 on behalf of the Ten Hours movement in the factory districts; see C. Driver, *Tory Radical: the Life of Richard Oastler* (Oxford. Oxford University Press, 1946), ch. 14.

87 C. Cole, 'The Spirit of Wat Tyler', *Northern Star*, 16 September 1848, p. 3.

88 *Poor Man's Guardian*, 27 August 1831, p. 63.

89 *National Reformer*, 11 June 1871, p. 382 and for a re-examination of Cade's reputation, J. Clayton, 'Shakespeare's Jack Cade', *Socialist Review*, 4 (1909–10), 457–62.

90 *New Statesman*, 17 May 1913, p. 173.

91 J. Walker, 'Chartist Ecologue', in *The Bard* (London: Simpkin, Marshall and Co., 1842), p. 2.

92 Watkins often gave readings from his poem on Wat Tyler: see the *Northern Star*, 10 December 1842, p. 1. He was also the editor of the short-lived *Chartist Journal*. For Watkins more generally, see D. Goodway, *London Chartism, 1838–1848* (Cambridge: Cambridge University Press, 1982), pp. 57–8 and M. Chase, *Chartism: A New History* (Manchester: Manchester University Press, 2007), pp. 17–25.

93 *Labour Leader*, 19 October 1906, p. 337 and for more on Ball the *English Labourers' Chronicle*, 6 July 1878, p. 1 and B. Villiers, *The Socialist Movement in England* (London: T.F. Unwin, 1908), pp. 19–20.

94 *Northern Star*, 22 July 1848, p. 3.

95 For Walpole's comparison of the Gordon riots to the Ket rising, see I. McCalman, 'Mad Lord George and Madame La Motte: riot and sexuality in the genesis of Burke's *Reflections on the Revolution in France*', *Journal of British Studies*, 35 (1996), 343–67 and I. Haywood, *Bloody Romanticism: Spectacular Violence and the Politics of Representation, 1776–1832* (London: Macmillan, 2006), p. 185.

96 See for the same point made about the William Courtenay revolt in rural Kent in 1838, *Is Jack Cade Coming? A Question Considered by the Age Newspaper of Sunday June 10 1838* (London: Holt, 1838), especially pp. 5–6.

97 J.A. Sutherland, *The Longman Companion to Victorian Fiction* (London: Longman, 1988), p. 209. The success of Egan's *Robin Hood and Little John* in 1840 contributed to a revival of interest in the career of the famous outlaw. See a gathering of Hood devotees at Sherwood Forest in the *Sheffield Iris*, 9 November 1841.

98 There is a short sketch of Pierce Egan Jr in J. Dix, *Lions Living and Dead or Personal Recollections of the Great and the Gifted* (London: W. Tweedie, 1854), p. 291. Pierce Egan Jr illustrated the work of his more famous father in woodblock prints for P. Egan, *The Pilgrims of the Thames in Search of the National* (London: Thomas Tegg, 1838).

99 J.C. Reid, *Bucks and Bruisers: Pierce Egan and Regency England* (London: Routledge and Kegan Paul, 1971), pp. 194–5.

100 'The Working-Man in History', *National Reformer*, 13 January 1867, pp. 20–1.

101 P. Egan Jr., *Wat Tyler* (London: Simpkin, Marshall and Co., 1841), chs.3 and 4 and p. 465. The 'history' of Tyler's career as a soldier and retainer to the Black Prince resurfaces in other popular treatments of this period, notably in the American work by W. Hilliard, *Life and Adventures of Wat Tyler* (London: Collins, 1851), especially pp. 57–87. Here there is a particular American inflection in the hostility displayed towards hereditary aristocracy, described as 'a useless, idle and profligate oligarchy' (p. 157). Wat Tyler's revolt against tax exactions also harmonized well with political preoccupations in the United States. Admiration for 'Wat Tylerism' was very nearly respectable in the United States. See P. Linebaugh, *The Magna Carta Manifesto* (Berkeley: University of California Press, 2008), p. 127, and for the diffusion of literature about him as 'the first martyr of socialism', the *International Socialist Review*, 14 (1913), 260.

102 See T. Costley, *Lancashire Poets and Other Literary Sketches* (Manchester: Abel Heywood and Son, 1897), p 128.

103 J. Cooke, *Jack Cade, the Insurrectionist: An Historical Romance* (London: T. White, 1840), p. 246.

104 Egan Jr., *Wat Tyler*, p. 493.

105 J. Leatham, *The Peasants' Revolt or the Tragedy of a Nation* (London: Twentieth Century Press, 1899), pp. 6–7.

106 There remain echoes of the 'good' Tyler whose 'personal influence seems to have been exercised on the side of discipline' of the mob in C.E. Maurice, *Lives of English Popular Leaders in the Middle Ages: Tyler, Ball and Oldcastle* (London: H.S. King and Co., 1875), pp. 178 and 182.

107 See the *Northern Star*, 5 February 1848, p. 4, 22 July 1848, p. 3, and a speech by Thomas Slingsby Duncombe in ibid, 30 September 1848, p. 4.

108 William Napier's comments on Cade are recorded in P. Napier, *Revolution and the Napier Brothers, 1820–1840* (London: Michael Joseph, 1973), p. 185.

109 Haywood, *Bloody Romanticism*, p. 105.

110 Ibid., pp. 112–13.

111 M. Elliott, *Robert Emmet: The Making of a Legend* (London: Profile Books, 2004), ch. 5. Emmet, like Tyler, was frequently toasted at radical gatherings. See a report of the Barnsley Radical Dinner in the *London Dispatch*, 20 November 1836. My thanks to Matthew Roberts for this reference.

112 See I. Dyck, '"Rural war" and the missing revolution in early nineteenth-century England', in Michael T. Davis (ed), *Radicalism and Revolution in Britain, 1775–1848* (London: Macmillan, 2000), pp. 176–90.

113 S.K. Hocking, *The Broken Fence* (London: Sampson Low, 1928), p. 12 and C. Gleig, *When All Men Starve* (London: John Lane, 1898), p. 150.

114 Loc cit and Morris, *Dream of John Ball*, p. 58.

115 *The History of Wat Tyler and Jack Straw* (Stirling: C. Randall, 1803), pp. 9. and 13.

116 For Henty as an advocate of empire and Christian virtues, see G.M. Fenn, *George Alfred Henty: The Story of an Active Life* (London: Sampson Low, Marston and Company, 1907) and J.M. MacKenzie, *Propaganda and Empire: The Manipulation of British Public Opinion, 1880–1960* (Manchester: Manchester University Press, 1984), pp. 209–13.

117 There was a tradition of patriotic and loyalist figures identifying with Richard II during periods of political turmoil and foreign policy adventurism. In the 1850s Lord Palmerston depicted himself as a 'modern Richard II' at the height of the Crimean War. See the *People's Paper*, 24 February 1855, p. 3. Radicals routinely represented Richard II as a symbol of reaction. In 1911, MPs who voted in favour of a bill for the creation of a strike-breaking volunteer police force were seen as likely to defend 'Richard II from Wat Tyler and [to hang] the followers of Jack Cade, the Captain of Kent'. See *The Eye Witness*, 21 December 1911.

118 G.A. Henty, *A March on London: A Tale of Wat Tyler's Rising* (New York: Charles Scribner's Sons, 1897), pp. 45–7 and 151–2.

119 Ibid., p. 119.

120 Ibid., p. 177.

121 This term is used for political nostalgia on the left in R. Samuel, *Island Stories: Unravelling Britain* (London: Verso, 1998), pp. 272–5.

122 M. Finn, *After Chartism: Class and Nation in English Radical Politics, 1848–1874* (Cambridge: Cambridge University Press, 1993), ch.1 and p. 67.

123 Egan Jr., *Wat Tyler*, p. 462.

124 Leatham, *The Peasants' Revolt*, pp. 13–18.

125 See comments by Karl Blind and a review of his work in the *National Reformer*, 8 November 1874, pp. 298–9.

126 *People's Paper*, 14 January 1854, p. 1. Ernest Jones frequently made reference to the history of peasant revolt. See respectively for articles on Wat Tyler, the 1536 Lincolnshire Rising, and the French *jacquerie*, the *London News*, 15 May 1858, p. 2, 22 May 1858, p. 2 and 29 May 1858, p. 2. For a full account of Jones's relationship with the Medieval past, see M. Taylor, *Ernest Jones, Chartism and the Romance of Politics 1819–1869* (Oxford: Oxford University Press, 2003), pp. 92–5.

127 See R.L. Outhwaite, *The Land Revolution* (London: George Allen and Unwin, 1917), pp. 8 and 49.

128 See on this point the ideas of the Tyneside antiquarian and Jacobin, Joseph Ritson, in B. H. Bronson, *Joseph Ritson, Scholar-at-Arms* 2 vols. (Berkeley, CA: University of California Press, 1938) I, p. 220.

129 Bede Jarrett believed that the English peasant revolts were very English in style, observing the constitutional proprieties, and using accepted petitioning techniques and methods of public assembly, in marked contrast to the tone of the excessively violent French *jacquerie*; see Jarrett, *Medieval Socialism*, p. 25.

130 For an excellent attempt to summarize the nature of the traditions bequeathed by the Tudor 'Revolt of the Commons' see M.L. Bush, 'The risings of the commons in England, 1381–1549', in J. Denton (ed), *Orders and Hierarchies in Late Medieval and Renaissance Europe* (London: Macmillan, 1999), pp. 109–25.

131 *Reynolds's Newspaper*, 27 January 1884, p.3. For more in the paper on Wat Tyler as an antidote to the court flattery and royal obeisance of Queen Victoria's 1887 jubilee, see ibid, 13 March 1887, p. 2.

Notes to Chapter 2: Anarchism and the Literature of Terror in the Metropolitan Imagination

1   C. Stein in R.H. Savage, *The Anarchist: A Story of To-Day* (2 vols., Leipzig: Bernhard Tauchniiz, 1894), i, p. 97.

2   J. Lyons and C. Raleigh, *The Master Crime* (London: Cassell and Company, Ltd., 1907), p. 1.

3   *Saturday Review*, 11 August 1900, pp. 166–7.

4   *Reynolds's Newspaper*, 7 March 1880, p. 4.

5   B. Anderson, *Under Three Flags: Anarchism and the Anti-Colonial Imagination* (London: Verso, 2005), pp. 113–15.

6   W E. Adams, *Memoirs of a Social Atom* (2 vols., London: Hutchinson and Co., 1903), ii, p. 566. Anarchists as 'uneasy human vampires' or 'unclean social spectres' also feature in Savage, *The Anarchist*, ii, pp. 228 and 239.

7   P. Marshall, *Demanding the Impossible: A History of Anarchism* (London: Fontana Press, 1992), p. 4.

8   D. Weir, *Anarchy and Culture: The Aesthetic Politics of Modernism* (Amherst: University of Massachusetts Press, 1997), ch. 2.

9   V. Serge, *Memoirs of a Revolutionary* (Iowa City: University of Iowa Press, 2002), p. 18.

10 There is a wide literature on the history and ideas of anarchism. The best introductions remain the following: D. Guerin, *Anarchism* (New York: Monthly Review Press, 1970); I.L. Horowitz (ed.), *The Anarchists* (New York: Dell Publishing Ltd., 1964), pp. 15–65, J. Joll, *The Anarchists* (New York: Grosset and Dunlap, 1964), chs. 4 and 5; S.M. Sheehan, *Anarchism* (London: Reaktion, 2003), chs. 2 and 4; F. Venturi, *Roots of Revolution: A History of the Populist and Socialist Movements in Nineteenth Century Russia* (Princeton: Princeton University Press, 1960), chs. 15 and 21; C. Ward, *Anarchism: A Very short Introduction* (Oxford: Oxford University Press, 2005), C. Ward and D. Goodway, *Talking Anarchy* (Nottingham: Five Leaves Press, 2005); G. Woodcock, *Anarchism: A History of Libertarian Ideas and Movements* (London: Penguin, 1986), chs. 5 and 6.

11 W. Wolfe, *From Radicalism to Socialism: Men and Ideas in the Formation of Fabian Socialist Doctrines 1881–1889* (London: Yale University Press, 1975), p. 134.

12 Bakunin recommended recruitment amongst the urban under-class usually ignored by reformist progressive parties: see R. de Jong, 'Provos and Kabouters', in D.E. Apter and J. Joll (eds), *Anarchism Today* (London: Macmillan, 1971), p. 172.

13 For pacifist anarchism, see G. Aldred, *At Grips with War* (Glasgow: Bakunin Press, 1932).

14 *Labour Leader*, 25 July 1912, p. 476.

15 See M. Bevir, 'The rise of ethical anarchism in Britain, 1885–1900', *Historical Research*, 69 (1996), 143–65 and M. Thomas, ' "No-one telling us what to do": Anarchist Schools in Britain, 1890–1916', *Historical Research*, 77 (2004), 405–36.

16 H. Gustav Klaus and S. Knight, 'Introduction', in Klaus and Knight (eds), *'To Hell with Culture': Anarchism and Twentieth Century Literature* (Cardiff: University of Wales Press, 2005), pp. 1–10.

17 The refusal of anarchists to vote put them at odds with all other British movements of radical reform in the nineteenth century. Not casting the ballot was a mark of pride for anarchists. When the committed anarchist Dr John Mclean Hayward died in 1886, his self-penned epitaph boasted: 'Here lies the body of John Mclean Hayward who Never Voted. Of such is the kingdom of heaven'. See *The Anarchist*, 1 July 1886, p. 1.

18 See G B Shaw, *The Impossibilities of Anarchism* (Fabian Society: London, 1893), especially pp. 4–5.

19 For Bakunin, see I Berlin, *Russian Thinkers* (London: Penguin, 1978), pp. 82–113 and S. Dolguff (ed.), *Bakunin on Anarchism* (Montreal: Black Rose Books, 1980), pp. 3–21. For Russian anarchism as a form of secularized religious faith, see M. Burleigh, *Earthly Powers: The Conflict between Religion and Politics from the French Revolution to the Great War* (London: Harper Perennial, 2005), pp. 299–310.

20 Quoted in J.W. Hulse, *Revolutionists in London: A Study of Five Unorthodox Socialists* (Oxford: Oxford University Press, 1970), p. 53.

21 For the Bonnot Gang, see H. Ashton-Wolfe, *Outlaws of Modern Days* (London: Cassell and Company Ltd., 1927), pp. 47–70. For the background to French anarchism more generally, see L. Proal, *Political Crime* (New York: D. Appleton and Co., 1898), ch. 3 and R.D. Sonn, *Anarchism and Cultural Politics in Fin de Siecle France* (Lincoln: University of Nebraska Press, 1989), chs, 1–3. For a first hand account, see Serge, *Memoirs of a Revolutionary*, passim.

22 J. Bruce Glasier, *William Morris and the Early Days of the Socialist Movement* (London: Longmans, Green and Co, 1921), p. 126.

23 H. Kennedy, *Anarchist of Love: The Secret Life of John Henry Mackay* (New York: Mackay Society, 1983) and A. Wexler, *Emma Goldman: An Intimate Life* (London: Virago, 1984), ch. 7.

24 Comfort had a long literary pedigree of writing and campaigning against oppressive religious and social institutions; see D. Goodway, *Anarchist Seeds beneath the Snow: Left Libertarian Thought and British Writers from William Morris to Colin Ward* (Liverpool: Liverpool University Press, 2009), ch. 11.

25 W.C. Hart, *Confessions of an Anarchist* (London: E Grant Richards, 1906), p. 9.

26   *Justice*, 25 May 1895, p. 1. For warnings against police spies and informers in the anarchist movement see ibid, 5 November 1892, p. 1 and the *Newcastle Weekly Chronicle*, 11 October 1884, p. 1, which accused continental governments of 'adopting precisely the same tactics as those which were adopted by Sidmouth and Castlereagh in this country in the early days of popular agitation'.

27   E. Bland and H. Bland, *The Prophet's Mantle* (London: Drane, 1885), p. 68.

28   This point is made in Edward Bellamy's utopian vision of a futuristic Boston in the year 2000. Dr Leete, the protagonist's guide to the future, comments of the nineteenth-century anarchist movement: 'No historical authority nowadays doubts that they were paid by the great monopolies to wave the red flag and talk about burning, sacking, and blowing people up, in order, by alarming the timid, to head off any real reforms'. See E. Bellamy, *Looking Backward, 2000–1887* (London: William Reeves, 1908), pp. 188–9. For the internal security world where Secret Service agents freely rubbed shoulders with anarchists, see B. Porter, *Plots and Paranoia: A History of Political Espionage in Britain, 1790–1988* (Boston: Unwin Hyman, 1989).

29   See A. Houen, *Terrorism and Modern Literature: From Joseph Conrad to Ciaron Carson* (Oxford: Oxford University Press, 2002).

30   Conrad's *The Secret Agent* had a very significant impact, particularly on the anarchists themselves. A popular parlour game in radical circles was to try to identify the personalities alluded to in the book; see *Lansbury's Labour Weekly*, 29 January 1927, p. 11.

31   For the Siege of Sidney Street and its aftermath, see C. Holmes, *The Battle of Stepney: The Sidney Street Siege, Its Causes and Consequences* (London: Robert Hale, 1981), ch. 17 and D. Rumbelow, *The Houndsditch Murders and the Siege of Sidney Street* (London: W.H. Allen, 1988), chs. 7 and 8. The Sidney Street siege is fictionalized in E. Litvinoff, *A Death Out of Season* (London: Michael Joseph, 1973) and F. Oughton, *The Siege of Sidney Street* (London: Pan, 1960). For Litvinoff see V. Cunningham, 'Litvinoff's Room: East End Anarchism', in Klaus and Knight (eds), *'To Hell with Culture'*, pp. 141–61.

32   For moral panics about anarchism, see H. Shpayer-Makov, 'Anarchism in British Public Opinion 1880–1914', *Victorian Studies*, 31 (1988), 487–516, and A.D. Pionke, *Plots of Opportunity: Representing Conspiracy in Victorian England* (Columbus: Ohio State University Press, 2004), chs. 2 and 5.

33   For invasion panic literature more generally, see P. Panayi, *The Enemy in our Midst: Germans in Britain during the First World War* (Oxford: Berg Publishers Ltd., 1991), ch. 6 and E.S. Turner, *Boys will be Boys: The Story of Sweeney Todd, Deadwood Dick, Sexton Blake, Billy Bunter, Dick Barton, et al* (London: Penguin, 1975), ch. 11.

34   H Shpayer-Makov, 'A traitor to his class: the anarchist in British fiction'. *Journal of European Studies*, 26 (1996), 299–325.

35   G. Boothby, *The League of Twelve* (London: F.V. White and Co., 1903), pp. 151–61 and 201.

36   J. Buchan, *The Power-House* (London: Pan, 1961), p. 44.

37   Ibid., p. 104. In Buchan's *The Thirty-Nine Steps* the cover story originally revealed by Scudder to Richard Hannay concerns an anarchist conspiracy: see Buchan, *The Thirty-Nine Steps* (London: Penguin, 1993), pp. 10–15.

38   E. Nesbit, *The Railway Children* (London: Penguin, 1993), p. 83. Edith Bland (later Nesbit)'s involvement in Fabianism and support for nihilism is discussed in J. Briggs, *A Woman of*

Passion: The Life of E. Nesbit, 1858–1924 (London: Penguin Books, 1989), pp. 72–7. The anarchist in the book is an amalgam of several different figures, but his career bears some similarity to Stepniak (Sergei Kravachinski) who was imprisoned for his work, *The Russian Peasantry, Their Agrarian Condition, Social Life and Religion* (Cambridge: Cambridge Scholars' Publishing, 2009). Stepniak was an author of terrorist manuals, but had a softer side displayed by his hosting of tea parties for female undergraduates from Lady Margaret Hall, Oxford; see Joll, *The Anarchists*, p. 147, Anderson, *Under Three Flags*, pp. 72–3 and *Freedom*, 1 January 1893, p. 7 and 1 March 1893, p. 15.

39   Blands, *The Prophet's Mantle*, pp. 1–4 and 64–5.

40   E. Wallace, *People: A Short Autobiography* (New York: Doubleday, Doran and Company, 1929), pp. 188–9. Also see M. Lane, *Edgar Wallace: The Biography of a Phenomenon* (New York: Doubleday, Doran and Company, 1938), pp. 159–61 and for the eyewitness account of the young George V, who was in the wedding cortege, J. Gore, *King George V: A Personal Memoir* (London: John Murray, 1941), p. 212.

41   Wallace, *People*, p. 247.

42   Wallace's interest in anarchism and its equation with criminality in his writings is surprisingly overlooked in D. Glover, 'Looking for Edgar Wallace', *History Workshop Journal*, 37 (1994), 143–64. Wallace himself was widely read, and was a favourite author of George VI; see J.T. Gorman, *George VI, King and Emperor* (London: W.G Foyle Ltd., 1937), p. 24.

43   *The Spectator*, 24 February 1894, p. 256.

44   G.H.R. Dabbs, *The Ladder of Pain* (London: Charles William Deacon and Co., 1902), p. 109.

45   E.B. Baker, *Robert Miner, Anarchist* (London: Ward, Lock and Co., 1902), pp. 156–7.

46   J. Hocking, *David Baring* (London: George Newnes, Ltd., 1900), p. 145.

47   Some contemporary authorities, striking a more moderate tone, questioned whether anarchists were really as dangerous as they seemed, seeing them as simple fantasists who thrived when their fantasies were reinforced by hysterical group dynamics; see O. Malagodi, 'The psychology of anarchist conspiracies', *Westminister Review*, 147 (1897), 87–91.

48   S. Winsten, *Days with Bernard Shaw* (London: Hutchinson and Co., 1951), p. 100. For Kropotkin more generally see P. Kropotkin, *Memoirs of a Revolutionist* (London: Hutchinson, 1988), especially pp. 231–59, G. Woodcock and I. Avakumovic, *The Anarchist Prince: The Biography of Prince Peter Kropotkin* (London: Boardman and Company, 1950), ch. 7 and Hulse, *Revolutionists in London*, pp. 68–71. For a sober reassessment of Kropotkinite anarchism, see A. Cahm, *Kropotkin and the Rise of Revolutionary Anarchism* (Cambridge: Cambridge University Press, 1989).

49   Harry Quelch's 'The Dynamiter' was first published in *The Social Democrat*, 1 April 1897, pp. 124–8 and reprinted in E.B. Bax (ed.), *Harry Quelch: Literary Remains* (London: Grant Richards, 1914), pp. 46–55. A short story 'Vive l'Anarchy' by 'Yorrick the Younger', which revolves around the deaths of two lonely and dispirited anarchists, casts them in a more positive light than is usual as the unfortunate victims of poverty and injustice; see the *Labour Leader*, 14 July 1894, p. 10.

50   *Freedom*, 1 November 1886, p. 7, and 1 June 1897, p. 43; J.H. Mackay, *The Anarchists* (New York: The Revisionist Press, 1972), p. 24. The anarchists' unique loathing for London is made clear in a curious tale 'By the Thames' by an anonymous anarchist author in which a

talking bench alongside the River Thames lures the hopeless and the depressed into drowning themselves; see *The Free Commune*, 1 February 1899, pp. 1–16.

51   R. Rocker, *The London Years* (Nottingham: Five Leaves Publications, 2005), pp. 108–9.

52   See K. Beckson, *London in the 1890s: A Cultural History* (New York: W.W. Norton and Co., 1992), ch. 1, C. Bloom, *Violent London: 2000 Years of Riots, Revels and Revolts* (London: Sidgwick and Jackson, 2003), ch. 12, C. Coroneos, 'Conrad, Kropotkin and anarchist geography', *The Conradian*, 18 (1994), 17–30, H. Epstein, '"A pier glass in the cavern": the construction of London in *The Secret Agent*', in G.M. Moore (ed.), *Conrad's Cities: Essays for Hans Van Marle* (Amsterdam: Rodopi, 2002), pp. 175–96, and D. Erdinast-Vulcan, '"Sudden holes in time and space": Conrad's anarchist aesthetics in *The Secret Agent*', in ibid, pp. 207–21.

53   The only full-length study of the Walsall anarchist case is in J. Quail, *The Slow-Burning Fuse: The Lost History of the British Anarchists* (London: Paladin, 1978), especially ch. 6.

54   See L.Trilling, *The Liberal Imagination: Essays on Literature and Society* (London: Penguin Books, 1970), pp. 69–101 and W.H. Tilley, *The Background of the Princess Casamassima* (Gainesville: University of Florida Press, 1961), ch. 3.

55   M. Davitt, *The Fall of Feudalism in Ireland* (New York: Harper and Brothers, 1904), ch. 35, C. Campbell, *Fenian Fire: The British Government Plot to Assassinate Queen Victoria* (London: Harper Collins, 2002), chs. 14–19 and B.A. Melchiori, *Terrorism in the Late Victorian Novel* (Brighton: Harvester, 1985), pp. 13–18. For an anarchist view of the 1885 Irish bombing campaign, see *The Commonweal*, 1 February 1885, p. 6.

56   D.D. Gray, *London's Shadows: The Dark Side of the Victorian City* (London: Hambledon Continuum, 2010), pp. 14–21.

57   N. Whelehan, '"Cheap as soap and common as sugar": the Fenians, dynamite and scientific warfare', in F. McGarry and J. McConnel (eds), *The Black Hand of Republicanism: Fenianism in Modern Ireland* (Dublin: Irish Academic Press, 2009), pp. 105–20.

58   M O'Cathain, '"The black hand of Irish republicanism"? Transcontinental Fenianism and Theories of Global Terror', in ibid, pp. 135–46.

59   D. Mackay, *The Dynamite Ship* (New York: Page, Pratt and Turner, 1888).

60   W.J. Fishman, *East End Jewish Radicals, 1875–1914* (London: Duckworth, 1975), chs. 2 and 3 and D. Glover, 'Aliens, Anarchists and Detectives: Legislating the Immigrant Body', *New Formations*, 32 (1997), 22–33.

61   *The King's Reign Told in Pictures* (Manchester: Sankey, Hudson and Co., 1935), p. 7.

62   *The Clarion*, 16 January 1892.

63   Baker, *Robert Miner, Anarchist*, p. 154 and pp. 156–7.

64   A. Morrison, 'The Red Cow Group', in *Tales of Mean Streets* (London: Methuen and Co., 1894), pp. 173–95. For anarchists as buffoonish wastrels see A. Robinson, *Imagining London, 1770–1900* (Basingstoke: Macmillan, 2004), chs. 5 and 6.

65   See for the iconography and social symbolism of the 'visit' to the East End, S. Koven, *Slumming: Sexual and Social Politics in Victorian London* (Princeton, 2004), ch. 5.

66   H. James, *The Princess Casamassima* (London: Penguin, 1977), p. 166.

67   Joseph Hocking, part of a West Country dynasty of Methodist writers, drew on the experiences of his sister, Salome Hocking, who lived at the Whiteway anarchist colony, and who recorded her impressions of it as a fictionalized and ironic 'Strangeways'. See

S. Hocking, *Belinda the Backward: A Romance of Modern Idealism* (London: Arthur C. Fifield, 1905). For the Hockings more generally, see A.M. Kent, *Pulp Methodism: The Lives and Literature of Silas, Joseph and Salome Hocking* (St. Austell: Cornish Hillside Publications, 2002), ch. 4.

68 Hocking, *David Baring*, p. 79.

69 Mackay, *The Anarchists*, p. 5. For the connections between prostitution and anarchist theory, see Sonn, *Anarchism and Cultural Politics*, pp. 111–12 and *The Walsall Anarchist*, 27 February 1892, p. 2.

70 Rocker, *The London Years*, p. 24.

71 The destruction of London is a long-standing motif of much popular fiction dealing with the capital: see J. White, 'Unreal city: reflections on London and the novel in the twentieth century', *History Workshop Journal*, 56 (2003), 1–32.

72 For open spaces and metropolitan radicalism, see A. Taylor, ' "Commons-stealers", "land-grabbers" and "jerry-builders": space, popular radicalism and the politics of public access in London, 1848–1880', *International Review of Social History*, 40 (1995), 383–407.

73 See S. Inwood, *A History of London* (Basingstoke: Macmillan, 1998), chs. 17 and 19; A. Palmer, *The East End of London* (London: John Murray, 1999); A. Taylor, ' "A melancholy odyssey among London public houses": radical club life and the unrespectable in mid-nineteenth century London', *Historical Research*, 78 (2005), 74–95 and J. Walkowitz, *City of Dreadful Delight* (London: Verso, 1992), ch. 1.

74 For the denizens of 'underground' London, see Pike, *Subterranean Cities*, ch.2 and for representations of the Chinese in London lore, J. Seed, 'Chinatown in the London docks, 1900–1940', *History Workshop Journal*, no. 62 (2006), 58–85.

75 See 'The Recrudescence of Anarchism', in the *Labour Leader*, 12 July 1907, p. 36.

76 'I. Meredith' (Olivia and Helen Rossetti), *A Girl Among the Anarchists* (Lincoln: University of Nebraska Press, 1992), pp. 43–4. For the Rossetti clan's involvement in anarchism, see W. M. Rossetti, *Some Reminiscences* (New York: Charles Scribner and Sons., 2 vols.,), i, p. 219.

77 Baker, *Robert Miner, Anarchist*, p. 156–7.

78 Ibid., p. 85 and pp. 153–4.

79 E. Wallace, *The Council of Justice* (Pan Books Ltd., 1973), pp. 46 and 106.

80 For the background to *The Princess Casamassima*, see J.A. Clymer, *America's Culture of Terrorism: Violence, Capitalism and the Written Word* (Chapel Hill: University of North Carolina Press, 2003), ch. 2.

81 For the Chicago Haymarket Martyrs, see P. Avrich, *The Haymarket Tragedy* (New Jersey: Princeton University Press, 1984), especially chs. 14, 15 and 23; C.S. Smith, 'Cataclysm and cultural consciousness: Chicago and the Haymarket Trial', *Chicago History*, XV (1986), 36–53, *The Anarchist*, 1 June 1886, p. 1, 1 December 1886, p. 1, 1 January 1888, p. 1, and 1 July 1888, p. 2; *Freedom*, 1 October 1887, p. 49, 1 December 1887, p. 59, 1 January 1888, p. 63, 1 November 1888, p. 5 and 1 December 1888, p. 9 and *Mother Earth*, 1 November 1907, pp. 368–74. There is an obituary of Jim Connell and an account of the inspiration for 'The Red Flag', in *The London News*, 1 March 1929, p. 6.

82 See *Justice*, 28 June 1884, p. 1.

83 B. Porter, *The Refugee Question in Mid-Victorian Politics* (Cambridge: Cambridge University Press, 1979), ch. 6.

84 P. Kropotkin, *Fields, Factories and Workshops* (London: Swan Sonnenschein and Co., 1901), ch. 6.

85 R. Jefferies, *After London: Wild England* (Oxford: Oxford University Press, 1980), vii–viii and for an analysis of *After London*, Pike, *Subterranean Cities*, p. 277.

86 Hart, *Confessions of an Anarchist*, p. 73.

87 E. Douglas Fawcett, *Hartmann the Anarchist, or the Doom of a Great City* (New York: Arno Press, 1975), p. 102.

88 Lyons and Raleigh, *The Master Crime*, p. 90.

89 *Freedom*, 1 March 1894, p. 9 and for the annual anarchist celebration of the Paris Commune, ibid, 1 March 1888, p. 69.

90 Savage, *The Anarchist*, vol. ii, p. 215.

91 M.J. Schaack, *Anarchy and Anarchists: A History of the Red Terror and the Social Revolution in America and Europe* (Chicago: F.J. Shulte and Co., 1889), pp. 682–3.

92 The elderly '48 veteran is the eccentric anarchist, Daniel Chatterton, see A. Whitehead, 'Dan Chatterton and his "atheistic communisitic scorcher"', *History Workshop*, 25 (1988), 83–99.

93 R. Whiteing, *No. 5 John Street* (London: Thomas Nelson and Sons, 1902), pp. 66 and 218. The name 'Azrael' also features in Gustave Linbach's thriller, *The Azrael of Anarchy* (London: Simpkin and Marshall, 1894).

94 R. Whiteing, *My Harvest* (London: Macmillan, 1915), p. 49. For the ideas of the Reclus brothers, see Hulse, *Revolutionists in London*, p. 54 and E Reclus, 'Anarchy: by an Anarchist' *Contemporary Review*, 45 (1884), 627–41. For the work of Whiteing more generally, see D. Smith, *Socialist Propaganda in the Twentieth-Century British Novel* (London: Macmillan, 1978), pp. 12–14.

95 James, *The Princess Casamassima*, pp. 283–4.

96 E. Thomas, *The Women Incendiaries* (New York: Haymarket Books, 2007).

97 B. Hemyng's *The Commune in London, or Thirty Years Hence* (London: C.H. Clarke, 1871) and 'Grip' (John Drew Gay), *How John Bull Lost London, or the Capture of the Channel Tunnel* (London: Sampson Low, 1882), pp. 2–8. For metropolitan invasion panic literature see I.F. Clarke, *Voices Prophesying War 1763–1984* (Oxford: Oxford University Press, 1966), chs. 1 and 2.

98 C. Gleig, *When All Men Starve* (London: John Lane, 1898), pp. 166 and 192.

99 Douglas Fawcett, *Hartmann the Anarchist*, p. 139. Anarchists themselves invoked Macaulay's vision of the end of the metropolis; see *The Anarchist*, 14 March 1886, p. 1. For Macaulay's New Zealander see Nead, *Victorian Babylon*, pp. 212–15.

100 M.I. Cole (ed), *Beatrice Webb's Diaries, 1912–1924* (London: Longmans, Green and Co., 1952), p. 109. For arguments about non-violent anarchism see R.W. Burnie, 'Peaceful Anarchists', *Justice*, 7 May 1892, p. 4. One review of Hart, *Confessions of an Anarchist*, bemoaned 'that Mr Hart has not done justice to the other and more estimable section of anarchists, those, for instance, who form farm colonies and who read and talk about Tolstoy.' See the *Labour Leader*, 12 October 1906, p. 323.

101 For rural anarchist colonies see W.H.G. Armytage, *Heavens Below: Utopian Experiments in England* (London: Routledge and Kegan Paul, 1961), pp. 305–15 and pp. 342–58, and note 67 above.

102 Hocking, *David Baring*, p. 154.

103 Kropotkin, *Fields, Factories and Workshops*, pp. 112–18 and 235–6.

104 Savage, *The Anarchist*, vol. ii, p. 86. See for the history of dynamite, A Marshall, *Explosives* (2 vols., London: J and A. Churchill, 1917) II, p. 342 and for an examination of explosive techniques as hinted at in Conrad's The Secret Agent, J. Sutherland, *Where Was Rebecca Shot: Puzzles, Curiosities and Conundrums in Modern Fiction* (London: Weidenfeld and Nicolson, 1998), pp. 22–6.

105 Present-day car bombs are in a direct line of descent from the anarchist carts laden with explosives; see M. Davis, *Buda's Wagon: A Brief History of the Car Bomb* (London: Verso, 2007).

106 Savage, *The Anarchist*, vol. ii, p. 160.

107 Wallace, *The Council of Justice*, pp. 72–3. The Bonnot gang also hoped to deploy aeroplanes in their attacks on French banks. There was a long literature linking anarchism with the new technology of airships and dirigibles. This plot was used in a number of novels in the 1890s by George Griffith, notably, *The Angel of the Revolution: A Tale of the Coming Terror* (New York: Heliograph Books, 2003), especially ch. 2. The image of anarchists attacking London from the air persisted in the film *The Aerial Anarchists* directed by Walter Booth in 1911 in which St. Paul's Cathedral is destroyed by aerial bombardment; see M. Paris, *Warrior Nation: Images of War in British Popular Culture 1850–2000* (London: Reaktion, 2000), pp. 100–1. For terrorism and technologies of mass destruction more generally, see Laqueur, *The New Terrorism*, ch. 2.

108 Dabbs, *The Ladder of Pain*, p. 116.

109 A. Morrison, 'The Case of the Lost Foreigner', in *The Chronicles of Martin Hewitt* (New York: Books for Libraries Press, 1971), p. 250.

110 *The Anarchist*, 1 March 1885, p. 4.

111 Ibid., 13 February 1885, p. 1 and 20 April 1886, pp. 1–2.

112 F. Dubois, *The Anarchist Peril* (London: T. Fisher Unwin, 1894), ch. 9.

113 For Johann Most, see H. Becker, 'Johann Most in Europe', *The Raven: Anarchist Quaterly*, 1 (1988), 291–321; B. Porter, 'The Freiheit persecutions, 1881–1882', *The Historical Journal*, 23 (1980), 833–56, for Ravachol and Henry see Joll, *The Anarchists*, ch. 5 and for Lucheni see A. Sinclair, *Death by Fame: A Life of Elizabeth, Empress of Austria* (New York: St. Martin's Press, 1998), ch. 12.

114 Joll, *The Anarchists*, p. 223.

115 See R. Kedward, *The Anarchists: The Men Who Shocked an Era* (Leiden: Sijthoff, 1970), pp. 5–33.

116 Hocking, *David Baring*, chs. 1–6 and 'Meredith', *A Girl Amongst the Anarchists*, ch. 1. Emma Goldman's vision of the anarchist commune was as a surrogate family; see Wexler, *Emma Goldman*, p. 280.

117 Dabbs, *The Ladder of Pain*, p. 132.

118 See Venturi, *Roots of Revolution*, ch. 15, and G. Fellner (ed.), *Life of an Anarchist: The Alexander Berkman Reader* (New York: Four Walls Eight Windows, 1992), pp. 5–106.

119 See Sonn, *Anarchism and Cultural Politics in Fin de Siecle France*, p. 261.

120 A L. Vago, *Orthodox Phrenology* (London: Simpkin, Marshall and Co., 1871), p. 46. For Lombroso, see D. Pick, 'The faces of anarchy: Lombroso and the politics of criminal science in post-unification Italy', *History Workshop*, no. 21 (1986), 60–86.

121 'Meredith', *A Girl Amongst the Anarchists*, p. 153.

122 Savage, *The Anarchist*, vol. i, p. 5, and ii, p. 70.

123   R. Magraw, *France 1815-1914: The Bourgeois Century* (London: Fontana, 1983), pp. 206–7 and Dubois, *The Anarchist Peril*, p. 47.

124   Baker, *Robert Miner, Anarchist*, pp. 9–15. On tramps and their relationships with anarchists more generally, see T. Cresswell, *The Tramp in America* (London: Reaktion Books, 2001), chs. 2 and 3 and H. Gustav Klaus, *Tramps, Workmates and Revolutionaries* (London: Journeyman Press, 1993). Victor Serge recalled the presence of tramps at the anarchist commune he visited in Belgium administered by Emile Henry's brother, Fortune: Joll, *The Anarchists*, p. 173.

125   The Rossetti sisters, Helen and Olivia, are very much 'New Women' types; see *A Girl Amongst the Anarchists*, v–xvii.

126   See the role of Virginia Clare in J.H. Shorthouse, *Sir Percival: A Story of the Past and of the Present* (London: Macmillan, 1894), pp. 149–53.

127   H. Oliver, *The International Anarchist Movement in Late Victorian London* (London: Croom and Helm, 1983). A quarter of Nihilists in Russia were allegedly female: see Laqueur, *The New Terrorism*, p. 38.

128   *Daily Telegraph*, 19 December 1910.

129   E. Thomas, *Louise Michel* (Montreal: Black Rose Books, 1980), intro and ch. 1, *The Anarchist*, 1 August 1886, p. 1 and 1 February, 1888, p. 5, *The Sunday World*, 3 May 1891, p. 5, Margaret McMillan, 'Louise Michel', *Labour Prophet*, 1 December 1892 and 1 January 1893, and for Michel's inflammatory speeches which predicted that the English people would rise up and 'choke the Thames with the corpses of the capitalists', Adams, *Memoirs of a Social Atom*, I, p. 566.

130   For Chernyshevsky see Venturi, *Roots of Revolution*, ch. 5.

131   For Petrovskaya, see *The Social Democrat*, 1 June 1897, pp. 194–7, and the *Labour Leader*, 19 October 1906, p. 337 and for the reverence in which she and Zasulich were held by a later generation of both female and male anarchists, Wexler, *Emma Goldman*, pp. 24–7 and Kropotkin, *Memoirs of a Revolutionist*, pp. 269–70. Vera Zasulich was the model for the Russian Nihilist heroine in Oscar Wilde's first play to be given a public performance, *Vera, or the Nihilists* written in 1881 and which fared badly on both the British and American stage; it's sometimes described as 'having bombed'; see for the play R. Ellman, *Oscar Wilde* (New York: Random House, 1987), pp. 116–19. Nihilist drama with romantic undertones was very prevalent in the theatre of the day; see for a review of one such production at the Britannia Theatre in the East End, *Our Corner*, 8 (1886), pp. 109–10.

132   See Schaack, *Anarchy and Anarchists*, p. 207.

133   Baker, *Robert Miner, Anarchist*, pp. 87–9.

134   G.A. Henty, *Condemned as a Nihilist: A Story of Escape from Siberia* (London: Blackie and Sons, 1892), p. 67.

135   Savage, *The Anarchist*, vol.ii, p. 254.

136   Whiteing, *No. 5 John Street*, pp. 271–3.

137   Wallace, *The Council of Justice*, pp. 12–13.

138   *Justice*, 14 February 1885, p. 5.

139   D. Rooum (ed.), *What is Anarchism? An Introduction* (London: Freedom Press, 1993), p. 4 and S.J. Ross, *Working-Class Holywood: Silent Film and the Shaping of Class in America* (New Jersey: Princeton University Press, 1998), pp. 64–7.

Notes to Chapter 3: Red Scares and Inter-War London

1   The Duc de Reichleau in D. Wheatley, *The Forbidden Territory* (London: Arrow Books Ltd., 1961), p. 20.

2   Mollie Lenden in N. Shute, *So Disdained* (London: House of Stratus, 2000), pp. 164–5.

3   The definitive statement of this position remains A. Light, *Forever England: Femininity, Literature and Conservatism between the Wars* (London: Rouledge, 1991), pp. 76–82, but also see for a humorous contribution to this critique, C. Watson, *Snobbery with Violence: English Crime Stories and Their Audience* (London: Methuen, 1971), especially ch. 8.

4   J. Symonds, *Bloody Murder: From the Detective Story to the Crime Novel* (London: Penguin. 1972), p. 96.

5   See, for introductions to this material, S. Knight, *Crime Fiction, 1800–2000: Detection, Death, Diversity* (London: Macmillan, 2004), chs. 2 and 3 and Priestman, *Crime Fiction*, chs. 4 and 5.

6   R. Usborne, *Clubland Heroes: A Nostalgic Study of Some Recurrent Characters in the Romantic Fiction of Dornford Yates, John Buchan and Sapper* (Barrie and Jenkins, 1953), pp. 39–40, 97–9 and 161–3.

7   K. Boyd, *Manliness and the Boys' Story Paper in Britain: A Cultural History, 1855–1940* (London: Palgrave-Macmillan, 2003), especially ch. 6 and M. Paris (2005), 'Red menace: Russia and British juvenile fiction', *Contemporary British Fiction*, 19, 117–32 and Turner, *Boys Will Be Boys*, chs. 8 and 9.

8   *Tribune*, 14 January 1944, p. 11.

9   See the entry on William Le Queux in D. McCormick, *Who's Who in Spy Fiction* (London: Sphere, 1977), p. 139.

10   A. Lownie, *John Buchan: The Presbyterian Cavalier* (London: Pimlico, 2002), pp. 162–3.

11   G. Orwell, 'Boys' Weeklies', in *Critical Essays* (London: Secker and Warburg, 1946), pp. 57–88. An exception to this general rule is provided by the children's stories of Geoffrey Trease. In *Bows Against the Barons* in 1934 he pained the story of Robin Hood as a people's national epic. In it Hood famously asserts that 'We are equal in Sherwood. What is the sense of getting rid of one master and taking a new one?' See G. Trease, *Bows Against the Barons* (Leningrad: Enlightenment Press, 1968), p. 18. The book became popular in the Soviet Union where it circulated without copyright. It was used as an English language primer and teaching aid. There is a review of the book by Harry Pollitt in the *Daily Worker*, 10 April 1934, p. 3 and a further commentary on the work, comparing it to the 'Penny Bloods', in ibid, 4 April 1934, p. 4.

12   See Lownie, *John Buchan*, chs. 9 and 10 and for the persistent anti-radical Edwardianism of Dornford Yates, A.J. Smithers, *Dornford Yates: A Biography* (London, 1982), pp. 32–5 and 212–15. Dennis Wheatley made his name with an anti-Bolshevik romp, *The Forbidden Territory* that introduced his long-running and popular character, the Duc de Reichleau, who was a veteran of Denikin's White armies in the Russian Civil War (p. 87). For Wheatley's anti-socialism, see Baker, *The Devil Is a Gentleman*, ch. 35.

13   A. Ridley, *The Ghost Train: A Drama in Three Acts* (London: Samuel French, 1931), p. 61. Ridley went on to play the part of Private Godfrey in 'Dad's Army'.

14   Priestman, *Crime Fiction*, p. 45.

15   Lord Willoughby de Broke, *The Passing Years* (London: Constable, 1924), p. 13.

16   For the pragmatic nature of Labour's economic and social ideas, see Jose Harris, 'Labour's Political and Social Thought', in D. Tanner, P. Thane and N. Tiratsoo (eds.), *Labour's First Century* (Cambridge: Cambridge University Press, 2000), pp. 8–45. Even attempts to locate a 'Labour Socialism' have acknowledged the weakness of this concept. See D. McHugh, *Labour in the City: The Development of the Labour Party in Manchester 1918–31* (Manchester: Manchester University Press, 2006), ch. 7.

17   J. Clayton, The Rise and Decline of Socialism in Great Britain, 1884–1924 (London: Faber and Gwyer, 1926), p 14.

18   J.R. Clynes, *Memoirs* (London: Hutchinson, 1937, 2 vols.,), I, pp. 124–5 and the *Maoriland Worker*, 28 July 1911, p. 10.

19   S. Grahame, *Where Socialism Failed: An Actual Experiment* (London: John Murray, 1912), p. 238. Anti-socialist rhetoric emerged very strongly in local elections after the emergence of the first Labour-controlled councils after 1926; see T.M. Willis, 'The Politics and Ideology of Local Authority Health Care in Sheffield, 1918–1948.' (PhD thesis, Sheffield Hallam University, 2009), pp. 28–32.

20   F. Brockway, *Bermondsey Story: The Life of Alfred Salter* (London: George Allen and Unwin, 1949), p. 35.

21   H.G. Wells, *Will Socialism Destroy the Home?* (London: ILP, 1904), p. 1.

22   For these ideas amongst employers' associations, see A.J. McIvor, 'Employers' Associations and Industrial Relations in Lancashire, 1890–1939' (PhD thesis, University of Manchester, 1983) and S. Berger, *The British Labour Party and the German Social Democrats, 1900–1931* (Oxford: Oxford University Press, 1994), pp. 50–60.

23   Critics of socialism reported with particular glee, the theft of Keir Hardie's watch during a visit to Winnipeg in Canada, depicting it as just desserts after his preaching of redistributionist doctrines; see the *Maoriland Worker*, 2 June 1911, p. 7.

24   A. Hopkinson, *The Hope of the Workers* (Manchester: Hopkinson, 1923), p. 12.

25   *The Individualist*, 1 October 1907, p. 72. See for similar sentiments, ibid, 1 March 1907, pp. 19–20 and 1 October 1907, pp. 18–19.

26   For the Army League, the Navy League and the National Service League, see J.M. Mackenzie, *Propaganda and Empire: The Manipulation of British Public Opinion, 1880–1960* (Manchester: Manchester University Press, 1984), pp. 151, 154–5, 183 and 229.

27   See K.D. Brown, 'The Anti-Socialist Union, 1908–49', in K.D. Brown (ed.), *Essays in Anti-Labour History: Responses to the Rise of Labour in Britain* (London: Macmillan, 1974), pp. 234–61.

28   *Labour Leader*, 17 November, 1911.

29   Brown, 'The Anti-Socialist Union', p. 238.

30   See for the Economic League, A. McIvor, 'Essays in anti-Labour history', *Society for the Study of Labour History Bulletin*, 53 (1988), 18–26.

31   For Herbert Morrison's opposition to Communism, see *Unity, Peace and Security: Pollitt's Reply to Morrison* (London: Workers' Bookshop, 1936), pp. 2–7 and for attempts to purge Communists from the Labour Party, N. Branson, *History of the Communist Party of Great Britain 1927–1941* (London: Weidenfeld and Nicholson, 1985), ch. 1.

32   See K. Morgan, *The Webbs and Soviet Communism* (London: Lawrence and Wishart, 2007), chs, 7, 8 and 9.

33 H.G. Williams, *Why I Am Not A Socialist* (London: The Anti-Socialist and Anti-Communist Union, 1930), p. 1.

34 *Real Socialism: Authenticated Extracts from Socialist Leaders' Speeches and Writings* (London: National Union of Conservative and Unionist Associations, 1924), and L. Beers, *Your Britain: Media and the Making of the Labour Party* (Cambridge, MA: Harvard University Press, 2010), pp. 59–67.

35 See W.P. Coates, *The 'Zinoviev Letter': The Case for a Full Investigation* (London: The Anglo-Russian Parliamentary Committee, 1928), pp. 25–7, Lewis Chester, S. Fay and H. Young, *The Zinoviev Letter: A Political Intrigue* (London: Heinemann, 1967), chs. 2 and 3, and Clynes, *Memoirs*, I, pp. 63–6.

36 Nevil Shute's novel *So Disdained*, about an ex-Royal Flying Corps airman lured into spying for the Bolsheviks, was written in the aftermath of the Arcos crisis, which is alluded to in the text (pp. 253–4).

37 Clynes, *Memoirs*, I, p. 102.

38 A. Clarke, 'What's the matter wi' th' country: Tum Fowt debatin' club an ' anti-henpeck mission', *Teddy Ashton's Lancashire Annual* (Blackpool: Palatine Books Co., 1925), p. 22.

39 D. Kiberd, *Inventing Ireland: The Literature of the Modern Nation* (London: Vintage, 1996), pp. 481–529.

40 A. Christie, *The Secret Adversary* (London: Triad Granada, 1982), p. 57.

41 L. O'Flaherty, *The Informer* (London: New English Library, 1971), p. 52.

42 D. Goldstein and M. Moore Avery, *Socialism: The Nation of Fatherless Children* (Boston: Thomas J. Flynn and Co., 1911), p. 18. This book is reviewed in *The International Socialist Review*, vol. 4 (1903–4), pp. 715–16.

43 For a summary of the major stories in this genre see C. Waters, *British Socialists and the Politics of Popular Culture, 1884–1914* (Manchester: Manchester University Press, 1990), ch. 2 and D. Smith, *Socialist Propaganda in the Twentieth-Century British Novel* (London: Macmillan, 1978), chs. 2–4, and for the continuation of such literature into the inter-war period, A. Croft, 'World without end foisted upon the future – some antecedents of *1984*', in C. Norris (ed.), *Inside the Myth; Orwell: Views from the Left* (London: Lawrence and Wishart, 1984), pp. 183–216.

44 *The Open Road*, vol. 9 (1911), pp. 86–90.

45 Croydon at the beginning of the twentieth-century was an appropriate place for musings on the genesis of a new society. It had a reputation for extreme radicalism, anarchism, alternative community-building and oppositional politics of every kind; 'in fact every kind of "anti" had a welcome and a hearing', in the radical societies in the town: see N. Shaw, *Whiteway: A Colony in the Cotswolds* (London: C.W. Daniel, 1935), p. 21.

46 *The Worker*, 4 April 1908, p. 2. The story was serialized in the Huddersfield *Worker* between 22 February 1908, p. 3, and 13 June 1908, p. 2. A large number of such stories appeared in 1907–8, following the gain of 29 Labour seats in the 1906 election, the formal establishment of the party machine in that year, and the build-up to the twentieth anniversary of the events at the 'Bloody Sunday' riot in Trafalgar Square in 1887. The centenary was marked by much introspection on socialist methods and tactics: see R.B. Cunningham Graham, 'Bloody Sunday, 13 November 1887', *New Age*, 12 November 1908, p. 49 and G.R.S. Taylor, 'The First Socialist Cabinet, 1912', ibid, 10 December 1908, p. 125.

47 *Labour Leader*, 20 March 1913, p. 4 and for praise of Jack London more generally, *The Worker*, 5 September 1908, p. 2 and the *Maoriland Worker*, 28 July 1911, p. 6 and 22 December 1911, p. 8. For the British readership of London's *The Iron Heel*, see J. Rose, *The Intellectual Life of the British Working Classes* (New Haven, CT: Yale University Press, 2001), pp. 83, 246 and 261, and Wilding, *Political Fictions*, ch. 3. See J. London, *The Iron Heel* (New York: Grayson Publishing Corp., 1948), ch. 22 for the destruction of the Chicago Commune.

48 Alexander Joyce, *Land Ho! A Conversation of 1933 on the Results of the Adoption of the System of Nationalising the Land of New Zealand adopted in 1883* (Lyttleton: Lyttleton Press, 1881), pp. 7–15. For similar speculative and utopian fiction in the Australian colonies see J. Docker, *The Nervous Nineties: Australian Cultural Life in the 1890s* (Oxford: Oxford University Press, 1991), chs. 8 and 9, and *The Commonweal* (Wellington), 1 February 1907, p. 6 for a futuristic depiction of the Australian colonies in AD 2006.

49 *The New Age*, 2 May 1908, p. 13.

50 Ibid., 16 May 1908, p. 52. The full text of the story is in *The New Age*, 2 May, 9 May and 16 May 1908.

51 C. Chesterton. 'The Defeat of Charles Murray', in ibid, 11 March 1909, pp. 403–4.

52 The phrase is used in J. Lawrence, *Speaking for the People: Party, Language and Popular Politics in England, 1867–1914* (Cambridge: Cambridge University Press, 1998), p. 201.

53 For a discussion of the 1926 radio panic in London see J. Bourke, *Fear: A Cultural History* (London: Virago, 2005), pp. 167–81, and the *Manchester Guardian*, 18 January 1926, p. 6.

54 J. Sommerfield, *May Day* (London: Lawrence and Wishart, 1984), p. 28.

55 J.D. Beresford, *Revolution* (London: W. Collins, Sons and Co, 1921), p. 74.

56 Ibid., pp. 210–12.

57 For British Communism's insistence on the inevitability of a rapid and cleansing revolutionary change, see R. Samuel, *The Lost World of British Communism* (London: Verso, 2006), pp. 35–6 and 54–5.

58 See, for example, H.R. Barbor, *Against the Red Sky: Silhouettes of Revolution* (London: Noel Douglas, 1922) ch.1, which opens with a street brawl in London which rapidly spirals out of control into outright revolution once the police intervene. For studies of this novel, see H.G. Klaus, *The Literature of Labour: 200 Years of Working- Class Writing* (Brighton: Harvester, 1985), pp. 97–101, Smith, *Socialist Propaganda*, p. 47, and for a contemporary review, *The Times Literary Supplement*, 3 August 1922, p. 507.

59 Sommerfield, *May Day*, p. 242.

60 Philip Toynbee's novel, *These Savage Days*, had an appeal to a Communist student audience in the 1930s; Denis Healey recalled reading it at Oxford and the hero, Simon Lawrence, who had read 'The *Daily Worker* from cover to cover on the train between Oxford and Paddington': D. Healey, *The Time of My Life* (London: Penguin, 1989), p. 34.

61 P. Toynbee, *These Savage Days* (London: Hamish Hamilton, 1937), pp. 305–6.

62 Ibid., pp. 312–14.

63 H. Addison, *The Battle of London* (London: Herbert Jenkins Ltd., 1926) p. 291. In this they bear comparison with pre-1914 invasion literature; see I.F. Clarke, 'Introduction: The paper warriors', in Clarke (ed.), *The Tale of the Next War, 1871–1914* (Liverpool: Liverpool University Press, 1995), pp. 1–28.

64 See for the image of the Paris Commune in the imagined British Revolution of 1940, a review of B. Wootton's *London's Burning* (London: Allen and Unwin, 1936) in *The Times Literary Supplement*, 16 May 1936, p. 418.

65 J.D. Mayne, *The Triumph of Socialism and How it Succeeded* (Amsterdam: Fredonia Books, 2003), p. 4.

66 D. Wheatley, *Black August* (London: Arrow Books Ltd, 1965), pp. 70 and 73.

67 Addison, *The Battle of London*, p. 124.

68 M. Ceadel, 'Popular Fiction and the Next War, 1918–39', in F. Gloversmith (ed.), *Class, Culture and Social Change: a New View of the Nineteen Thirties* (Brighton: Harvester, 1980), pp. 161–84.

69 The hero of Beresford's *Revolution*, Paul Leaming, reveals that he had read and been much inspired by the book. See *Revolution*, p. 239.

70 E. Shanks, 'The People of the Ruins', *Famous Fantastic Mysteries*, vol. 8, 1947, p. 12.

71 Ibid., p. 51.

72 See Clarke, *Voices Prophesying War*, pp. 166–9.

73 G. Household, *A Time to Kill* (London: Penguin, 1971), p. 17.

74 Ibid., ch. 18 and Wheatley, *Black August*, 231–2 and 304.

75 Viscount Hailsham, 'The Middle Way', in Newton Branch (ed.), *This Britain, Tradition and Achievement* (London: Macdonald, 1951), pp. 77–83. For discussion of the 'Middle Way', see P. Mandler, *The English National Character: The History of an Idea from Edmund Burke to Tony Blair* (New Haven, CT: Yale University Press, 2006), pp. 202–3.

76 See the opening statement in Pelling, *The British Communist Party*, p. 1, and the assertion by Walter Hannington that the National Government of 1931 was 'the worst since Pitt or Castlereagh', in the *Daily Worker*, 16 April 1934, p. 1.

77 J. Buchan, *Mr Standfast* (London: Wordsworth Classics, 1988), p. 62.

78 Ibid., p. 99.

79 J. Shaw, 'Land, People and Nation: Historicist Voices in the Highland Land Campaign, c.1850–1883', in E. Biagini (ed.) *Citizenship and Community: Liberals, Radicals and Collective Identities in the British Isles, 1865–1931* (Cambridge: Cambridge University Press, 1996), pp. 305–24.

80 Christie, *The Secret Adversary*, pp. 178–9. Christie occasionally succumbed to anti-Labour and anti-socialist themes in her crime fiction; see especially the Hercule Poirot mystery, *The Hollow* (London: Collins, 1946), which provides in David Ankatell, an image of a sneering and affected young Left-winger at the height of the post-1945 Labour government (p. 114).

81 Christie, *The Secret Adversary*, p. 59.

82 H. Bertens, 'A Society of Murderers Run on Sound Conservative Lines: The Life and Times of Sapper's Bulldog Drummond', in C. Bloom (ed.), *Twentieth Century Suspense: The Thriller Comes of Age* (London: Macmillan, 1990), pp. 51–68.

83 J. Buchan, *Huntingtower* (London: Thomas Nelson and Sons Ltd., 1927), p. 276 and for a review of the book, *The Times Literary Supplement*, 1 August 1922, p. 520.

84 Baker, *The Devil is a Gentleman*, p. 344.

85 G.L. Mosse, *Fallen Soldiers: Reshaping the Memory of the World Wars* (Oxford: Oxford University Press, 1990), p. 161. Paul Leaming, the hero of J.D. Beresford's Revolution, presents a rare example of a shell-shocked veteran who seeks restitution through conflict resolution and pacifism.

86   Shute, *So Disdained*, p.171.

87   E. Linklater, *The Impregnable Women* (London: Penguin, 1959), p. 43.

88   Buchan, *Huntingtower*, p. 193.

89   Eric Linklater, *Magnus Merriman* (London: Penguin, 1959), p. 70.

90   See M. Denning, *Cover Stories: Narrative and Ideology in the British Spy Thriller* (London: Routledge and Kegan Paul, 1987), pp. 56–7 and 46–9.

91   'Sapper', *Bulldog Drummond* (London: Hodder and Stoughton, 1933), p. 5.

92   Ibid., p. 24.

93   'Sapper', *The Black Gang* (London: Hodder and Stoughton, 1956), pp. 309–11. Bulldog Drummond's irregulars wear masks and theatrical cloaks, that give them the feeling of vigilantes, the Ku Klux Klan, or of super-heroes; see Priestman, *Crime Fiction*, p. 45.

94   J. Buchan, *The Three Hostages* (London: Wordsworth Classics, 1995), pp. 17–18.

95   For the discipline and loyalty to theory of the Communist Party of Great Britain, see Samuel, *The Lost World of British Communism*, pp. 100–20 and 186–202 and E.E. Hobsbawm, *Interesting Times: A Twentieth Century Life* (London: Allen Lane, 2002), pp. 66–76.

96   D. Wheatley, *Contraband* (London: Arrow Books Ltd., 1971), p. 195.

97   Christie, *The Secret Adversary*, p. 184.

98   Ibid., pp. 58–9.

99   'Sapper', *The Black Gang*, p. 258. For Jesuit fears about the threat posed to the young by Socialist Sunday Schools, see Goldstein and Avery, *Socialism*, pp. 228–36.

100   Buchan, *Huntingtower*, p. 190.

101   Christie, *The Secret Adversary*, p. 54.

102   Addison, *The Battle of London*, p. 14.

103   Ibid., p. 164.

104   See S. Collini, *Absent Minds: Intellectuals in Britain* (Oxford: Oxford University Press, 2006), p. 84.

105   'Sapper', *Bulldog Drummond*, p. 171.

106   *The Worker*, 1 June 1910, p. 2. See also for warnings about 'propaganda work . . . carried on earnestly and seriously at half the street corners of England', *The Individualist*, 1 October 1907, pp. 68–9. For the significance of outdoors propaganda work for both Edwardian Socialism and British Communism, see H. Pollitt, *Serving My Time: An Apprenticeship to Politics* (London: Lawrence and Wishart, 1940), chs. 2 and 3.

107   'Sapper', Bulldog Drummond, p. 117. The open air agitators at Hyde Park corner were frequently regarded as dangerous and inflammatory, see the reference to 'the republican, the crank, the anarchist, the revolutionary [who] . . . pour[s] out his frothy torrent in Hyde Park or on Tower Hill', in C. Cox, *For Ever England: An Anthology* (London: Cassell and Company Ltd., 1943), p. 160.

108   Shute, *So Disdained*, pp. 148–9.

109   E. Bramah, *The Secret of the League: The Story of a Social War* (London: Thomas Nelson and Sons, 1907), p. 167.

110   Ibid., p. 105.

111   Christie, *The Secret Adversary*, p. 209.

112   Buchan, *Huntingtower*, p. 272.

113   'Sapper, *The Black Gang*, pp. 291, 258–9 and 289–90.

114   Ibid., p. 292.

115   Wheatley, *Black August*, p. 159.

116   See for hostility to bohemianism, E. Wilson, *Bohemians: The Glamorous Outcasts* (London: Macmillan, 2003), ch. 13, V. Nicholson, *Among the Bonemians: Experiments in Living, 1900-1939* (London: Penguin, 2002), ch. 2 and C. Hilliard, 'The Literary Underground of 1920s London', *Social History*, 33 (2008), pp. 164-82.

117   Collini, *Absent Minds*, chs. 4 and 5.

118   Buchan, *Mr Standfast*, p. 33.

119   J. Buchan, *The Island of Sheep* (London: Wordsworth Classics, 1995), pp. 63 and 80. Dislike of 'arty' types also featured in the novels of Dorothy L. Sayers and Sax Rohmer. In one of Sax Rohmer's series of Fu Manchu novels, Nayland Smith and Dr. Petrie disguise themselves as 'Futurists'. See Watson, *Snobbery with Violence*, pp. 199-200.

120   For radical and liberal philanthropic brotherhoods and the culture of 'slumming', in the East End into the twentieth century, see Koven, *Slumming*, especially ch. 5.

121   See for socialist clerics, Conrad Noel, 'Why Churchmen become Socialists', *New Age*, 14 January 1908, pp. 240-1 and for criticism of Christian Socialism more generally, Ray B. White, *The False Christ of Communism and the Social Gospel* (London: Pillar of Fire, 1946), pp. 214-15.

122   E. Phillpotts ('Harrington Hext'), *The Thing at their Heels* (London: Macmillan, 1923), p. 298.

123   Buchan, *The Three Hostages*, p. 50.

124   Ibid., p. 118.

125   Mayne, *The Triumph of Socialism*, pp. 111-28.

126   Bramah, *The Secret of the League*, pp. 171-80.

127   H. Edmonds, 'The North Sea Mystery', in *Chums Annual 1934-5* (London, 1935), p. 346. See for the full story, pp. 3-10, 67-74, 151-8, 215-22, 279-85 and 343-8.

128   Addison, *The Battle of London*, pp. 248-85.

129   Quoted in R. Blythe, *The Age of Illusion: England in the Twenties and Thirties, 1919-40* (London: Penguin, 1963), p. 130.

130   D. Yates, *Lower than Vermin* (London: Ward, Lock and Co., Ltd, 1950), pp. 318-23.

Notes to Chapter 4: Fascist Britain

 1   G. Freeman, *The Leader* (London: New English Library, 1965), pp. 51-2.

 2   R. Muller, *After All, This Is England: The Lost Diaries of Albert Smith* (Harmondsworth: Penguin, 1967), p. 43.

 3   O. Sheers, *Resistance* (London: Faber and Faber, 2007), p. 32.

 4   See for these concerns, Calder, *The Myth of the Blitz*, ch. 5.

 5   See especially, A. Roberts and N. Ferguson, 'Hitler's England: What if Germany had Invaded Britain in May 1940?', in N. Ferguson (ed.), *Virtual History: Alternatives and Counterfactuals* (London: Basic Books, 1997), pp. 281-320.

 6   J. Clute and P. Nicholls (eds), *An Encyclopaedia of Science Fiction* (London: St. Martin's Press, 1993), pp. 572-3 and G.D. Rosenfeld, *The World Hitler Never Made* (Cambridge: Cambridge University Press, 2005), pp. 34-5.

7   There is a wide literature on Le Queux. See, for example, Clarke, *Voices Prophesying War*, pp. 144–54, P. Fleming, *Operation Sea Lion* (London: Pan, 1975), ch. 2, J. Ramsden, *Don't Mention the War: The British and the Germans Since 1890* (London: Little Brown, 2007), ch. 2 and Turner, *Boys Will Be Boys*, ch. 15.

8   Fleming, *Operation Sea Lion*, pp. 28–9.

9   For the debates around this subject see A.L. Friedberg, *The Weary Titan: Britain and the Experience of Relative Decline, 1895–1905* (Princeton: Princeton University Press, 1988).

10. A. Sykes, *The Radical Right in Britain: Social Imperialism to the BNP* (London: Palgrave, 2001), p. 28.

11 Ramsden, *Don't Mention the War*, pp. 75–6.

12 *Britain's Fifth Column: A Plain Warning!* (London: Workers' Bookshelf, 1940), p. 3.

13 There is now a considerable literature on the origins of British Fascism, but see for general accounts, R. Benewick, *The Fascist Movement in Great Britain* (London: Allen Lane, 1972), S. Dorril, *Blackshirt: Sir Oswald Mosley and British Fascism* (Viking: London, 2006), ch. 3, M. Pugh, *Hurrah for the Blackshirts: Fascists and Fascism in Britain between the Wars* (London: Pimlico, 2006), chs. 1–6 and R. Thurlow, *Fascism in Britain: From Oswald Mosley's Blackshirts to the National Front* (London: I.B. Tauris, 1998), chs, 1–3.

14 *The Blackshirt*, 8–14 July 1933, p, 1.

15 The *North Kensington Citizen*, quoted in ibid, 13 August 1934, p. 3.

16 J. Cameron, *How Long Do We Ignore the Lessons of Bethal Green?* (London: *Daily Express*, 1947), p. 2. Also see his article in the *Daily Express*, 5 September 1947. For a general account of the Union Movement, see Dorril, *Blackshirt*, ch. 25, and for first hand memories of involvement in it, T. Grundy, *Memoirs of a Fascist Childhood* (London: Heinemann, 1998), ch. 2.

17 *Blood on the Streets: A Report by Bethnal Green and Stepney Trades Council on Racial Attitudes in East London* (London: Bethnal Green and Stepney Trades Council, 1978), pp. 3–9.

18 See for the formation of the National Front, M. Durham, 'The Conservative Party, the British extreme right and the problem of political space, 1967–83', in M. Cronin (ed.), *The Failure of British Fascism: The Far Right and the Fight for Political Recognition* (Basingstoke: Macmillan, 1996), pp. 81–98; Sykes, *The Radical Right*, pp. 93–114; Thurlow, *Fascism in Britain*, chs. 9 and 10; M. Walker, *The National Front* (London: Fontana, 1977), chs. 2 and 3, and for the role of John Tyndall as an ideologue of resurgent British Fascism from the 1960s, N. Copsey, *Contemporary British Fascism: The British National Party and the Quest for Legitimacy* (Basingstoke: Macmillan, 2004), pp. 82–7.

19 For organized working-class opposition to the National Front see D. Renton, 'Guarding the barricades: working-class anti-Fascism', in N. Copsey and D. Renton (eds), *British Fascism, the Labour Movement and the State* (Basingstoke: Palgrave, 2005), pp. 141–59.

20 J. Herbert, *The Spear* (London: Pan Books, 1998), p. 147.

21 M. Drabble, *The Ice Age* (London: Penguin, 1977), p. 210.

22 A. Beckett, *When the Lights Went Out: What Really Happened to Britain in the Seventies?* (London: Faber and Faber, 2009), pp. 1–6. For comparisons between Britain in the 1970s and Weimar Germany more generally, see R. Weight, *Patriots: National Identity in Britain, 1940–2000* (London: Macmillan, 2002), pp. 536–7.

23 Sheers, *Resistance*, p. 104.

24 G. J. Renier, *The English: Are They Human?* (Leipzig: Bernhard Tauchnitz, 1932), pp. 151–2.

25 See C. M. Dolan, *The Blackshirt Racket: Mosley Exposed* (Reading: Workers' Bookshelf, 1935), p. 5. Dolan had worked as the propaganda chief for the British Union of Fascists. For similar sentiments from a Fascist point of view see C.F. Melville, *The Truth about the New Party* (London: Wishart and Co., 1931), pp. 25–6.

26 I. Montagu, *Blackshirt Brutality: The Story of Olympia* (London: Workers' Bookshop, 1934), p. 4 and R. A. Palmer, *Co-operation under the Nazis* (Manchester: Co-operative Union Ltd., 1939), pp. 6–8.

27 See Dorril, *Blackshirt*, ch. 15 and J. Lawrence, 'Fascist violence and the politics of public order in inter-war Britain: the Olympia debate revisited', *Historical Research*, 76 (2003), 238–67.

28 See the derisory account of the 'budding Mussolinis' of the British Fascist movement who hatched a plot to kidnap Harry Pollitt in 1925 in *Freedom*, 1 May 1925, p. 21. There is an account of this episode in Pugh, *Hurrah for the Blackshirts*, p. 51.

29 A. Huxley, *Point Counter Point* (London: Flamingo, 1994), pp. 53 and 72.

30 P. G. Wodehouse, 'The Code of the Woosters', in *The Wodehouse Omnibus* (London: Penguin, 2001), p. 386.

31 G. Orwell, 'England, your England', in *Inside the Whale and Other Essays* (London: Penguin, 1979), pp. 63–90.

32 R. Cook, *A State of Denmark* (London: New English Library, 1973), p. 167. Robin Cook was the pen-name of Derek Raymond, who went on to achieve considerable success as a crime writer under his own name.

33 G. Orwell, 'Prophecies of Fascism', *Tribune*, 12 July 1940, pp. 16–17. Orwell had witnessed Mosley speaking at a meeting in Barnsley in 1936; see B. Crick, *George Orwell: A Life* (London: Penguin, 1982), pp. 291–2.

34 Bramah, *The Secret of the League*, pp. 259–60.

35 The tactical problems posed by a potential German invasion attempt across the Channel are outlined in Fleming, *Operation Sea Lion*, chs. 3 and 4.

36 The most frequently cited work of this nature is Katharine Burdekin, *Swastika Night* (London: Victor Gollancz, 1937). Set 700 years in the future, it envisages a world of quasi-permanent Nazi rule in which women are subjugated to the level of mere breeders for the Nazi empire. Dealing mainly with events in Germany, it is not included here for that reason. For discussion of this work, see Rosenfeld, *The World Hitler Never Made*, pp. 35–7 and D. Patai, 'Imagining reality: the utopian fiction of Katharine Burdekin', in A. Ingram and D. Patai (eds), *Rediscovering Forgotten Radicals: British Women Writers, 1889–1939* (Chapel Hill: University of North Carolina Press, 1993), pp. 226–43. For a recent extract from the novel, see J. Carey (ed.), *The Faber Book of Utopias* (London: Faber and Faber, 1999), pp. 412–18.

37 G. Cooper, *The Other Man* (London: Panther, 1964), p. 5.

38 N. Mitchison, *We Have Been Warned* (London: Constable, 1935), pp. 536–53.

39 Ibid., pp. 552–3.

40 *Daily Worker*, 8 May 1935, p. 4.

41 N.H. Reeve, *The Novels of Rex Warner: An Introduction* (New York: St. Martin's Press, 1989), pp. 75–6.

42 For the significance of flight for European Fascism, see Mosse, *Fallen Soldiers*, pp. 120–4, and for British Fascism's interest in flight, C. Hopkins, *English Fiction in the 1930s* (London: Continuum, 2006), pp. 13–53 and the special RAF pageant edition of *The Blackshirt*, 24 June–1 July 1933, p. 1. For an aerial display at a British Fascist rally, see ibid, 1 June 1934, p. 1.

43 *The Blackshirt*, 16–22 February 1934, p. 1.

44 A. Harris, *Romantic Moderns: English Writers, Artists and the Imagination from Virginia Woolf to John Piper* (London: Thames and Hudson, 2010), pp. 176–8.

45 See Reeve, *The Novels of Rex Warner*, p. 79.

46 R. Warner, *The Aerodrome* (London: Penguin Books, 1944), p. 112.

47 Ibid., p. 191.

48 E. Ambler, *Background to Danger* (New York, Dell Publishing Co., 1965), p. 9.

49 See for the dubious reputation of London's night-clubs in the 1920s, G.H. Fosdike Nichols, 'A Round of the Night-Clubs', in J. Adcock (ed.), *Wonderful London*, 3 vols. (London: Fleetway House, 1927) 1, pp. 940–52.

50 Buchan, *The Three Hostages*, p. 85. Buchan's only contribution to the 'Hitler Wins' genre, was set abroad, in *The House of the Four Winds* (London: Thomas Nelson and Sons, 1935), in which a republic in the fictional Eastern European state of Evallonia, is undermined by monarchists working in conjunction with the militarized extreme nationalist movement, 'Juventus'. Even so, the model for a future Evallonia, is essentially that of the British state. The leader of Juventus, Jaikie declares: 'Some things we will not have – Communism for one – of that folly Europe contains too many awful warnings. We have had enough talk of republics, which are the dullest species of oligarchy. Evallonia, having history in her bones, is a natural monarchy. Her happiest destiny would be to be like England' (p. 111).

51 See *The Blackshirt*, 5–11 August 1933, p. 2.

52 The timing and publication date for this novel strongly suggests that the author had the Ugandan Asian crisis in mind when he wrote it. C. Priest, *Fugue for a Darkening Island* (London: New English Library, 1972), pp. 6–11 and 26–8.

53 Ibid, pp. 17 and 44–5.

54 R. Saw, 'Fascism and our Cultural Heritage', *The Blackshirt*, 13 July 1934, p. 6.

55 Sheers, *Resistance*, p. 201. For speculation about the fate of Nelson's Column under German rule, see Roberts and Ferguson, 'Hitler's England', pp. 318–19.

56 Sheers, *Resistance*, p. 201.

57 'Saki' (H.H. Munro), 'When William Came', in M. Moorcock (ed.), *England Invaded: A Collection of Fantasy Fiction* (London: W.H. Allen and Co., 1980), p. 91.

58 G. Walters, *The Leader* (London: Headline, 2003), p. 3.

59 L. Deighton, *SS-GB: Nazi Occupied Britain, 1941* (London: Jonathan Cape, 1978), p. 158.

60 One exception that does compare occupied London to occupied Paris is G. Stevens, *And All the King's Men* (London: Pan Books, 1990), pp. 419–20.

61 Deighton, *SS-GB*, p. 207.

62 Cook, *A State of Denmark*, p. 118.

63 See R. Skidelsky, *Oswald Mosley* (London: Macmillan, 1975), ch. 21, T. Lineham, *East London for Mosley: The British Union of Fascists in East London and South-West Sussex*,

1933–1940 (London: Frank Cass, 1996), and G. C. Webber, 'Patterns of membership and support for the British Union of Fascists', *Journal of Contemporary History*, 19 (1984), 575–606, and for a treatment of similar conditions that have favoured recent electoral successes by the British National Party in the area, M. Hillier, 'The British National Party: a view from the East End', in F. Grindrod and M. Rusling (eds), *Stopping the Far Right: How Progressive Politics Can Tackle Political Extremism* (London: Fabian Society, 2007), pp. 13–24.

64 E.A. Dickenson, *Legion of Blue and White Shirts: An Exposure of Fascism* (London: Epworth Press, 1936), p. 2. The author proposed a patriotic Legion of anti-Fascist campaigners, wearing blue and white shirts adorned with union jacks.

65 R. Clews, *The Rise of Cromwell Jones* (London: Warner Books, 1995), p. 23.

66 See D. Stone, 'The far right and the back-to-the-land movement', in J.V. Gottlieb and T. P. Lineham (eds), *The Culture of Fascism: Visions of the Far Right in Britain* (London: I.B. Tauris, 2004), pp. 182–98 and R. Moore-Colyer, 'Towards "mother earth": J. Jenks, organicism, the right and the British Union of Fascists', *Journal of Contemporary History*, 39 (2004), 353–71. The National Front manifesto for the October 1974 election stressed the movement's commitment to curbing developers, and hoped for a Britain in which all cities looked like Edinburgh's old town; see *A New Britain: The Manifesto of the National Front* (London: National Front, October 1974), p. 22.

67 See Sykes, *The Radical Right*, p. 107.

68 M. Billig, *Fascists: A Social Psychological View of the National Front* (New York: Harcourt Brace Jovanovich, 1978), pp. 105–9, 160–1, and 207–10.

69 B. Wohl, *The Ten-Tola Bars* (Feltham: Hamlyn, 1978), pp. 58–9.

70 J. G. Ballard, *Kingdom Come* (London: Harper Perennial, 2007), p. 168.

71 See Hugh Trevor Roper's comments at the time of the Suez Crisis that 'there is in England, as in other countries, a Fascist world: the world of lower middle-class conservatives who have no intelligence, but a deep belief in violence as a sign of self-importance' and who moreover 'hate foreigners, especially if they come from "inferior races"', in R. Davenport-Hines (ed.), *Letters from Oxford: Hugh Trevor-Roper to Bernard Berensen* (London: Heinemann, 2007), pp. 209–10.

72 P. Hamilton, *Hangover Square* (London: Penguin, 2001), p. 128.

73 Cook, *A State of Denmark*, pp. 153–4.

74 Muller, *After All, This Is England*, pp. 95–6, 111, and 160.

75 Ibid., pp. 21–2.

76 Ibid., pp. 168–9.

77 *The Blackshirt*, 1 February 1933, p. 1.

78 Ibid., 8–14 July, 1933, p. 3 and 2–9 December 1933, p. 1.

79 Deighton, *SS-GB*, pp. 180–1 and 209.

80 K. Macksey, *Invasion: The German Invasion of England, July 1940* (Barnsley: Greenhill Books, 1980), especially, pp. 133–87.

81 Sheers, *Resistance*, pp. 7 and 30–41.

82 Ibid., p. 216.

83 Cooper, *The Other Man*, p. 64.

84 Cook, *A State of Denmark*, p. 112.

85 Muller, *After All This Is England*, pp. 244–6.

86 Walters, *The Leader*, pp. 25–32. This study is heavily influenced by recent media exposures about Edward VIII's affinities with European Fascism. The abdicated Edward VIII also returns as a Nazi puppet in Sheers' *Resistance*, p. 217 and in R. Harris, *Fatherland* (London: Arrow Books, 1992), p. 40.

87 For these bodies see Sykes, *The Radical Right*, p. 113, and *The Observer*, 9 January 2005.

88 A. Wise, *Who Killed Enoch Powell?* (London: Weidenfeld and Nicolson, 1970), pp. 121–7 and 133–41.

89 Ibid., p. 39.

90 G. Shipway, *The Chilian Club* (London: Mayflower Books, 1972), pp. 24–5.

91 Blurb to the 1973 reprinted edition of the above.

92 *The Blackshirt*, 16 November 1934, p. 6. For the impact of Carlyle's pro-Teutonism in Britain, see Ramsden, *Don't Mention the War*, pp. 34–6.

93 J. Buchan, *John Macnab* (Ware: Wordsworth Classics, 1996), p. 99.

94 See Skidelsky, *Oswald Mosley*, ch. 17.

95 See *The Blackshirt*, 8 June 1934, p. 10 and 29 July–4 August 1933, p. 3.

96 Clews, *The Rise of Cromwell Jones*, pp. 148–51.

97 Ibid., p. 360.

98 P. Van Greenaway, *The Man who Held the Queen to Ransom and Sent Parliament Packing* (London: Penguin, 1968), p. 246.

99 Ibid., p. 12.

100 Such characters feature in discussion of models for a 'British Petain' who might have acted as an intermediary and collaborator with the German High Command in 1940. The tank strategist and BUF member Brigadier J.F.C. Fuller is sometimes cited as a possible candidate for this task; see Macksey, *Invasion*, pp. 201–3.

101 Wise, *Who Killed Enoch Powell?*, p. 30.

102 Freeman, *The Leader*, pp. 13–14.

103 The position in the German occupied Channel Isles is often seen as a proxy for the form a British Fascist state might take. See M. Bunting, *The Channel Islands under German Rule, 1940–45* (London: Granta Books, 1996) and for personal memories of the concentration camps there, J. Dalmou, *Slave Worker in the Channel Isles* (Guernsey: The Guernsey Press Company, 1955), pp. 3–16.

104 S. Jameson, *In the Second Year* (Nottingham: Trent Editions, 2004), p. 95.

105 Such allegations of 'betrayal' tend to be targeted at Mosley, who turned his back on the Labour Party to found the BUF; see *Who Backs Mosley? Fascist Promise and Fascist Performance* (London: Labour Research Department, 1934), pp. 4–8 and for the notion of betrayal more broadly in the British labour tradition, J. Lawrence, 'Labour – the myths it has lived by', in Tanner, Thane, Tiratsoo (eds), *Labour's First Century*, pp. 341–66.

106 Jameson, *In the Second Year*, pp. 46–7.

107 Ibid., pp. 98–9.

108 Ibid., pp. 38–48.

109 Recently a series about a successful Nazi invasion of Britain raising this theme has been launched for children, written by the former Grange Hilll actor, Michael Cronin; the first part is called *Against the Day* (Oxford: Oxford University Press, 1998).

110 Sheers, *Resistance*, p. 310.

111 Cooper, *The Other Man*, pp. 47–8.

112 Ibid., 77–8.

113 Deighton, *SS-GB*, p. 21.

114 B. 'Yank' Levy, *Guerrilla Warfare* (London: Penguin, 2008), pp. 71–2.

115 See Macksey, *Invasion*, pp. 186–7.

116 Levy, *Guerrilla Warfare*, p. 21.

117 Stevens, *And All the King's Men*, p. 376.

118 See P. Laity (ed.), *Left Book Club Anthology* (London: Gollancz, 2001), xi.

119 J. Herbert, *'48* (London: Harper Collins 1996), p. 28. R.C. Sherriff's *The Cataclysm* (London: Pan Books Ltd, 1958) imagines perhaps the most unlikely scenario for the emergence of a successful British Fascism. In the aftermath of a collision between the earth and the moon, survivors fight for the mineral wealth the former moon holds, leading to a steady drift into militarism by a reconstruction government in the British Isles, and the dictatorship of a British Hitler (pp. 212–17).

120 See N. Freeman, ' "A decadent appetite for the lurid"?: James Herbert, *The Spear* and "Nazi Gothic"', *Gothic Studies*, 8 (2006), 80–97.

121 Anthony Blond, 'Sub-Hitler', *Times Literary Supplement*, 2 September 1965, p. 749.

Notes to Chapter 5: Revolution and Counter-Revolution in London in the 1960s and 1970s

1   A. Waugh, *A Bed of Flowers* (London: Robin Clark Ltd., 1985), p. 188.

2   Drabble, *The Ice Age*, pp. 151–2.

3   A. Gamble, *Britain in Decline: Economic Policy, Political Strategy and the British State* (London: Macmillan, 1981), ch. 1.

4   See A.W. Turner, *Crisis? What Crisis? Britain in the 1970s* (London: Aurum, 2008), pp. 44–5, 108–9 and 156–9.

5   For the best general treatments of the period and its popular fears, see Beckett, *When the Lights Went Out*, especially ch. 1, J. Black, *Britain since the Seventies: Politics and Society in the Consumer Age* (London: Reaktion, 2004), chs. 4 and 5, and D. Sandbrook, *State of Emergency: The Way We Were: Britain, 1970–74* (London: Little Brown, 2010).

6   M. Edelman, *The Prime Minister's Daughter* (London: Panther, 1968), pp. 27–8.

7   C. Booker, *The Seventies: Portrait of a Decade* (London: Allen Lane, 1980), p. 5.

8   See D. Coates, 'Politicians and the Sorceror', in A. King (ed.), *Why is Britain Becoming Harder to Govern?* (London: British Broadcasting Corporation, 1976), pp. 31–57.

9   See I. Kramnick, 'Introduction: the making of a crisis', in Kramnick (ed.), *Is Britain Dying? Perspectives on the Current Crisis* (Ithaca, NY: Cornell University Press, 1979), pp. 11–27.

10 The term 'banana republic' to describe an ailing Britain entered popular parlance in the 1970s and 1980s; see C. Mullin, *A Very British Coup* (London: Politico's, 2006), p. 98.

11 G.R. Searle, *Country Before Party: Coalition and the Idea of "National Government" in Britain 1885–1987* (London: Longman, 1995), pp. 235–46.

12 G. Lean, *Rebirth of a Nation* (Poole: Blandford Press, 1976), pp. 15–16.

13 C. Smith, *Big Cyril: The Autobiography of Cyril Smith* (London: W.H. Allen, 1977), p. 223.

14 Quoted in R. McIntosh, *Challenge to Democracy: Politics, Trade Union Power and Economic Failure in the 1970s* (London: Politico's, 2006), p. 172.

15 P. Johnson, *Enemies of Society* (London: Weidenfeld and Nicolson, 1977). Johnson was an apostate leftist and former editor of the *New Statesman* who, repelled by the trades unionism of the Seventies, migrated towards Conservatism. See Booker, *The Seventies*, pp. 238–44.

16 Searle, *Country Before Party*, p. 246.

17 *The Times Literary Supplement*, 6 May 1960, p. 285. See C. Fitz Gibbon, *When the Kissing Had to Stop* (London: Pan, 1962).

18 P. Bryers, *Hollow Man* (London, 1976), p. 274.

19 See R. S. Grayson, 'Britain and the Channel Tunnel', *Twentieth Century British History*, 7 (1996), p. 387, T. Whiteside, *The Tunnel under the Channel* (London: Rupert Hart-Davis, 1962), pp. 48–73, and K. Wilson, *Channel Tunnel Visions, 1850–1945: Dreams and Nightmares* (London: Hambledon, 1994), ch. 1.

20 Ibid., p. 51.

21 R. Byrne, *The Tunnel* (London: Michael Joseph, 1975), p. 72. For fears about potential terrorist attacks on the Channel Tunnel in the 1990s see 'How Safe is the Channel Tunnel?', *The Sunday Times*, 8 May 1994, p. 5 and Weight, *Patriots*, pp. 490–1 and 654–7.

22 J. Burmeister, *The Weatherman Guy* (London: Michael Joseph Ltd., 1975), p. 47.

23 Drabble, *The Ice Age*, p. 93.

24 P. Bailey, *Old Soldiers* (London: Fourth Estate , 1999), ch. 1.

25 D. Seaman, *The Committee* (London: Futura, 1979), p. 38.

26 Booker, *The Seventies*, p. 104. See for the political and social impact of decolonization on Britain, J. Darwin, *Britain and Decolonisation: The Retreat from Empire in the Post-War World* (London: Macmillan, 1987) and W.D. McIntyre, *British Decolonisation, 1946–1997* (New York: St. Martin's Press, 1998).

27 These contemporary fears are outlined in R. Colls, *Identity of England* (Oxford: Oxford University Press, 2002), chs. 21 and 22.

28 Van Greenaway, *The Man who Held the Queen to Ransom*, p. 57.

29 A. Wilson, *The Old Men at the Zoo* (London: Penguin, 1961), p. 275.

30 Ibid., pp. 324–9. The fears about European integration that united both left and right in Britain in the 1960s and 1970s are outlined in T. Nairn, *The Left Against Europe* (London: Penguin, 1973), M. Garnett, *From Anger to Apathy: The Story of Politics, Society, and Popular Culture in Britain since 1975* (London: Vintage, 2008), pp. 31–5 and 38–41, and Weight, *Patriots*, pp. 475–516.

31 See W. Webster, *Englishness and Empire, 1939–1965* (Oxford: Oxford University Press, 2005), pp. 112–18. For anti-Americanism in Britain and Europe more generally, see J. Ceaser, 'The philosophical origins of anti-Americanism in Europe', in P. Hollander (ed.), *Understanding Anti-Americanism: Its Origins and Impact* (Chicago: Ivan R. Dee, 2004), pp. 51–70 and J. C. E. Gienow-Hecht, 'Always blame the Americans: anti-Americanism in Europe in the twentieth century', *The American Historical Review*, 3 (4) (2006), 1067–91. There is also a voluminous pamphlet literature on this subject from the Communist Party of Great Britain; see especially for the 'plague centres' of American airforce bases, A.L. Morton, *Get Out* (Ipswich: CPGB, 1953), p. 3 and more generally *Uncle Sam* (London: CPGB, 1947), *America Go Home* (London: CPGB, 1951) and A. Clegg, *American Spider* (London: CPGB, 1947).

32 D. Du Maurier, *Rule Britannia* (London: Victor Gollancz, 1973), pp. 246–9.

33 Ibid., pp. 126–7.

34 Ibid., pp. 266–73 and 283–5 and for Du Maurier's romantic vision of the West Country, Light, *Forever England*, pp. 204–5.

35 For example, R. Maby, *The Unofficial Countryside* (London: Little Toller Books, 2010), and E. Holden, *The Country Diary of an Edwardian Lady* (London: Michael Joseph, 1977), a notable publishing phenomenon in the 1977 Jubilee Year. British ecological ruralism in the 1970s is discussed in Beckett, *When the Lights Went Out*, ch. 10.

36 The book is referred to as a possible guide towards the future development of Britain in the 1970s in R. Moss, *The Collapse of Democracy* (London: Sphere Books Ltd., 1977), p. 21.

37 A.G. Elliot, *The Guilty Madmen of Whitehall* (Kingswood: Elliot Right Way Books, 1969), p. 19.

38 Fitz Gibbon, *When the Kissing Had to Stop*. The term 'Socialist Megalomaniac' is taken from the back cover of the 1962 Pan edition.

39 Concerns about defence and the Labour Party's unilateralist tendencies were particularly apparent during the late 1970s. See for Labour's stance on the arms race and negotiations with the Soviet Union in 1977, I. Mikardo (ed.), *Sense about Defence: The Report of the Labour Party Defence Study Group* (London: Quartet Books, 1977), pp. 51–69.

40 *The Times Literary Supplement*, 6 May 1960, p. 285.

41 Fitz Gibbon, *When the Kissing Had to Stop*, p. 31. The novel misses or is unaware of the political orientation of both first and second wave CND which reflected a traditional British patriotic Whiggism, rather than ultra-left militancy: see H. Nehring, 'The British and West German protests against nuclear weapons and the cultures of the Cold War, 1957–1964', *Contemporary British History*, 19, 2 (2005), 223–41, H. Nehring, 'National internationalists: British and West German protests against nuclear weapons: the politics of transnational communications and the social history of the Cold War, 1957–1964', *Contemporary European History*, 14, 4 (2005), 559–82 and M. Phythian, 'CND's Cold War", *Contemporary British History*, 15, 3 (2001), 133–56.

42 Fitz Gibbon, *When the Kissing Had to Stop*, p. 5.

43 Ibid., pp. 250–1.

44 W. Greatorex, *1990* (London: Sphere Books Ltd., 1977), pp. 28–9.

45 These features of the regime reflect the methods used to discipline internal dissenters revealed by Alexander Solzhenitsyn in his *The Gulag Archipelago* (London: Harper and Row, 1973), which was widely read in the 1970s. For the publishing history of Solzhenitsyn's works see his obituaries in *The Guardian*, 5 August 2008, pp. 30–1 and *The Independent*, 5 August 2008, pp. 32–3.

46 Greatorex, *1990*, pp. 112–13.

47 Ibid., p. 130.

48 Ibid., p. 127.

49 Moss, *The Collapse of Democracy*, pp. 23–34.

50 A. Burgess, *1985* (London: Little Brown, 1978), p. 118.

51 Ibid., pp. 120–4.

52 Ibid., p. 136.

53 See Burgess's outrage at the Tuc state's adoption of a 'proletarianised' ungrammatical English in his 'A Note on Worker's English', in ibid., pp. 221–6 and for a review of the novel, Michael Irwin, 'Tucland, their Tucland', *Times Literary Supplement*, 6 October 1978, p. 1109.

54 Burgess, *1985*, p. 205. For dirt, decay, rubbish and rats as the cipher for the decade, see Turner, *Crisis? What Crisis?*, pp. 43–6.

55 See R. Williams (ed.), *May Day Manifesto, 1968* (London: Penguin, 1968), pp. 155–9.

56 See the model for a successful uprising by Black American activists in Philadelphia in M. Oppenheimer, *Urban Guerrilla* (London: Penguin, 1970), pp. 102–6.

57 See J. Becker, *Hitler's Children: The Story of the Baader-Meinhof Gang* (Philadelphia: J.P. Lippincott, 1978), pp. 13–42.

58 A. Burns, *The Angry Brigade* (London: Allison and Busby, 1973), G. Carr, *The Angry Brigade: A History of Britain's first Urban Guerrilla Group* (London: Victor Gollancz, 1973) and *The Observer Magazine,* 3 February, 2002, pp. 17–22. British anarchism in the 1970s produced a lively series of book and pamphlets on notions of civil resistance and practical guerrilla warfare strategies. See *Towards a Citizens' Militia: Anarchist Alternatives to NATO and the Warsaw Pact* (Cienfuegos Press: Orkney, 1980), especially pp. 2–4.

59 See for the revival in anarchist ideas in the 1960s and 1970s, S. Christie and A. Meltzer, *The Floodgates of Anarchy* (London: Sphere Books Ltd, 1970), especially chs. 10 and 11. Stuart Christie was a defendant in the Angry Brigade trial of 1972. He has written an account of his anarchist past in *My Granny Made Me an Anarchist: General Franco, the Angry Brigade and Me* (Edinburgh: Scribner, 2002).

60 Bryers, *Hollow Target*, p. 97.

61 Burmeister, *The Weatherman Guy*, p. 106.

62 H. Innes, *North Star* (London: William Collins Sons and Co., Ltd., 1975), pp. 96–7.

63 The disaster is mentioned by name in ibid., p. 32 and in Bryers, *Hollow Target*, pp. 256–7, 269 and 270.

64 See for the new environmental agenda of the nineteen seventies and the success of environmentalist novels like *Watership Down*, Booker, *The Seventies*, ch. 36.

65 Innes, *North Star*, pp. 96–7.

66 Bryers, *Hollow Target*, pp. 257–8.

67 See P. Cosgrove, 'Could the Army Take Over?', *The Spectator*, 22 December 1973, p. 806.

68 Waugh, *A Bed of Flowers*, p. 32.

69 B. Pimlott, *Harold Wilson* (London: Harper Collins, 1992), pp. 505–6. In his account of his 1964–70 premiership Wilson alludes to the King circle's attempt to depose him in favour of a 'coalition of all the talents', but says that the group couldn't agree on a 'Prime Talent' to lead it; see H. Wilson, *The Labour Government 1964–1970: A Personal Record* (London: Weidenfeld and Nicolson, 1971), pp. 493–4.

70 Wright provides the most sensationalist accounts of MI5 conspiracies against Wilson. See P. Wright with P. Greengrass, *Spycatcher* (Richmond: William Heinemann, Australia, 1987), pp. 369–70. A number of leading figures recorded their involvement in such conspiracies in their memoirs, stoking subsequent fears that Britain only narrowly avoided a drift into political extremism. See for a novelistic treatment of the alleged plotting and conspiracies that surrounded Harold Wilson's governments in particular, M. Lawson, *Enough is Enough, or the Emergency Government* (London: Picador, 2004). An inquiry, however, found no evidence of any plot against Wilson.

71 Weight, *Patriots*, p. 537.

72 J. Rogaly, *Grunwick* (London: Penguin, 1977), pp. 73 and 78.

73 The best example of this genre remains, F Forsyth, *The Dogs of War* (London: Corgi, 1974). For the drift away from liberalism in Britain in the seventies, see Beckett, *When the Lights Went Out*, p. 287, and for a contemporary view, Tom Nairn, 'The Future of Britain's Crisis: A Political Analysis', in Kramnick (ed.), *Is Britain Dying?*, pp. 233–68.

74 All these aspects of Britain were widely derided in the late 1960s and the 1970s: see, for example, Christopher Hollis, 'Parliament and the Establishment', in H. Thomas (ed.), *The Establishment* (London: New English Library, 1960), pp. 158–74.

75 The backcover of Maurice Edelman's *The Prime Minister's Daughter*, thunders, 'Are *these* the men and women who control our destinies? Naked, weak, corrupt . . .'.

76 Van Greenaway, *The Man Who Held the Queen to Ransom*, p. 96.

77 Ibid., pp. 242–51.

78 See for ultra-Left entryism into the Labour Party in the late 1970s and early 1980s, D Hayter, *Fightback: Labour's Traditional Right in the 1970s and 1980s* (Manchester: Manchester University Press, 2005).

79 Mullin, *A Very British Coup*, p. 10.

80 Ibid., p. 218.

81 Drabble, *The Ice Age*, p. 165.

82 Bryers, *Hollow Target*, pp. 105–6.

83 Ibid., p. 200.

84 See for an account of the Grosvenor Square protests, P. Hain, *Radical Regeneration: Protest, Direct Action and Community Politics* (London: Quartet Books, 1975), pp. 2–4.

85 Van Greenaway, *The Man who Held the Queen to Ransom*, p. 59.

86 Burmeister, *The Weatherman Guy*, p. 101.

87 Van Greenaway, *The Man who Held the Queen to Ransom*, p. 56.

88 Bryers, *Hollow Target*, p. 21.

89 Drabble, *The Ice Age*, pp. 201–4.

90 Ibid., p. 66.

91 H. Kunzru, *My Revolutions* (London: Penguin, 2007), p. 109.

92 Van Greenaway, *The Man Who Held the Queen to Ransom*, p. 179.

93 See for the communes of the 1970s N. Dunn, *Living Like I Do* (London: Futura Publications Ltd., 1977), pp. 9–10, A. Rigby, *Communes in Britain* (London: Rouledge and Kegan Paul, 1974), pp. 1–22, and for a first hand account of a squat in Islington, S. Rowbotham, *Promise of a Dream: Remembering the Sixties* (London: Verso, 2001), pp. 117–21; for the South London squatting movement see N. Cohen, 'What did the Squatters do for Us', *New Statesman*, 23 January 2006, pp. 28–30.

94 See G. McKay, 'DiY Culture: Notes Towards an Intro', in McKay (ed.), *DiY Culture: Party and Protest in Nineties Britain* (London: Verso, 1998), pp. 7–9.

95 D. Lessing, *The Good Terrorist* (London: Grafton, 1985), p. 249.

96 Waugh, *A Bed of Flowers*, p. 41.

97 Drabble, *The Ice Age*, pp. 10–11.

98 Bryers, *Hollow Target*, p. 13.

99 See P. Magee, *Gangster Guerrillas: Representations of Irish Republicans in 'Troubles' Fiction* (Belfast: Beyond the Pale, 2001).

100 Ulster Unionism, following the prejudices of the period, features almost nowhere during these years either as a potential threat or a destabilising element despite strikes by Ulster power workers in the early 1970s. By the 1990s, however, loyalist paramilitary violence is more marked in popular fiction. See in particular D. Silva, *The Marching Season* (London: Weidenfeld and Nicolson, 1999), in which loyalist paramilitaries plot to de-rail the peace process in Northern Ireland by bombing Heathrow airport.

101 Innes, *North Star*, p. 140.

102 Bryers, *Hollow Target*, pp. 282–3.

103 Byrne, *The Tunnel*, p. 5.

104 Ibid., p. 152.

105 P. Theroux, *The Family Arsenal* (London: Penguin, 1977), p. 97.

106 Weight, *Patriots*, p. 412.

107 Weight, *Patriots*, pp. 403–72 and Colls, *Identity of England*, ch. 17.

108 J. Summers, *The Disaster* (London: New English Library, 1969), pp. 118–19 and 130–44. For the Free Wales Army and nationalist extremism in Wales in the 1960s, see J. Davies, *A History of Wales* (London: Penguin, 1994), pp. 670–2.

109 S. Mayse, *Merlin's Web* (Toronto: Seal Books, 1987), p. 36.

110 Ibid., p. 117.

111 Ibid., p. 288.

112 Weight, *Patriots*, pp. 408–11. For analysis of the emergence of the SNP and debates about Scottish devolution, see Jack Brand, 'From Scotland with Love', in Kramnick (ed.), *Is Britain Dying?*, pp. 169–82 and T. Nairn, *After Britain: New Labour and the Return of Scotland* (London: Granta, 2000), ch. 2.

113 N. Tranter, *The Freebooters* (Edinburgh: B & W Publishing Ltd., 1997), p. 33.

114 Ibid., p. 72. In fact interest in stealing the Stone of Scone preceded the 1950s. Romantic Irish nationalists like Maud Gonne had also talked about securing the stone to establish Irish claims to its lineage which predated the Scottish ones. Unable to carry it away she left 'its cold, dead weight under the chair in cold, dead, London'; R. Reynolds, *My Life and Crimes* (London: Jarrolds Publishers, 1956), pp. 231–2.

115 D. Hurd and A. Osmond, *Scotch on the Rocks* (London: Fontana/Collins, 1971), pp. 40–1.

116 Ibid., p. 195. The theme of paramilitary militias and demagoguery in Scottish politics is a persistent one; see H. Liddell, *Elite* (London: Rowan, 1990).

117 W. Besant, *The Revolt of Man* (Leipzig: Berhard Tauchnitz, 1882).

118 In the novel militant women deny their husbands and partners their conjugal rights until they renounce war: see Linklater, *The Impregnable Women*, ch. 3.

119 There was, however, a move towards popular fiction that reprized and reclaimed the role of women in the suffragette movement; see M. Darke, *A Question of Courage* (London: William Collins Sons and Co., 1978).

120 Some of the anti-Feminist fiction of the seventies drew on US models. See, for example, P.J. Cooper, *The Feminists* (New York: Pinnacle, 1971).

121 P. Kettle, *The Day of the Women* (London: New English Library, 1969), p. 46.

122 Ibid., pp. 86, 99, 120, 131, 133, 135, and 139. The term 'high-heeled Fascism' is taken from the back-cover of the 1970 New English Library version of this book.

123 Ibid., pp. 174–5.

124 J. Harmon, *W.I.T.C.H* (London: New English Library, 1971), pp. 111 and 114–18.

125 Ibid., pp. 124–6.

126 Ibid., p. 124.

127 Herbert, *The Spear*, p. 153.

128 H. Young, *One of Us: A Biography of Margaret Thatcher* (London: Pan,, 1989), pp. 408–9. David Cameron also professes a fondness for 'a really trashy novel', see *The Guardian*, 28 July 2009, p. 2.

Notes to Chapter 6: Post 9/11 : Radical Islamism in Recent Metropolitan Fiction

1 J. Kennedy, *Armed and Dangerous* (London: Mandarin, 1996), p. 281.

2 D. Delillo, *Mao II* (London: Vintage, 1992), p. 157.

3 L. Maguire, 'The destruction of New York City: a recurrent nightmare of American cold war cinema', *Cold War History*, 9 (2009), 513–24.

4 D. Holloway, *9/11 and the War Against Terror* (Edinburgh: Edinburgh University Press, 2008), ch. 5.

5 C. McCarthy, *The Road* (London: Picador, 2006), p. 192.

6 J. Burke, *Al-Qaeda: The True Story of Radical Islam* (London: I.B. Tauris, 2003), pp. 283–91.

7 L. Wright, *The Looming Tower: Al-Qaeda and the Road to 9/11* (London: Allen Lane), 2006, ch. 1.

8 J. Updike, *The Terrorist* (New York: Ballantine Books, 2006), p. 196.

9 M. Hamid, *The Reluctant Fundamentalist* (London: Penguin, 2007), pp. 93–5.

10 *New Statesman*, 14 May 2007, pp. 57–8.

11 Kennedy, *Armed and Dangerous*, p. 298.

12 Delillo, *Mao II*, p. 120.

13 D. Silva, *The Secret Servant* (London: Penguin, 2007), p. 84.

14 C. Forbes, *The Cell* (London: Pocket Books, 2002), p. 381.

15 C. Cleave, *Incendiary* (London: Vintage, 2005), p. 63.

16 M. Gilbert, *Trouble* (London: Gainsborough Press, 1996), pp. 198–225.

17 Delillo, *Mao II*, p. 41.

18 Fears of nuclear, chemical or biological weapons deployed by secret terrorist cells in attacks on London became a feature of British press reporting of Islamic terrorism in the first decade of the twenty-first century; see *The Guardian*, 3 June 2006, pp. 1, 4 and 5.

19 B.S. Turner, 'New and old xenophobia: the crisis of liberal multiculturalism', in S. Akbarzadeh and F. Mansouri (eds), *Islam and Political Violence: Muslim Diaspora and Radicalism in the West* (London: I. B. Tauris, 2010), pp. 65–86.

20 M. Phillips, *Londonistan: How Britain Created the Terror State Within* (London: Encounter Books, 2006), ch. 1.

21 'For jihadist, read anarchist', *The Economist*, 18 August 2005 and the *New Statesman*, 8 August 2005, p. 40.

22 J.L. Gelvin, *The Modern Middle East: A History* (Oxford: Oxford University Press, 2007), p. 7.

23 C. Caldwell, *Reflections on the Revolution in Europe: Immigration, Islam and the West* (London: Allen Lane, 2010).

24 E. Husain, 'Radical Departure', *New Statesman*, 15 February 2010, p. 29.

25 P. Berman, *Terror and Liberalism* (New York: Norton, 2003), ch. 2.

26 *The Guardian Review*, 3 November 2006, p. 8.

27 These were the named targets of the Islamist terrorist ring arrested in London in 2006; see Bill Durodie, 'We are the enemies within', *The Times Higher Education Supplement*, 22 September, 2006, pp. 16–17. Michael Burleigh speculates about a 'compensatory, born-again mechanism' for Islamists who rebel against Western immorality. He notes that the prominent Islamist preacher, Abu Hamza, once worked as a doorman at a 'London strip-joint'; see M. Burleigh, *Blood and Rage: A Cultural History of Terrorism* (London: Harper Perennial, 2009), p. 306.

28 E. Ambler, *The Care of Time* (London: Fontana, 1982), p. 24.

29 R. English, *Terrorism: How to Respond* (Oxford: Oxford University Press, 2007), pp. 97–8.

30 Burleigh, *Blood and Rage*, pp. 487–517.

31 N. Ferguson, 'Clashing civilisations or mad mullahs: the United States between informal and formal empire', in S. Talbot and N. Chana (eds), *The Age of Terror* (New York: Perseus, 2001), pp. 18–19.

32 Quoted in *The Guardian*, 21 March, 2004, p. 27.

33 Burke, *Al-Qaeda*, pp. 290–1.

34 *The Guardian*, 26 February 2005, p. 7.

35 Ibid., 11 September 2006, p. 30.

36 O. Nahiri, *Inside the Jihad: My Life with Al-Qaeda* (New York: Basic Books, 2006), p. 279.

37 Husain, 'Radical Departure', p. 29. The proliferation of these reminiscences of time spent in Islamist organizations by apostate militants is also reminiscent of insider accounts of time spent in anarchist groups at the end of the nineteenth century.

38 E. Husain, *The Islamist: Why I Joined Radical Islam in Britain, What I Saw and Why I Left* (London: Penguin Books, 2007), ch. 1.

39 For arguments about the construction of 'the West', see I. Morris, *Why the West Rules – for Now* (London: Profile, 2010).

40 See W.M. Flinders Petrie, *The Revolutions of Civilisation* (New York: Harper, 1911), pp. 2–5.

41 For a detailed examination of these themes see R. Overy, *The Morbid Age: Britain Between the Wars* (London: Allen Lane, 2009), ch. 1.

42 Light, *Forever England*, p. 99.

43 *The Guardian*, 8 March, 2011, p. 14.

44 A. Christie, *They Came to Baghdad* (London: Harper, 2003), pp. 313–23.

45 M.P. Shiel, *The Purple Cloud* (London: Allison and Busby, 1901), p. 93.

46 J. Buchan, *Greenmantle* (London: Penguin, 2008), p. 8. See also for analysis of the significance of this quotation, English, *Terrorism*, p. 121.

47 Sax Rohmer, *The Mask of Fu Manchu* (New York: Pyramid Publications, 1962), p. 19. For the significance of Fu Manchu and his legions to the stability of the West, see Taylor, ' "And I am the God of Destruction!" ', passim.

48 Sherriff, *The Great Catastrophe*, p. 250.

49 Ibid., p. 253.

50 J. White, *London in the 20th Century* (London: Vintage, 2001), p. 140.

51 Ibid., p. 140.

52   Bailey, *Old Soldiers*, p. 18.

53   Drabble, *The Ice Age*, p. 62.

54   Burgess, *1985*, p. 121.

55   Loc cit.

56   Ibid., pp. 190–4.

57   J. Patterson, *London Bridges* (London: Headline, 2004), p. 210.

58   Burleigh, *Blood and Rage*, pp. 152–7.

59   Ambler, *The Care of Time*, p. 76.

60   P. Niesewand, *The Underground Connection* (London: Pan, 1978), p. 163.

61   Ibid., p. 111.

62   S. Rimington, *At Risk* (London: Hutchinson, 2004), pp. 68–71.

63   Ibid., p. 356.

64   Forbes, *The Cell*, pp. 71–3.

65   Ibid., p. 14.

66   K. Macleod, *The Execution Channel* (London: Orbit, 2007), p. 257.

67   *The Guardian Review*, 7 July, 2006, p. 8.

68   Cleave, *Incendiary*, pp. 44–51.

69   Ibid., p. 219.

70   Ibid., pp. 65–6.

71   Macleod, *The Execution Channel*, p. 301.

72   Ibid., pp. 139–40.

73   Ibid., p. 270.

Notes to Conclusions

1   Colls, *Identity of England*, p. 213.

2   R.A. Soloway, *Demography and Degeneration: Eugenics and the Declining Birthrate in Twentieth Century Britain* (Chapel Hill: University of North Carolina Press, 1995, pp. 39–41.

3   See Charles Booth's suggestions for re-settling the East End poor on the land, C. Booth, *In Darkest England and the Way Out* (London: International Headquarters of the Salvation Army, 1890), pp. 125–31.

4   See F. Jameson, *Archaeologies of the Future: The Desire Called Utopia and Other Science Fiction* (London: Verso, 2007), ch. 2.

5   R. Nadelson, *Londongrad* (London: Atlantic Books, 2009), p. 148.

6   W. Boyd, *Ordinary Thunderstorms* (London: Bloomsbury Publishing, 2009), pp. 232–3.

Bibliography

PRIMARY SOURCES

Document and Manuscript Collections

Marx Memorial Library, Communist Party of Great Britain ephemera.
Norwich City Library, Manuscript materials and poetry relating to Robert Ket.
Sheffield City Library, Local History collection, broadsides and songs.

NEWSPAPERS

Anarchist, 1885–8.
Bee-Hive, 1874.
Blackshirt, 1933–4.
Clarion, 1892.
Commonweal, 1885–9.
Commonweal, 1907.
Commonwealth, 1866–7.
Daily Mirror, 1934.
Daily Telegraph, 1910.
Daily Worker, 1934–5.
De Morgan's Monthly, 1876.
Eastern Daily Post, 1949.
Economist, 2005.
English Chartist Circular, 1841.
English Labourers' Chronicle, 1878.
Eye Witness, 1911.
Free Commune, 1899.
Freedom, 1886–1927.
Guantlet, 1834.
Guardian, 1981–2009.
Individualist, 1907.
International Socialist Review, 1913.
Justice, 1884–95.
Kentish Mercury, 1876.
Labour Leader, 1894–1913.

Labour Pioneer and Yorkshire Factory Times, 1921.

Labour Prophet, 1892–3.

Lansbury's Labour Weekly, 1925–7.

London Dispatch, 1836.

London News, 1858.

London News, 1929.

Manchester Guardian, 1926.

Maoriland Worker, 1911.

Mother Earth, 1907.

National Reformer, 1867–79.

New Age, 1908–9.

Newcastle Weekly Chronicle, 1866–84.

New Statesman, 1913–2007.

Northern Star, 1848.

Odd Fellow, 1840.

Open Road, 1911.

Our Corner, 1886.

Our Land, 1909.

People's Paper, 1853–5.

Poor Man's Guardian, 1831.

Radical, 1881.

Reynolds's Newspaper, 1858–80.

Reynolds's Political Instructor, 1850.

Saturday Review, 1900.

Sheffield Iris, 1841.

Sherwin's Political Register, 1817.

Social Democrat, 1897.

Socialist, 1897.

Spectator, 1894–1973.

Sunday Times, 1994.

Sunday World, 1891.

The Times, 1822.

Times Literary Supplement, 1921–78.

Tribune, 1937–44.

Walsall Anarchist, 1892.

War Commentary, 1941.

Weekly Tribune, 1904.

Worker (Huddersfield), 1908.

Worker, 1910.

CONTEMPORARY BOOKS AND PAMPHLETS

A Dialogue between Wat Tyler, Mischievous Tom and an English Farmer (London: John Stockdale, 1793).

A New Britain: The Manifesto of the National Front (London: National Front, October, 1974).

Adams, W. E. *Memoirs of a Social Atom* (2 vols., London: Hutchinson and Co., 1903).

Adcock, J. (ed.), *Wonderful London* (3 vols., London: Fleetway House, 1927).

Addison, H. *The Battle of London* (London: Herbert Jenkins Ltd., 1926).

Aldred, G. *At Grips with War* (Glasgow: Bakunin Press, 1932).

Allingham, M. *The Tiger in the Smoke* (London: Penguin, 1957).

Ambler, E. *The Dark Frontier* (London: Hodder and Stoughton, 1959).

Ambler, E. *Background to Danger* (New York, Dell Publishing Co., 1965).

Ambler, E. *The Care of Time* (London: Fontana, 1982).

Ambler, E. *Here Lies: An Autobiography* (London: Harper Collins, 1985).

America Go Home (London: CPGB, 1951).

ARP: The Practical Air Raid Protection Britain Needs (London: Communist Party of Great Britain, 1939).

Ashton-Wolfe, H. *Outlaws of Modern Days* (London: Cassell and Company Ltd., 1927).

Bailey, P. *Old Soldiers* (London: Fourth Estate, 1999).

Baker, B. *Robert Miner, Anarchist* (London: Ward, Lock and Co., 1902).

Ballard, J. G. *Kingdom Come* (London: Harper Perennial, 2007).

Barbor, H. R. *Against the Red Sky: Silhouettes of Revolution* (London: Noel Douglas, 1922).

Bax E. B. (ed.), *Harry Quelch: Literary Remains* (London: Grant Richards, 1914).

Becker, J. *Hitler's Children: The Story of the Baader-Meinhof Gang* (Philadelphia: J.P. Lippincott, 1978).

Beer, M. *Social Struggles and Socialist Forerunners* (London: Leonard Parsons, 1924).

Bellamy, E. *Looking Backward, 2000–1887* (London: William Reeves, 1908).

Benn, T. *Fighting Back: Speaking Our for Socialism in the Eighties* (London: Hutchinson, 1988).

Beresford, J. D. *Revolution* (London: W. Collins, Sons and Co, 1921).

Besant, W. *The Revolt of Man* (Leipzig: Berhard Tauchnitz, 1882).

E. and H. Bland, *The Prophet's Mantle* (London: Drane, 1885).

Blood on the Streets: A Report by Bethnal Green and Stepney Trades Council on Racial Attitudes in East London (London: Bethnal Green and Stepney Trades Council, 1978).

Booth, W. *In Darkest England and the Way Out* (London: International Headquarters of the Salvation Army, 1890).

Boothby, G. *The League of Twelve* (London: F.V. White and Co., 1903).

Boyd, W. *Ordinary Thunderstorms* (London: Bloomsbury Publishing, 2010).

Bramah, E. *The Secret of the League: The Story of a Social War* (London: Thomas Nelson and Sons, 1907).

Bramley, T. *We Are Many* (London: Communist Party of Great Britain, 1941).

Britain's Fifth Column: A Plain Warning! (London: Workers' Bookshelf, 1940).

Brockway, F. *Bermondsey Story: The Life of Alfred Salter* (London: George Allen and Unwin, 1949).

Bronson, B. H. *Joseph Ritson, Scholar-at-Arms*, 2 vols. (Berkeley: University of California Press, 1938).

Burns, A. *The Angry Brigade* (London: Allison and Busby, 1973).

Bryers, P. *Hollow Man* (London: Hodder and Stoughton, 1976).

Buchan, J. *Mr. Standfast* (Ware: Wordsworth Classics, 1988).

Buchan, J. *Huntingtower* (London: Thomas Nelson and Sons Ltd., 1927).

Buchan, J. *The Three Hostages* (Ware: Wordsworth Classics, 1995).

Buchan, J. *The Island of Sheep* (Ware: Wordsworth Classics, 1995).

Buchan, J. *The House of the Four Winds* (London: Thomas Nelson and Sons, 1935).

Buchan, J. *John Macnab* (Ware: Wordsworth Classics, 1996).

Buchan, J. *The Power-House* (London: Pan, 1961).

Buchan, J. *The Thirty-Nine Steps* (London: Penguin, 1999).

Buchan, J. *Greenmantle* (London: Penguin, 2008).

Burdekin, K. *Swastika Night* (London: Victor Gollancz, 1937).

Burgess, A. *1985* (London: Little Brown, 1978).

Burmeister, J. *The Weatherman Guy* (London: Michael Joseph Ltd., 1975).

Byrne, R. *The Tunnel* (London: Michael Joseph, 1975).

Lord Byron, *The Vision of Judgement by Quevedo Redivivus Suggested by the Composition So Entitled by the Author of Wat Tyler* (London: L. Hunt, 1824).

Cameron, J. *How Long do we Ignore the Lessons of Bethal Green?* (London: *Daily Express*, 1947).

Carnie, E. *This Slavery* (London: Labour Publishing Co., 1925).

Cheyney, P. *The Urgent Hangman* (London: Penguin, 1938).

Christie, A. *The Secret Adversary* (London: Triad Granada, 1982).

Christie, A. *The Hollow* (London: Collins, 1946).

Christie, A. *They Came to Baghdad* (London: Harper, 2003).

Christie S. and A. Meltzer, *The Floodgates of Anarchy* (London: Sphere Books Ltd.).

Christie, S. *My Granny Made Me an Anarchist: General Franco, the Angry Brigade and Me* (Edinburgh: Scribner, 2002).

Christopher, J. *The Death of Grass* (London: Penguin, 2009).

Clarke, A. 'What's the matter wi' th' country: Tum Fowt debatin' club an ' anti-henpeck mission', *Teddy Ashton's Lancashire Annual* (Blackpool: Palatine Books Co., 1925).

Clayton, J. *Wat Tyler and the Great Uprising* (London: Francis Griffiths, 1909).

Clayton, J. *The True Story of Jack Cade, Captain of Kent A.D. 1450: A Vindication* (London: Frank Palmer, 1909).

Clayton, J. *Leaders of the People: Studies in Democratic History* (London: Martin Secker, 1910).

Clayton, J. *Robert Ket and the Norfolk Rising* (London: Martin Secker, 1912).

Clayton, J. *Father Stanton of St. Albans, Holborn: A Memoir* (London: Wells, Gardner, Darton and Co., 1913).

Clayton, J. *The Rise and Decline of Socialism in Great Britain, 1884–1924* (London: Faber and Gwyer, 1926).

Cleave, C. *Incendiary* (London: Vintage, 2005).

Clegg, A. *American Spider* (London: CPGB, 1947).

Cleveland, J. *The Rustick Rampant, or Rural Anarchy Affronting Monarch in the Insurrection of Wat Tyler: An Edition of the Idol of the Clownes* (London: John Cleveland, 1658).

Clews, R. *The Rise of Cromwell Jones* (London: Warner Books, 1995).

Clynes, J. R. *Memoirs* (London: Hutchinson, 1937, 2 vols.).

Coates, W. P. *The 'Zinoviev Letter': The Case for a full Investigation* (London: The Anglo-Russian Parliamentary Committee, 1928).

Cole, M. I. (ed), *Beatrice Webb's Diaries, 1912–1924* (London: Longmans, Green and Co., 1952).

Collings, J. *Land Reform: Occupying Ownership, Peasant Proprietorship and Rural Education* (London: Longmans, 1906).

Conrad, J. *The Secret Agent* (London: Penguin, 1980).

Cook, R. *A State of Denmark* (London: New English Library, 1973).

Cooke, J. *Jack Cade, the Insurrectionist: An Historical Romance* (London: T. White, 1840).

Cooper, G. *The Other Man* (London: Panther, 1964).

Cooper, P. J. *The Feminists* (New York: Pinnacle, 1971).

Cooper, T. *Captain Cobler or the Lincolnshire Rebellion: An Historical Romance of the Reign of Henry VIII* (London: J. Watson, 1850).

Cooper, T. *Poetical Works* (London: Hodder and Stoughton, 1877).

Costley, T. *Lancashire Poets and Other Literary Sketches* (Manchester: Abel Heywood and Son, 1897).

Cowen, J. *Tales of Revolution and of Patriotism* (London: Walter Scott, 1884).

Cox, C. *For Ever England: An Anthology* (London: Cassell and Company Ltd., 1943).

Cox, H. *Land Nationalisation* (London: Land Nationalisation Society, 1892).

Cronin, M. *Against the Day* (Oxford: Oxford University Press, 1998).

Dabbs, G. H. R. *The Ladder of Pain* (London: Charles William Deacon and Co., 1902).

Dalmou, J. *Slave Worker in the Channel Isles* (Guernsey: The Guernsey Press Company, 1955).

Darke, M. *A Question of Courage* (London: William Collins Sons and Co., 1978).

Davenport-Hines, R. (ed.), *Letters from Oxford: Hugh Trevor-Roper to Bernard Berensen* (London: Heinemann, 2007).

Davidson, J. M.*Eminent Radicals In and Out of Parliament* (London: W. Stewart and Co., 1880).

Davidson, J. M. *Annals of Toil: Labour History Outlines, Roman and British* (London: William Reeves, 1899).

Davitt, M. *The Fall of Feudalism in Ireland* (New York: Harper and Brothers, 1904).

Lord Willoughby de Broke, *The Passing Years* (London: Constable, 1924).

de Gibbins, H. D. *English Social Reformers* (London: Methuen and Co., 1892).

Deighton, L. *SS-GB: Nazi Occupied Britain, 1941* (London: Jonathan Cape, 1978).

Delillo, D. *Mao II* (London: Vintage, 1992).

Dick, P. K. *The Man in the High Castle* (London: Penguin, 2001).

Dickens, C. *A Child's History of England* (London: Thomas Nelson and Sons, 1900).

Dickens, C. *Bleak House* (Oxford: Oxford World's Classics, 1996).

Dickenson, E. A. *Legion of Blue and White Shirts: An Exposure of Fascism* (London: Epworth Press, 1936).

Dix, J. *Lions Living and Dead or Personal Recollections of the Great and the Gifted* (London: W. Tweedie, 1854).

Dolan, C. M. *The Blackshirt Racket: Mosley Exposed* (Reading: Workers' Bookshelf, 1935).

Dolguff, S. (ed.), *Bakunin on Anarchism* (Montreal: Black Rose Books, 1980).

Drabble, M. *The Ice Age* (London: Penguin, 1977).

Dubois, F. *The Anarchist Peril* (London: T. Fisher Unwin, 1894).

Du Maurier, D. *Rule Britannia* (London: Victor Gollancz, 1973).

Dunn, N. *Living Like I Do* (London: Futura Publications Ltd., 1977).

Edelman, M. *The Prime Minister's Daughter* (London: Panther, 1968).

Edmonds, H. 'The North Sea Mystery', in *Chums Annual 1934–5* (London, 1935).

Egan, P. Jr., *The Pilgrims of the Thames in Search of the National* (London: Thomas Tegg, 1838).

Egan, P. Jr., *Wat Tyler* (London: Simpkin, Marshall and Co., 1841).

Elliot, A. G. *The Guilty Madmen of Whitehall* (Kingswood: Elliot Right Way Books, 1969).

Evans, R. H. H. (ed.), *Thomas Evans, Old Ballads, Historical and Narrative* (London: R. H. H. Evans, 1810).

Fawcett, E. D. *Hartmann the Anarchist, or the Doom of a Great City* (New York: Arno Press, 1975).

Fellner G. (ed.) *Life of an Anarchist: The Alexander Berkman Reader* (New York: Four Walls Eight Windows, 1992).

Fenn, G. M. *George Alfred Henty: The Story of an Active Life* (London: Sampson Low, Marston and Company, 1907).

Fitz Gibbon, C. *When the Kissing Had to Stop* (London: Pan, 1962).

Fleming, I. *Moonraker* (London: Penguin, 2004).

Forbes, C. *The Cell* (London: Pocket Books, 2002).

Forsyth, F. *The Dogs of War* (London: Corgi, 1974).

Freeman, G. *The Leader* (London: New English Library, 1965).

Froude, J. A. *Oceana* (London: Longmans, Green and Co., 1886).

Fyfe, J. (ed.), *Autobiography of John McAdam (1806–1883)* (Edinburgh: Clark Constable Ltd., 1980).

Gallacher, W. *The Case for Communism* (London: Penguin, 1948).

Gammage, R. G. *History of the Chartist Movement* (London: Merlin Press, 1976).

Gilbert, M. *Trouble* (London: Gainsborough Press, 1996).

Glasier, J. B. *William Morris and the Early Days of the Socialist Movement* (London: Longmans, Green and Co., 1921).

Glasspool, A. J. *The Corporation of the City of London: Its Ceremonies and Importance* (London: Effingham Wilson, 1924).

Gleig, C. *When All Men Starve* (London: John Lane, 1898).

Glover, H. *Wat Tyler: A Play in Three Acts* (London: Kegan Paul, Trench, Trubner, 1925).

Goldstein, D. and M. Moore Avery, *Socialism: The Nation of Fatherless Children* (Boston: Thomas J. Flynn and Co., 1911).

Gore, J. *King George V: A Personal Memoir* (London: John Murray, 1941).

Gorman, J. T. *George VI, King and Emperor* (London: W.G Foyle Ltd., 1937).

Grahame, S. *Where Socialism Failed: An Actual Experiment* (London: John Murray, 1912).

Greatorex, W. *1990* (London: Sphere Books Ltd., 1977).

Griffith, G. *The Angel of the Revolution: A Tale of the Coming Terror* (New York: Heliograph Books, 2003).

'Grip' (John Drew Gay), *How John Bull Lost London, or the Capture of the Channel Tunnel* (London: Sampson Low, 1882).

Grundy, T. *Memoirs of a Fascist Childhood* (London: Heinemann, 1998).

Hain, P. *Radical Regeneration: Protest, Direct Action and Community Politics* (London: Quartet Books, 1975).

Hamid, M. *The Reluctant Fundamentalist* (London: Penguin, 2007).

Keir Hardie, J. *From Serfdom to Socialism* (London: Gorge Allen, 1907).

Harmon, J. *W.I.T.C.H* (London: New English Library, 1971).

Harris, R. *Fatherland* (London: Arrow Books, 1992).

Hamilton, P. *Hangover Square* (London: Penguin, 2001).

'Harrington Hext' (E. Phillpotts), *The Thing at Their Heels* (London: Macmillan, 1923).

Hart, W. C. *Confessions of an Anarchist* (London: E Grant Richards, 1906).

Hay, W. D. *The Doom of the Great City* (London: Newman and Co., 1880).

Healey, D. *The Time of My Life* (London: Penguin, 1989).

Heath, R. *The English Peasant; Studies, Historical, Local and Biographic* (London: T. Fisher Unwin, 1893).

Hemyng, B. *The Commune in London, or Thirty Years Hence* (London: C.H. Clarke, 1871).

Henty, G. A. *A March On London: Being a Story of Wat Tyler's Insurrection* (New York: Charles Scribner's Sons, 1897).

Henty, G. A. *Condemned as a Nihilist: A Story of Escape from Siberia* (London: Blackie and Sons, 1892).

Herbert, J. *The Spear* (London: Pan Books, 1998).

Herbert, J. *'48* (London: Harper Collins 1996).

Hilliard, W. *Life and Adventures of Wat Tyler* (London: Collins, 1851).

Hocking, J. *David Baring* (London: George Newnes, Ltd., 1900).

Hocking, S. *Belinda the Backward: A Romance of Modern Idealism* (London: Arthur C. Fifield, 1905).

Hocking, S. K. *The Broken Fence* (London: Sampson Low, 1928).

Holden, E. *Country Diary of an Edwardian Lady* (London: Michael Joseph, 1977).

Hone, W. *The Political "A, Apple-Pie"; or the Extraordinary Red Book Versified* (London: Adams and Dart, 1971).

Hopkinson, A. *The Hope of the Workers* (Manchester: Hopkinson, 1923).

Household, G. *A Time to Kill* (London: Penguin, 1971).

Hurd, D. and A. Osmond, *Scotch on the Rocks* (London: Fontana/Collins, 1971).

Husain, E. *The Islamist: Why I Joined Radical Islam in Britain, What I Saw and Why I Left* (London: Penguin Books, 2007).

Huxley, A. *Point Counter Point* (London: Flamingo, 1994).

Hyndman, H. *The Historical Basis of Socialism in England* (London: Kegan Paul, 1883).

Innes, H. *North Star* (London: Willliam Collins Sons and Co., Ltd., 1975).

Is Jack Cade Coming? A Question Considered by the Age Newspaper of Sunday June 10, 1838 (London: Holt, 1838).

James, H. *The Princess Casamassima* (London: Penguin, 1977).

Jameson, S. *In the Second Year* (Nottingham: Trent Editions, 2004).

Jarrett, B. *Medieval Socialism* (London: Burns Oates and Washbourne Ltd., 1913).

Jefferies, R. *After London: Wild England* (Oxford: Oxford University Press, 1980).

Johnson, P. *Enemies of Society* (London: Weidenfeld and Nicolson, 1977).

Joyce, A. *Land Ho! A Conversation of 1933 on the Results of the Adoption of the System of Nationalising the Land of New Zealand adopted in 1883* (Lyttleton: Lyttleton Publishing, 1881).

Kettle, P. *The Day of the Women* (London: New English Library, 1969).

Kropotkin, P. *Fields, Factories and Workshops* (London: Swan Sonnenschein and Co., 1901).

Kropotkin, P. *Memoirs of a Revolutionist* (London: Hutchinson, 1988).

Kunzru, H. *My Revolutions* (London: Penguin, 2007).

Lane, M. *Edgar Wallace: The Biography of a Phenomenon* (New York: Doubleday, Doran and Company, 1938).

Larwood, J. and J. C. Hotten, *English Inn Signs* (London: Chatto and Windus, 1951).

Lawson, M. *Enough is Enough, or the Emergency Government* (London: Picador, 2004).

Lean, G. *Rebirth of a Nation* (Poole: Blandford Press, 1976).

Leatham, J. *The Peasants' Revolt or the Tragedy of a Nation* (London: Twentieth Century Press, 1899).

Lessing, D. *The Good Terrorist* (London: Grafton, 1985).

Liddell, H. *Elite* (London: Rowan, 1990).

Linbach, G. *The Azrael of Anarchy* (London: Simpkin and Marshall, 1894).

Linklater, E. *The Impregnable Women* (London: Penguin, 1959).

Linklater, E. *Magnus Merriman* (London: Penguin, 1959).

Litvinoff, E. *A Death Out of Season* (London: Michael Joseph, 1973).

London, J. *The Iron Heel* (New York: Grayson Publishing Corp., 1948).

Lyons, J. and C. Raleigh, *The Master Crime* (London: Cassell and Company, Ltd., 1907).

Maby, R. *The Unofficial Countryside* (London: Little Toller Books, 2010).

Mackay, J. H. *The Anarchists* (New York: The Revisionist Press, 1972).

MacLeod, K. *The Execution Channel* (London: Orbit, 2007).

A Marshall, *Explosives*, 2 vols. (London: J and A. Churchill, 1917).

Maurice, C. E. *Lives of English Popular Leaders in the Middle Ages: Tyler, Ball and Oldcastle* (London: H.S. King and Co., 1875).

Mayne, J. D. *The Triumph of Socialism and How it Succeeded* (Amsterdam: Fredonia Books, 2003).

Mayse, S. *Merlin's Web* (Toronto: Seal Books, 1988).

McCarthy, C. *The Road* (London: Picador, 2006).

Melville, C. F. *The Truth about the New Party* (London: Wishart and Co., 1931).

'I. Meredith' (Olivia and Helen Rossetti), *A Girl Among the Anarchists* (Lincoln: University of Nebraska Press, 1992).

Mitchison, N. *We Have Been Warned* (London: Constable, 1935).

Mikardo, I. (ed.), *Sense about Defence: The Report of the Labour Party Defence Study Group* (London: Quartet Books, 1977).

Montagu, I. *Blackshirt Brutality: The Story of Olympia* (London: Workers' Bookshop, 1934).

Morris, W. *News from Nowhere* (London: Penguin, 1993).

Morrison, A. *Tales of Mean Streets* (London: Methuen and Co., 1894).

Morrison, A. 'The Case of the Lost Foreigner' in *The Chronicles of Martin Hewitt* (New York: Books for Libraries Press, 1971).

Morrison, H. *Unity, Peace and Security: Pollitt's Reply to Morrison* (London: Workers' Bookshop, 1936.

Morton, A. L. *Get Out* (Ipswich: CPGB, 1953).

Moss, R. *The Collapse of Democracy* (London: Sphere Books Ltd., 1977).

Mottram, R. H. *Bowler Hat: A Last Glance at the Old Country Banking* (London: Hutchinson, 1940).

Muller, R. *After All, This Is England: The Lost Diaries of Albert Smith* (Harmondsworth: Penguin, 1967).

Mullin, C. *A Very British Coup* (London: Politico's, 2006).

Nadelson, R. *Londongrad* (London: Atlantic Books, 2009).

Nahiri, O. *Inside the Jihad: My Life with Al-Qaeda* (New York: Basic Books, 2006).

Nesbit, E. *The Railway Children* (London: Penguin, 1993).

Niesewand, P. *The Underground Connection* (London: Pan, 1978).

Noel, C. *Autobiography* (London: J. M. Dent and Sons Ltd., 1945).

O'Flaherty, L. *The Informer* (London: New English Library, 1971).

O'Neill, H. C. *Can Britain be Invaded?* (London: Dent, 1941).

Oppenheimer, M. *Urban Guerrilla* (London: Penguin, 1970).

Orwell, G. 'Boys' Weeklies' in *Critical Essays* (London: Secker and Warburg, 1946).

Orwell, G. 'England, your England' (1941), in *Inside the Whale and Other Essays* (London: Penguin, 1979), pp. 63–90.

Oughton, F. *The Siege of Sidney Street* (London: Pan, 1960).

Outhwaite, R. L. *The Land Revolution* (London: George Allen and Unwin, 1917).

Paine, T. *The Rights of Man* (London: Penguin, 1979).

Palmer, R. A. *Co-operation under the Nazis* (Manchester: Co-operative Union Ltd., 1939).

Flinders Petrie, W. M. *The Revolutions of Civilisation* (New York: Harper, 1911).

Poll-Tax Riot: Ten Hours that Shook Trafalgar Square (London: Acab Press, 1990).

Pollitt, H. *Serving My Time: An Apprenticeship to Politics* (London: Lawrence and Wishart, 1940).

Priest, C. *Fugue for a Darkening Island* (London: New English Library, 1972).

Proal, L. *Political Crime* (New York: D. Appleton and Co., 1898).

Real Socialism: Authenticated Extracts from Socialist Leaders' Speeches and Writings (London: National Union of Conservative and Unionist Associations, 1924).

Renier, G. J. *The English: Are They Human?* (Leipzig: Bernhard Tauchnitz, 1932).

Reynolds, R. *My Life and Crimes* (London: Jarrolds Publishers, 1956).

Rickword, E. *A Handbook of Freedom: A Record of English Democracy through Twelve Centuries* (London: Lawrence and Wishart, 1939).

Ridley, A. *The Ghost Train: A Drama in Three Acts* (London: Samuel French, 1931).

Ridley, F. A. *The Revolutionary Tradition in England* (London: National Labour Press, 1948).

Rimington, S. *At Risk* (London: Hutchinson, 2004).

Robert Ket, *The Wyndham Tanner: A Poem* (London: A. Brown, 1869).

Rocker, R. *The London Years* (Nottingham: Five Leaves Publications, 2005).

Rogaly, J. *Grunwick* (London: Penguin, 1977).

Thorold Rogers, J. E. *Six Centuries of Work and Wages: The History of English Labour* (London: T. Fisher and Unwin, 1903).

Rossetti, W. M. *Some Reminiscences*, 2 vols (New York: Charles Scribner and Sons., 1906).

Roth, P. *The Plot Against America* (London: Vintage, 2005).

Rowbotham, S. *Promise of a Dream: Remembering the Sixties* (London: Verso, 2001).

Russell, F. W. *Ket's Rebellion* (London: Longman, Brown and Green, 1859).

'Saki' (H.H. Munro), 'When William Came' in M. Moorcock (ed.), *England Invaded: A Collection of Fantasy Fiction* (London: W.H. Allen and Co., 1980).

'Sapper' (Herman Cyril McNeile), *Bulldog Drummond* (London: Hodder and Stoughton, 1933).

'Sapper' (Herman Cyril McNeile), *The Black Gang* (London: Hodder and Stoughton, 1956).

Savage, R. H. *The Anarchist: A Story of To-Day* (2 vols., Leipzig: Bernhard Tauchniiz, 1894).

'Sax Rohmer' (Arthur Sarsfied Ward), *The Mask of Fu Manchu* (New York: Pyramid Publications, 1962).

Schaack, M. J. *Anarchy and Anarchists: A History of the Red Terror and the Social Revolution in America and Europe* (Chicago: F.J. Shulte and Co., 1889).

Seaman, D. *The Committee* (London: Futura, 1979).

Serge, V. *Memoirs of a Revolutionary* (Iowa City: University of Iowa Press, 2002).

Shanks, E. 'The People of the Ruins', *Famous Fantastic Mysteries*, vol. 8, 1947.

Shaw, C. *When I Was a Child* (London: Caliban Books, 1983).

Shaw, G. B. *The Impossibilities of Anarchism* (London: Fabian Society, 1893).

Shaw, N. *Whiteway: A Colony in the Cotswolds* (London: C.W. Daniel, 1935).

Sheers, O. *Resistance* (London: Faber and Faber, 2007).

Sherriff, R. C. *The Cataclysm* (London: Pan Books Ltd, 1958).

Shiel, M. P. *The Purple Cloud* (London: Allison and Busby, 1901).

Shipway, G. *The Chilian Club* (London: Mayflower Books, 1972).

Shorthouse, J. H. *Sir Percival: A Story of the Past and of the Present* (London: Macmillan, 1894).

Shute, N. *In the Wet* (New York: Permabooks, 1957).

Shute, N. *So Disdained* (London: House of Stratus, 2000).

Silva, D. *The Secret Servant* (London: Penguin, 2007).

Silva, D. *The Marching Season* (London: Weidenfeld and Nicolson, 1999).

Smith, C. *Big Cyril: The Autobiography of Cyril Smith* (London: W.H. Allen, 1977).

Solzhenitsyn, A. *The Gulag Archipelago* (London: Harper and Row, 1973).

Sommerfield, J. *May Day* (London: Lawrence and Wishart, 1984).

Spring, H. *Fame is the Spur* (London: Fontana/Collins, 1982).

'Stepniak' (Sergei Kravachinski), *The Russian Peasantry: Their Agrarian Condition, Social Life and Religion* (Cambridge: Cambridge Scholars' Publishing, 2009).

Summers, J. *The Disaster* (London: New English Library, 1969).

Tansley, F. C. *For Kett and Countryside* (London: Jarrold and Sons, 1910).

The History of Wat Tyler and Jack Straw (Stirling: C. Randall, 1803).

The King's Reign Told in Pictures (Manchester: Stanley, Hudson and Co., 1935).

The Rebellion of Norwich in 1549, A Drama Interspersed with Music First Acted on Monday April 17 1815 at the Theatre Royale, Norwich: With Notes, Historical and Explanatory by George P. Bromley (Norwich: Bacon, Kinnebrook and Co., 1815).

Theroux, P. *The Family Arsenal* (London: Penguin, 1977).

Thomas, D. *Y Werin a'i Theyrnas* (The Common People and their Kingdom) (Caernarfon: Cyhoeddwyd gan yr Awdur, 1910).

Thomas, H. (ed.), *The Establishment* (London: New English Library, 1960).

Toynbee, P. *These Savage Days* (London: Hamish Hamilton, 1937).

Tranter, N. *The Freebooters* (Edinburgh: B & W Publishing Ltd., 1997).

Trease, G. *Bows Against the Barons* (Leningrad: Enlightenment Press, 1968).

Towards a Citizens' Militia: Anarchist Alternatives to NATO and the Warsaw Pact (Cienfuegos Press: Sandy, Orkney, 1980).

Turner, C. *Land Problems and National Welfare* (London: John Lane, 1911).

Uncle Sam (London: CPGB, 1947).

Updike, J. *The Terrorist* (New York: Ballantine Books, 2006).

Vago, A L. *Orthodox Phrenology* (London: Simpkin, Marshall and Co., 1871).

Van Greenaway, P. *The Man who Held the Queen to Ransom and Sent Parliament Packing* (London: Penguin, 1968).

Villiers, B. *The Socialist Movement in England* (London: T. F. Unwin, 1908).

Vizetelly, E. A. *The Anarchists: Their Faith and Their Record* (Edinburgh: Turnbull and Spears Printers, 1911).

Wakeman, J. *Anarchism and Democracy* (London: Freedom Press, 1920).

Walker, J. 'Chartist Ecologue', in *The Bard* (London: Simpkin, Marshall and Co., 1842).

Wallace, E. *People: A Short Autobiography* (New York: Doubleday, Doran and Company, 1929).

Wallace, E. *The Council of Justice* (Pan Books Ltd., 1973).

Walters, G. *The Leader* (London: Headline, 2003).

Warner, R. *The Aerodrome* (London: Penguin Books, 1944).

Wat Tyler and Jack Straw, or the Mob Reformers, a Dramatic Entertainment as It Is Perform'd at Pinkethman's and Giffard's Great Theatrical Booth in Bartholomew Fair (London: J. W., 1730).

'Wat Tyler', *Two Essays: The Earth Question or Landlords and People, and the Capital Question or Employers and Workers* (Belfast: Reid, 1889).

Waugh, A. *A Bed of Flowers* (London: Robin Clark Ltd., 1985).

Wells, H. G. *Will Socialism Destroy the Home?* (London: ILP, 1904).

Wheatley, D. *Black August* (London: Arrow Books Ltd, 1965).

Wheatley, D. *The Forbidden Territory* (London: Arrow Books Ltd, 1961).

Wheatley, D. *Contraband* (London: Arrow Books Ltd., 1971).

Wheeler, J. M. *A Biographical Dictionary of Freethinkers of all Ages and Nations* (London: Progressive Publishing Company, 1889).

Wheelwright, J. *Landlordism: Its Origins and Growth* (London: English Land Restoration League, 1896).

White, Ray B. *The False Christ of Communism and the Social Gospel* (London: Pillar of Fire, 1946).

Whiteing, R. *No. 5 John Street* (London: Thomas Nelson and Sons, 1902).

Whiteing, R. *My Harvest* (London: Macmillan, 1915).

Who Backs Mosley? Fascist Promise and Fascist Performance (London: Labour Research Department, 1934).

Wilkins, W. G. *The Penny History of the Poor People of England: The Rise and Progress of Poverty in England from the Norman Conquest to Modern Times* (London: Headley Brothers, 1911).

Williams, F. *Fifty Years' March: The Rise of the Labour Party* (London: Odhams Press Ltd., 1950).

Williams, H. G.*Why I Am Not A Socialist* (London: The Anti-Socialist and Anti-Communist Union, 1930).

Williams, R. (ed.), *May Day Manifesto, 1968* (London: Penguin, 1968).

Wilson, A. *The Old Men at the Zoo* (London: Penguin, 1961).

Wilson, H. *The Labour Government, 1964–1970: A Personal Record* (London: Weidenfeld and Nicolson, 1971).

Winsten, S. *Days with Bernard Shaw* (London: Hutchinson and Co., 1951).

Wise, A. *Who Killed Enoch Powell?* (London: Weidenfeld and Nicolson, 1970).

Wodehouse, P. G. 'The Code of the Woosters' in *The Wodehouse Omnibus* (London: Penguin, 2001).

Wright, P. with P. Greengrass, *Spycatcher* (Richmond: William Heinemann, Australia, 1987).

Wohl, B. *The Ten-Tola Bars* (Feltham: Hamlyn, 1978).

Wootton, B. *London's Burning* (London: Allen and Unwin, 1936).

Wyndham Lewis, P. *Rotting Hill* (Santa Barbara: Black Sparrow Press).

Yates, D. *Lower than Vermin* (London: Ward, Lock and Co., Ltd, 1950).

SECONDARY SOURCES

Anderson, B. *Under Three Flags: Anarchism and the Anti-Colonial Imagination* (London: Verso, 2005).

Armytage, W. H. G. *Heavens Below: Utopian Experiments in England* (London: Routledge and Kegan Paul, 1961).

Avrich, P. *The Haymarket Tragedy* (New Jersey: Princeton University Press, 1984).

Baker, P. *The Devil is a Gentleman: The Life and Times of Dennis Wheatley* (Cambridge: Dedalus, 2010).

Baxendale, J. *Priestley's England: J.B. Priestley and English Culture* (Manchester: Manchester University Press, 2007).

Beaumont, M. *Utopia Ltd.: Ideologies of Social Dreaming in England 1870–1900* (New York: Haymarket Books, 2005).

Beckett, A. *When the Lights Went Out: What Really Happened to Britain in the Seventies?* (London: Faber and Faber, 2009).

Beckson, K. *London in the 1890s: A Cultural History* (New York: W.W. Norton and Co., 1992).

Beers, L. *Your Britain: Media and the Making of the Labour Party* (Cambridge, Massachusetts: Harvard University Press, 2010).

Belich, R. *Making Peoples: A History of the New Zealanders* (Rosedale: Penguin, 1996).

Benewick, R. *The Fascist Movement in Great Britain* (London: Allen Lane, 1972).

Berger, S. *The British Labour Party and the German Social Democrats, 1900–1931* (Oxford: Oxford University Press, 1994).

Berlin, I. *Russian Thinkers* (London: Penguin, 1978).

Berman, P. *Terror and Liberalism* (New York: W.W. Norton and Company, 2003).

Billig, M. *Fascists: A Social Psychological View of the National Front* (New York: Harcourt Brace Jovanovich, 1978).

Black, J. *Britain since the Seventies: Politics and Society in the Consumer Age* (London: Reaktion, 2004).

Bloom, C. *Cult Fiction: Popular Reading and Pulp Theory* (London: Macmillan, 1996).

Bloom, C. *Violent London: 2000 Years of Riots, Revels and Revolts* (London: Sidgwick and Jackson, 2003).

Blythe, R. *The Age of Illusion: England in the Twenties and Thirties, 1919–40* (London: Penguin, 1963).

Booker, C. *The Seventies: Portrait of a Decade* (London: Allen Lane, 1980).

Bourke, J. *Fear: A Cultural History* (London: Virago, 2005).

Boyd, K. *Manliness and the Boys' Story Paper in Britain: A Cultural History, 1855–1940* (London: Palgrave-Macmillan, 2003).

Briggs, J. *A Woman of Passion: The Life of E. Nesbit, 1858–1924* (London: Penguin Books, 1989).

Bunting, M. *The Channel Islands under German Rule, 1940–45* (London: Granta Books, 1996).

Burke, J. *Al-Qaeda: The True Story of Radical Islam* (London: I.B. Tauris, 2003).

Burleigh, M. *Earthly Powers: The Conflict between Religion and Politics from the French Revolution to the Great War* (London: Harper Perennial, 2005).

Burleigh, M. *Blood and Rage: A Cultural History of Terrorism* (London: Harper Perennial, 2009).

Cahm, A. *Kropotkin and the Rise of Revolutionary Anarchism* (Cambridge: Cambridge University Press, 1989).

Calder, A. *The Myth of the Blitz* (London: Jonathan Cape, 1991).

Caldwell, C. *Reflections on the Revolution in Europe: Immigration, Islam and the West* (London: Allen Lane, 2010).

Campbell, C. *Fenian Fire: The British Government Plot to Assassinate Queen Victoria* (London: Harper Collins, 2002).

Cannadine, D. *In Churchill's Shadow: Confronting the Past in Modern Britain* (London: Allen Lane, 2002).

Carr, G. *The Angry Brigade: A History of Britain's First Urban Guerrilla Group* (London: Victor Gollancz, 1973).

Chase, M. *Chartism: A New History* (Manchester: Manchester University Press, 2008).

Chester, L. S. Fay and H. Young, *The Zinoviev Letter: A Political Intrigue* (London: Heinemann, 1967).

Clarke, I. F. *Voices Prophesying War 1763–1984* (Oxford: Oxford University Press, 1966).

Clarke, I. F. 'Introduction: The paper warriors' in Clarke (ed.), *The Tale of the Next War, 1871–1914* (Liverpool: Liverpool University Press, 1995), pp. 1–28.

Clymer, J. A. *America's Culture of Terrorism: Violence, Capitalism and the Written Word* (Chapel Hill: University of North Carolina Press, 2003).

Collini, S. *Absent Minds: Intellectuals in Britain* (Oxford: Oxford University Press, 2006).

Colls, R. *Identity of England* (Oxford: Oxford University Press, 2002).

Copsey, N. *Contemporary British Fascism: The British National Party and the Quest for Legitimacy* (Basingstoke: Macmillan, 2004).

Cresswell, T. *The Tramp in America* (London: Reaktion Books, 2001).

Crick, B. *George Orwell: A Life* (London: Penguin, 1982).

Darwin, J. *Britain and Decolonisation: The Retreat from Empire in the Post-War World* (London: Macmillan, 1987).

Davies, J. *A History of Wales* (London: Penguin, 1994).

Davis, M. *Buda's Wagon: A Brief History of the Car Bomb* (London: Verso, 2007).

Davison, G. *The Rise and Fall of Marvellous Melbourne* (Carlton: Melbourne University Press, 2004).

Denning, M. *Cover Stories: Narrative and Ideology in the British Spy Thriller* (London: Routledge and Kegan Paul, 1987).

Diemert, B. *Graham Greene's Thrillers and the 1930s* (Belfast: McGill-Queen's University Press, 1996).

Docker, J. *The Nervous Nineties: Australian Cultural Life in the 1890s* (Oxford: Oxford University Press, 1991.

Dorril, S. *Blackshirt: Sir Oswald Mosley and British Fascism* (Viking: London, 2006).

Driver, C. *Tory Radical: the Life of Richard Oastler* (Oxford: Oxford University Press, 1946).

Elliott, M. *Robert Emmet: The Making of a Legend* (London: Profile Books, 2004).

Ellman, R. *Oscar Wilde* (New York: Random House, 1987).

English, R. *Terrorism: How to Respond* (Oxford: Oxford University Press, 2007).

Epstein, J. *Radical Expression: Political Language, Ritual, and Symbolism in England, 1790-1850* (Oxford: Oxford University Press, 1994).

'Fagin', *'Reds on the Green': A Short Tour of Clerkenwell Radicalism* (London: South London Radical History Group, 2005).

Finn, M. *After Chartism: Class and Nation in English Radical Politics, 1848–1874* (Cambridge: Cambridge University Press, 1993).

Fishman, W. J. *East End Jewish Radicals, 1875–1914* (London: Duckworth, 1975).

Fleming, P. *Operation Sea Lion* (London: Pan, 1975).

Foster, R. F. *Lord Randolph Churchill* (Oxford: Clarendon Press, 1981).

Friedberg, A. L. *The Weary Titan: Britain and the Experience of Relative Decline, 1895–1905* (Princeton: Princeton University Press, 1988).

Gamble, A. *Britain in Decline: Economic Policy, Political Strategy and the British State* (London: Macmillan, 1981).

Garnett, M. *From Anger to Apathy: The Story of Politics, Society, and Popular Culture in Britain since 1975* (London: Vintage, 2008).

Gelvin, J. L. *The Modern Middle East: A History* (Oxford: Oxford University Press).

Girouard, M. *The Return to Camelot: Chivalry and the English Gentleman* (New Haven: Yale University Press, 1981).

Goodway, D. *London Chartism, 1838–1848* (Cambridge: Cambridge University Press, 1982).

Goodway, D. *Anarchist Seeds Beneath the Snow: Left Libertarian Thought and British Writers from William Morris to Colin Ward* (Liverpool: Liverpool University Press, 2009).

Gray, D. D. *London's Shadows: The Dark Side of the Victorian City* (London: Hambledon Continuum, 2010).

Gray, J. *Al-Qaeda and What it Means to be Modern* (London: Faber, 2003).

Griffiths, C. V. J. *Labour and the Countryside: The Politics of Rural Britain, 1919–1939* (Oxford: Oxford University Press, 2007).

Guerin, D. *Anarchism* (New York: Monthly Review Press, 1970).

Viscount Hailsham, 'The Middle Way' in Newton Branch (ed.), *This Britain, Tradition and Achievement* (London: Macdonald, 1951), pp. 77–83.

Hajdu, D. *The Ten-Cent Plague: The Great Comic Book Scare and How it Changed America* (New York: Farrar, Straus and Giroux, 2008).

Harris, A. *Romantic Moderns: English Writers, Artists and the Imagination from Virginia Woolf to John Piper* (London: Thames and Hudson, 2010).

Harrison, M. *Peter Cheyney: Prince of Hokum* (London: Neville Spearman, 1954).

Harrison, R. *The English Defence of the Commune (1871)* (London: Merlin Press Ltd., 1971).

Hayter, D. *Fightback: Labour's Traditional Right in the 1970s and 1980s* (Manchester: Manchester University Press, 2005).

Haywood, I. *The Revolution in Popular Literature: Print, Politics and the People, 1790–1860* (Cambridge: Cambridge University Press, 2004).

Haywood, I. *Bloody Romanticism: Spctacular Violence and the Politics of Representation, 1776–1832* (London: Palgrave, 2006).

Hepburn, A. *Intrigue: Espionage and Culture* (London: Yale University Press, 2005).

Hilliard, C. *To Exercise Our Talents: The Democratisation of Writing in Britain* (Cambridge, Mass.,: Harvard University Press, 2006).

Hobsbawm, E. *Interesting Times: A Twentieth Century Life* (London: Allen Lane, 2002).

Hodgkinson, T. *How to be Idle* (London: Penguin, 2004).

Hoggart, R. *The Uses of Literacy* (London: Penguin, 1962).

Holloway, D. *9/11 and the War Against Terror* (Edinburgh: Edinburgh University Press, 2008).

Holmes, C. *The Battle of Stepney: The Sidney Street Siege, Its Causes and Consequences* (London: Robert Hale, 1981).

Hopkins, C. *English Fiction in the 1930s* (Continuum: London, 2006).

Horowitz, I. L. (ed.), *The Anarchists* (New York: Dell Publishing Ltd., 1964).

Houen, A. *Terrorism and Modern Literature: From Joseph Conrad to Ciaron Carson* (Oxford: Oxford University Press, 2002).

Hulse, J. W. *Revolutionists in London: A Study of Five Unorthodox Socialists* (Oxford: Oxford University Press, 1970).

Ignatieff, M. *The Lesser Evil: Political Ethics in an Age of Terror* (New Jersey: Princeton University Press, 2004).

Inwood, S. *A History of London* (London: Macmillan, 1998).

Jameson, F. *Archaeologies of the Future: The Desire Called Utopia and Other Science Fictions* (London: Verso, 2007).

Joll, J. *The Anarchists* (New York: Grosset and Dunlap, 1964).

Karsten, P. *Patriot-Heroes in England and America: Political Symbolism and Changing Values over Three Centuries* (Madison: University of Wisconsin Press, 1978).

Kedward, R. *The Anarchists: The Men Who Shocked an Era* (Leiden: Sijthoff, 1970).

Kennedy, H. *Anarchist of Love: The Secret Life of John Henry Mackay* (New York: Mackay Society, 1983).

Kent, A. M. *Pulp Methodism: The Lives and Literature of Silas, Joseph and Salome Hocking* (St. Austell: Cornish Hillside Publications, 2002).

Kent, W. *John Burns: Labour's Lost Leader* (London: Williams and Norgate Ltd., 1950).

Kiberd, D. *Inventing Ireland: The Literature of the Modern Nation* (London: Vintage, 1995).

Klaus, H. G. (ed.), *The Socialist Novel in Britain* (Hassocks: Harvester, 1982).

Klaus, H. G. *The Literature of Labour: 200 Years of Working- Class Writing* (Hassocks: Harvester, 1985).

Klaus, H. G. *Tramps, Workmates and Revolutionaries* (London: Journeyman Press, 1993).

Knight, S. *Crime Fiction, 1800–2000: Detection, Death, Diversity* (London: Macmillan, 2004).

Koven, S. *Slumming: Sexual and Social Politics in Victorian London* (Princeton: Princeton University Press, 2004).

Laclau, E. *On Populist Reason* (London: Verso, 2005).

Laqueur, W. *The New Terrorism: Fanaticism and the Arms of Mass Destruction* (London: Phoenix Press, 2001).

Lawrence, J. *Speaking for the People: Party, Language and Popular Politics in England, 1867–1914* (Cambridge: Cambridge University Press, 1998).

Lees, A. *Cities Perceived: Urban Society in European and North American Thought* (Manchester: Manchester University Press, 1985).

Light, A. *Forever England: Femininity, Literature and Conservatism between the Wars* (London: Rouledge, 1991).

Linebaugh, P. *The London Hanged: Crime and Civil Society in the Eighteenth Century* (London: Penguin, 1991).

Linebaugh, P. *The Magna Carta Manifesto* (Berkeley: University of California Press, 2008).

Lineham, T. *East London for Mosley: The British Union of Fascists in East London and South-West Sussex, 1933–1940* (London: Frank Cass, 1996).

Lloyd, A. L. *Folk Song in England* (London: Panther, 1967).

Lownie, A. *John Buchan: The Presbyterian Cavalier* (London: Pimlico, 2002).

MacCarthy, F. *William Morris: A Life for Our Time* (London: Faber and Faber, 1994).

Mackenzie, J. M. *Propaganda and Empire: The Manipulation of British Public Opinion, 1880–1960* (Manchester: Manchester University Press, 1984).

Macksey, K. *Invasion: The German Invasion of England, July 1940* (Barnsley: Greenhill Books, 1980).

Magee, P. *Gangster Guerrillas: Representations of Irish Republicans in 'Troubles' Fiction* (Belfast: Beyond the Pale, 2001).

Magraw, R. *France 1815–1914: The Bourgeois Century* (London: Fontana, 1983).

Mandler, P. *The English National Character: The History of an Idea from Edmund Burke to Tony Blair* (New Haven: Yale University Press, 2006).

Marlowe, J. *The Tolpuddle Martyrs* (London: Deutsch, 1971).

Marshall, P. *Demanding the Impossible: A History of Anarchism* (London: Fontana Press, 1992).

McCormick, D. *Who's Who in Spy Fiction* (London: Sphere, 1977).

McHugh, D. *Labour in the City: The Development of the Labour Party in Manchester 1918–31* (Manchester: Manchester University Press, 2006).

McIntosh, R. *Challenge to Democracy: Politics, Trade Union Power and Economic Failure in the 1970s* (London: Politico's, 2006).

McIntyre, W. D. *British Decolonisation, 1946–1997* (New York: St. Martin's Press, 1998).

McKay, G. *Senseless Acts of Beauty: Cultures of Resistance Since the Sixties* (London: Verso, 1996).

McWilliam, R. *The Tichborne Claimant: A Victorian Sensation* (London: Hambledon Press, 2007).

Melchiori, B. A. *Terrorism in the Late Victorian Novel* (Brighton: Harvester, 1985).

Morgan, K. *The Webbs and Soviet Communism* (London: Lawrence and Wishart, 2007).

Morris, I. *Why the West Rules – for Now* (London: Profile, 2010).

Morton, A. L. *When the People Arose: The Peasants Revolt of 1381* (London: CPGB, 1981).

Morton, A. L. *A People's History of England* (London: Lawrence and Wishart, 1986).

Mosse, G. L. *Fallen Soldiers: Reshaping the Memory of the World Wars* (Oxford: Oxford University Press, 1990).

Nairn, T. *The Left Against Europe* (London: Penguin, 1973).

Nairn, T. *After Britain: New Labour and the Return of Scotland* (London: Granta, 2000).

Napier, P. *Revolution and the Napier Brothers, 1820–1840* (London: Michael Joseph, 1973).

Nead, L. *Victorian Babylon: People, Streets, and Images in Nineteenth-Century London* (New Haven: Yale University Press, 2000).

Nicholson, V. *Among the Bonemians: Experiments in Living, 1900–1939* (London: Penguin, 2002).

Oliver, H. *The International Anarchist Movement in Late Victorian London* (London: Croom and Helm, 1983).

Overy, R. *The Morbid Age: Britain Between the Wars* (London: Allen Lane, 2009).

Page, M. *The City's End: Two Centuries of Fantasies, Fears, and Premonitions of New York's Destruction* (New Haven, CT: Yale University Press, 2008).

Palmer, A. *The East End of London* (London: John Murray, 1999).

Panayi, P. *The Enemy in our Midst: Germans in Britain during the First World War* (Oxford: Berg Publishers Ltd., 1991).

Paris, M. *Warrior Nation: Images of War in British Popular Culture 1850–2000* (London: Reaktion, 2000).

Pelling, H. *The British Communist Party: A Historical Profile* (London: Adam and Charles Black, 1958).

Phillips, J. *A Man's Country: The Image of the Pakeha Male* (Auckland: Penguin, 1987).

Phillips, M. *Londonistan: How Britain Created the Terror State Within* (London: Encounter Books, 2006).

Pike, D. L. *Subterranean Cities: The World Beneath Paris and London, 1800–1945* (New York: Cornell University Press, 2005).

Pimlott, B. *Harold Wilson* (London: Harper Collins, 1992).

Pionke, A. D. *Plots of Opportunity: Representing Conspiracy in Victorian England* (Columbus: Ohio State University Press, 2004).

Porter, B. *The Refugee Question in Mid-Victorian Politics* (Cambridge: Cambridge University Press, 1979).

Porter, B. *Plots and Paranoia: A History of Political Espionage in Britain, 1790–1988* (Boston: Unwin Hyman, 1989).

Priestman, M. *Crime Fiction: From Poe to the Present* (Plymouth: Northgate House, 1998).

Pugh, M. *Hurrah for the Blackshirts: Fascists and Fascism in Britain between the Wars* (London: Pimlico, 2006).

Quail, J. *The Slow-Burning Fuse: The Lost History of the British Anarchists* (London: Paladin, 1978).

Ramsden, J. *Don't Mention the War: The British and the Germans Since 1890* (London: Little Brown, 2007).

Rance, N. *The Historical Novel and Popular Politics in Nineteenth-Century Britain* (London: Vision, 1975).

Read, D. *Cobden and Bright: A Victorian Political Partnership* (London: Edward Arnold Ltd., 1967).

Readman, P. *Land and Nation in Britain: Patriotism, National Identity, and the Politics of Land, 1880–1914* (Woodbridge: Boydell and Brewer, 2008).

Reeve, N. H. *The Novels of Rex Warner: An Introduction* (New York: St. Martin's Press, 1989).

Reid, J. C. *Bucks and Bruisers: Pierce Egan and Regency England* (London: Routledge and Kegan Paul, 1971).

Rigby, A. *Communes in Britain* (London: Rouledge and Kegan Paul, 1974).

Robinson, A. *Imagining London, 1770–1900* (Basingstoke: Macmillan, 2004).

Rooum, D. (ed.), *What is Anarchism? An Introduction* (London: Freedom Press, 1993).

Rose, J. *The Intellectual Life of the British Working Classes* (New Haven: Yale University Press, 2001).

Rosenfeld, G. D. *The World Hitler Never Made* (Cambridge: Cambridge University Press, 2005).

Ross, K. *May '68 and its Afterlives* (Chicago: Chicago University Press, 2002).

Ross, S. J. *Working-Class Hollywood: Silent Film and the Shaping of Class in America* (New Jersey: Princeton University Press, 1998).

Royle, E. *Revolutionary Britannia? Reflections on the Threat of Revolution in Britain 1789–1848* (Manchester: Manchester University Press, 2000).

Rumbelow, D. *The Houndsditch Murders and the Siege of Sidney Street* (London: W.H. Allen, 1988).

Samuel, R. *Island Stories: Unravelling Britain* (London: Verso, 1998).

Samuel, R. *The Lost World of British Communism* (London: Verso, 2006).

Sandbrook, D. *State of Emergency: The Way We Were: Britain, 1970–74* (London: Little Brown, 2010).

Schneer, J. *London 1900: The Imperial Metropolis* (New Haven: Yale University Press, 1999).

Schoyen, A. R. *The Chartist Challenge: A Portrait of George Julian Harney* (London: Heinemann, 1958).

Searle, G. R. *Country Before Party: Coalition and the Idea of "National Government" in Britain 1885–1987* (London: Longman, 1995).

Shannon, R. *Gladstone and the Bulgarian Agitation, 1876* (London: Hamish Hamilton, 1963).

Sheehan, S. M. *Anarchism* (London: Reaktion, 2003).

Sinclair, A. *Death by Fame: A Life of Elizabeth, Empress of Austria* (New York: St. Martin's Press, 1998).

Skidelsky, R. *Oswald Mosley* (London: Macmillan, 1975).

Smith, D. *Socialist Propaganda in the Twentieth-Century British Novel* (London: Macmillan, 1978).

Smith, F. B. *Radical Artisan: William James Linton, 1812–97* (Manchester: Manchester University Press, 1973).

Smithers, A. J. *Dornford Yates: A Biography* (London, 1982).

Soloway, R. A. *Demography and Degeneration: Eugenics and the Declining Birthrate in Twentieth Century Britain* (Chapel Hill: University of North Carolina Press, 1995).

Sonn, R. D. *Anarchism and Cultural Politics in Fin de Siecle France* (Lincoln: University of Nebraska Press, 1989).

Souter, G. *A Peculiar People: The Australians in Paraguay* (Sydney: Angus and Robertson Ltd., 1968).

Speck, W. A. *Robert Southey: Entire Man of Letters* (New Haven: Yale University Press, 2006).

St. Clair, W. *The Reading Nation in the Romantic Period* (Cambridge: Cambridge University Press, 2004).

Storey, M. *Robert Southey: A Life* (Oxford, 1997).

Sutherland, J. *Where was Rebecca Shot?: Puzzles, Curiosities and Conundrums in Modern Fiction* (London: Weidenfeld and Nicolson, 1998).

Sykes, A. *The Radical Right in Britain: Social Imperialism to the BNP* (London: Palgrave, 2001).

Symonds, J. *Bloody Murder: From the Detective Story to the Crime Novel* (London: Penguin. 1972).

Tanner, D. P. Thane and N. Tiratsoo (eds.), *Labour's First Century* (Cambridge: Cambridge University Press, 2000).

Taylor, M. *Ernest Jones, Chartism and the Romance of Politics 1819–1869* (Oxford: Oxford University Press, 2003).

Thomas, E. *Louise Michel* (Montreal: Black Rose Books, 1980).

Thomas, E. *The Women Incendiaries* (New York: Haymarket Books, 2007).

Thomas, P. D. G. *John Wilkes: A Friend to Liberty* (Oxford: Oxford University Press, 1996).

Thompson, D. *Popular Politics in the Industrial Revolution* (Aldershot: Wildwood House Ltd., 1984).

Thompson, J. *Fiction, Crime and Empire: Clues to Modernity and Postmodernism* (Chicago: University of Illinois Press, 1993).

Thurlow, R. *Fascism in Britain: From Oswald Mosley's Blackshirts to the National Front* (London: I.B. Tauris, 1998).

Tilley, W. H. *The Background of the Princess Casamassima* (Gainesville: University of Florida Press, 1961).

Trilling, L. *The Liberal Imagination: Essays on Literature and Society* (London: Penguin Books, 1970).

Turner, A. W. *Crisis? What Crisis? Britain in the 1970s* (London: Aurum, 2008).

Turner, E. S. *Boys will be Boys: The Story of Sweeney Todd, Deadwood Dick, Sexton Blake, Billy Bunter, Dick Barton, et al.* (London: Penguin, 1975).

Urbainczyk, T. *Spartacus* (Bristol: Bristol University Press, 2004).

Usborne, R. *Clubland Heroes: A Nostalgic Study of Some Recurrent Characters in the Romantic Fiction of Dornford Yates, John Buchan and Sapper* (Barrie and Jenkins, 1953).

Venturi, F. *Roots of Revolution: A History of the Populist and Socialist Movements in Nineteenth Century Russia* (Princeton: Princeton University Press, 1960).

Walker, M. *The National Front* (London: Fontana, 1977).

Walkowitz, J. *City of Dreadful Delight* (London: Verso, 1992).

Waller, P. *Writing, Reading and Reputations: Literary Life in Britain, 1870–1914* (Oxford: Oxford University Press, 2006).

Ward, C. *Anarchism: A Very Short Introduction* (Oxford: Oxford University Press, 2005).

Ward, C. and D. Goodway, *Talking Anarchy* (Nottingham: Five Leaves Press, 2005).

Ward, P. *Red Flag and Union Jack: Englishness, Patriotism and the British Left, 1881–1924* (Woodbridge: Boydell and Brewer, 1998).

Waters, C. *British Socialists and the Politics of Popular Culture, 1884–1914* (Manchester: Manchester University Press, 1990).

Watson, C. *Snobbery with Violence: English Crime Stories and Their Audience* (London: Methuen, 1971).

Webster, W. *Englishness and Empire, 1939–1965* (Oxford: Oxford University Press, 2005).

Weight, R. *Patriots: National Identity in Britain, 1940–2000* (London: Macmillan, 2002).

Weir, D. *Anarchy and Culture: The Aesthetic Politics of Modernism* (Amherst: University of Massachusetts Press, 1997).

Wexler, A. *Emma Goldman: An Intimate Life* (London: Virago, 1984).

White, J. *London in the 20th Century* (London: Vintage, 2001).

White, R. *Inventing Australia: Images and Identity, 1688–1980* (St. Leonards: Allen and Unwin, 1981).

Whiteside, T. *The Tunnel under the Channel* (London: Rupert Hart-Davis, 1962).

Wilson, A. *The Search for Ernest Bramah* (London: Creighton and Reed, 2007).

Wilson, E. *Bohemians: The Glamorous Outcasts* (London: Macmillan, 2003).

Wilson, K. *Channel Tunnel Visions, 1850–1945: Dreams and Nightmares* (London: Hambledon, 1994).

Windscheffel, A. *Popular Conservatism in Imperial London, 1868–1906* (Woodbridge: Boydell and Brewer, 2007).

Wolfe, W. *From Radicalism to Socialism: Men and Ideas in the Formation of Fabian Socialist Doctrines 1881–1889* (London: Yale University Press, 1975).

Wood, A. *The 1549 Rebellions and the Making of Early Modern England* (Cambridge: Cambridge University Press, 2007).

Woodcock, G. *Anarchism: A History of Libertarian Ideas and Movements* (London: Penguin, 1986).

Woodcock G. and I. Avakumovic, *The Anarchist Prince: The Biography of Prince Peter Kropotkin* (London: Boardman and Company, 1950).

Worden, B. *Roundhead Reputations: The English Civil War and the Passions of Posterity* (London: Penguin, 2001).

Wright, L. *The Looming Tower: Al-Qaeda and the Road to 9/11* (London: Allen Lane).

Wright, P. *On Living in An Old Country* (London: Verso, 1985).

Wright, P. *A Journey Through Ruins: The Last Days of London* (London: Radius, 1991).

Young, H. *One of Us: A Biography of Margaret Thatcher* (London: Pan, 1989).

ARTICLES IN BOOKS AND JOURNALS

Becker, H. 'Johann Most in Europe', *The Raven: Anarchist Quarterly*, 1 (1988), 291–321.

Bertens, H. 'A society of murderers run on sound conservative lines: the life and times of Sapper's Bulldog Drummond', in Clive Bloom (ed.), *Twentieth Century Suspense: The Thriller Comes of Age* (London: Macmillan, 1990), pp. 51–68.

Betts, R. F. 'The allusion to Rome in British imperialist thought of the late nineteenth and early twentieth centuries', *Victorian Studies*, 15 (1971), 149–59.

Bevir, M. 'The rise of ethical anarchism in Britain, 1885–1900', *Historical Research*, 69 (1996), 143–65.

Bratton, J. S. 'Of England, home and duty: the image of England in Victorian and Edwardian juvenile fiction' in J. M. Mackenzie (ed.), *Imperialism and Popular Culture* (Manchester: Manchester University Press, 1986), pp. 73–93.

Broadbridge, H. 'The turning of the worm' in *Fifty Mutinies, Rebellions and Revolutions* (London: Odhams Press Ltd., 1933), pp. 371–84.

Brown, K. D. 'The Anti-Socialist Union, 1908–49', in Brown (ed.), *Essays in Anti-Labour History: Responses to the Rise of Labour in Britain* (London: Macmillan, 1974), pp. 234–61.

Bush, M. L. 'The risings of the Commons in England, 1381–1549' in J. Denton (ed.), *Orders and Hierarchies in Late Medieval and Renaissance Europe* (London: Macmillan, 1999), pp. 109–25.

Castle, K. 'Imperial legacies, new frontiers: children's popular literature and the demise of empire', in S. Ward (ed.), *British Culture and the End of Empire* (Manchester: Manchester University Press, 2001), pp. 145–62.

Ceadel, M. 'Popular fiction and the next war, 1918–39', in F. Gloversmith (ed.), *Class, Culture and Social Change: a New View of the Nineteen Thirties* (Brighton: Harvester, 1980), pp. 161–84.

Ceaser, J. 'The philosophical origins of anti-Americanism in Europe', in P. Hollander (ed.), *Understanding Anti-Americanism: Its Origins and Impact* (Chicago: Ivan R. Dee, 2004), pp. 51–70.

Clayton, J. 'Shakespeare's Jack Cade', *Socialist Review*, 4 (1909–10), 457–62.

Coates, D. 'Politicians and the sorcerer', in A. King (ed.), *Why is Britain Becoming Harder to Govern?* (London: British Broadcasting Corporation, 1976), pp. 31–57.

Cohen, N. 'What did the Squatters do for Us', *New Statesman*, 23 January 2006, 28–30.

Coroneos, C. 'Conrad, Kropotkin and anarchist geography', *The Conradian*, 18 (1994), 17–30.

Cosgrove, P. 'Could the Army Take Over?', *The Spectator*, 22 December 1973, 806.

Croft, A. 'World without end foisted upon the future – some antecedents of 1984', in C. Norris (ed.), *Inside the Myth; Orwell: Views from the Left* (London: Lawrence and Wishart, 1984), pp. 183–216.

de Jong, R. 'Provos and kabouters', in D. E. Apter and J. Joll (eds), *Anarchism Today* (London: Macmillan, 1971), pp. 164–80.

Dobson, R. B. 'Remembering the peasants' revolt', in W. H. Liddell and R .G. E. Wood, (ed.), *Essex and the Great Revolt of 1381: Lectures Celebrating the Sixth Hundreth Anniversary* (Chelmsford: Essex Record Office, 1982), pp. 1–15.

Dingley, R. 'The ruins of the future: Macaulay's New Zealander and the spirit of the age', in A. Sanderson and R. Dingley (eds), *Histories of the Future: Studies in Fact, Fantasy and Science Fiction* (London: Palgrave, 2005), pp. 15–33.

Durham, M. 'The conservative party, the British extreme right and the problem of political space, 1967–83', in M. Cronin (ed.), *The Failure of British Fascism: The Far Right and the Fight for Political Recognition* (Basingstoke: Macmillan, 1996), pp. 81–98.

Dyck, I. ' "Rural war" and the missing revolution in early nineteenth-century England', in Michael T. Davis (ed.), *Radicalism and Revolution in Britain, 1775–1848* (London: Macmillan, 2000), pp. 176–90.

Epstein, H. ' "A pier glass in the cavern": the construction of London in *The Secret Agent*', in G. M. Moore (ed.), *Conrad's Cities: Essays for Hans Van Marle* (Amsterdam: Rodopi, 2002), pp. 175–96.

Fahrmeir, A. 'The London lord mayor's show in the nineteenth century: celebrating achievement or glorifying tradition', in J. Neuheiser and M. Schaich (eds), *Political Rituals in Great Britain, 1700–2000* (Augsburg: *Arbeitskreis Deutsche England-Forschung*, 2006), pp. 55–73.

Ferguson, N. 'Introduction' to Ferguson (ed.), *Virtual History: Alternatives and Counterfactuals* (London: Macmillan, 1997), pp. 7–8.

Ferguson, N. 'Clashing civilisations or mad mullahs: the United States between informal and formal empire', in S. Talbot and N. Chana (eds), *The Age of Terror* (New York: Perseus, 2001), pp. 113–41.

Freeman, N. ' "A decadent appetite for the lurid"?: James Herbert, *The Spear* and "Nazi gothic" ', *Gothic Studies*, 8 (2006), 80–97.

Gienow-Hecht, J. C. E. 'Always blame the Americans: anti-Americanism in Europe in the twentieth century', *The American Historical Review*, 3 (2006), 1067–91.

Glover, D. 'Looking for Edgar Wallace', *History Workshop Journal*, 37 (1994), 143–64.

Glover, D. 'Aliens, anarchists and detectives: legislating the immigrant body', *New Formations*, 32 (1997), 22–33.

Grayson, R. S. 'Britain and the channel tunnel', *Twentieth Century British History*, 7 (1996), 387.

Grindrod, F. and M. Rusling (eds), *Stopping the Far Right: How Progressive Politics Can Tackle Political Extremism* (London: Fabian Society, 2007), pp. 13–24.

Hall, R. 'Creating a people's history: political identity and history in Chartism, 1832–1848', in O. Ashton, R. Fyson and S. Roberts (eds), *The Chartist Legacy* (Woodbridge: Merlin, 1999), pp. 255–85.

Hilliard, C. 'The literary underground of 1920s London', *Social History*, 33 (2008), 164–82.

Hilliard, C. 'Producers by hand and by brain: working-class writers and left-wing publishers in 1930s Britain', *The Journal of Modern History*, 78 (2006), 37–64.

Kellett, J. 'William Lane and "New Australia": a reassessment', *Labour History* (Australia), 72 (1997), 19–34.

Klaus H. G.and S. Knight, 'Introduction', in *'To Hell with Culture': Anarchism and Twentieth Century Literature* (Cardiff: Cardiff University Press, 2005), pp. 1–10.

Kramnick, I. 'Introduction: the making of a crisis', in Kramnick (ed.), *Is Britain Dying? Perspectives on the Current Crisis* (Ithaca: Cornell University Press, 1979), pp. 11-27.

Laqueur, W. 'Interpretations of terrorism: fact, fiction and political sense', *Journal of Contemporary History*, 12 (1977), 1–42.

Lawrence, J. 'Fascist violence and the politics of public order in inter-war Britain: The Olympia debate revisited', *Historical Research*, 76 (2003), 238–67.

Malagodi, O. 'The psychology of anarchist conspiracies', *Westminister Review*, 147 (1897), 87–91.

McCalman, I. 'Mad Lord George and Madame La Motte: riot and sexuality in the genesis of Burke's *Reflections on the Revolution in France*', *Journal of British Studies*, 35 (1996), 343–67.

McIvor, A. 'Essays in anti-Labour history', *Society for the Study of Labour History Bulletin*, 53 (1988), 18–26.

McKay, G. 'DiY culture: notes towards an intro', in McKay (ed.), *DiY Culture: Party and Protest in Nineties Britain* (London: Verso, 1998), pp. 7–9.

Moore-Colyer, R. 'Towards "mother earth": J. Jenks, organicism, the right and the British Union of Fascists', *Journal of Contemporary History*, 39 (2004), 353–71.

Nehring, H. 'The British and West German protests against nuclear weapons and the cultures of the cold war, 1957–1964', *Contemporary British History*, 19, 2 (2005), 223–41.

Nehring, H. 'National internationalists: British and West German protests against nuclear weapons: the politics of transnational communications and the social history of the cold war, 1957–1964', *Contemporary European History*, 14, 4 (2005), 559–82.

Ober, J. 'The triumph of Anthony and Cleopatra at Actium in 31 BC' in R. Cowley (ed.), *More What If? Eminent Historians Imagine What Might Have Been* (London: Macmillan, 2001), pp. 23–47.

O'Cathain, M. '"The black hand of Irish republicanism"? Transcontinental Fenianism and theories of global terror', in F. McGarry and J. McConnel (eds), *The Black Hand of Republicanism: Fenianism in Modern Ireland* (Dublin: Irish Academic Press, 2009), pp. 135–46.

Orwell, G. 'Prophecies of Fascism', *Tribune*, 12 July 1940, 16–17.

Paris, M. 'Red menace: Russia and British juvenile fiction', *Contemporary British Fiction*, 19 (2005), 117–32.

Patai, D. 'Imagining reality: the utopian fiction of Katharine Burdekin', in A. Ingram and D. Patai (eds), *Rediscovering Forgotten Radicals: British Women Writers, 1889–1939* (Chapel Hill: University of North Carolina Press, 1993), pp. 226–43.

Phythian, M. 'CND's Cold War", *Contemporary British History*, 15, 3 (2001) 133–56.

Pick, D. 'The faces of anarchy: Lombroso and the politics of criminal science in post-unification Italy', *History Workshop*, 21 (1986), 60–86.

Poole, R. 'French Revolution or peasants' revolt?: petitioners and rebels in England from the Blanketeers to the Chartists', *Labour History Review*, 74 (2009), 6–26.

Porter, B. 'The Freiheit persecutions, 1881–1882', *The Historical Journal*, 23 (1980), 833–56.

Prescott, A. 'Writing about rebellion: using the records of the peasant revolt of 1381', *History Workshop Journal*, 45 (1998), 1–29.

Readman, P. 'The place of the past in English culture c.1890–1914', *Past and Present* 186 (2005), 147–99.

Reclus, E. 'Anarchy: by an anarchist', *Contemporary Review*, 45 (1884), 627–41.

Renton, D. 'Guarding the barricades: working-class anti-fascism', in N. Copsey and D. Renton (eds), *British Fascism, the Labour Movement and the State* (Basingstoke: Palgrave, 2005), pp. 141–59.

Rickword, E. 'Culture, progress and English tradition', in C. Day Lewis (ed.), *The Mind in Chains: Socialism and the Cultural Revolution* (London: Frederick Muller, 1937), pp. 237–56.

Roberts A. and N. Ferguson, 'Hitler's England: what if Germany had invaded Britain in May 1940?', in N. Ferguson (ed.), *Virtual History: Alternatives and Counterfactuals* (London: Basic Books, 1997), pp. 281–320.

Ruskin History Workshop Students Collective, 'Worker-historians in the 1920s', in R. Samuel (ed.), *People's History and Socialist Theory* (History Workshop, 1981), pp. 17–20.

Samuel, R. 'British Marxist historians, 1880–1980', *New Left Review*, 1 (1980), pp. 21–96.

Schneer, J. 'London's docks in 1900: nexus of empire', *Labour History Review*, 59 (1994), 20–33.

Seed, J. 'Chinatown in the London docks, 1900–1940', *History Workshop Journal*, 62 (2006), 58–85.

Shaw, J. 'Land, people and nation: historicist voices in the Highland land campaign, c.1850–1883', in E. Biagini (ed.), *Citizenship and Community: Liberals, Radicals and Collective Identities in the British Isles, 1865–1931* (Cambridge: Cambridge University Press, 1996), pp. 305–24.

Shpayer-Makov, H. 'Anarchism in British public opinion 1880–1914', *Victorian Studies*, 31 (1988), 487–516.

Shpayer-Makov, H. 'A traitor to his class: the anarchist in British fiction', *Journal of European Studies*, 26 (1996), 299–325.

Smith, C. S. 'Cataclysm and cultural consciousness: Chicago and the Haymarket Trial', *Chicago History*, XV (1986), 36–53.

Smith, T. B. 'In defence of privilege: the City of London and the challenge of municipal reform, 1875–1890', *Journal of Social History*, 27 (1993), 59–83.

Smith, T. B. 'A grand work of noble conception: the Victoria memorial and imperial London', in F. Driver and D. Gilbert (eds), *Imperial Cities* (Manchester: Manchester University Press, 1999), pp. 21–39.

Stone, D. 'The far right and the back-to-the-land movement', in J. V. Gottlieb and T. P. Lineham (eds), *The Culture of Fascism: Visions of the Far Right in Britain* (London: I.B. Tauris, 2004), pp. 182–98.

Taylor, A. ' "A melancholy odyssey among London public houses": radical club life and the unrespectable in mid-nineteenth century London', *Historical Research*, 78 (2005), 74–95.

Taylor, A. ' "Commons-stealers", "land-grabbers" and "jerry-builders": space, popular radicalism and the politics of public access in London, 1848–1880', *International Review of Social History*, 40 (1995), 383–407.

Taylor, A. ' "And I am the god of destruction!": Fu Manchu and the construction of Asiatic evil in the novels of Arthur Sarsfield Ward', in T. Crook, R. Gill and B. Taithe (eds), *Evil, Barbarism and Empire: Britain and Abroad, c.1830–c.2000* (Basingstoke: Palgrave-Macmillan, 2011), pp. 73–95.

Thomas, M. ' "No-one telling us what to do": anarchist schools in Britain, 1890–1916', *Historical Research*, 77 (2004), 405–36.

Turner, B. S. 'New and old xenophobia: the crisis of liberal multiculturalism', in S. Akbarzadeh and F. Mansouri (eds), *Islam and Political Violence: Muslim Diaspora and Radicalism in the West* (London: I. B. Tauris, 2010), pp. 65–86.

Ward, S. 'Introduction' to Ward (ed.), *British Culture and the End of Empire* (Manchester: Manchester University Press, 2001), pp. 1–20.

Webber, G. C. 'Patterns of membership and support for the British Union of Fascists', *Journal of Contemporary History*, 19 (1984), 575–606.

Weitzman, A. J. 'Eighteenth century London: urban paradise or fallen city?', *Journal of the History of Ideas*, 36 (1975), 469–80.

Whelehan, N. ' "Cheap as soap and common as sugar": the Fenians, dynamite and scientific warfare', in F. McGarry and J. McConnel (eds), *The Black Hand of Republicanism: Fenianism in Modern Ireland* (Dublin: Irish Academic Press, 2010), pp. 105–20.

White, A. 'England and America: strangers yet', *Anglo-Saxon Review*, 7 (1900), 8–18.

White, J. 'Unreal city: reflections on London and the novel in the twentieth century', *History Workshop Journal*, 56 (2003), 1–32.

Whitehead, A. 'Dan Chatterton and his "Atheistic Communisitic Scorcher"', *History Workshop*, 25 (1988), 83–99.

Windscheffel, A. '"In darkest Lambeth": Henry Morton Stanley and the imperial politics of London Unionism', in M. Cragoe and A. Taylor (eds), *London Politics, 1760–1914* (London: Palgrave, 2005), pp. 191–210.

THESES

McIvor, A. J. 'Employers' Associations and Industrial Relations in Lancashire, 1890–1939' (Ph.D thesis, University of Manchester, 1983).

Smith, D. L. 'Mirrors of Inscrutability: British Textual Representations of China and the Chinese, 1880–1940' (Ph.D thesis, University of Birmingham, 1998).

Willis, T. M. 'The Politics and Ideology of Local Authority Health Care in Sheffield, 1918–1948' (Ph.D thesis, Sheffield Hallam University, 2009).

WORKS OF REFERENCE

Breuilly, J. G. Niedhart and A. Taylor (eds), *The Era of the Reform League: English Labour and Radical Politics 1857–1872: Documents Selected by Gustav Mayer* (Mannheim: *Mannheimer Historische Forschungen*, 1995).

Clute J. and P. Nicholls (eds), *An Encyclopaedia of Science Fiction* (London: St. Martin's Press, 1993).

Laity P. (ed.), *Left Book Club Anthology* (London: Gollancz, 2001).

Sutherland, J. A. *The Longman Companion to Victorian Fiction* (London: Longman, 1988).

Index

Page numbers in **bold** denote illustration.